COUNTY COLLEGE OF MORRIS

D0088010

'*Political Marketing: Principles and applications*, second stop guide to the discipline of political marketing. The recent campaigns across the globe, and the scholarship is

Travis N. Ridout, Thomas S. Foley Distinguished
Professor of Government and Public Policy,
Washington State University, USA

'Lees-Marshment's *Political Marketing* is authoritative and accessible, combining rich analysis with case studies added by practitioners and academics. The book is an indispensable resource for anyone interested in contemporary political marketing research and application.'

Dr Darren G. Lilleker, Bournemouth University, UK

'An indispensable textbook of political campaigning, based on the most recent international evidence about what does and doesn't work.'

Tom Flanagan, former National Campaign
Manager, Conservative Party of Canada

'Political marketing has become the most relevant field of study to those of us who cover politics and Jennifer Lees-Marshment's work is crucial to our understanding of how this world works – not just in theory, but also in practice.'

Susan Delacourt, Senior Political Writer, Toronto Star,
and Author of Shopping For Votes: How politicians
choose us and we choose them

'*Political Marketing* is a must-have textbook. It combines politics and marketing theory with experience to simply and clearly explain the concept and practice of political marketing. As a consequence, it will be a vital tool for students of political science, marketing and political marketing. This second edition expertly combines a breadth of understanding with the latest thinking in the field. Concepts are explained well, the case studies provide insight and the range of classroom activities provides clear direction for learning.'

Dr Nigel Jackson, Reader in Persuasion and
Communication, Plymouth University, UK

COUNTY COLLEGE OF MORRIS

Political Marketing

Substantially revised throughout, *Political Marketing*, second edition, continues to offer students the most comprehensive introduction to this rapidly growing field. It provides an accessible but in-depth guide to what political marketing is and how it is used in practice, and encourages reflection on how it should be used in the future.

Features and benefits of the second edition include:

- New chapters on political branding and delivery marketing;
- Expanded discussion of political public relations, crisis management, marketing in the lower levels of government and volunteer-friendly organizations;
- Examination of the new research on emerging practices in the field, such as interactive and responsive leadership communication, mobile marketing, co-creation market research, experimental and analytic marketing, celebrity marketing and integrated marketing communications; and
- Extensive pedagogical features, including 21 detailed case studies from around the world, practitioner profiles, best practice guides, class discussion points, an online resource site and both applied and traditional assessment questions.

Written by a leading expert in the field, this textbook is essential reading for all students of political marketing, parties and elections and comparative politics.

Jennifer Lees-Marshment is an Associate Professor at Auckland University, New Zealand, and is an international expert in political marketing.

Political Marketing

Principles and applications

Second edition

Jennifer Lees-Marshment

Routledge
Taylor & Francis Group

LONDON AND NEW YORK

First edition published 2009
by Routledge

This edition published 2014
by Routledge
2 Park Square, Milton Park, Abingdon, Oxon OX14 4RN

and by Routledge
711 Third Avenue, New York, NY 10017

Routledge is an imprint of the Taylor & Francis Group, an informa business

© 2014, 2009 Jennifer Lees-Marshment

The right of Jennifer Lees-Marshment to be identified as author of this
work has been asserted by her in accordance with the Copyright, Designs
and Patents Act 1988.

All rights reserved. No part of this book may be reprinted or
reproduced or utilised in any form or by any electronic, mechanical,
or other means, now known or hereafter invented, including photocopying
and recording, or in any information storage or retrieval system,
without permission in writing from the publishers.

Trademark notice: Product or corporate names may be trademarks
or registered trademarks, and are used only for identification and
explanation without intent to infringe.

British Library Cataloguing in Publication Data
A catalogue record for this book is available from the British Library

Library of Congress Cataloging in Publication Data
Lees-Marshment, Jennifer.
  Political marketing: principles and applications/Jennifer Lees-Marshment.
  – Second edition.
  pages cm
  Includes bibliographical references and index.
  1. Campaign management. 2. Political campaigns. 3. Marketing –
  Political aspects. I. Title.
  JF2112.C3L44 2014
  324.7′3 – dc23
  2013045369

ISBN: 978-0-415-63208-9 (hbk)
ISBN: 978-0-415-63207-2 (pbk)
ISBN: 978-1-315-77504-3 (ebk)

Typeset in Times New Roman and Helvetica Neue
by Florence Production Ltd, Stoodleigh, Devon, UK

Printed and bound in the United States of America by
Edwards Brothers Malloy

JF
2112
.C3
L44
2014

This book is dedicated to my graduate students at Auckland University in New Zealand, who kept my faith in the importance of teaching political marketing, stimulated new thinking with their own ideas and maintained my passion for the field between 2006 and 2013. This provided the energy to complete this revised second edition.

They include Edward Elder, Sophia Blair, Phillip Wakefield, Laura Young, Lisa Kemp, Renisa Maki, Rachael Crosby, Thomas Seeman, Nicholas Mignacca, John Wilcox, Jack Davies, Elijah Pear, Matthew Jackson, Melanie Tuala, Bailey Duggan, Shawn Moodie, Fraser Nicholas, Michelle Craig, Glenn Lamont, Randall Potter, Daria Gorbonova and Jamie Turner.

2/10/15

Contents

Figures

Case studies

Practitioner perspectives

Practitioner profiles

1 Introduction to political marketing

Political marketing is a fundamental part of political life. Presidents and prime ministers; politicians and parties; government departments and councils all use marketing in their pursuit of political goals. Market research is used, when deciding on policies and service design, to understand what the people they serve and seek votes from want and need; voter profiling helps create new segments to target; strategy guides creation of the political brand to develop an attractive vision; internal marketing guides the provision of volunteer involvement; analytics and experimental research test and refine communication messages; and delivery management sets expectations and helps to convey progress once a politician is elected or a programme has begun.

As an area of academic research and teaching, political marketing is a modern and dynamic field that seeks to understand, learn from, comment on and even influence such behaviour. As Butler and Harris (2009, 149) observe, 'political marketing research has made significant progress in recent years as evidenced by its own dedicated journal, special issues of international marketing journals, handbooks and edited volumes, special research interest groups of the academy, dedicated academic and practitioner conferences and articles in leading field journals'. Political marketing explores a range of political behaviour from a strategic perspective that is both analytical and applied: it considers what works, not just what has happened in the past; and what should be as well as what might have gone wrong. It is continually updated with new elections and technologies. Political marketing is applicable to the real world, so it attracts students who want to explore literature they can use after graduation. It offers fresh perspectives on old questions; taking the normally profit-oriented marketing analysis into the arena of conviction and values and contributing applied research to classical political science questions of leadership, citizenship and democracy itself.

Political marketing also attracts public attention and debate. It has become the focus of many recent movies such as *Game Change*, *The Iron Lady*, *The Ides of March* and *No*; and TV series such as *The West Wing*, *VEEP* and *Scandal* which cover strategy, branding, positioning, crisis management and polling, and raise ethical issues of authenticity, targeting ethnic minorities and gender. Issenberg's book *The Victory Lab* (published by Crown in 2012) which explores the rise of analytical and experimental marketing has become a bestseller. Mainstream media regularly discuss political marketing: CNN ran a feature on the weaknesses of GOP (Grand Old Party) branding in 2012; the Australian Broadcasting Corporation discussed the loss of the Rudd brand in 2012; the BBC ran a section on the targeting of 'motorway man' in the UK 2010 general election; and in 2011 the Canadian newspaper *The Toronto Star* dedicated an online blog to political marketing whilst the Canadian Broadcasting Corporation radio station featured a programme critiquing targeted communication to ethnic minorities.

This book synthesises academic research on political marketing, featuring theories and empirical examples from around the world. It seeks to explain what political marketing is, show how it is used in practice, and encourage reflection on how it should be used in future. The book is organised into nine chapters: Chapter 2 explores political strategy; Chapter 3, political market research; Chapter 4, political branding; Chapter 5, internal political marketing; Chapter 6, static political marketing communication; Chapter 7, relational and interactive communication; Chapter 8 looks at political delivery marketing and the final chapter focuses on political marketing and democracy. This introductory chapter explains the basic components of political marketing, its relationship to its parent disciplines political science and marketing; studying and researching political marketing including why marketing and politics students should study it and barriers to researching and teaching the field.

What is political marketing?

Political marketing is about how political elites use marketing tools and concepts to understand, respond to, involve and communicate with their political market in order to achieve their goals. Political elites include candidates, politicians, leaders, parties, governments, government departments and programmes, NGOs and interest groups. Their political marketing goals, market, product, tools and approaches are wide-ranging.

Political goals

Political goals are wide-ranging. The most obvious is to get votes to get elected – but as in business where goals include long-term sustainability not just profit politics is about more than just winning power. Politicians and political parties have a range of ambitions and dreams:

1 Get a new issue onto the political agenda.
2 Create more understanding of a complex policy such as security policy.
3 Stimulate action on a growing problem like climate change.
4 Ensure an emerging new group in society is better represented.
5 Pass legislation such as gay marriage.
6 Change behaviour in society such as reducing drink driving.
7 Gain support from new segments in the market such as the healthy pensioners.
8 Create a long-term positive relationship with voters in a constituency.
9 Increase the number and activity of volunteers in a campaign or party.
10 Become a coalition partner in government.
11 Win control of government.
12 Gain support for a vision such as universal health care.
13 Manage expectations of leaders.
14 Get credit for delivery.
15 Increase the vote at the next election.
16 Make the world a better place.

The relative importance of such goals varies of course, depending on the party, candidate, electoral environment, and the rules of the marketplace, its size, its philosophy, resources, political system or country. For major parties (i.e. those who win control of government with the largest share of the vote), the goal is to win enough votes in general elections to win control of government and do whatever is necessary to achieve this. Minor parties tend to be more interested in advancing a particular cause or influencing debate. And, of course, individual candidates are more interested in their particular seat than the overall party's success. And once a party or candidate gets into power, the priority of goals can change again. But it is important to understand that it is not just about winning an election – political goals are more intangible, normative and values based than that. For some, getting into power is just the means to an end; whereas others may never stand a chance of getting into government but can nevertheless exert significant influence on debate and policy.

The political market

The political market is also more complex than just voters: Mortimore and Gill (2010, 257) argue that 'a wise party will not confine its opinion research to the voting public. Political parties, like companies, are dependent on various stakeholders and suppliers.' Political stakeholders include all those interested and with an investment in the party or candidate such as members or volunteers within a political party or campaign, other politicians, lobbyists, interest groups, donors, the media, professional associations or unions, electoral commission and party or government staff: see Figure 1.1.

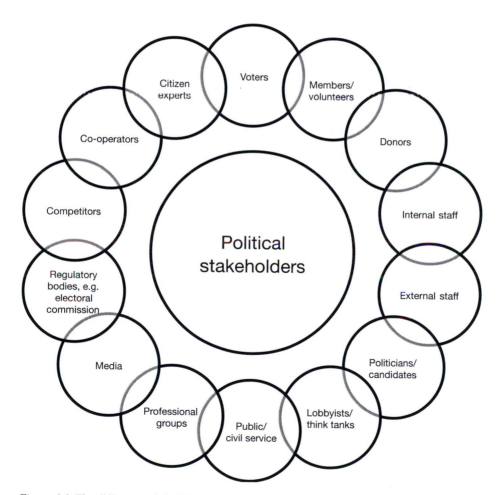

Figure 1.1 The different stakeholders in politics

The importance of different stakeholders differs from one organisation to another; and for politicians and parties, between opposition and government. Hughes and Dann (2009, 252) argue that in elections parties might tailor their product to suit key target markets but once in government politicians need to meet 'the broader stakeholder needs of society'. Research by de Bussy and Kelly (2010) into the perceptions of 23 politicians and political advisors in Western Australia as to what constitutes stakeholders in government concludes that government favours some more than others, so some groups may be excluded, especially if they are less organised and do not have the same ability to communicate with the elite. Politicians in power need to take care to identify all potential stakeholders. Thus as Temple (2010, 272) notes, 'the relationship between politicians and voters is more complex than the marketing models acknowledge and the preferences of traditional voters, interest groups, other political leaders and, as argued, the media, must be taken into consideration'. All stakeholders could potentially impact on the ability of a political organisation or actor to achieve their goals. If candidates want to employ sophisticated market research to understand voters better, they need to obtain financial donations to fund such research, so they need to identify potential donors; if they want to 'get out the vote' (GOTV), they need to recruit high-quality volunteers; if they want to communicate with the electorate, they need to consider the media; and once in government, politicians need to consult with key groups affected by proposed policy and will get lobbied by interest groups regarding their proposed legislation – otherwise delivery will be impaired.

One other aspect of the political market is culture: Kiss (2013, 71) notes that cultural factors also influence political marketing activities, as leaders adopt certain messages, gestures and deeds to respond to social, sports and cultural aspects of the country they are campaigning in. This can include traditional cultural activities such as baseball in the US, hockey in Canada, football in the UK and rugby in New Zealand; or it can be targeted at sub-national ethnic groups with politicians appearing at religious festivals and events or sampling traditional food. Understanding both who the stakeholders are and what the culture is like can inform the creation of political marketing activities that help political elites be seen to understand, represent and connect with their different publics.

The political product

The political product is extremely complex. The most obvious components are policy proposals, put forward by politicians; but it also includes a person – the politician or party leader – and everything else a political organisation or politician does. In other words, its entire behaviour is the product; and uncontrollable aspects such as the behaviour of members or volunteers can influence public perception of a product, as can more intangible factors including the emotive imagery of a political party brand. The political product is also constantly evolving and changing over time and is never complete – it isn't like an iPhone that is manufactured and can be picked up from a shop, and thus there is an end point to the design of the product. There are certain aspects of the political product which are more visible, including:

1   Leadership/the candidate – their powers, image, character, support/appeal, relationship with the rest of the party organisation (advisers, cabinet, members, MPs), media relationship.
2   Members of the legislature (senators, MPs)/candidates for election – e.g. their nature, activity, how representative of society they are.

3   Membership or official supporters – their powers, recruitment, nature (ideological character, activity, loyalty, behaviour, relationship to leader).
4   Staff – researchers, professionals, advisers, etc. – their role, influence, office powers, relationship with other parts of the party organisation.
5   Symbols – name, logo, anthem.
6   Constitution/rules.
7   Activities – meetings, conferences, rallies.
8   Policies – proposed, current and those implemented in power.

However, as Lloyd (2005, 41–3) argues, a political product includes even broader aspects:

Services offering: the identification of the services (including policy) that the country/ electorate *really* needs (as opposed to what parties believe it needs), delivery of policy *and* the effective management of its implementation (involving appropriate management skills and expertise).

Representation: the way that all aspects of the political party, its policies and its members are represented to the electorate on a number of interrelated levels, from the political sector as a whole, through individual parties to individual politicians. It includes controlled and uncontrolled communication.

Accommodation: how parties understand and respond appropriately to the needs of the electorate, with their members, MPs and members of the government being accessible and open and the party encouraging participation at all levels across the community.

Investment: concerns the stakeholder-type relationship that the electorate has with its political representatives; it can be a direct financial payment in the form of subscriptions to a political party or candidate, or a delayed financial 'investment', for example, likely changes in tax or welfare benefits; or non-monetary investment, such as time, effort and emotion. Either way, electors expect to see a return, either tangible or intangible, on their investment.

Outcome: the ability to deliver on policy issues and election promises; a tangible measurement of performance by electors.

Sansom (2009) applied Lloyd's concept of the political product to the UK Conservative Party in the 2001 election and identified the weaknesses in the product offered to voters. The *services* offering of the Conservative Party included a set of ideological beliefs and policies associated with the management of national security, social stability and economic growth such as firmer immigration controls, a stronger emphasis on law and order and a tax-cutting policy, as well as an assurance that Britain would not be involved in the European single currency. However the Conservatives failed to convey that they had the managerial skills to implement these measures. The tax-cutting ideas were compromised by suggestions that there was a more radical agenda to slash the tax burden which would negatively affect public service provision; other initial ideas such as the 'tax guarantee' had been retracted, raising doubts about what the final product would really be; and there was disunity over European policy. This disunity, as well as negative associations from the previous time in government and negative campaigning, prevented the party conveying *representation*. The Conservatives also failed to convey *accommodation* as they adopted a core vote strategy in the campaign. In the election the Conservatives portrayed the *investment* of a vote for their party as a voice against the increasing European influence in British society, as well as for halting crime and improving education standards; but this was a very narrow appeal, and when they lost the election they could not deliver the promised *outcome*. Political parties and candidates are not just judged on their current product but on their previous performance and their ability to deliver.

Political marketing functional tools

Marketing techniques ubiquitous in business are increasingly common in politics, offering politicians new ways of engaging with and responding to an increasingly demanding electorate. Political marketing offers political elites a range of functional tools they can use to achieve their goals of obtaining support from their market for their product: see Figure 1.2.

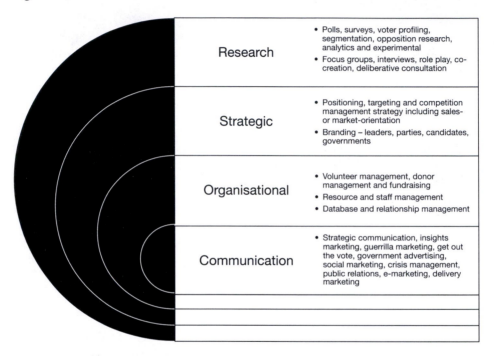

Research
- Polls, surveys, voter profiling, segmentation, opposition research, analytics and experimental
- Focus groups, interviews, role play, co-creation, deliberative consultation

Strategic
- Positioning, targeting and competition management strategy including sales- or market-orientation
- Branding – leaders, parties, candidates, governments

Organisational
- Volunteer management, donor management and fundraising
- Resource and staff management
- Database and relationship management

Communication
- Strategic communication, insights marketing, guerrilla marketing, get out the vote, government advertising, social marketing, crisis management, public relations, e-marketing, delivery marketing

Figure 1.2 Political marketing functional tools

First, there are a range of political market research tools to identify and understand the public and other markets. Market research includes the usual quantitative and qualitative techniques such as polls and focus groups but also role play and deliberation and, more recently, experimental and analytical marketing research. Segmentation and voter profiling helps understand voters and volunteers at an individual level to then connect them into new groups politicians can target. Strategies include: positioning, which suggests that parties and candidates need to take account of the competition and ensure they occupy a distinctive, superior position from which they can attract support; adopting a sales or market orientation towards electioneering, which involves either focusing on using research to create effective communication to sell the product to the voter or utilising the results of research to create a product that the voter will want because it meets their needs and wants; and political branding to create a long-term sustainable relationship with voters. Strategies for communication include e-marketing, market-oriented political advertising, delivery management and public relations, and not just short-term sales but longer-term communication that suits the receiver (not just the producer) and develops a positive long-term relationship between politicians and the public. Political marketing also offers tools for how to organise effectively, such as GOTV campaigns, internal party marketing and volunteer management. All of these tools work in relation to each other; so whilst segmentation might take place under market research it is then used to inform communication, strategic product development and voter profiling in GOTV campaigns. To be most effective, political marketing is not just about cherry-picking one or two tools from marketing; it is about an overall framework of interrelated activities that politicians can use to achieve a range of goals in a way they are comfortable with. Lees-Marshment *et al.* (2014) conclude from their new study of political marketing in the US that each element of political marketing – from the four areas of researching, strategising, organising and communicating – connects with and influences each other.

Political marketing approaches

Furthermore, political marketing is not just about a series of tools or techniques, it is also about concepts – a way of thinking, doing and being that is more philosophical in nature. Political marketing approaches are less tangible and are harder to measure academically but they can have a profound impact on the effectiveness of political marketing tools. Political marketing approaches also have normative implications and thus consequences for democracy.

Political marketing as selling

Political marketing is commonly seen as being about selling. One concept that has gained traction in academic discussion is the Sales-Oriented Party, which argues that parties should utilise market research to make their communication more effective, enabling them to test the effectiveness of both the message and the medium in persuading key voters to switch their support for a policy, politician or party. Political market research is conducted after the product is developed; it does not affect the decisions of elites on policy but how they are sold.

Political marketing communications remains a key part of both practice and research, and whilst persuasive forms remain common, more recent practice and research suggests that communication can be used to: create a long-term positive relationship with voters that can be sustained even when voters do not agree, and cannot be made to agree, with the decisions of political elites; or to enable contributions towards elite thinking before such decisions are made.

Political marketing as a product-based transaction strategy

Practitioner perspective 1.1 on the importance of strategy in political marketing

Strategy is the most important thing for winning and losing elections by any measure. [That's what I think, but other people argue . . .] Well, they're wrong.

The Late Lord Philip Gould, advisor to UK PM Tony Blair, interviewed in 2007

Source: Lees-Marshment (2011)

Political marketing is not just about communication, and some academics and practitioners argue that strategy or the actual product is more important in determining effectiveness: see Practitioner perspective 1.1. A dominant theme in political marketing practice and research is that elites will use marketing to identify voter demands and then design their product to suit this. In academic research, this concept is called the Market-Oriented Party. Political market research is conducted before the design and development of the product or brand to enable elites to create something the public will want to vote for. The focus is on elites changing what they do to suit voters instead of the other way round. As Newman (1999, 39) notes, 'marketing research is used by political leaders to shape policy. Bill Clinton and presidents before him have relied extensively on opinion polls to help determine the direction of their presidencies'.

The concept of a market orientation in politics has attracted a lot of attention and discussion as it changes the relationship and status of political elites vis-à-vis the public; on one hand meaning politicians listen to voters more, and on the other meaning that elected officials have less room to show leadership and make the 'right' decisions for the country. Market-oriented approaches are more transactional in focus: *let us know what you want, and we will offer it to you, and then you can vote for it.*

Relational political marketing

Very recent literature has suggested that political marketing is moving to a more relational strategy, where marketing is used to create long-term positive relationships between voters and political elites that help sustain politicians in times of crisis or failure and enable them to enact transformational leadership decisions. Yes, voters are still listened to, but as Jackson (2013, 252) notes, the approach is to build 'relationships centred on dialogue, which leads to trust and empathy'. In 2010, Anita Dunn, who was President Obama's first White House Communications Director and Senior Strategic Adviser for the 2008 Obama campaign, delivered a keynote at the APSA (American Political Science Association) Political Marketing Workshop. Dunn said that political marketing is changing from being transaction based (this is the product I offer to you) – to transformational (work with me to create change) and argued that this was the difference between Hillary Clinton and Barack Obama. She also argued that there was an emergent change in the relationship between voters and politicians whereby voters are being asked to be engaged and get involved, rather than just being treated as political consumers of a political product.

Several authors have argued for more of a relationship approach in political marketing. Johansen (2012) argues that relationship marketing would advise parties to strengthen their grass-roots organisation. The collection of new research in the *Routledge Handbook of Political Marketing* published in 2012 suggested that there has been a movement from neglecting members to seeing internal stakeholders as integral to successful political marketing; from short-term sales to long-term, mutual and interactive communication; and from campaigning to governing necessitating greater integration of political marketing into leadership (Lees-Marshment 2012). Internal marketing within parties and campaigns therefore becomes more about building mutually beneficial relationships that show respect for, and offer support to, volunteers and staff to help them become effective political marketers in their own right. Practitioners can therefore choose more dialogical and transformational approaches to achieve and maintain relationships with political consumers over the long term.

A relational form of political marketing may be particularly appropriate for government. Hughes and Dann (2010, 92) note how the Australian Labor Party used the relationship

Authors' corner 1.1

Political Marketing: Theoretical and Strategic Foundations
By Wojciech Cwalina, Andrzej Falkowski, and Bruce I. Newman
Published in 2011 by M. E. Sharpe

Political Marketing: Theoretical and Strategic Foundations is a comprehensive treatment of political marketing as an applied science. With insights, empirical research and concepts drawn from marketing, psychology, and political science, this book covers every aspect of marketing's infiltration into politics.

The authors define political marketing as 'the processes of exchanges and establishing, maintaining, and enhancing relationships among objects in the political market (politicians, political parties, voters, interests groups, institutions), whose goal is to identify and satisfy their needs and develop political leadership' (p.17). Political marketing is then conceptualized as a permanent element of governance rather than a discrete element of election campaigns. Thus, the authors present an advanced model of political marketing that brings together, into a single framework, the two campaigns: the permanent marketing campaign and the political marketing process. These two components are realized within a particular country's political system – 'democracy orientation'. This determines how the functions of the authorities are implemented, who is the dominant object in the structure of government, and, on the other hand, defines whom the voters focus on during elections. From this perspective, they distinguish four main types of democracy orientation: candidate oriented, party leader oriented, party oriented, and government oriented. Depending on this orientation, political campaigns may focus on different goals and different means of reaching them. Nevertheless, the political campaigns are always permanent. The political marketing process contains three key elements: politician/party message development, dissemination and relationship building. The goals of message development are elaboration and establishing the campaign platform. The campaign platform is defined in terms of candidate leadership, image, and issues and policies he/she advocates. Message development refers to distinguishing particular groups of voters for whom an individualized and appropriate campaign platform will be designed (segmentation) and candidate/party positioning (image and issue positions) in targeted segments.

The established politician or party message is then distributed on the voter market via personal (direct) campaigns (e.g. grass-roots efforts, election events and meetings) and mediated (indirect) campaigns that make use of electronic and printed media outlets (e.g. advertisements, debates, sponsored press releases), direct mail, the Internet (e.g. email, websites, blogs, social network sites), campaign literature (e.g. flyers, brochures), billboards, etc. The third element of the political marketing process and the goal of political party or candidate is to establish, maintain, and enhance relationships with voters and other political power brokers (media, party organisations, sponsors, lobbyists and interest groups, etc.), so that the objectives of the parties involved are met. This is achieved by an exchange which is based on mutual trust and fulfilling promises.

Using examples and empirical research drawn from countries around the globe, the authors elucidate the importance of political marketing techniques for the stability of democratic institutions. They also note the potential threats to democracy, especially the use of marketing techniques to manipulate voters at the subconscious level. They conclude with a set of normative 'do's and don'ts' for political marketing practice that strengthens civic education and democratic governance.

marketing paradigm of 'trust, reciprocity and commitment' in the first year of the Rudd government through 'the rapid implementation of election promise and the delivery of high profile trust-building policy initiatives', such as the apology to Australia's indigenous peoples at the opening of the first parliamentary session. Lees-Marshment (2012, 373) argues that in this way governing becomes a 'more mutualistic, organic, nuanced process'. Cwalina *et al.* (2011, 74) argue that government needs relationship building including delivery to build mutual trust: see Authors' corner 1.1 to learn more about their book in this area.

Experiential or co-creation

An alternative concept is experiential marketing, discussed by Jackson (2013), which is focused on involving the consumer in an active experience with the brand. Voters are not just spectators but feel part of the event. Similarly the *Routledge Handbook of Political Marketing* suggested that political market research was increasingly used to involve the political consumer in creating the solution to how to meet voter demands, with the public asked to step into the decision-makers' shoes and help to solve the problems (Lees-Marshment 2012, 373). Figure 1.3 integrates all of these approaches to show a potential pathway from sales-oriented political marketing to one that is more about co-production.

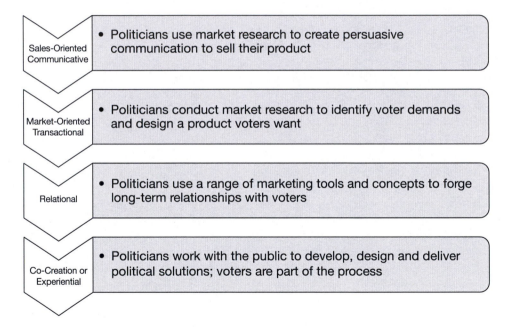

Figure 1.3 The development of political marketing approaches

The relationship between political marketing and its parent disciplines, political science and marketing

The basic notion that an area such as politics could use marketing was first suggested in the 1960s by Kotler and Levy, who argued that marketing, previously confined to commercial and business organisations, could be used by all organisations, including non-profit, state, public sector and charitable ones:

> The [marketing] concept of sensitively serving and satisfying human needs . . . provides a useful concept for all organisations. All organisations are formed to serve the interest of particular groups: hospitals serve the sick, governments serve the citizens, and labour unions serve the members . . . Marketing is that function of the organisation that can keep in constant touch with the organisation's consumers, read their needs, develop 'products' that meet these needs, and build a program of communications to express the organisation's purposes.
>
> (Kotler and Levy 1969, 15)

What makes politics amenable to a marketing perspective is its interest in the relationship between elites and the market: electorate and candidates; volunteers and campaigns; audience and media. The two disciplines aim to understand how an organisation or elite acts in relation to their market and vice versa. Marketing provides tools and ideas about how an organisation can understand and respond to its market more effectively to achieve its goals.

However, politics is very different to business in many respects. Politics links marketing to elections and therefore to government and the decision as to who ultimately controls the world. Politics is not about making money and it isn't even just about getting votes. Politics is about principles, ideals and ideology. As Savigny (2006, 83) notes, values and beliefs 'about the proper distribution of resources, and what a society should look like, underpins the notion of politics'. The political product has symbolic value, is intangible as well as tangible and is continually evolving. There is only a limited range of political products available to 'buy' and political consumers often support one political product simply to avoid another. Volunteers make up the producers' labour force, and the product is difficult to deliver. Normatively, politicians are duty bound to show political leadership and judgment rather than just offer voters what they want. Political parties are there to provide representation, serving to ensure there is an effective link between citizens and the government; and to aggregate interests by reconciling a variety of conflicting individual demands, which aids governing and facilitates political socialisation and mobilisation. The apparent ethos and certainly the language of business can therefore appear at odds with politics. As Maurice Saatchi (2008), both a businessman and political advisor noted, politics and business 'are parallel universes with their own solar systems, time zones and laws of gravity'.

Given these differences, when applying concepts and techniques which originated in business to politics, they need to be adapted if they are to be of value in understanding political behaviour. As Scammell's review of the field observes, the four Ps (product, pricing, promotion and place) 'need considerable stretching to make much sense in politics' (1999, footnote 50). Political marketing is created by applying marketing concepts from business to politics but not by simply imposing one over the other. There is also an older discipline, political science, that existed before the emergence of management or marketing research, and thus political science literature needs to be considered when researching political marketing. Lees-Marshment (2001) calls this process of combining the two disciplines a 'marriage', because political marketing literature needs to draw on both disciplines. Or, to put it another way, perhaps politics and marketing are the parents, and political marketing is the baby resulting from the marriage which has some of its parents' traits but is its own separate entity.[1]

Political marketing is concerned with all aspects of political behaviour by politicians, parties and governments. It is about the design of the political product, its relationship to market demands, and the relationship between political elites and the public. Communication is a key part of political marketing, but not the only one; and marketing extends beyond elections to governments and groups. Political practitioners and organisations use all aspects of marketing to help them achieve their goals. Lees-Marshment (2003) argues that to make the marriage of politics and marketing work political marketing research needs to be comprehensive and thus:

1   Apply marketing to the whole behaviour of a political organisation, not just how it communicates or campaigns.
2   Use marketing concepts, not just techniques.
3   Integrate political science literature into the analysis.
4   Adapts marketing theory to suit the differing nature of politics.
5   Apply marketing to all political organisational behaviour: interest groups, policy, the public sector, the media, parliament and local government, as well as parties/elections.

Political marketing research has broadened out beyond communication and applied a wider range of marketing concepts, and this book explores how marketing permeates all aspects of the political product. Butler and Harris (2009) discuss how new disciplines develop over time, citing Mullins (1973) who argues there are four stages: normal, network, cluster and specialty. In the first stage, isolated scholars begin to discuss and share published work and attempt to agree a direction; by the third stage there are more formal organisational and relational arrangements which attract recognition from the parent discipline. The final stage sees work become institutionalized with clear research parameters and an agenda, with a growth in university courses and textbooks. Butler and Harris's (2009, 154) conclusion that political marketing is currently about the third stage is appropriate, though we are seeing signs of it moving to the fourth as it is now taught and studied all around the world in political science, marketing and communication departments, and in applied politics or political management programmes in the US and Canada.

Studying and researching political marketing

Why marketing and politics students should study political marketing

As Savigny and Temple (2010, 1049) observe, 'contemporary politics has become dominated by the use of marketing strategies, techniques and principles'. Politicians, parties, consultants and governments are all aware of the potential benefit of marketing tools to help them in their work. For political science students, studying political marketing will ensure they are aware of a profound area of practice in the political sphere, and not only get to understand this behaviour but to critique its nature and impact on democracy. Teaching political marketing also significantly enhances the employability of political science students because they gain knowledge of an area where there are a range of jobs in government and political organisations: see Figure 1.5.

For marketing students, political marketing has become more widespread in research, with Harris and Lock (2010, 43) noting that political marketing is now 'a significant area of international research in contemporary marketing'. Marketing students will gain knowledge of an important area of marketing activity which adds further strength to their employability skills by preparing them for working in a political as well as corporate organisations; they gain understanding of the potential problems with transferring marketing into a non-business sphere and acquire a deeper, more critical and reflective insight into marketing itself in doing so. Baines (2012) argues in *The Financial Times* that political marketing should be taught on MBA programmes, arguing that 'political marketing, when it is good, has an uncanny ability to market ideology. Business schools should take note. After all, their students, many of whom will in time become managers and chief executives, will have to develop and market ideology internally, usually in the form of missions, visions and values, to gee up their constituent employees, supply-chain partners and shareholders.' One of the challenges for marketing students can be to understand politics quickly enough, and students may want to access introductory politics texts – see Figure 1.4 – and need to watch the news and follow politics more closely. Marketing students also might like to consult the book by Ormrod *et al.* (2013) which is written from a marketing management perspective.

Introductions to politics for marketing students

Stephen D. Tansey and Nigel Jackson (2008). *Politics: The Basics*, 4th edn. Routledge.
Robert Garner *et al.* (2012). Introduction to Politics. Oxford University Press.
Benjamin Ginsberg *et al.* (2012) *We the People: An Introduction to American Politics*. W. W. Norton & Company.
Gillian Peele *et al.* (eds) (2014) *Developments in American Politics 7*. Palgrave.
Richard Heffernan *et al.* (eds) (2011) *Developments in British Politics 9*. Palgrave.
Erik Jones *et al.* (eds) (2011) *Developments in European Politics 2*. Palgrave.
Alistair Cole *et al.* (eds) (2013) *Developments in French Politics 5*. Palgrave.

Figure 1.4

Both marketing and political science students will gain a range of benefits from studying political marketing. This book and any course on political marketing will enable students to:

- appreciate how and why political marketing has developed over time and its relation to party decline, increase in electoral volatility, and so forth;
- comprehend the concept of political marketing, understanding that political marketing is not just about spin or election campaigns;
- understand how marketing may be used within the political environment, but also appreciate the differences between marketing business and marketing politics;
- learn about the difficulties in introducing marketing into politics, questioning the ethical issues arising from marketing politics and arguing the benefits marketing may bring to politics;
- gain knowledge about comparative political behaviour by utilising international case studies and learning about the global transfer of ideas and consultants;
- encourage broader thinking about the practice of modern-day politics;
- comprehend the potential and limitations of marketing politics, both practically and normatively;
- gain knowledge of another discipline;
- reflect on practical experience in politics.

Both sets of students will also gain significant transferable skills by studying political marketing, such as: intellectual agility and interdisciplinary understanding; comparative analysis, by examining the use of political marketing in a number of countries and systems;

Student comments on the value of studying political marketing

Political marketing is relevant to politics today
- Political marketing you see every day in the news, everyone talks about it.
- It's about understanding what goes on in the world today.
- You're not studying, doing your hobby.

Political marketing has a direct career/practice link
- It's useful for future career . . . the research is something you can apply in politics.
- It opens doors . . . it's opened a lot of doors for me.
- It's a skill in demand.
- With political marketing you get out there and talk to people.
- It's a contribution . . . not just theoretical; can recommend how to improve things.
- In political marketing you can take the things you study and learn and put them into practice.
- It has practical applications – not only in elections but also in internal party political matters as well.

As a new field there are more opportunities to make an impact
- Political marketing is not a dinosaur field.
- You can contribute to a field you are working on . . . so many areas where there's a gap.

Figure 1.5

Source: Graduate students' comments during a presentation to undergraduates about studying political marketing at postgraduate level, 2011, Auckland University; and comments from Daniel Mann on the Political Marketing Group Facebook page

balanced consideration, by learning about the different academic perspectives in the field of political marketing; debating skills, by discussing topical issues that arise from political marketing; critical analysis, through considering both the effectiveness and the democratic implications of political marketing; applied analysis and report writing skills, by completing applied assessment. Figure 1.5 reports what students themselves have found valuable about studying political marketing.

One of the most heartening comments from students is that studying political marketing increases their employability. Students go from this to working in government, parties and marketing companies with a clear understanding of how political marketing can work. In other words, political marketing it is not just knowledge for it's own sake; it is applicable to the real world and useful after graduation. Students taught political marketing will be better prepared for the workforce.

Barriers to researching and teaching political marketing

Studying and conducting cross-disciplinary research is not easy. Part of the problem is practical – political marketing requires scholars and students to learn and understand two disciplines, not just one. As Butler and Harris (2009, 158) note, it needs scholars not just to cross-reference ideas and methods but to genuinely engage with the other discipline's philosophical base.

Defending of academic territory can also present barriers. Like most new ideas in academia, the suggestion by Kotler and Levy (1969) that marketing be broadened beyond business aroused tremendous controversy. Luck (1969) argues that no benefit would come from this: 'marketer's self image may be pleasurably inflated by claiming that political campaigns are just another part of marketing, but what progress is to be gained by such reasoning?' Arndt (1978) objects on academic discipline grounds that such 'a combined semantic and territorial expansion may threaten the conceptual integrity of marketing, add to the confusion in terminology, and widen the gulf between marketing theory and practice'. Thankfully such fears have proved incorrect, and political marketing research has not damaged marketing! Scholars and students have also faced barriers in political science to working on political marketing, with more traditional academics claiming this is not political science, not 'what we do', or dismissing it as being simply about advertising. The more the field grows, and attracts growing numbers of students, the harder is it for such claims to persist. However, in publishing terms, articles and books on political marketing are increasing in political science outlets and as Savigny and Temple (2010, 1049) observe recently, 'political marketing has become an important sub-field in the discipline of politics'.

There is also an institutional barrier. Universities are not well equipped for cross-disciplinary teaching. It should be the case that political marketing programmes and supervision at UG, MA and PhD level can be taught by either a political scientist or marketing scholar yet be open to students from both those disciplines and faculties; but this rarely happens. Instead, barriers form to prevent one discipline teaching a course as it relates to the other discipline too. The hierarchical and siloed nature of universities sadly puts up many barriers to cutting-edge teaching.

A fourth problem is that the very appeal of political marketing – that is applicable to the real world – can be at odds with more traditional views of academia: that our purpose is to create knowledge for its own sake and not to understand and improve practice. In centres and programmes of applied politics in the US, political marketing is more likely to be taught by practitioners than academics. Practitioner-focused teaching in public sector management, which trains government staff, is often found in business schools instead of political science departments. Political marketing and management may well end up following the same trend, which is a shame for political science. Institutions which are prepared to be more open and buck this trend will however be able to be ahead of the game in capturing student interest in political marketing and enjoy significant success as a result – as shown by the programmes on political management at George Washington University and Carleton University in Canada.

Another obstacle concerns the democratic implications of political marketing. The democratic problems political marketing cause can create exciting and interesting debates in class but can also be used as a reason to thwart research and teaching on the topic. Many of the academic critiques focus around the basic core of political marketing, that politicians should listen to voters. For example, Walsh (1994, 68) argues that 'the central questions of politics, the nature of punishment, the organisation of health and education, foreign relations and the formation of law cannot be settled on the basis of consumers'; Smith and Saunders (1990, 298) that 'pandering to the prejudices of the majority might herald a tyranny of the ill informed'; and Coleman (2007, 181) that 'voters are promiscuous and rationally irresponsible in the range of inconsistent views they hold at any one time, and rarely think about long-term policy consequences in ways that politicians and their advisors are required to do'. The strongest counter argument to this is if you think political marketing is seen as a problem for democracy, then that is all the more reason universities need to be teaching students about it so they can be well informed before they begin to practice it themselves.

The last chapter of this textbook focuses on political marketing and democracy and consider both the problems and potential of marketing politics so that readers can make their own choices about what to think and do about political marketing.

Political marketing: a dynamic field

Political marketing is a substantial aspect of modern politics; politicians, advisors, parties and governments themselves use segmentation, market research, branding, and public relations to help them win and maintain support from the public. It attracts significant attention from politicians, academics, journalists and the public. Political marketing also has profound impact on the way the political world operates. Through reading this textbook, readers will be able to better understand the concepts, techniques and ramifications of political marketing. The book synthesises a wide range of literature and provide a diverse group of empirical applications of political marketing to ensure that whether readers are students, scholars or practitioners, they become properly informed about scholarly research, and the pragmatic application and principled implications of political marketing so they can make appropriate choices as to what they think, study, research and practice when marketing politics.

Discussion points

1   In your own words, describe what political marketing is about. What tools do political marketers use and what do you think is the best approach they should take – sales-oriented communicative, market-oriented transactional, relational or co-creation/experiential?
2   What are the most important goals for world leaders such as President Obama? Which goals do you think are most important for the parties in your country?
3   Identify the potential stakeholders for a party or candidate, and then debate which are more important and why.
4   Describe and evaluate the product for the governing party or local candidate in your country.
5   Discuss and debate why some academics object to marketing permeating politics.
6   Identify and discuss the careers that studying political marketing might be useful preparation for.

Assessment questions

Essay/exam

1   Define political marketing, and explain what it involves in terms of tools and approaches.
2   What are the differences between business and politics, and how does political marketing have to be adapted in light of this?
3   Discuss what factors make up the political product, considering both theoretical concepts and empirical examples.
4   Explore and evaluate the nature and varying importance of the different stakeholders a political party, candidate or government needs to consider.
5   'The election campaign is the least important part of political marketing.' Explain and critique the validity of this statement, illustrating your argument with examples and theory.

6 Drawing on cases and theory, write a ten-point statement of 'political marketing principles': a list of the most important lessons and advice for how a candidate, political party, group or government should use political marketing.

Applied

1 Identify the goals, product and stakeholders of a political party, candidate or government, noting the relative importance of each, and from this suggesting what they need to take into account when deciding how to use political marketing.
2 Assess the extent to which a political organisation or figure has used the different political marketing approaches – sales-oriented communicative, market-oriented transactional, relational or co-creation/experiential – and how effective each has been, making recommendations for future action.
3 Analyse the behaviour of a political organisation or figure in a recent period (whether the last election, or last year) and critique how well they responded to their stakeholders, designed their political product and achieved their goals.

Note

1 I remain grateful to an anonymous reviewer of the first edition of this textbook who suggested this analogy.

References

Arndt, Johan (1978). 'How broad should the marketing concept be?' *Journal of Marketing*, 42(1) (January): 101–3.

Baines, Paul (2012). 'Political marketing has lessons for business schools'. *The Financial Times*, 12 November. http://www.ft.com/cms/s/2/e58afb24–2755–11e2-abcb-00144feabdc0.html#axzz2 C01AiNze (accessed 7 June 2013)

Butler, Patrick and Phil Harris (2009). 'Considerations on the evolution of political marketing theory'. *Marketing Theory*, 9(2): 149–64.

Coleman, Stephen (2007). 'Review of Lilleker and Lees-Marshment (2005) Political Marketing: A Comparative Perspective'. *Parliamentary Affairs*, 60(1): 180–6.

Cwalina, Wojciecj, Andrzej Falkowski and Bruce I. Newman (2011). *Political Marketing: Theoretical and Strategic Foundations*. Armonk, NY: M. E. Sharpe.

de Bussy, Nigel M. and Lorissa Kelly (2010). 'Stakeholders, politics and power: towards an understanding of stakeholder identification and salience in government'. *Journal of Communication Management*, 14(4): 289–305.

Harris, Phil and Andrew Lock (2010). 'EDITORIAL: "Mind the gap": The rise of political marketing and a perspective on its future agenda'. *European Journal of Marketing*, 44(3/4): 297–307.

Hughes, Andrew and Stephen Dann (2009). 'Political marketing and stakeholder engagement'. *Marketing Theory*, 9(2): 243–56.

Hughes, Andrew and Stephen Dann (2010). 'Australian political marketing: substance backed by style'. In Jennifer Lees-Marshment, Jesper Strömbäck and Chris Rudd (eds) *Global Political Marketing*. London: Routledge, 82–95.

Jackson, Nigel (2013). 'General election marketing – selling a can of beans, building a favours bank or managing an event?' *Journal of Public Affairs*, 13(3): 251–9.

Johansen, Helene. P. M. (2012). *Relational Political Marketing in Party-Centred Democracies: Because We Deserve It*. Farnham, Surrey: Ashgate.

Kiss, Balázs (2013). 'Cultural paradigm contra political marketing or two answers to the same question'. In Kōstas Gouliamos, Antonis Theocharous and Bruce Newman (eds) *Political Marketing Strategic 'Campaign Culture'*. London: Routledge: 57–73.

Kotler, Philip and Sidney J. Levy (1969). 'Broadening the concept of marketing'. *Journal of Marketing*, 33(1): 10–15.

Lees-Marshment, Jennifer (2001). 'The marriage of politics and marketing'. *Political Studies*, 49(4): 692–713.

Lees-Marshment, Jennifer (2003). 'Political marketing: How to reach that pot of gold'. *Journal of Political Marketing*, 2(1): 1–32.

Lees-Marshment, Jennifer (2011). *The Political Marketing Game*. Houndmills and New York: Palgrave Macmillan.

Lees-Marshment, Jennifer (ed.) (2012). *The Routledge Handbook of Political Marketing*. London and New York: Routledge.

Lees-Marshment, Jennifer, Brian Conley and Kenneth Cosgrove (eds) (2014). *Political Marketing in the US*. New York: Routledge.

Lloyd, Jenny (2005). 'Marketing politics . . . saving democracy'. In Adrian Sargeant and Walter Wymer (eds) *The Routledge Companion to Nonprofit Marketing*. New York: Routledge, 317–36.

Luck, David J. (1969). 'Broadening the concept of marketing – too far'. *Journal of Marketing*, 33: 53–5.

Mortimore, Roger and Mark Gill (2010). 'Implementing and interpreting market orientation in practice: lessons from Britain'. In Jennifer Lees-Marshment, Jesper Strömbäck and Chris Rudd (eds) *Global Political Marketing*. London: Routledge, 249–62.

Mullins, Nicholas C. (1973). *Theories and Theory Groups in Contemporary American Sociology*. New York: Harper and Row.

Newman, Bruce I. (1999). *The Mass Marketing of Politics*. Thousand Oaks, CA: Sage.

Ormrod, Robert P., Stephan C. M. Henneberg and Nicholas O'Shaughnessy (2013). *Political Marketing: Theory and Concepts*. London: Sage.

Saatchi, Maurice (2008). 'Business and politics are worlds apart'. *The Financial Times*, 24 March. http://www.ft.com/cms/s/0/cb090874-fa0d-11dc-9b7c-000077b07658.html#axzz2nNkzAuy1 (accessed 15 May 2008)

Sansom, Tim (2009). 'An application of Lloyd's product concept: the UK Conservative Party in 2001'. Case study 2.1 in Jennifer Lees-Marshment, *Political Marketing: Principles and Applications*. London and New York: Routledge, 35–7.

Savigny, Heather (2006). 'Political marketing and the 2005 election: what's ideology got to do with it?' In D. Lilleker, N. Jackson and R. Scullion (eds) *The Political Marketing Election? UK 2005*. Manchester: Manchester University Press, 81–100.

Savigny, Heather and Mick Temple (2010). 'Political marketing models: the curious incident of the dog that doesn't bark'. *Political Studies*, 58(5): 1049–64.

Scammell, Margaret (1999). 'Political marketing: lessons for political science'. *Political Studies*, 47(4): 718–39.

Smith, Gareth and John Saunders (1990). 'The application of marketing to British politics'. *Journal of Marketing Management*, 5(3): 295–306.

Temple, Mick. (2010). 'Political marketing, party behaviour and political science'. In Jennifer Lees-Marshment, Jesper Strömbäck and Chris Rudd (eds) *Global Political Marketing*. London: Routledge, 263–77.

Walsh, Kieron (1994). 'Marketing and public sector management'. *European Journal of Marketing*, 28(3): 63–71.

2 Political strategy

Practitioner perspective 2.1 on the importance and complexity of strategy

Strategy is the most important thing for winning and losing elections by any measure. Unless you've got a strategy that is robust, long term, linked to serious political projects, you're not going to win elections.

The Late Lord Philip Gould, advisor to UK PM Tony Blair, interviewed in 2007

Without a clear strategy, you have to jump from stump to stump. A strategy helps you to prioritise between the important and the insignificant.

Claus Hjort Frederiksen, a minister in the Danish government led by Fogh

The first thing that you need to identify about the process of formulating strategy is that there is no one model and no one process.

Murray McCully, New Zealand National strategist & MP/ Foreign Minister, interviewed in 2007

Sources: Lees-Marshment (2011); Lindholm and Prehn (2007, 20)

Political marketing strategy is about how parties, candidates and governments think and plan in order to achieve their goals. It requires consideration of many different factors such as the nature of the market, history, culture, governance, stakeholders, competitors, resources and goals. Therefore, as Barber (2005, 212) defines it, political strategy is about 'the forming of objectives and implementing the tasks necessary to achieve those objectives with a pattern of consistency over time given the limitations of available resources'. Strategy is not just used to win power; Fischer *et al.*'s (2007) comparative study suggests that strategy was the key to ensuring effective focus in government. Practitioner perspective 2.1 indicates that not only is strategy important, it is hard to model, and Winther Nielsen (2012, 301) notes that political strategy is 'often an iterative process ... whenever new information is obtained, it might change the strategy outlook'. Nonetheless, political marketing has developed a number of concepts and frameworks to help us understand strategy. This chapter will discuss targeting, positioning strategies, attack and defence strategies, sales and market-orientations, populist strategies, strategy and the environment, measuring and implementing strategy.

Targeting

Targeting is about strategic resource allocation and focusing products where there is a market for them and it will win necessary support to achieve goals. Targeting ensures that resources go where they will be most useful and effective.

Practitioners firstly need to decide who to target. There are a number of ways to do this, drawing on a wide range of data to divide the electorate into smaller groups. At its most basic, targeting involves dividing the electorate according to traditional supporters who, if they vote, will support the candidate/party but need to be persuaded to get out and actually vote, and floating voters who have not yet decided who to vote for, as these two groups might influence the election outcome. But political marketers now engage in diverse and detailed targeting. Voters can be targeted by specific demographic groups: for example, when President Bill Clinton was trying to build support to pass his health-care bill during his first term, advertisements were produced featuring middle-aged women sitting around the kitchen table. In the 2012 US presidential election both Obama and Romney targeted single women voters in the styling and message of their advertisements;[1] and Michelle Obama encouraged the public to join 'Women for Obama' to help the campaign.[2] The campaigns also divided the women target group further into single women voters – swinglers – because their vote was more unpredictable. Rosin (2012) argues that they 'switch alliances, hold out for the best deal, express their outrage by suddenly going cold on a candidate who has irritated them and then warm up quickly to a new one who makes a better offer'; and they make up a fast-growing voting bloc of over 55 million voters in the US. Furthermore, there was a long-term strategy at play: Obama may have wanted their vote in 2012, but the Democratic Party also wants to attract them to turn them into more loyal voters in the long term.

Davidson and Binstock (2012, 25) note how parties and candidates have targeted seniors in the US since John F. Kennedy's campaign for presidency in 1960. Events are held in places such as nursing homes, senior centres, congregate meal sites, and retirement and assisted living communities. Some states have a higher proportion of seniors and are also swing states with large electoral votes, and thus it is worth political marketers targeting these. For example, Florida had 27 electoral votes in 2008 and 25 percent of its voting-age population was aged 65 and older; Pennsylvania had 21 electoral votes and 23 percent of its voting-age population was in this age range. Research can also identify diverging policy needs within the senior target group. Davidson and Binstock (2012, 26) note that 'poor and wealthy older Americans have substantially different stakes in issues concerning Social Security' because those who are least well off will rely more on social security, and this needs to be taken into account when planning strategy and communication: see Figure 2.1.

Targeting is arguably even more important for smaller parties as it helps conserve precious resources and deploy them more effectively. The UK Liberal Democrats increased their power by focusing on target areas, so that campaign efforts were placed in areas that had a chance of winning instead of being spread evenly through the country. They built up geographical clusters which, as Russell and Fieldhouse (2005, 210) note, enabled grass-roots supporters to work across seats if needed and helped to build up 'shared credibility from having a historical and realistic chance of winning seats in the region'.

Targeting is an effective strategy when communication and product targeting are linked: Tony Blair succeeded through displaying his policy promises to reduce class sizes on glossy billboards to appeal to traditional Tory voters in middle England (Lees-Marshment 2001). Kiss (2009) observed how the Hungarian Socialist Party (HSP) targeted the youth through communication and behaviour. In 2004 a new prime minister, Ferenc Gyurcsány, was elected and the party chose a new president, István Hiller, and each worked to respond to the youth

---

Advice for practitioners on how to reach senior voters

1 Pay serious attention to the greying electorate, especially given that older voters are more likely to pay attention to campaigns, get involved, donate and actually vote.
2 Utilise online forms of communication to reach senior voters.
3 Research actual needs and behaviours of seniors, instead of relying on myths and stereotypes.
4 Segment deeply, as there are varying needs within the senior group, with some fit and able to work and fully engage in society and others badly affected by low income and ill health.
5 Be open to new ways of viewing seniors – engage in 'a process of ongoing discovery'.
6 Be aware that retirement is changing, and it is not just about old-age benefit and concessions on public transport.

Figure 2.1

Source: Adapted from Davidson and Binstock (2012, 29)

segment though both product development and communication. Gyurcsány's youth, his passion for youthful pastimes such as partying and sport, and his frequent jogging were communicated through the media or directly on the internet and via direct mail; and he was regularly seen in universities, in pubs, and at rock festivals. The party abolished policies unpopular with the youth such as compulsory military service and created programmes to help young people with housing problems and support Hungarian pop music instead. The image of the party was also rejuvenated to show it was more modern and dynamic: using new colours and slogans, emphasising the youth of the party by seating young people, particularly girls, on the stage behind the speakers, publishing a CD of pop hits with the evocative picture of a young woman with chillis in her mouth and using a picture of a condom on the youth organisation's website. This targeting strategy was successful: the HSP achieved a larger majority with increased support from the youth segment at the next election and thus remained in government.

As well as creating large target groups, parties and candidates also divide the electorate up into micro- and nano-target groups using complex computerised data processing, as Practitioner perspective 2.2 indicates. In the 2005 UK election, all of the three main parties identified key target groups (see Figure 2.2), and such groups were then targeted with direct mail and telemarketing (Savigny 2005).

Practitioner perspective 2.2 on the move to micro targeting in the US

It was fascinating to watch – but too much . . . We were going after voters with a meat cleaver, they were going after them with a scalpel.

Richard Beeson, Romney Campaign Director, 2012

If you don't know anything about campaigns you would assume it's national, but a successful campaign is highly, highly local, down to the Zip code. The revolution in technology is to understand where the undecideds are in this district and how you reach them.

Eric Schmidt, who offered advice to the Obama Campaign, 2013

Sources: Balz (2013); Zeleny (2012)

Examples of target groups identified by UK parties in the 2005 election

Labour	Conservative	Liberal Democrats
Upscaling new owners Don't believe in consumption as means of expression. Busy people, so convenience is the watchword.	**Corporate chieftains** Senior business people living in large detached houses in outer metropolitan suburbia. Tend to have four-bedroom homes surrounded by trees and protected from view by laurels and rhododendrons. Drive Lexus or BMW cars.	**Golden empty nesters** Wealthy older people living in provincial regions in 1930s houses. Lib Dems have strong challenge to Tories in this sort of neighbourhood. Support the National Trust. They are not concerned about the economy but rather with value for money.
Coronation St Found in northern maritime and industrial regions. Represent good market for mass brands.	**Burdened optimists** Modest qualifications. Many have built up debts. Made the Thatcher revolution. No belief in collective social responsibility. Place high value on personal freedom. Indulgence and immediate gratification sets the trend for everything.	**University challengers** Mostly aged 18 to 24, in areas of provincial cities which contain halls of residence. Much less ideologically driven than previous generations.
Rustbelt resilience Found in traditional mining communities, gardens well tended with newly painted house exteriors. Few read books or travel to offbeat holiday locations. They eat fish and chips. Solidly Labour.		

Source: Excerpts from Patrick Wintour, (2005). 'Postcode data could decide next election'. *The Guardian*. http://www.spinwatch.org/content/view/613/9/ (accessed May 8 2008)

Figure 2.2

Friesen (2011) notes how in the Canadian 2011 federal election, Canadian parties utilised highly focused targeted campaigning and created policies and messages to suit narrow bands of the population to shift just enough votes to win, utilising commercial market research data on buying and lifestyle habits along with their own party's canvassing data and polling. This can make a big difference in a close race. Friesen noted how in Canada, a firm called Environics Analytics broke voters down into 66 types. Such methods were also used to a great extent in the 2012 US presidential election, and this is discussed in detail in the chapter on political market research.

Positioning strategies

Positioning is about where parties or candidates place themselves in the marketplace in relation to the competition. Bannon (2004) argues there are five principles for successful positioning: see Figure 2.3.

Bannon's five principles for successful political positioning

1 **Clarity of the position**: know what the competitive advantage is and what voters think of this.

2 **Consistency of position**: a voter needs to know where they are; the organisation needs to offer a consistent and sustained approach.

3 **Credibility of positioning**: the voters' judgment of the quality of political proposals will always prevail.

4 **Competitiveness**: offer value that competing products do not.

5 **Communicable**: position must be easily communicated to targets.

Figure 2.3

Source: Bannon (2004)

Devine (2013) discusses how, in 2012, the Obama campaign positioned him as being the best candidate to take the country forward in the *next* four years. The campaign adopted the keyword 'forward' in speeches, ads and the podium to keep the focus on the future, not the *past* four years. Devine (2013, 145) argues that this positioning worked as it convinced voters that Obama had a better plan for the second term, and even voters who viewed his first term negatively were willing to trust him to move in the right direction after 2012. Applying Bannon's principles of successful positioning, Obama's position was seen as credible; it was consistent and clear, easy to communicate, and seen as superior to Romney's slogan which was a more vague 'Believe in America'.

Collins and Butler's (Butler and Collins 1996; Collins and Butler 2002) theory of market positioning explains the difference a position can make in terms of the strategic options available: see Figure 2.4. They argue that candidates need to be realistic and take this into account – for example, nichers are unlikely to move to being a leader in a single electoral period.

Hillary Clinton's failed bid to win the Democratic presidential nomination could be argued to be partly because she began the primaries in the leader position as the most well known candidate due to her time as First Lady when her husband Bill Clinton was president. Gorbounova and Lees-Marshment (2009) note how the Clinton product was largely informed by market intelligence, promoting the theme of responsiveness and emphasising Clinton's proposals on issues that worried voters most: ending the Iraq war, universal health care and reviving the economy. In terms of Clinton herself, the campaign strategy focused on characteristics such as her experience, having been tested and vetted already. However, Hillary Clinton met a surprise challenger: the, then, unknown Barack Obama who appeared as very fresh and energetic in comparison with her longevity as a political figure. Experience is a very apt product feature to emphasise for a leader, but it can weaken the candidate if voters prefer the 'change' theme which the Obama campaign adopted very effectively. The Clinton response was to attack, arguing that Obama was unelectable, inconsistent, hypocritical and, above all, untested and inexperienced, capable only of inspiring oratory rather than governing. However Obama responded with a counter-attack on her leader position, painting her as a stale Washington insider. Each market position has advantages and limitations.

Niche political marketing is about strategically developing your product and communication to suit a small defined group with relatively homogenous members. Harada and Morris (2012, 93) explored the use of niche marketing by the Canadian and Scottish

Collins and Butler's constraints and options for each market position

	Constraints	Options
Market leader	Has to appeal to a broad range of voters, and their interests conflict. Subject to continuous attack.	Defensive strategies to maintain and/or expand market share.
Challenger	Champions new issues which can make challenger appear to be out of step with public opinion; but otherwise has a similar product to leader and needs to convey differentiation or superiority.	Characterises leader negatively (e.g. as corrupt or incompetent). Brand position on new issue early to gain support once the issue becomes more salient.
Follower	Insecure position as follows the leader, but lacks the marketing resources to do so and is subject to losing their market support to challengers.	Can use cloning and copy the leader; or imitate them by adapting product aspects so they still differentiate or seek support from distinctive segments. They also need to protect their market share and thus avoid too much radical change.
Nicher	Specialises in serving the needs of a niche better than other competitors.	Can transform through radical strategic change and new product positioning but needs to communicate it effectively.

Figure 2.4

Source: Adapted from Collins and Butler (2002, 7–13)

Green parties. They argue that effective parties will follow niche market-oriented behaviour with four key principles: see Figure 2.5.

They noted how the two parties followed these principles with mixed effect. In the 2004 and 2008 federal elections, the Canadian Green Party was successful at being specialised, promoting ecology-based policies with a unique grass-roots approach, but did not use market research to inform the product. It showed some signs of forging strong relationships with its volunteers, but this was mitigated by a centralised top-down campaign organisation; and product adjustment of policies in response to public critique was only carried out in a limited way. The Scottish Green Party was also a classic specialised party, focused on ecology with the same grass-roots approach; but it was more effective in solidifying constituent relations. However, it did not attempt to change or adjust the product in response to market research at all. Harada and Morris concluded that the strong principles of Green parties present a challenge to them seeking to expand their market through adjustment of the product in response to public opinion.

Strategies are also formed in how to co-operate or compete with other parties. Barber (2009) notes how in the lead up to the 1997 UK election, the leader of the Liberal Democrats, Paddy Ashdown, asked his party to accept co-operation with Labour in order to defeat the

---

Harada and Morris's principles of effective niche market-oriented behaviour

1 Identify a focused area of specialisation.
2 Develop an organisation capable of forging a unique party reputation and fostering long-lasting relationships with supporters.
3 Utilise market research to inform a product that will maintain and expand support.
4 Actively resist niche incursions by other parties by adjusting the product in response to market research.

Figure 2.5

Source: Adapted from Harada and Morris (2012)

Conservatives. The Lib Dems doubled their seats in the House of Commons in 1997. They then pursued a strategy of *constructive opposition* to the Labour Government. Under a new party leader, Charles Kennedy, the party became more opposed to Labour as they moved closer to the centre ground and the Conservatives, opposing Blair taking Britain into an unpopular war in Iraq, which gained them more support in the 2001 election. In 2010, they formed a coalition with the Conservatives under David Cameron to get into power to enact some of their policy goals. The party has therefore exhibited a wide range of strategies in response to their own policy goals and ideals, the competition and their changing position in the political market place.

Case study 2.1 by Lorann Downer explores the use of positioning by the Australian Labor Party in 2007 and 2010. It notes how in 2007 the new leader, Kevin Rudd, was positioned as the challenger, as both socially progressive and economically conservative with specific points of difference from the Liberal opposition. Each election presents new market circumstances, however; so after Julia Gillard took over as leader following Rudd's fall in popularity she was positioned as the market leader, forward focused and having superior points of difference on education and health.

Attack and defence strategies

Political strategy always needs to be changing to suit different circumstances; sometimes it is about co-operating and sometimes, directly opposing. There are a range of ways to attack and defend a political organisation or figure. Marland (2003) suggests that when attacking and defending themselves in response to the competition, parties can take a range of military strategies: see Figure 2.6.

Market- and sales-oriented strategies

One of the most dominant theories of political marketing is a market-orientation, which argues that for politicians and parties to win elections, they need to use market research to inform how they design their product and brand, thus creating something voters want to support and reducing the need for communication. The basic principle is that a market-orientation involves the politician or party being in touch with ordinary voter concerns; interested in public views; responsive to what the public are concerned about; and demonstrating this in the way they *behave* – or in the political product they design, offer and

Marland's concepts of political attack and defence

Military strategy	Political marketing description	Political example
Bypass attack	Attack in an unexpected way, such as seeking the support of previously ignored market segments	A mainstream party promoting environmental policies to attract green voters, such as the UK Conservatives under David Cameron in the lead up to the 2010 election
Counter-offensive defence	Use head-on counter-attacks to equal or exceed opponent's action	A centrist party targeting centre-right and centre-left voters
Diplomacy	Collaborate with opponent	Party enters coalition or seeks agreement on specific policies, such as the decision by New Zealand's National Party to work with the Labor Government to support the anti-smacking bill in the lead-up to the 2008 election
Encirclement attack	Direct marketing at all areas using superior resources	Governing party utilises government resources to engage in public opinion research and government advertising
Flank attack	Use marketing to win support from segments where an opponent is most vulnerable	Left-leaning party targets competitors' female supporters as they are more likely to value social programmes
Flanking defence	Defend previously undefended segments	Marketing targets core supporters, such as through GOTV or internal political marketing
Frontal attack	Launch a direct attack on an opponent, and the one with the greatest resources wins	Heavily funded campaign overwhelms an opponent
Guerrilla attack	Weaken and demoralise an opponent through a series of small, unpredictable efforts to secure permanent elector support	Use of testimonials, case studies and special events to suggest grass-roots frustration with an incumbent; or using the jujitsu move to undermine an opponent's strengths, such as the UK Liberals questioning the Conservative's traditionally strong record on crime
Mobile defence	Diversify support by attracting targeted new voters when	Targets at recent immigrants, youth, seniors

Figure 2.6

Source: Adapted from and building on Marland (2003, 111–12)

Military strategy	Political marketing description	Political example
	party traditionalists have been attacked	
Position defence	Reinforce weakest supporters to prevent loss of core supporters	Marketing is targeted at own soft supporters through specific policies and communication
Pre-emptive defence	Attack opponents before you are attacked	Use of public relations and attack advertising to suggest flaws of opponents
Strategic withdrawal	Focus on core supporters and give up attracting new, but weaker, supporters	Appeasement and reassurance of the party faithful; another example of this is the UK Conservatives under William Hague abandoning market-oriented strategy, originally adopted after losing in 1997, and instead focusing on core supporters for the 2001 election

Figure 2.6—continued

implement, in order to ensure the product satisfies market demands in order to achieve the desired goals. This kind of behaviour is distinct from seeing marketing as being about selling; it is more concerned with the product and what voters want. However, market-orientation is not just about doing what everyone wants, as the market can be segmented and it involves needs as well as wants. And as the product is broad, the overall image, or brand, of the party can affect whether the public perceives the political leader to be in touch.

There are several models of market-orientation in politics: Newman's (1994) model of political marketing based in the USA, Lees-Marshment's (2001) Market-Oriented Party framework based in the UK and Ormrod's (2005a, 2005b) political market-orientation model which is European. The theoretical foundations of this model have been the subject of significant debate. Lees-Marshment's (2001) model of a Market/Sales/Product-Oriented Party framework has become one of the most cited – and critiqued – theories in political marketing. It has also been applied empirically to parties around the world (see Lilleker and Lees-Marshment 2005 and Lees-Marshment *et al.* 2010) as well as being applied to and cited in other arenas such as the European Parliament, and other fields including economics, law, medicine, urban studies and social work. Working from a political science perspective, this model applied marketing concepts as well as techniques to the overall behaviour of political parties and suggested a stage-by-stage process to show what a party with each one of the three orientations might do from the beginning of an electoral term through to election and delivery in government: see Figure 2.7.

A Product-Oriented Party (POP) is a traditional party, making the case for what it believes in elections without reflecting on what voters want or how they react to its product even

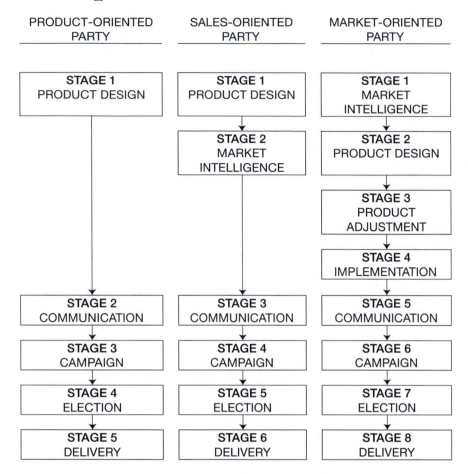

Figure 2.7 Lees-Marshment's (2001) model of the political marketing process for Product-, Sales- and Market-Oriented Parties

if it fails to gain support. It argues for what it stands for, believing its product is of such value that people will vote for it because it is right. Many smaller parties adopt this approach, particularly if their goal is to represent a particular section of society or put issues on the agenda, as opposed to winning power.

A Sales-Oriented Party (SOP) is also reluctant to change its product, but it uses marketing to identify persuadable voters and design more effective communication to sell the party to them. A SOP does not change its behaviour to suit what people want, but tries to make people want what it offers. Using market intelligence to understand voters' response to its behaviour, the party employs the latest advertising and communication techniques to persuade voters that it is right: see Figure 2.8.

An example of a Sales-Oriented Party is the UK Labour Party in 1992. Lees-Marshment (2001) explains how the Labour leader, Neil Kinnock, was elected in 1987 to unite the party and appease its left wing, but lacked wider electoral appeal. A number of other product weaknesses were apparent, such as unpopular policies in the manifesto including a unilateralist policy on defence, expansion of state ownership and intervention in the economy. The party also had a poor image on economic management, and strong party

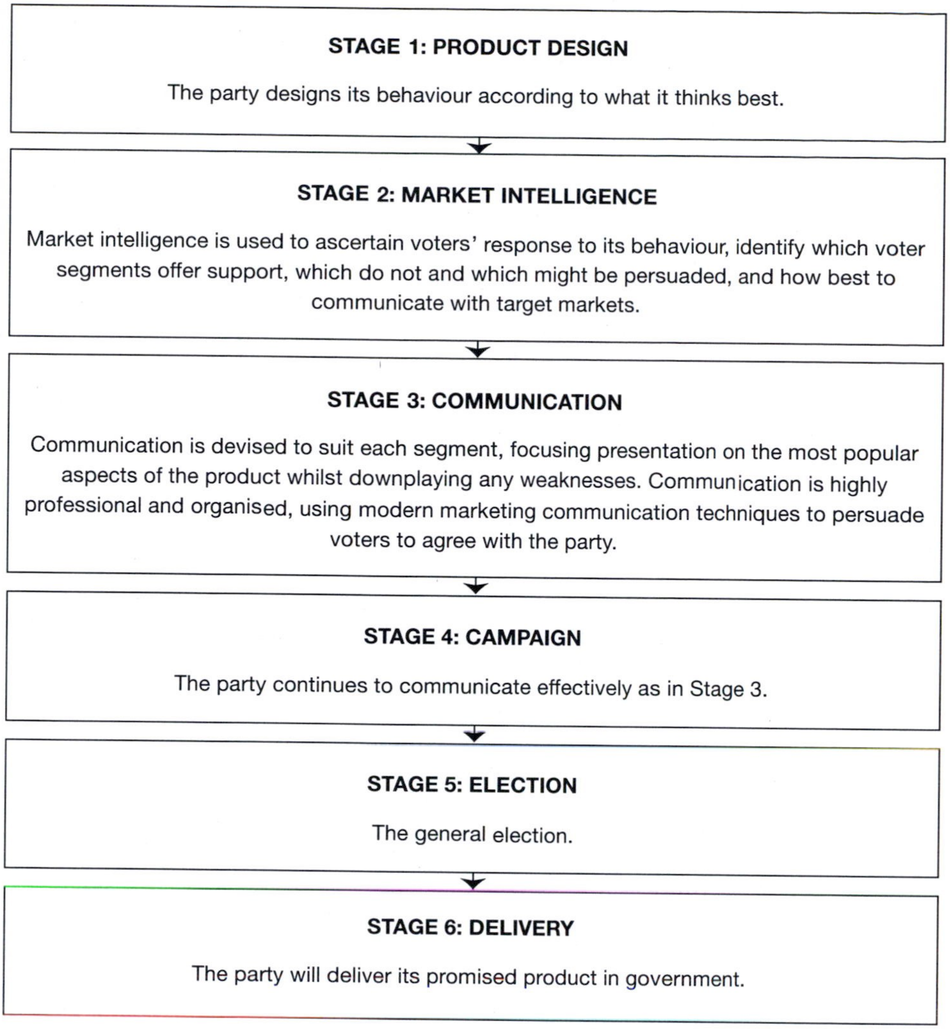

STAGE 1: PRODUCT DESIGN

The party designs its behaviour according to what it thinks best.

STAGE 2: MARKET INTELLIGENCE

Market intelligence is used to ascertain voters' response to its behaviour, identify which voter segments offer support, which do not and which might be persuaded, and how best to communicate with target markets.

STAGE 3: COMMUNICATION

Communication is devised to suit each segment, focusing presentation on the most popular aspects of the product whilst downplaying any weaknesses. Communication is highly professional and organised, using modern marketing communication techniques to persuade voters to agree with the party.

STAGE 4: CAMPAIGN

The party continues to communicate effectively as in Stage 3.

STAGE 5: ELECTION

The general election.

STAGE 6: DELIVERY

The party will deliver its promised product in government.

Figure 2.8 The political marketing process for a Sales-Oriented Party
Source: Lees-Marshment (2001)

links with the unions were still apparent. However, the party put significant effort into communication. Staff with professional expertise were recruited to reorganise communications; an advertising agency was appointed, and a new symbol was adopted: a red rose. Labour appointed MORI to conduct surveys, polling and a panel study, especially of target groups and marginal seats, to inform campaign design. However, Labour still lost, with polls indicating public dissatisfaction with the product. The party had only used marketing to inform the communication rather than the product design itself. Other examples of parties following a sales-orientation have been identified in comparative studies. Maier *et al.* (2010) conclude that whilst German parties use market research all the time, the focus is on communication and campaigning. Kiss and Mihályffy's analysis of Hungarian parties in the 2006 elections found that most were sales-orientated with the focus on using more sophisticated communication through an 'expanding arsenal and paraphernalia of campaigning techniques . . . strategies and tactics, activists and managers, advisors and counsels'

(2010, 155). Strömbäck (2010b, 59) concludes that in Sweden although the New Moderates moved towards a market-orientation the dominant trend is sales-orientation, and no party admitted to using research when developing policies.

In contrast, a Market-Oriented Party designs its behaviour to provide voter satisfaction to reach its goal. It uses market intelligence to identify voter demands, then designs a product that meets their needs and wants, which is supported and implemented by the internal organisation, and is deliverable in government. It does not attempt to change what people think, but to deliver what they need and want.

This concept is very different from more traditional views of political parties as organisations that seek to pursue their ideological vision. It also differs from the narrow view that marketing, if used, would be used in political communication. Instead, the MOP concept places emphasis on the development of a product, and market intelligence, rather than communication and campaigning.

Understanding that political parties are different to businesses – having complex products, markets as well as goals and, in particular, having members, more informed politicians and ideological history – a MOP does not simply offer voters what they want, or simply follow opinion polls, because it needs to ensure that it can deliver the product on offer. A MOP needs to ensure that its product will be accepted within the party and so needs to adjust it carefully to take account of this, using party views and political judgment to inform how it responds to public concerns. Parties may use their ideology as a means to create effective solutions to public demands but without trying to shape opinion. Therefore MOPs will not all become the same, nor assume the characteristics of catch-all parties, nor simply move to the Downsian centre ground.

The MOP political marketing process shows the different activities parties would carry out to achieve a market-orientation: see Figure 2.9.

Lees-Marshment (2001) argues that Labour became a Market-Oriented Party by the 1997 UK election. It conducted extensive market intelligence that informed the development of the product, particularly amongst traditional Labour supporters who had voted Tory in 1992. The party elected a new leader, Tony Blair, who was pro change and popular with voters. The party distanced itself from trade unions in response to market research telling them this had lost them votes in 1992. Clause IV of the constitution was altered to remove unpopular commitment to state ownership, and the slogan 'New Labour, New Britain' was adopted. Specific pledges were made in areas most important to voters, such as education and the health service, and the party made a commitment to fiscal prudence, low government spending and income tax in line with voter demands rather than party ideology. A mini-manifesto was launched a year before the election to pretest policies. Product adjustment was carried out with specific pledges for delivery kept short and limited, and details on how they would be achieved were added such as cutting waiting lists in the NHS by reducing money spent on bureaucracy. Reassurances were made on income tax and economic management. 'Middle England' voters were targeted, especially in communications. A strong leadership style ensured high party unity; the public accepted the party had changed. The product was well communicated to voters before the campaign even started and thus the campaign was uneventful. Labour won the 1997 election and attracted an increase in membership, and they won subsequent elections in 2001 and 2005 (see Lees-Marshment 2001).

The Market-Oriented Party (MOP) and Sales-Oriented Party (SOP) concepts suggest very different relationships between parties and voters. The SOP's main aim is to persuade and change voters' minds, while, in contrast, the MOP aims to respond to their views. Lees-Marshment argued that marketing sales techniques cannot make up for the lack of a

---

STAGE 1: MARKET INTELLIGENCE

The party aims to understand and ascertain market demands. Informally it 'keeps an ear to the ground', talks to party members, creates policy groups and meets with the public. Formally it uses methods such as polls, focus groups and segmentation to understand the views and behaviour of its market, including the general public, key opinion influencers, MPs and members. It uses market intelligence continually and considers short- and long-term demands.

STAGE 2: PRODUCT DESIGN

The party then designs 'product' according to the findings from its market intelligence before adjusting it to suit several factors explored in Stage 3.

STAGE 3: PRODUCT ADJUSTMENT

The party then develops the product to consider:

Achievability: ensures promises can be delivered in government. In an era of pledges, annual reports, and timetables for action, delivery capability is a big issue. The factors that go into this include the overall leadership team, economic management, capability, party unity and voters perception of the party's ability to deliver their desired outcome.

Internal reaction: ensures changes will attract adequate support from MPs and members to ensure implementation, taking into account a party's ideology and history and retaining certain policies to suit the traditional supporter market where necessary. Changes in policy thus need to be placed within, or with reference to, the party's traditional ideological framework wherever possible. This will be a sometimes delicate, yet essential, balancing act between the demands of external and internal supporters. This is, in effect, about internal marketing – and applying the same concepts for the wider public to those within the party organisation.

Competition: identifies the opposition's weaknesses and highlights the party's own corresponding strengths, ensuring a degree of distinctiveness.

Support: segments the market to identify untapped voters necessary to achieve goals, and then develop targeted aspects of the product to suit them. The party does not adopt the 'catch-all' approach of trying to get everyone on board. It is more 'traditional market plus'.

STAGE 4: IMPLEMENTATION

Changes are implemented throughout the party, needing careful party management and leadership over an appropriate time frame to obtain adequate acceptance to create party unity and enthusiasm for the new party design.

STAGE 5: COMMUNICATION

Communication is carefully organised to convey the new product so that voters are clear before the campaign begins. Not just the leader but all MPs and members send a message to the electorate. It involves media management but is not just about spin-doctoring; it should be informative rather than manipulative and built on a clear internal communication structure.

STAGE 6: CAMPAIGN

The party repeats its communication in the official campaign, reminding voters of the key aspects and advantages of its product.

STAGE 7: ELECTION

The party should win not just votes but attract positive perception from voters on all aspects of behaviour including policies, leaders, party unity and capability; as well as increasing the quality of its membership.

STAGE 8: DELIVERY

The party then needs to deliver its product in government.

Figure 2.9 The political marketing process for a Market-Oriented Party

Source: Lees-Marshment (2001)

comprehensive, unified political product that offers a positive, achievable alternative to an existing government and responds effectively to the concerns and demands of the public. Political marketing is more effective for major parties if it is used to inform how the product on offer is designed.

Comparative political marketing research has uncovered a range of examples of Market-Oriented Party/candidate behaviour around the world. Newman (1999) and Ingram and Lees-Marshment (2002) observe how, in 1992, Bill Clinton created the 'New Democrats', distancing himself from traditional Democrat large government programmes which were unpopular; and differentiated himself from the Republican President Bush by attacking his economic record and encouraging voters to view the election as a referendum on Bush's economic management. The policy focus was on issues of concern to both target middle-class voters and traditional Democrat supporters, such as the economy and health care; and a detailed economic plan was created that scaled back a number of Clinton's spending pledges and other promises, including his plans for infrastructure spending and deficit reduction, in order to make them more believable.

Knuckey and Lees-Marshment (2005) explored how, in 2000, George W. Bush came into power after adopting a compassionate conservative position that appealed both to swing voters and the Republican base, and portraying himself as a different type of Republican and as a different type of politician – a uniter not a divider. Policy evolved to focus on issues that opinion polls showed to be of paramount concern, as well as where Democrats were traditionally strong, such as education, social security and health care. Bush included traditional Republican themes, such as tax cuts, smaller government and a stronger military as well, to appeal to internal markets. On the competition, he criticised Al Gore as an 'Old Democrat' whose 'Big Government' programmes and tax plan showed that he did not trust the people and the contest became one between a 'New Republican' and an 'Old Democrat'. The campaign also targeted new market segments, including blacks and especially the growing Hispanic vote. Positive ads also targeted three other markets among the white electorate: women, moderates and independents.

Matuskova *et al.* (2010) explored how the Czech Social Democratic Party (CSSD) adopted a market-orientation and substantially increased its support, coming close to winning the 2006 parliamentary general elections. It analysed the market and used the results to develop a product and strategy in response, aimed at specific target groups of voters. Keenan (2007) explored how the Australian Labor Party won power after several election losses in the 2007 federal election under Kevin Rudd by responding to research that found people wanted vision and hope for the future but reassurance there would be continued competent economic management. Rudd proclaimed to be an economic conservative and reassured there would be no change from the economic management approach of the existing Liberal government, under Howard. Labor also downplayed or ignored its founding principles related to the working class, adopted some socially conservative policies and focused on education and other public service issues; but he also provided differentiation on issues such as the environment, ratifying Kyoto, and withdrawal from the Iraq war.

Lees-Marshment (2009a) argues that the New Zealand National Party became market-oriented between 2005 and 2008. The new leader, John Key, appealed to ordinary voters across different market segments, being both an extremely successful businessman and the son of an immigrant single mother. The opening address of the campaign showed a group of multicultural children, followed by a range of visuals showing Key amidst varied groups in society. Election adverts ended with the phrase: 'You've just got to choose it', giving the power to the voter. The National Party's political product appealed to traditional conservative voters with lower taxes and promises to act on crime; and the less well off by maintaining Labour's Working For Families benefit scheme for working parents on low to medium incomes and Key visiting 'struggle street' – low socio-economic areas. The Nationals succeeded in being elected, both in 2008 and again in 2011, and polled well against a fragmented Labour opposition.

Market-oriented behaviour can also be seen in newer democracies. Patrón Galindo (2009) explored how the Peruvian centre-left party APRA (People's Revolutionary American Alliance) adapted a market-oriented strategy in the Peruvian context to reorganise and relaunch after losing popularity in government during the late 1980s. After the collapse of the Fujimori regime in 2000, APRA openly utilised various means of data collection among different voter segments, separated by geography, gender, age, etc. APRA sought to fill the gap left by parties of the left, neglecting the poorest in Peruvian society and ideologically positioning itself on the centre-left as a reflection of the specific circumstances of the political situation. However they avoided being too left wing as they were also seeking support from key sectors, such as the private sector, and international organisations and corporations. Internally, the whole organisation of the party was changed with a new School of Training in Municipal Issues and branches tasked with creating new policy positions and preparing party members for campaigning and governing. The leader, Alan García, communicated a new image as a *mature* and *centred* politician to counteract negative voter perception from when he was in power. The party and García won power in 2006 (see also Patrón Galindo 2005).

Wakefield (2009) observed how the Japanese Liberal Democratic Party (LDP) adapted the MOP concept to suit the political system. LDP candidates developed and nurtured 'kōenkai' – private support organisations affiliated with individual candidates rather than the party – to campaign as it was illegal for volunteers to do so for the party. Kōenkai Aksi provided a source of market research about voter preferences. LDP candidates engaged in ongoing communication with voters – rather than the differentiated step in the MOP model. LDP candidates used their influence in Tokyo to secure lucrative public construction projects which rewarded loyal voters and businesses with jobs and contracts, thus creating satisfaction. At a national level, meanwhile, the party emphasised the economic gains felt by the voter, and voters responded positively to the economic inducements offered by LDP (see also Asano and Wakefield 2010). Fell and Cheng (2010) note how parties in Taiwan have sought to use political marketing research since the early 1990s to improve their understanding of voter preferences, and they used the results to develop targeted communication messages. The KMT (the Kuomintang or the Chinese Nationalist Party) moved towards an MOP approach after losing the 2000 presidential election, reforming its leadership, campaign style and policy positions with the help of consultants, polling and targeting, which helped it regain governing status in 2008.

Incomplete and short-lived market-oriented parties

However, few parties follow the market-oriented concept in full, and maintaining it once in government is difficult. Political marketing is often criticised because of its association with Tony Blair's UK New Labour design in 1997. Lees-Marshment (2001) argues that New Labour was not a perfect example of a MOP. Blair followed some, but not all, aspects of the MOP model. The main weaknesses were that, in terms of internal reaction analysis, changes Blair made to the party's product to increase its external support created significant dissatisfaction within the party; in particular the change in Clause IV, a constitutional clause that was of ideological, emotive importance, embodying what members had been fighting for during all their years of involvement in the party. As for competition analysis, Blair accepted the achievements of Thatcherism without saying how Labour would be that different; policy positions were extremely close to those of the Conservatives and failed to differentiate the New Labour product. Similarly, New Zealand National's orientation in 2008 wasn't a perfect example of a Market-Oriented Party as it lacked distinctiveness from Labour, failed to convey delivery management, sought more to show Key was an ordinary, in touch Kiwi bloke (based on the given communication), and produced a Commitments Card that had a long, rather than focused, list of promises. An overall weakness was that there was no clear vision, and expectations were not managed well, which could have led to voter disappointment once the party was in power. Mortimore and Gill (2010, 258) argue that 'a successful market orientation does not entail a party being led by the nose by its pollsters. The optimal strategy will involve taking into account ideology and party traditions, the historical context of the political party and party system and broader considerations of party and leader image – unless the voters themselves reject these as irrelevancies.'

In Peru, APRA lost support in government because they delivered different policies to what they promised (Patrón Galindo 2010). If the major weakness in MOP strategies is delivery, this can cause problems for governing – both pragmatically and normatively. Kotzaivazoglou and Zotos's (2010) analysis of the 2004 elections in Greece identified that New Democracy (ND) used market research and then designed its electoral product on clearly market-oriented lines, focusing on issues that were important to the voters, and the leader Karamanlis adopted an issue-focused, specific-audience targeted communication strategy. The ND won the election but once in government failed to deliver on most of its election promises, leading to significant voter discontent. In Australia, although Hughes and Dann (2010, 88) contended that 'the 2007 campaign of Kevin Rudd will likely go down in Australian political marketing history as the turning point in the acceptance and use of marketing strategy at a national level by a major political party', their predictions that internal debates within the Labor Party about being driven by the market or historical party ideology would cause challenges for it to remain market-oriented in government proved correct, as the Rudd/Gillard/Rudd government 2007–2013 demonstrated. In the US, Bush's 'Compassionate Conservative' strategy in 2000 gave way to a focus on defence after 9/11. Other difficulties with market-oriented politics include, as noted by Wakefield (2009), that the Japanese-style use of the MOP concept had problems as it led to corruption from close working relationships between government and business interests. This eroded public faith in the LDP at the same time that central government lost its ability to 'buy' voter support with economic projects during poor economic times in the 1990s, and in 1993 the LDP fell from power.

Critiques of the Lees-Marshment Market-Oriented Party model

The Lees-Marshment model has been subject to a range of criticisms (see Coleman 2007 and Ormrod 2006). For example, no party ever follows the MOP model 100 per cent. Case Study 2.2 by Gordica Karanfilovska discusses how, although a party in Macedonia has utilised the MOP concept, voters themselves have not absorbed such a change, and overall the party does not follow the model 100 per cent. Political marketing is increasingly relevant in new democracies, but it does not dominate the whole political system.

Parties do not always fit 100 per cent into a sales or market-orientation; behaviour is always evolving; and internally a party may engage in a divisive debate about whether to take one or the other approach to electioneering. Parties often adopt a hybrid approach, implementing either sales or market-orientation, depending on the individual policy area. Case Study 2.3 by John Wilcox explores how the New Zealand Greens utilised elements of both SOP and MOP in the 2011 election. On one hand this demonstrates that even minor parties can benefit from market-oriented concepts and strategies, as the party enjoyed a significant increase in voter support and seats, but it also demonstrates the difficulties of fitting a party into one category.

Comparative studies of market-orientation have found a mixed pattern of market-oriented behaviour: parties may adopt different orientations at different times, moving back and forth. The George W. Bush/Karl Rove strategy, once in power, could be viewed as a more sales-oriented approach, which won and maintained control of the presidency (see Knuckey 2010) – although given that public satisfaction with the Bush government declined it could still be concluded that a more responsive, market-oriented strategy may have generated greater voter satisfaction. A 14-nation study of political market-orientation by Lees-Marshment *et al.* (2010) concludes that whilst political marketing is a global activity and political parties around the world all utilise marketing techniques and concepts, the extent to which marketing is used to design the political product varies from one election to the next. The trend in orientation is 'diverse and fluctuating'; not dependent on being an established versus a new democracy; or limited to countries with a particular political system.

Furthermore, the MOP model does not consider the influence of a wider range of stakeholders other than voters and members; nor does it take account of the media. Savigny and Temple (2010, 1056) note how 'in Lees-Marshment's examination of the genesis of New Labour one crucial set of actors is missing from the analysis. At no stage is there any systematic examination of the role and power of the media.' They conclude that 'in any model of political marketing, the media must be more than one of the many factors impacting on the likelihood of parties or candidates becoming market oriented'. Additionally, it does not allow for party behaviour in PR (proportional representation) systems where parties may co-operate with each other; it also fails to consider the wide range of stakeholders parties need to consider other than voters and members which Ormrod's (2005a) model of political market-orientation does.

Other criticisms of the model echo those of Kotler and Levy's (1969) early article on broadening the concept of marketing and are linked to concerns about the democratic consequences of political marketing. As Temple argued, 'the main impact and importance of Lees-Marshment's work may well be the debate it has engendered about the role of political marketing in modern democracies' (2010, 274).

The market-oriented politics model applied more widely

The market-oriented concept has been applied to other areas of politics, not just political parties. Balestrini and Gamble (2011) applied the MOP model to the European Union (EU) to explore the link between the electorate's needs and wants and EU policymaking, arguing that public discontent with the EU reflects lack of responsiveness. They argue that the EU needs to adopt a market-orientation to policymaking to address the democratic deficit and propose a new model of a market-oriented European Union (2011, 97). This suggests that the EU should consider the electorate's needs and wants as well as the ideology and goals of the governing political parties; and then go through a series of stages:

Stage 1: Identify the problem;
Stage 2: Build a policy agenda;
Stage 3: Explore policy options and make selections;
Stage 4: Implement the policy;

Stage 5: Evaluate the policy.

This model could be applied to empirical analysis of the EU. Balestrini and Gamble theorise that the EU needs to consider macro and micro environmental factors of an economic, social and political nature, such as professional organisations which can influence the desirability and feasibility of an EU policy. The EU would need to manage the same dilemma of balancing conflicting public opinion of individual voters with the collective interest and governing constraints that political parties face. For example, if the EU promised to stop immigration altogether, even though it might be popular with some voters it could be detrimental to the EU not only in philosophical and human terms but also economically. Instead, it might argue that carefully managed immigration can also help to foster greater understanding, co-operation and friendship between individuals of different races and religions. The institution would also need to adjust their policies in response to internal reactions, balancing the demands of external (voters) and internal (members) supporters. The EU does not face the same competition as parties in an election, as there is no alternative, but it would still benefit from adjusting its product to suit key groups through segmentation, especially given public opinion data indicating dissatisfaction with the EU.

Populist strategies

Marketing can be linked to populism, and Winder and Tenscher's (2012) analysis of populism argues that parties and candidates can engage in a populist form of market-orientation by going through three phases: see Figure 2.10.

Winder and Tenscher (2012) explored cases such as Ross Perot's independent candidacy in the 1992 US presidential elections, Venuzuelan leader Hugo Chávez and Austrian FPÖ's leader Jörg Haider. They note, for example, how Perot's campaign was effective because it showed him to be 'in touch with ordinary people's needs and fears (inclusion) and against

---

Market intelligence
To identify counter consumers, understand their moods and frustrations, and identify simple solutions

Product design and communication
The leadership drives adjusting the product to suit the internal market creating clear-cut messages through skilled communicators

Election and post election
Maximising the vote, evaluating and then creating stable relationships

---

Figure 2.10 Winder and Tenscher's (2012) populist marketing strategy

the ruling class (exclusion)'; and his communication reflected the growing dissatisfaction amongst the people (2012, 237). Their discussion demonstrates that populist marketing can be used to good effect, but it tends not to have a long-term lasting impact; and thus populist marketing needs to move closer to the market-oriented model.

Strategy and the environment

Ideal types of political marketing strategies by Winther Nielsen (2013)

Entrepreneurial   If an organisation adopts an entrepreneurial strategy, it thinks it can control its environment and thus is willing to engage in more innovative strategy even if it might lose resources. An example is how the, then, president for the European Commission Jacques Delors pushed to create the single market in the EU to stimulate economic growth.

Decoupling   The decoupling strategy is where an organisation feels in control but decides to avoid risk.

Defense   Organisations that take a defence strategy feel their lack of control and thus carry on as before, avoiding risk, but also refusing to change and sticking to their old habits (e.g. if a political party continues to ignore low polling numbers and refuses to change its policies and so continues to lose public support).

Conformity   A political organisation that knows it can't control its' environment and thus decides to comply with the prevailing culture and norms, and is thus very risk averse (e.g. UK New Labour's decision to change the party to suit public opinion after losing three elections in a row).

Figure 2.11

Strategy is about responding to the environment, and Winther Nielsen (2013) argues there are four ideal types of political marketing strategies: see Figure 2.11.

Winther Nielsen expands on the idea that strategy depends at least partly on the environment – or how practitioners conceive it – in his book *Marketised Politics: Party Marketing Strategy and Voter Brand Consumption* – see Authors' corner 2.1 for more information.

Winther Nielsen (2012) argues there are three faces of political marketing strategy: design, emergent and interpretive, which all offer various thoughts on assumptions of individual political actors, the political environment in which they operate, their strategic political behaviour (varying from forming a clear long-term plan to being ad hoc, or norm/ritual based), and objectives including goals, learning and creating legitimacy. *Design* political strategies create a clear plan from the start, which appears most logical but, as Winther Nielsen notes, may be unrealistic to apply to politics because it is not possible to foresee events and markets are unstable. Bill Clinton's 1992 campaign, for example, was carefully planned to focus on the economy.

Authors' corner 2.1

Marketized Politics: Party Marketing Strategy and Voter Brand Consumption
By Sigge Winther Nielsen
Published by Copenhagen University Press in 2013

This book explores two core concepts from the international literature on political marketing: (1) the marketing strategy concept in relation to party behaviour, and (2) the brand consumption concept in relation to voting behaviour. Employing survey panel data, survey experiment and elite interviewing, this research unpacks the dynamics of modern politics through the lens of these two marketing concepts. This investigation makes three overall contributions – theoretical, methodological and empirical.

Theoretically, it rigorously examines the concepts of strategy and brand to illuminate the tacit intellectual presuppositions that flourish within these two literatures: in the strategy literature we identify three distinct perspectives, *and* in the brand literature we identify six distinct perspectives. This conceptual groundwork enables a purified ground to work from when carrying out future research. This conceptual groundwork is built on in the rest of the book by singling out specific perspectives of strategy and brand. Particularly, in the chapters on brands, the book employs a voter-centric political brand perspective premised on cognitive psychology, *and* in the articles on strategy, it employs an interpretive marketing strategy perspective premised on social psychology. Theoretically, it concludes that when scholars are more precise about their epistemological foundation, the scientific community has a better chance of undertaking comparisons and documenting contingencies because we can clearly distinguish different notions. Ultimately, the delineated categorizations of different perspectives within the strategy and brand concept will hopefully help to speed up the accumulation of knowledge in the field of political marketing.

Methodologically, it draws on the conceptual groundwork outlined above. When grappling with the strategy concept, the book uses a survey experiment and elite interviews to untangle the delicate interplay between decision-maker cognition of the organisational environment and the chosen strategic action. Obviously, examining decision-maker cognition is complicated, but the integration of a survey experiment and elite interviews move us closer to an explanation of the mechanisms guiding party strategists. When grappling with the brand concept, the research employs open-ended category data from a survey panel. As such, through a representative survey, the book attempts to integrate ideas from qualitative and quantitative research by eliciting voters' associations about parties in open categories, in contrast to closed categories that are typically utilised in questionnaire surveys. With numerous associations, the book develops a novel measure of political brand value which captures public sentiments attached to the parties.

Empirically, it delivers two primary findings related to strategy. Party strategists are influenced by how they cognitively frame their environment as a threat or an opportunity in relation to resources and control. That is, a cognitive deep structure exists which drives parties against a particular marketing strategy when trying to make sense of the organisational environment through their cognitive schemas. This social psychological influence on strategy selection is a novel finding in the literature that adds decision-maker cognition to the existing rational focus on competitors and capabilities. Even so, this effect is mediated by context-specific variables embedded in the political science tradition, such as historical tensions, coalition partners, or the ideology, goal and organisational structure of the party. In sum, there is a link between cognition and strategy selection.

Emergent political strategies are 'carried out on the run', so there is no clear logical flow but instead behaviour is more reactive to a wide range of information and intelligence. Political organisations therefore draw on old knowledge, learning through feedback mechanisms such as market research. It is a pragmatic approach to the complexity of politics, but the lack of a clear long-term direction might result in less effective behaviour. Winther Nielson suggests that UK New Labour's attempts to change policies to suit voters under Tony Blair was an emergent strategy – there is certainly evidence of them using political market research extensively.

Interpretive political marketing strategy is where political organisations such as a political parties try to influence and change their environment rather than just responding to it. The example provided is the Obama 2008 campaign's ability to transform the playing field, in the primaries and then in the presidential election, using language symbols and norms. His advisors decided that the political environment had changed in just the last two years and thus created the possibility that a strategy focused on change might work for a candidate who was, at the start of the race, unknown. Of course, changing the environment might be hard – however it may be where politicians get to show their true leadership.

Measuring political strategy

Political strategy is not easily discernable or measurable, and is rarely public – parties and candidates don't tend to publish their strategy documents. Partly this is because they don't want the other side to know what they plan, but mostly it is because in political strategy needs to be flexible to changing circumstances. Given this, it is difficult to measure scientifically for research purposes. Some scholars have tried to develop more quantitative measurements of market-orientation. Ormrod and Henneberg (2006) analysed UK party manifestos in the 2005 election, applying Ormrod's concepts through QSR NVivo, a qualitative analysis tool, to examine number of occurrences and relationships between concepts; and assessing whether they were not developed, somewhat developed or highly developed. O'Cass (1996) also developed quantitative measurements of market-orientation, conducting interviews and a survey in Australia. Strömbäck (2010a) created a survey to explore the extent to which parties in different countries both used political marketing techniques and adopted the orientations within the Lees-Marshment model and what affect the system might have on which orientation parties' chose. This survey can be used to assess elite attitudes towards market and sales-orientations: see Figure 2.12.

Implementing political strategy

Politicians and advisors have to ensure they can get enough political support for any proposals, otherwise they have no chance of being implemented (Glaab 2007, 67; Lindholm and Prehn 2007, 23): see Practitioner perspective 2.3. Even the best designed strategies fail because of unanticipated events or internal blockages (Barber 2005), especially in political parties.

Factors that hinder strategy implementation

Lindholm and Prehn (2007) studied strategy in Denmark and concluded that strategy is harder to develop when support is high, as there seems less need to innovate and reorientate. It is also much easier to gain support for change when the party has lost several elections. Barber (2005) notes how, when Tony Blair took over as leader of the UK Labour Party in 1995, he faced a very different set of circumstances to that of Neil Kinnock in 1992 and

Strömbäck's survey of political marketing practitioners or politicians

Section A asked respondents to rate the extent to which they agreed or disagreed with the statements:

1 It is important for a party to know the kinds of individual and group that are most likely to vote for the party, and target them accordingly.
2 When party policies are being formulated, a trade-off may have to be made between the opinions of voters in general and the core values of the party.
3 Opinion polls are indispensable for a party to determine the views of individuals and groups likely to support the party.
4 It would be unacceptable to change core policy positions because opinion polls suggest that it would convince more people to vote for the party.
5 A party that decides to revise its policies and programmes should first and foremost listen to, and discuss with, its own members and activists.
6 As a Member of Parliament it is my duty to follow my own ideas and opinions when voting in Parliament.
7 As a Member of Parliament it is my duty to follow the official party line when voting in Parliament.
8 As a Member of Parliament it is my duty to follow my voters' opinions when voting in Parliament.
9 The most important thing during an election campaign is to persuade people to want what the party has to offer.
10 The most important thing during an election campaign is to show people that the party offers what people want.

Section B asked respondents to rate the extent to which they thought the following aspects were important when people decided which party to vote for:

1 the trustworthiness of the party leader;
2 party identification;
3 the party's core values;
4 the party's performance since the last election;
5 the party's promises for the future;
6 the issues and policy positions that the party emphasises;
7 the candidates;
8 the party's image;
9 the party's ability to fulfil its promises.

Section C asked respondents to rate the extent to which they thought the following aspects were important in determining whether a party does well in an election:

1 identification of target groups;
2 using opinion polls;
3 using focus groups;
4 election advertisements;
5 direct marketing
6 the party leader;
7 individual candidates;
8 party's issue positions;
9 party ideology
10 access to, and use of, voter databases;
11 the use of campaign consultants;
12 the use of attack and defence strategies.

Figure 2.12

Source: Adapted from Strömbäck (2010a)

Practitioner perspective 2.3 on the difficulties of implementing political strategy

Strategy development in politics is never easy, never comfortable. It is always challenging, often frustrating, as the sheer complexity of the strategic task has to be first made comprehensible, then manageable, and finally simple, uncomplicated and decisive. Effective political strategy is the result of bruising months of argument, counterargument, testing, verification, endless meetings, constant setbacks and much frustration, attempting to tie together policy, politics, ideology and public opinion.

The Late Lord Philip Gould, advisor to UK PM Tony Blair, 2002

Source: Bartle, Atkinson and Mortimore (eds) (2002)

found it much easier to impose a voter-responsive strategy because the party was power-seeking after losing so many successive elections from 1979 to 1992. Strömbäck (2009) explained how the Moderate Party in Sweden turned to marketing in 2002 when it experienced its worst election result since 1973. The party was the biggest party on the right of Swedish politics and led the opposition to the Social Democrats; traditionally, it espoused typical conservative politics, but after its loss in 2002 the new leader Fredrik Reinfeldt led the repositioning of the party in the centre ground in response to mainstream concerns and voters' understandings of everyday reality. Strömbäck quotes Per Schlingmann, the party secretary, who said 'it is the voters' everyday experiences that guide the policy formation and how we express ourselves'. The repositioning enabled the Moderates to create a new coalition, 'Alliance for Sweden', of centre and right-wing parties which then won the 2006 Swedish election and formed a majority coalition government with Reinfeldt becoming the new prime minister.

There are also a number of barriers to effective positioning. It is difficult for incumbents to reposition because they are bound by their previous behaviour and record. In the UK 2005 election, this was illustrated in several respects. As Smith (2005, 1137–9) observes, if Labour moved to the left, it would open up the market for the Conservatives; if it moved to the right, it would open up other sections of the market to the Liberal Democrats. The Conservatives found it hard to show differentiation from Labour, because Labour took on very similar positions on choice and efficiency in the public sector. Nevertheless, Labour enjoyed positive points of difference over both competitors, being perceived to hold better policies on the two most important issues, health services and taxation/public services.

Strategy is harder in government than opposition. Fischer *et al.'s* (2007) comparative study of political strategy in government suggests that the power of a government to implement its chosen strategy depends on a number of factors, such as its existing power, the strategic qualities of the leaders and market conditions such as the economy and approaching elections. The nature of government also makes strategy, and indeed political marketing as a whole, more complex. First, the pressure of daily government business stops ministers having time to think about electoral considerations. When the firm 'Promise' about future strategy and rebranding was presented to UK Prime Minister Tony Blair in 2004, he asked his private secretary, Jonathan Powell, to make sure he had the time to think about it over the weekend (Promise 2006). Government can end up being driven more by crisis – where it doesn't want to be – and less by strategy – where it wants to go. In the US, Arterton (2007) found that strategy in government was hindered by the machinery of the US government, which works against cross-unit or state co-operation for long-term

---

Factors hindering maintenance of a market-orientation in government

1   Loss of objective advisors with that gut feel and ability to offer blunt criticism.
2   Realities and constraints of government.
3   Increasing knowledge and experience among leaders, encouraging feeling of invincibility and superiority.
4   Weak opposition, which encourages and facilitates complacency.
5   Difficulty and slow pace of delivery in government.
6   Lack of time to think about future product development.

Figure 2.13

Source: Adapted from Lees-Marshment (2008)

benefit. George W. Bush's attempt to push social security reform through in his second term of office is another example where, despite appealing to the public for support, the nature of government and special interests blocked the change. Other obstacles to effective strategy include departmentalism, separation of policy and delivery, short-term distractions and politicians' lack of skill (Boaz and Solesbury 2007, 123).

Research has also identified that parties and candidates struggle to maintain a market-orientation once in power. There are many forces that work against the maintenance of a market-orientation in government. Government is a very different environment; it brings into play a whole new set of resources, information and advice, including the civil service or bureaucracy but also think tanks who want to influence the detailed construction of legislation. Figure 2.13 outlines the range of factors working against maintaining a market-orientation.

Leaders in particular find it hard to remain in touch, as they enjoy power and also want to make a difference and impact during their time in office. A good example of this is Tony Blair: despite winning a landslide election in 1997 with market-oriented behaviour, in government Blair's popularity declined after decisions such as that to go to war in Iraq. Not only did his particular position prove unpopular, communication from him suggested he ignored the public's opposition, which made him seem dismissive and uncaring of public opinion, making the situation worse. Case study 2.4 by Elijah Pear discusses the difficulties that the Australian Labor Party had maintaining a market-orientation after being elected in 2010, including moving to a more product-oriented approach and failing to deliver certain promises such as repeal of the carbon tax.

Another example of losing touch is Arnold Schwarzenegger, governor of California (2003–2011). In 2005, he called a special election to allow voters to decide on propositions regarding teacher tenure requirements (Proposition 74), the use of union dues for political campaign contributions (Proposition 75), state budgetary spending limits (Proposition 76) and redistricting (Proposition 77), which ended up losing him considerable support. California voters rejected all eight ballot propositions, despite the election costing hundreds of millions of dollars. The main reason, according to Mehlman (2006, 12), was that he broke a number of rules such as forgetting who elected him. Schwarzenegger won office in 2003 by gaining support across several markets, from moderate and conservative Republicans, Independents and even some Democrats, through an appeal to be a different kind of politician. At first, he governed in a bipartisan way, gaining increases in approval ratings. However, he then moved to the right, working against his allies instead of with them and therefore abandoning his key supporter market.

Positive influences that aid strategy

The leader plays an important part in the success of political strategy. Fischer *et al.* (2007) conclude from their comparative study of strategy that leadership is important: the advantage with Tony Blair is that he was a prime minister 'who thinks and acts in strategic terms . . . [and] encourages others to do the same', whereas the former German Chancellor Schröder was noted to have 'a situational and not entirely consistent leadership style that focused on immediate needs rather than the big picture', and this was 'detrimental to the development of a coherent strategy' (2007, 185). Lees-Marshment *et al.*'s (2010, eds) comparative study identified that the attitude of the leader towards a market-orientation is a key factor in its implementation. In New Zealand, market-oriented development was constrained by Don Brash becoming leader in 2004 as he took a more right-wing approach to focus on traditional National issues: economic growth, welfare reform, education, law and order, and more generally security, and the Treaty of Waitangi. Lees-Marshment (2010, 71) interviewed Brash who recalled that his gut feel determined the major issues on which the party focused in the 2005 election and that he thought market research was less useful than other politicians did. When John Key took over as leader the party's approach became more responsive; Murray McCully, National MP and strategist, said when interviewed:

> At the end of the day this is a process that is about having respect for the views of the public . . . If you thumb your nose at the public and do things to them without seeking their consent then it comes back and bites your backside real quick . . . You should look respectfully about what you can learn about market research and polling and focus groups and so on. Not slavishly follow the detail but understand the substance of it.
>
> (Quoted in Lees-Marshment 2010, 74)

Political strategy also benefits from a focused group driving it. Both Glaab's (2007) and Lindholm and Prehn's (2007) analyses, of Germany and Denmark respectively, suggest that strategy tended to become associated with, and carried out by, a small informal group – usually around the leader; indeed strategy worked only if they too were able to think strategically. Boaz and Solesbury (2007, 123 and 132), and Glaab (2007, 100) suggest that a number of behaviours help strategy in government including effective stakeholder support and management; making sure leaders and other practitioners have time in the schedule away from daily government business to reflect about strategy; maintaining flexibility; having clear goals; and resisting the temptation to be diverted by short-term issues and problems. They also argue that leadership is crucial – there needs to be support from politicians and senior bureaucrats to other staff engaged in strategy.

Government strategy units help encourage new thinking and change the nature of the civil service to reward strategic thinking. The UK Labour government created the Prime Minister's Strategy Unit in 2003, its second term in office, which looked at spending reviews and five-year strategies for different departments. The role of the Strategy Unit was to provide strategy and policy advice to the prime minister/No. 10 and to support government departments in developing effective strategies and policies – including helping them to build their strategic capability and to identify and effectively disseminate emerging issues and policy challenges.

Governments can also encourage strategic skills amongst their staff or civil service. Boaz and Solesbury (2007, 121) note how the UK civil service provide a list of the core skills of a strategic thinker which include the ability to shape and set the long-term vision and

---

Lindholm and Prehn's advice for political strategists

1   Have the facts at your fingertips and know what you are talking about.
2   Create a simple policy you can explain.
3   Make a plan and write it down.
4   Define your target group and go after this group, not the entire electorate.
5   Absorb knowledge, learning from what you see.
6   Be pragmatic.
7   Be courageous and strong.
8   Reinforce your analytical skills and learn to read the interests of others.
9   Define where you see yourself in five to ten years and work to get there.
10 Be very patient.

Figure 2.14

Source: Adapted from Lindholm and Prehn (2007, 59–69)

direction for the department, taking into account both wider government priorities and delivery systems; make trade-offs between different policy areas and over different time scales; present ministers and colleagues with key choices based on robust evidence and champion the role of strategic thinking in the organisation, working effectively with relevant internal and external experts. Political strategists are a growing area of practice both in and out of government, and Lindholm and Prehn offer advice for how to be an effective strategist: see Figure 2.14.

Research has also suggested tactics to help politicians avoid losing a market-orientation in power. Conducting continual market intelligence is crucial – it can help ensure leaders remain aware of the impact their behaviour has on public support. Lilleker and Lees-Marshment (2005, 225–6) suggest strategies a government needs to implement to ensure it finds space and time to think about product design/development for the next election. Studying empirical examples from Blair and Clark, Lees-Marshment (2008) suggest a number of tools that can be used by governments: see Figure 2.15.

Governments need to adopt a learning orientation to maintain a market-orientation in power (Lees-Marshment 2009b, 215–16). Many governments have struggled to reinvent themselves and offer a newly developed product after winning the first election. To ensure effective redevelopment, governments need to proactively question whether existing behaviour and practices actually maximize their performance, thereby being willing to challenge the status quo and be open to new ideas. Parties in government need to ensure that consultation and market analysis results are disseminated to ensure politicians remain in touch, there are appropriate resources and time to maintain and develop a clear strategy, there is continual debate as to how to best serve the public and other markets to ensure continued reflective thinking and maintain a balance between leadership and following public opinion.

Summary

Political strategy is fundamental to political marketing: it determines how governments, parties and candidates think and behave in relation to the electorate. Strategy informs every other aspect of marketing, which will be explored in subsequent chapters. It includes

---

Tools to regain a market-orientation in government

1 **Conduct listening or consultation exercises to get back in touch:**
   e.g. UK Labour's 'The Big Conversation' in 2003 and 'Let's Talk' in 2005.

2 **Refresh the overall team:**
   e.g. the UK Labour 2005 campaign conveyed 'Team Labour', showing a range of politicians within the government, not just Blair; and NZ Labour refreshed the cabinet in 2007 and encouraged older MPs to retire, leaving room to promote those more junior.

3 **Use public-friendly, non-political communication:**
   Blair appeared on non-political television, such as the popular daytime programme *Richard and Judy*, and *Ant and Dec's Saturday Night Takeaway*, a mainstream Saturday evening programme, before the 2005 election; and after winning a third term took part in a comedy sketch with comedienne Catherine Tate for the charity television fundraising show *Comic Relief*.

4 **Acknowledge public concern with leaders' difficult, unpopular decisions or issues:**
   UK Labour enacted a 'masochism' strategy, where Blair met the public and listened to, and showed respect for, voters' disagreement with his decision to take the country into the Iraq war, explaining the pressures on a leader to take a decision whether it was popular or not.

5 **Develop new strategy for future terms, ensuring there is the space and time to think about product design/development for the next election:**
   In 2007, Clark implemented new policies such as KiwiSaver, free part-time child care and a new pension scheme; and acknowledged the need to reduce income tax in response to market demand and economic conditions; in the UK, the Strategy Unit established in Blair's second term helped provide a means by which new ideas from academia, think tanks, private industry and non-governmental organisations were integrated into government.

Figure 2.15

Source: Adapted from Lees-Marshment (2008)

targeting, positioning, defence/attack approaches and market-orientation. It is not easy to implement strategy but the support of leadership, teams and units, and maintaining research and reflection can all help strategy be implemented and maintained even in power.

Figure 2.16 provides a best practice guide for doing political strategy. This, and all those in the other chapters of the book, is derived from: Lees-Marshment (2011) which featured practitioner advice on what works; the *Routledge Handbook of Political Marketing* whose chapters provided recommendations for practice; and the material presented in this chapter.

Practitioners who have success at political strategy often end up in influential political positions, as they are able to offer advice on a number of interconnected areas of political marketing. The profiles of two strategists, Phillip Gould and James Carville, discuss their work and achievements. Before parties, candidates and governments can respond to what the market demands and how it behaves, they need to know what that is.

The next chapter will look at how political elites use political market research to understand the market.

Best practice guide to doing political strategy

1   Devise your strategy first – set achievable goals (not just to win votes) then figure out how to achieve them.

2   Allow time for strategy development: make it a core process with leadership support and internal resources.

3   Ensure the strategy is like a ship: so it can evolve and respond to change.

4   Consider a range of stakeholders: voters, members/volunteers, donors, internal staff, external staff, politicians and candidates, lobbyists and think tanks, public/civil service, professional groups, media, regulatory bodies, competitors, co-operators, citizen experts.

5   Also consider the candidate/organisation's history, beliefs and vision.

6   Create a targeting strategy using a range of data to identify and better understand different segments and potential supporters.

7   Break segments such as seniors and women voters down into smaller groups (micro or nano targeting) where resources will be most effective and diversify the product to better meet divergent needs within a segment.

8   When targeting, create a strategy for brand development, not just communication, so it will be convincing to new target groups.

9   Choose the right orientation strategy to suit the circumstances. A Sales-Oriented Party might not win against other market-oriented competitors; but if your goal is not to win, or the opposition is sales-oriented or product-oriented, then you do not need to adopt a market-orientation. However parties/candidates wishing to win control of government most likely do need to become market-oriented.

10 Minor parties or outsider candidates can adopt niche market-oriented behaviour and develop a product that responds to research into their specialist market.

11 Make the strategy localized: adapt ideas from global knowledge sharing to create a unique campaign each time.

12 When positioning, make sure the adopted position is consistent, credible, competitive, and communicable and stake your position early to force other parties to react to you.

13 Adopt a competition strategy that suits your market position; and use a wide range of attack and defence strategies.

14 Anticipate attacks and be proactive in response to them.

15 Do the jujitsu move: flip their strength over by attacking them on their usual strengths to undermine voter loyalty and get their traditional supporters to consider switching.

16 Co-operate with the competition if it brings benefits.

17 Make sure the product and positioning are authentic.

Figure 2.16

Practitioner profile 2.1

Name: Philip Gould, Baron Gould of Brookwood
Date of birth: 30 March, 1950 (to 6 November, 2011)
Most notable job: Strategy and Policy Advisor for the UK Labour Party

Description: Philip Gould was a political consultant and advertising executive best known for his work with the UK Labour Party from 1987 to 2005. After a career in advertising and founding his own polling and strategy company, Gould was appointed by Peter Mandelson to create and head the Shadow Communications Agency, a team of communication volunteers who created Labour's unsuccessful 1987 election campaign. While not successful, this did lead to Gould's position of influence within the Labour Party. Gould championed the use of focus groups, made up of ordinary voters, to track public opinion and reaction to particular policies. Importantly, Gould was a key advisor to newly appointed Labour leaders John Smith and subsequently Tony Blair, when he ran focus groups to help better understand why the British public, especially the all-important swing voter, had not supported the Labour Party in 1992 – despite their negative feelings towards the Conservative government. On the back of this, Gould was a key figure in 'modernising' the UK Labour Party's image, including abandoning Labour's attachment to nationalism and embracing market economics, in the lead up to their successful general election campaign in 1997 – their first in 18 years. Paying tribute to Gould after his death, Prime Minister Tony Blair noted that 'he was my guide and mentor, a wise head, a brilliant mind . . . [a] huge part of the renaissance of the Labour Party'. Lord Peter Mandelson described Gould as 'instrumental in driving a revolution that transformed not just our party but British politics as a whole'. See his books: *The Unfinished Revolution: How the Modernisers Saved the Labour Party* (published by Abacus in 1999) and *When I Die: Lessons from the Death Zone* (published by Little, Brown in 2012).

Practitioner profile 2.2

Name: Chester James Carville, Jr.
Date of birth: 25 October, 1944
Most notable job: Lead strategist for Bill Clinton in the 1992 US presidential campaign

Description: James Carville is a political commentator and media personality, but he is better known for his work as a key political advisor and strategist for many political campaigns around the world. Carville helped in the design of numerous campaign strategies over the last 30 years. After a number of successes at the gubernatorial level, Carville rose to national attention when, in 1991, he and his business partner Paul Begala helped incumbent Senator Harris Wofford of Pennsylvania claw back a 40-point deficit against Dick Thornburgh to win with 55 percent of the vote. It was during Wofford's campaign that the 'it's the economy, stupid' strategy, a strategy that would become commonplace in political campaigns worldwide, was first used by Carville. In 1992 Carville, as lead strategist, helped Bill Clinton win against George H. W. Bush in the US presidential election. His role in the Clinton campaign was documented in the documentary film *The War Room*. Having helped Clinton win the election, Carville was honoured as Campaign Manager of the Year by the American Association of Political Consultants. Since then Carville has worked on a number of high-profile campaigns, including Ehud Barack's successful campaign to become the Prime Minister of Israel in 1999, UK Prime Minister Tony Blair's successful re-election campaign in 2001, and Gonzalo Sánchez de Lozada's succesful bit to become president of Bolivia in 2002 – which was documented in the movie *Our Brand Is Crisis*. Carville was also an advisor in Hillary Clinton's unsuccessful 2008 presidential primaries campaign. While known for his active role in personalising politics and attacking his clients' opposition, Carville's most notable influence in political campaign strategies is probably a campaign formulation he used in the Clinton campaign in 1992. Derived from a list he posted in the 'war room' (Clinton's campaign HQ) to help himself and his staff focus, Carville's campaign formula started with the three points: 'Change vs. more of the same', 'The economy, stupid', and 'Don't forget health care'. Such a formula became commonplace in election campaigns around the world, many of which Carville played an active role in.

"
"
Discussion points

1   Think of examples where recent political candidates, leaders or parties have targeted certain groups – what were those targets, how did they respond to them, and how effective was their targeting strategy overall?
2   Consider the current positioning of particular candidates or parties. To what extent are they following criteria for successful positioning?
3   Which category (Product-, Sales- or Market-Oriented Party) do current parties/candidates/leaders best fit into?
4   Discuss the main differences between Lees-Marshment's model of Product-, Sales- and Market-Oriented parties, and debate which approach is more likely to win an election.
5   Think of governments that have won elections with significant public support, only to lose touch and, with it, lose votes over time. Identify and discuss any who have succeeded in regaining a market-orientation.
6   What obstacles are there to effective strategy and what tools can politicians use to maintain effective strategy, especially in government?

Assessment questions

Essays/exams
1   'Strategy is the most important part of political marketing.' Explain and critique the validity of this statement, illustrating your argument with examples and theory.
2   Discuss and evaluate the effectiveness of party positioning, utilizing theories by Bannon, Collins and Butler, and Harada and Morris.
3   Evaluate the nature and effectiveness of party competition strategies using Marland's political attack and defence strategies.
4   To what extent did the parties that won power in the last election follow the Lees-Marshment Market-Oriented Party model?
5   Discuss the effectiveness and limitations of the model of Market-, Sales- and Product-Oriented parties as a means of explaining modern party behaviour.
6   Discuss the extent to which the Lees-Marshment model of market-oriented parties is followed in detail, comparing examples such as UK Labour/Blair in 1997, Australia Labor/Rudd in 2007, and US Democrats/Obama in 2008, and noting where the cases do not follow the model as well as where they do.
7   Critically explore the effectiveness of the sales-oriented approach to political marketing, utilising case studies to support your answer and taking account of party goals.

8 Explore and evaluate the lessons that today's political leaders might learn from how former leaders such as Ronald Reagan, Margaret Thatcher, Bill Clinton and Tony Blair used political marketing strategy.

9 Considering a range of political marketing strategies, discuss what you consider to be the most effective strategy for political candidates or parties to adopt, and why.

10 Why is implementing political strategy difficult, and what can help it succeed?

Applied

1 Assess the extent to which *x* party or candidate(s) met Bannon's (2004) five principles for successful positioning (clarity, consistency, credibility, competitiveness and communication).

2 Identify and justify which position from Collins and Butler's theory you think the parties at the last national election fitted into (market leader, challenger, nicher, follower), and critique how effectively they managed the constraints and options for each market position.

3 Assess minor party or political movement against the criteria put forward by Harada and Morris and make recommendations for what they should improve.

4 Apply Marland's concepts of political attack and defence to political parties or candidates and assess how effectively they used the range of techniques available, making recommendations for the future.

5 Apply the Lees-Marshment model of a Market-Oriented Party in detail to Obama's 2008 campaign and first term of government, exploring the extent to which he maintained a market-orientation in government as well as campaigning.

6 Identify a range of empirical examples of political organisations or figures which fit the ideal types of political marketing strategies by Winther Nielsen and critique their effectiveness.

7 Assess whether the parties in *x* country fall into a Product-, Sales- or Market-Oriented Party, and make recommendations as to whether they should retain or change their orientation to achieve their goals in the future.

8 Interview/survey local politicians, electorate/party branch staff, or party members using Strömbäck's Survey of Political Marketing Practitioners or Politicians and analyse what the results indicate about the party's orientation.

9 Create a political marketing Strategic Plan: write an original, present-day political marketing plan that assesses how well a party uses marketing strategy, and give recommendations for how it can improve its use of marketing to achieve its goals or objectives. Write as if you were a marketing consultant, planning how the party can use marketing in the years leading up to the next election. The plan is not a traditional essay and can therefore be written in report style, although it should include references to academic literature, where relevant, and primary sources.

CASE STUDIES

Case study 2.1 Positioning for power in Australia

By Lorann Downer, The University of Queensland
lorann.downer@uqconnect.edu.au

Positioning – how a politician or party is presented to voters (Baines 1999, 413) – is critical to an election campaign. That's because positioning is about 'how a brand can effectively compete against a specified set of competitors in a particular market' (Keller 2008, 121). Keller (2008, 98) provides a comprehensive framework for understanding positioning, including in politics

(2008, 118–19). Positioning is determined by identifying the target customer market or segments, understanding the competition, then establishing points of difference with competitors and points of parity to neutralise advantages enjoyed by competitors (Keller 2008, 98, 99 and 107). Keller's framework is applied here to illustrate how the Australian Labor Party used positioning to gain and retain power in consecutive, but very different, campaigns.

The 2007 campaign

At the start of the 2007 election year, Labor campaigners were working on how best to position the new Opposition Leader, Kevin Rudd, to appeal to a range of voter segments. Most important were 'working families', described by Labor strategist Bruce Hawker as 'suburban mortgage holders with young families'. In 2007, Tim Gartrell, said the party also wanted to reclaim blue-collar workers, part of its traditional base, from the Liberal Party. Also vital were young people and voters in Rudd's home state of Queensland.

Having decided who to target, Labor then decided how to target them. Labor positioned Rudd as a challenger (Butler and Collins 1996, 30–1) to Liberal Prime Minister John Howard in a presidential-style contest. After a decade in office, Howard was seen as out of touch, especially over recently introduced industrial relations laws. Despite this, voters were still cautious about Labor according to Nick Martin. So, while Rudd was offered as a change, it was 'safe change' (Gartrell 2012). Accordingly, Rudd was socially progressive but economically conservative, a contemporary Labor leader but reassuring to soft Liberal voters who saw him as 'a mini John Howard but better' (Martin 2012).

Labor sought to develop several points of difference with Howard and the Liberals. The first high-level point of difference between Rudd and Howard boiled down to the future versus the past (Gartrell 2012). This was made tangible via policies to combat climate change, which became 'a metaphor for Rudd' (Gartrell 2012). Labor's 'historical association with fairness' (Gartrell 2012) meant it could capitalise on community concern over Howard's industrial relations laws. Thus, fairness, especially in the workplace, was the third point of difference. The final two relied on Labor's traditional strengths in education and health.

Rudd's 'more atypically conservative values' (Gartrell 2012), like his Christianity and lack of union and factional links, were deployed to create two points of parity with Howard. The higher-level point was the idea of 'safe change'. As campaign strategist Cameron Milner noted: 'The Sunday morning press conference outside church was Kevin talking about his values and letting the electorate know he wasn't just another union-backed, factional leader'. The second point of parity was on economic management, which Howard had owned for a decade. Rudd took this head-on, declaring himself to be 'an economic conservative'. Positioning was a cornerstone of Labor's year-long, disciplined and ultimately successful campaign for office. As Hawker (2012) said, the party 'never forgot the people we were trying to influence'.

The 2010 campaign

By June 2010, Labor had spent 15 months repositioning Prime Minister Rudd for a second-term campaign (Milner 2012). Rudd, however, had lost much public and party support and was replaced by his deputy, Julia Gillard. Campaigners scrambled to 'create continuity in the messages we'd already started to develop, albeit with a new leader delivering those messages' (Milner 2012). They had just 24 days to do so before Gillard called an election. Rather than seeking new voter segments, this campaign was about 'trying to protect what you've already got, trying to hold onto those groups which are by now disillusioned on a number of fronts' (Hawker 2012). Once again, middle Australian families, blue-collar workers and Queenslanders were important. Also targeted were voters in outer-suburban western Sydney, where Labor held ten seats, and inner-city progressives who were switching to the Greens.

Labor sought to position Gillard as the market leader (Butler and Collins 1996, 28–30) against opposition leader, Tony Abbott. Labor's National Secretary in 2010, Karl Bitar (2010), wanted 'a clear contest between Prime Minister Gillard's positive plan to move Australia forward and Tony Abbott who would take Australia backwards'. Gillard was styled as the new leader of a government that had rediscovered its purpose, after losing its way under Rudd. The task was made difficult by the fact and manner of Rudd's removal. Gillard could not campaign on some of the achievements of the man she deposed (Hawker 2012). And the dumping of Rudd with little public explanation bred some voter confusion and animosity, and left Gillard with 'a problem with legitimacy with a large section of the community' (Hawker 2012).

Labor sought to develop seven points of difference for the leader and the party. There was a high-level point between the forward-focused Gillard and the backward-looking Abbott (Hawker 2012). This was made tangible via Gillard's policy for a National Broadband Network (Hawker 2012), the second point. Next were the party's traditional advantages in education and health. In a sign of the challenging nature of this campaign, there is also evidence that Labor understood the need for points of difference with Rudd. The campaign sought to differentiate Gillard from Rudd on three points; border control, population control and environmental protection.

The campaign did want Gillard to be like Rudd, however, on the matter of legitimacy. Labor sought to establish legitimacy as a high-level point of parity, working to reinforce Gillard's authority throughout the campaign. Labor television commercials, for example, often showed Gillard with two potent symbols of authority, the Prime Minister's office and the Australian flag. As in 2007, Labor wanted a point of parity with the Liberals on economic management, citing its success in steering Australia through the global economic crisis of 2008 (Martin 2012). Positioning was much more difficult in 2010, because of limited preparation time and a challenging environment. As party pollster John Utting (2012) noted: 'You had the bizarre situation where a Labor leader was running not only against the conservatives but also against her own previous leader'. Labor emerged from the campaign having lost its majority, but eventually was able to form a minority government with the support of Greens and Independents.

Lessons for political marketing

These two cases show positioning can contribute to the electoral outcome, even in a difficult campaign. Labor developed different positioning strategies for two very different campaigns and, while execution was much more successful in 2007 than in 2010, the party had a return on its investment each time. In 2007, Rudd's presentation to the electorate added several vital percentage points to Labor's primary vote (Martin 2012). And in 2010, positioning helped Labor retain some of its target segments, notably western Sydney, which in turn allowed it to retain a hold on power.

Sources and further reading

Baines, Paul R. (1999). 'Voter Segmentation and Positioning'. In Bruce I. Newman (ed.) *Handbook of Political Marketing*. Thousand Oaks, CA: Sage Publications.

Bitar, Karl (2010). Address to the National Press Club, 9 November. http://australianpolitics.com/2010/11/09/karl-bitar-national-press-club-address.html (accessed 12 November, 2010)

Butler, Patrick and Neil Collins (1996). 'Strategic analysis in political markets'. *European Journal of Marketing*, 30(10/11): 25–36.

Gartrell, Tim (2012). *(Pers. Comm.)* Former National Secretary, Australian Labor Party. Interviewed by telephone by author. March 15, Sydney, Australia.

Hawker, Bruce (2012). *(Pers. Comm.)* Managing Director, Campaigns and Communications. Interviewed by author. March 12, Brisbane, Australia.

Keller, Kevin Lane (2008). *Strategic Brand Management: Building, Measuring and Managing Brand Equity*. New Jersey: Pearson Education Inc.

Martin, Nick. (2012). *(Pers. Comm.)* Assistant National Secretary, Australian Labor Party. Interviewed by author. October 11, Canberra, Australia.

Milner, Cameron (2012). *(Pers. Comm.)* Director, Milner Strategic Services. Interviewed by author. September 20, Brisbane, Australia.

Utting, John (2012). *(Pers. Comm.)* Managing Director Australia, UMR Australia. Interviewed by author. September 10, Bondi Junction, Australia.

Case study 2.2 Two sides of the 'political marketing coin' as key for winning elections in Macedonia

By Gordica Karanfilovska, Cabinet of the President of the Republic of Macedonia

gordicak@yahoo.com

In general, outcomes depend on our responses to challenges and adversity in the environment in which we live. When it comes to winning elections and getting into power, there are two sides to the political marketing coin that have to be taken into account: change and implementation of political marketing principles. Parties in general disregard this, yet they want to respond to the challenges and adversity in a manner that would secure them election victory and the opportunity to run the political affairs of the country.

In the case of the Republic of Macedonia, the door for implementing marketing concepts in politics opened in 1990 when the old monistic ideological monopoly of the Yugoslav federation was abandoned and political pluralism and democracy were welcomed among the multi-ethnic communities. Some political parties accepted the settings more successfully than others by using the new 'political marketing coin', in a complex reality which presented great challenges to build democracy and political pluralism.

Following 22 years of independence, when we review the 'political score sheet' of the two main parties in the Republic of Macedonia, VMRO-DPMNE and SDSM (within the ethnic Macedonian block) we can understand how effectively they have utilised the new 'currency' with two sides to the coin.[3]

List of parliamentary elections and the two biggest parties from the ethnic Macedonian block that led the coalition in the government

VMRO-DPMNE	SDSM
1998	11 November, 1990 (under the name SKM-PDP; Expert government, 20 March, 1991–17 August, 1992)
2006	1994
2008	2002
2011	

The seven parliamentary elections were conducted using three different electoral system models. Members of Parliament were elected by popular vote with a majority voting system (1990 and 1994), combined proportional and majority (1998), and proportional model with closed lists (2002, 2006, 2008 and 2011). The electoral system model affects the quality of communication between voters and MPs; hence the application of political marketing and the behaviour of political parties were also influenced. Each of the aforementioned electoral systems has its advantages and disadvantages with both parties beginning to use marketing techniques.

However, only one of them developed their use of the market-oriented concept. By assessing Macedonia and the political parties against structural and semi-structural factors systematized by Strömbäck (2010) that influence the likelihood of a party to be market-oriented, we can recognize that systemic factors such as the political system and culture, media systems, parliamentary arenas, the internal party's arena and the electoral arena encouraged the VMRO-DPMNE to become market-oriented.

Theoretical and empirical research was conducted for this case study including a representative sample of 1,000 responders in December 2012 which demonstrated that the VMRO-DPMNE is more market-oriented, leading the party into continuous electoral victories since 2006 onwards. However, this doesn't mean the party followed Lees-Marshment's model of MOP behaviour purely, as some of the figures representing citizens' perception and some of the party's activity show contrast and appear in opposition to one another.

Taking into consideration information from the media, party documents and information of the processes that are taking place, we can say that the party's behaviour is much closer to the market-oriented model. However, if we analyze only the citizen's perception, the results show that the party has inclinations towards sales-oriented models. This divergence can be explained by several factors:

- Extremely low-level of participation of citizens in sociopolitical life (89.4 per cent respond that citizens are not giving or proposing any ideas or projects to the local or central government led by VMRO-DPMNE).
- High percentages of respondents believe that the party does not show interest for demands and needs of the voters (58.9 per cent).
- Very high percentages of the respondents answered that the party does not ask for feedback of the implemented policies (80.6 per cent).

The former Secretary-General of the biggest opposition party SDSM (Spasov, 2013) explained that 'despite their constitutional rights, citizens are not in a position to bring any civic initiative in the Parliament for the amendment of certain laws. Regardless of who is in power, the parliamentary majority does not accept any draft laws from opposition, nor amendments or civil initiatives.' Other academic studies (see, for example, Ananiev, 2010) have also noted the limited democratic capacity at local level and for the low-level of political participative culture. Factors discussed include that:

- Macedonia's political tradition is still rooted in the previous political system, marked by enclosed decision-making processes and fear of proactivity;
- there is a resentment of local authorities towards civic ideas and proposals, due to the decades-long practice of meeting the interests of a narrow circle of people loyal to the Socialist Party;
- there is insufficient information on the municipal responsibilities and unawareness among local community members about their participative rights;
- there is also a predominant view that only political parties can serve as efficient and effective channels for problem solving, at the expense of personal citizens' initiatives; lack of understanding local problems as personal problems, as well as insufficient civic responsibilities;
- lacking organisation, local communities cannot impose themselves in the management of the entire process of implementation.

Lessons for political marketing

The aforementioned reasons have not prevented the parties attempt to be more market-oriented however. Overall, despite some deviations from the MOP model, VMRO-DPMNE is the first party on the Macedonian political market which has attempted to professionalize their political campaigns and communication with citizens, i.e. improving the use of marketing skills and techniques, and implementing long-term policies in which some are completely new for the citizens. This will, however, take time to be accepted by voters. If the party seeks to gain more trust and greater satisfaction among the voters, it needs to continue to implement the theory more fully and adopt market-oriented behaviour as the winning concept for the Macedonian political market. Declarative participative democracy has to become real, active and function for its citizens. In democratic society where only one 'wins', then both lose. This in turn means the principle has to be a powerful reminder for the political elite of VMRO-DPMNE to continue with their effort to be a Market-Oriented Party.

Further reading

Ananizv, J. (2010). 'Analysis of the democratic capacity of the units of local self-government in the Republic of Macedonia'. In Sasha Mitrev et al. 'Yearbook. Vol.2 (2)'. Faculty of Law, Goce Delcev University – Stip. http://e-lib.ugd.edu.mk/resursi/zbornici/praven/Godisen%20zbornik%20Praven%20fak.pdf (accessed 28 January 2013)
Karanfilovska, G. (2013). Politological aspects of Political Marketing – with special reference to the Republic of Macedonia. PhD thesis, Ss. Cyril and Methodius University.
Lees-Marshment, J. (2009). 'Political Marketing: Principles and Applications'. Abingdon, Oxon: Routledge.
Spasov, Gjorgji (2013). Former Secretary General to SDSM. Interviewed by Gordica Karanfilovska in Skopje, The Republic of Macedonia, 19 February.
Strömbäck, J. (2010). 'A framework for comparing political market orientation'. In J. Lees-Marshment, C. Rudd and J. Strömbäck (eds) Global Political Marketing, Abingdon: Routledge, 16–33.

Case study 2.3 The Green Party's SOP/MOP strategy at the 2011 general election in New Zealand

By John Wilcox, University of Auckland
jwil831@aucklanduni.ac.nz

This case study uses the Sales-Oriented Party (SOP) and Market-Oriented Party (MOP) frameworks to analyse the political strategy of the Green Party of New Zealand for the 2011 general election. This strategy is insightful as an example of how a strategy can effectively integrate the approaches of a SOP and a MOP. With the aid of such a strategy, the Green Party successfully increased their share of the party vote to 11.1 per cent at the 2011 election from 6.7 per cent in the earlier 2008 election: a 66 per cent increase. Under New Zealand's mixed-member-proportional representation system, this increase gave the party an additional five seats, raising their total number of seats to 14 of the 121 seats in the Parliament of New Zealand.

SOP aspects of the Green Party's strategy

The party's strategy generally resembles a SOP since market research succeeded the product design, but preceded and informed the communication and campaigning stages. The party's product design was largely what the party considered to be best for society rather than what was popular. Some examples of this are their non-priority policies, such as their policy to decriminalise personal use of cannabis (within some limits) and their ideological concern for the environment. Many of their values and policies have been long held, some of which are relatively unpopular when compared to that of New Zealand's centrist parties, Labour and National.

In some respects, market intelligence was used not to change the Green Party's product to what people want but to identify suasible voters and the best communication methods to attract them to their product. The most apparent example of this was the party's communication of their product in the form of priorities. After the 2008 election, the data from the New Zealand Election Study, a research institute which distributed questionnaires to voters, demonstrated that the Green Party had high voter volatility as approximately 50 per cent of previously Green Party voters had switched to supporting other parties. Hence, previous voters were identified as a suasible target. The party employed a market researcher who apprehended voters' responses to the party's key messages through focus groups. Their research found that to connect with these voters, they needed to know what the party's priorities were succinctly.

This market research changed their communication of their product design – in particular, their ideology – to most effectively connect with target audiences and win their vote. The party adjusted their communication to reflect three priorities – the economy, the environment and social justice. These priorities were encapsulated in the slogans 'Jobs, Rivers, and Kids' and a 'clean green economy that works for everyone'. The "clean green" component of the latter slogan expressed the values of environmental concern and New Zealand's national identity as a 'clean green' country. The 'works for everyone' component embodied their values of social justice and fairness. These and similar slogans highlighted the popular facets of their product and appeared in modern marketing approaches – billboards, social media, websites, and party member interactions with the public and media.

The party also used a SOP approach in downplaying the unpopular parts of their product. The party's charter, online, states that 'unlimited material growth is impossible' and environmental 'sustainability is paramount' given that we live in a finite world. Consequently, this implies tacit advocacy of a steady-state economic model in which economic growth does not continue indefinitely. This is an unpopular model since the dominant paradigm advocates continuous economic growth. Since this model is neither popular nor immediately feasible, the party intentionally did not emphasise such a model in their communication despite the economic and scientific evidence which they believe supports its wisdom. This can be seen through the party's omission of reference to such a model in their billboards, slogans, and other primary communication forms.

MOP aspects of the Green Party's strategy

However, the SOP model does not completely encompass the party's strategy since other aspects of it resembled a MOP. This is because the party used market research to design parts of their product and make them responsive to the voters' wants. For example, the New Zealand Election Study indicated that many Green Party voters switched to voting for other parties, citing economic management as the main cause. This indicated market demand for parties characterised by economic competency. As a result, the party developed their product to include a pronounced economic vision, a move they would not have made without the suggestion of market intelligence. This vision included a new policy to create 100,000 new 'green jobs' should they be in government. In this sense, market intelligence preceded and informed product development.

Market research also informed their communication of the new aspects of their product. Research suggested that their voter base was largely comprised of women between the ages of 18 and 40 and people who were professionals, tertiary-educated, and urban-based. Research also indicated that Green Party voters at the 2008 election resonated with a strong emotive and creative connection developed through inspirational imagery and wording. Hence, the branding of the party's product changed so that it was less fact-based and aimed to connect on an emotional level with these voters. The party's billboards especially reflected this emotional focus. One billboard featured a young boy smiling, a group of friends fishing in a typical Kiwi 'clean green' river, and the slogan, 'For a richer New Zealand', a slogan that was tested in focus groups and subtly communicated the Green Party's emphasis on both the economic and non-economic factors which contribute to a richer life. One could see how such happy and natural imagery with a child and a newly developed emphasis on economic prosperity would resonate with party voters. Thus, market research further informed the party's product communication.

Strategic evaluation

Some evidence suggests the Green Party's hybrid strategy was highly effective. Following the election stage, the party had a 66 per cent increase in their party vote by winning 11.1 per cent of the vote at the 2011 election. It was also clear that their communication was effective as well. For instance, one news item indicated that 'Jobs, Rivers, and Kids' had the best cut-through to voters when compared to the other political messages during the election campaigning. Additionally, the reasoning underpinning their hybrid strategy appears cogent and conducive to success. Political commentators also attributed the Green Party's success to their strategy, such as their newly developed economic orientation.

Lessons for political marketing

This case study has a number of implications for political marketing. First, the strategy of political parties might not exclusively fit into one category of approach, such as a SOP or MOP; rather, strategies can integrate aspects of different approaches. Furthermore, a hybrid SOP and MOP strategy can be effective in gaining votes. Our case also suggests that a SOP strategy is especially apposite for minor parties which advocate relatively unpopular values which they are committed to (like the decriminalisation of cannabis use); they would benefit from SOP tactics to gain the voter appeal and resulting power.

Sources and further reading

Anonymous source who was intimately acquainted with the Green Party's 2011 political strategy, interviews by the author, 26 March and 10 April, 2013.

Green Party of Aotearoa New Zealand. http://www.greens.org.nz/election (accessed September 28, 2013)
Jon Johansson and Stephen Levine (eds) (2012) *Kicking the Tyres: The New Zealand General Election and Electoral Referendum of 2011.* Wellington: Victoria University Press.

Case study 2.4 Maintaining a market-orientation in minority government

By Elijah Pear, University of Auckland
elijahpear@gmail.com

In the 2010 Australian election there was a hung parliament and the Australian Labor Party (ALP) under the leadership of Julia Gillard negotiated to form a minority government and experienced a number of difficulties maintaining a market-orientation thereafter.

Moving from market-orientation to product-orientation

The realities and constraints of governments, such as unpredictability, impede the maintenance of market-orientation (Lees-Marshment 2008, 533). As a minority government ALP held 72 seats. Their alliance with crossbenchers provided a barest majority of 76. Maintaining market-orientation becomes demanding, with the need to balance public expectations and product achievability.

During the 2010 elections, Gillard guaranteed a 'no carbon tax' government. However the necessity to remain in government entailed trade-offs between public approval and much needed support from the Greens. Upon entering a supply and confidence agreement, the Labor-Greens carbon tax was passed. This is an additional challenge for minority governments in maintaining market-orientation. To make an impression during their term, it is important to collaborate with alliances to ensure product achievability (Esselment 2012, 307).

On a related note, different expectations from voters can create potential disappointments (Lees-Marshment 2009, 216). In contradiction to ALP's 2010 election theme of a 'Small Australia', the Enterprise Migration Agreements (EMA) was announced to provide foreign immigration to mining sectors despite disapprovals from ALP-affiliated unions.

Such a shift from market-orientation towards product-orientation could be explained by the arrogance and superiority that follow knowledge and information parties attain when in power (Lees-Marshment 2008). Being in their second term, the ALP possibly developed a sense of superiority, becoming more introspective and less responsive towards its core support. On the other hand, marketing in government need not aim to satisfy everyone. Rather, when in government there are trade-offs between pleasing voters and successful product achievability (Lees-Marshment 2001, 118).

Managing a loss of a market-orientation

Market-back approach and learning orientation

Responding to public dissatisfaction towards the EMA, Gillard revealed in a press conference that a Jobs Board and sub-committee be established to ensure mining jobs remain favorable to domestic workers. Similarly, she debuted as a live blogger on http://www.thetelegraph.com.au answering questions on carbon tax. These reflect a masochism strategy, which conveys the acceptance and suffering of voters' discontent (Lees-Marshment 2008).

Likewise, in reality, governing parties usually end up making unpopular decisions. Even if parties do not intend to actually change their decisions, through marketing and adopting a learning orientation, they can identify and acknowledge public concerns by respecting criticisms (Lees-Marshment 2009). Equally, governing parties must proactively question existing behaviours and practices to maximize performance (Lees-Marshment 2009). By establishing the Jobs Board, the ALP adjusted their product (EMA) to suit the market, assuring voters that the government had learned from feedback. Responding to live feedbacks from voters indicates that communication in government not only includes demonstrating delivery, but also engagement in consultation and conveying products; ensuring a two-way communication (Lees-Marshment 2009).

Maintenance of market-oriented attitude among MPs and leadership

Seemingly, party unity is assured in a minority government because of the constant need to withstand a no confidence motion (Esselment 2012). Yet evidence suggests otherwise. The implication of this transpired when the EMA was announced without Gillard's knowledge. It also revealed internal dysfunctions within the party as other members, such as Labor Senator Doug Cameron, disclosed unfamiliarity and opposition towards the announcement.

This lack of internal consultation and consideration for both leadership and public opinion reflects complacency in some ALP members and a decline in Gillard's leadership. This overconfidence inhibits governing leaders and/or parties from maintaining responsiveness (Lees-Marshment 2008).

Such attitudes have also affected ALP's relationship with its partners. An agreement with cross-bencher Andrew Wilkie made during the elections to restrict gambling issues was later withdrawn when Clubs Australia launched a counteracting campaign to threaten Labor's marginal seats. Similar to the EMA, this was a move against market-orientation that significantly questioned ALP's commitments.

Parties in government often neglect their party organisations because too much of their focus is on daily government businesses (Lynch 2006). Rather than anticipating problems in advance, the here and now priorities can drive governments more towards managing crisis (to avoid where it does not want to be) and less towards strategy (where it wants to head in the future). As a minority government, the ALP's need for internal support is crucial. However feelings of superiority can erode internal cooperation and ultimately result in a motion of no confidence.

Developing long-term strategies

Leaders who stay in power for more than one term tend to only take actions after there has been a loss of responsiveness in the public's eyes (Lees-Marshment 2008, 530). Likewise the masochism strategy utilised by Gillard may seem more of a crisis management strategy rather than a future development plan. The lack of time to think about future product development is one of the challenges faced by governments. This is a challenge for maintaining market-orientation because there is a need to monitor the brand consistently and prepare to be responsive before the public perceives the government as out of touch.

Lessons for political marketing

Esselment (2012, 309) proposes that minority governments do not suffer as much as majority government from fatigue, inaction or lack of momentum because they are constantly on the edge to withhold a confidence motion. However Lees-Marshment's framework (2008) suggests that in practice, unlike in majority governments, retaining market-orientation in a minority government represents even more challenges. Minority governments face greater trade-offs if members develop complacency that can disrupt the unity of government, while still tackling the same challenges majority governments encounter.

Since mistakes are unavoidable when in government, there is a need to consistently resolve arising issues. Once in government, the ALP seemed to be trapped in crisis management situations as the masochism strategies utilised by Gillard suggests. Arguably this is required to show continued ability in responding, listening and assuring voters. But at the same time, this transpires at the cost of considerations for future developments to maintain a market-orientation. Although delivery is the key difference in political marketing, to maintain support, parties need to sustain market-orientation by balancing both the existing image of the party as well as progressing long-term strategies to redevelop their product (Lees-Marshment 2009, 211).

Further reading

Anna Esselment (2012). 'Delivering in government and getting results in minorities and coalitions'. In Jennifer Lees-Marshment (ed.) *Routledge Handbook of Political Marketing*. Abingdon and New York: Routledge, 307.

Lees-Marshment, Jennifer (2001) 'Blair and New Labour design: a classic Market-Oriented Party?' In Jennifer Lees-Marshment (ed.) *Political Marketing and British Political Parties: The Party's Just Begun*. Manchester and New York; Manchester University Press, 118.

Lynch, Richard, Paul Baines and John Egan (2006). 'Long-term performance of political parties: towards a competitive resources-based perspective'. *Journal of Political Marketing*, 5(3): 71–92.

Lees-Marshment, Jennifer (2008). 'Managing a Market-Orientation in government'. In Dennis W. Johnson (ed.) *The Routledge Handbook of Political Management*. USA: Taylor and Francis Group, 533.

Lees-Marshment, Jennifer (2009) 'Marketing after the election: the potential and limitations of maintaining a market orientation in government'. *Canadian Journal of Communication*, 34(2): 211.

Notes

1   See for example a collation of political ads for women Oct 2012, at http://www.youtube.com/watch?v=qUmh4KCzrjc
2   See Michelle Obama – Join Women for Obama, at http://www.youtube.com/watch?v=KaXtEwTszac&feature=relmf
3   Internal Macedonian Revolutionary Organization-Democratic Party for Macedonian National Unity (VMRO-DPMNE), the Social Democratic Union of Macedonia (SDSM). DUI (Democratic Union for Integration) and DPA (Democratic Party of Albanians) are representing the country's ethnic Albanian minority. Ethnic Albanian parties as well as other smaller parties could enter the parliament and participate only in coalition with some of the major Macedonian ethnic parties.

References

Arterton, Christopher F. (2007). 'Strategy and politics: the example of the United States of America'. In Thomas Fischer, Gregor Peter Schmitz and Michael Seberich (eds) *The Strategy of Politics: Results of a Comparative Study*. Butersloh: Verlag Bertelsmann Stiftung.

Asano, Masahiko and Bryce Wakefield (2010). 'Political market-orientation in Japan'. In Jennifer Lees-Marshment, Jesper Strömbäck and Chris Rudd (eds) *Global Political Marketing*. London: Routledge, 234–48.

Balestrini, Pierre P. and Paul R. Gamble (2011). 'Confronting EU unpopularity: the contribution of political marketing'. *Contemporary Politics*, 17(1): 89–107.

Balz, Dan (2013). 'How the Obama campaign won the race for voter data'. *The Washington Post*, 28 July. http://articles.washingtonpost.com/2013–07–28/politics/40858951_1_president-obama-david-plouffe-barack-obama

Bannon, Declan (2004). 'Marketing segmentation and political marketing'. Paper presented to the UK Political Studies Association, University of Lincoln, 4–8 April.

Barber, Stephen (2005). *Political Strategy: Modern Politics in Contemporary Britain*. Liverpool: Liverpool Academic Press.

Barber, Stephen (2009). 'The strategy of the British Liberal Democrats'. Case study 3.4 in Jennifer Lees-Marshment, *Political Marketing: Principles and Applications*. London and New York: Routledge, 73–4.

Bartle, J., S. Atkinson and R. Mortimore (eds) (2002). *Political Communications: The General Election Campaign of 2001*. London: Frank Cass.

Boaz, Annette and William Solesbury (2007). 'Strategy and politics: the example of the United Kingdom'. In Thomas Fischer, Gregor Peter Schmitz and Michael Seberich (eds) *The Strategy of Politics: Results of a Comparative Study*. Butersloh: Verlag Bertelsmann Stiftung, 107–32.

Butler, Patrick and Neil Collins (1996). 'Strategic analysis in political markets'. *European Journal of Marketing*, 30(10/11): 25–36.

Coleman, Stephen (2007). 'Review'. *Parliamentary Affairs*, 60(1): 180–6.

Collins, Neil and Patrick Butler (2002). 'Considerations on market analysis for political parties'. In Nicholas O'Shaughnessy and Stephan Henneberg (eds) *The Idea of Political Marketing*. London: Praeger, 1–18.

Davidson, Scott and Robert H. Binstock (2012). 'Political marketing and segmentation in aging democracies'. In Jennifer Lees-Marshment (ed.) *Routledge Handbook of Political Marketing*. London and New York: Routledge, 20–33.

Devine, Tad (2013). 'Obama campaigns for re-election'. In Dennis W. Johnson (ed.) *Campaigning for President 2012: Strategy and Tactics*. New York: Routledge, 137–50.

Downs, Anthony (1995). *An Economic Theory of Democracy*. New York: Harper & Row.

Fell, Dafydd J. and Isabelle Cheng (2010). 'Testing the market-oriented model of political parties in a non-Western context: the case of Taiwan'. In Jennifer Lees-Marshment, Jesper Strömbäck and Chris Rudd (eds) *Global Political Marketing*. London: Routledge, 175–88.

Fischer, Thomas, Gregor Peter Schmitz, and Michael Seberich (eds) (2007). *The Strategy of Politics: Results of a Comparative Study*. Butersloh: Verlag Bertelsmann Stiftung.

Friesen, Joe (2011). '"Micro-targeting" lets parties conquer ridings, one tiny group at a time'. *The Globe and Mail*, Friday, April 22. http://www.theglobeandmail.com/news/politics/micro-targeting-lets-parties-conquer-ridings-one-tiny-group-at-a-time/article1996155/ (accessed 20 June, 2013)

Glaab, Manuela (2007). 'Strategy and politics: the example of Germany'. In Thomas Fischer, Gregor Peter Schmitz, and Michael Seberich (eds) *The Strategy of Politics: Results of a Comparative Study*. Butersloh: Verlag Bertelsmann Stiftung, 61–106.

Gorbounova, Daria and Jennifer Lees-Marshment (2009). 'Political marketing strategy of Hillary Clinton in the 2008 Iowa and New Hampshire primaries'. Case study 5.3 in Jennifer Lees-Marshment, *Political Marketing: Principles and Applications*. London and New York: Routledge, 126–8.

Harada, Susan and Helen Morris (2012). 'Niche Marketing the Greens in Canada and Scotland'. In Jennifer Lees-Marshment (ed.) *Routledge Handbook of Political Marketing*. London and New York: Routledge, 93–106.

Hughes, Andrew and Stephen Dann (2010). 'Australian political marketing: substance backed by style'. In Jennifer Lees-Marshment, Jesper Strömbäck and Chris Rudd (eds) *Global Political Marketing*. London: Routledge, 82–95.

Ingram, Peter and Jennifer Lees-Marshment (2002). 'The Anglicisation of political marketing: how Blair "out-marketed" Clinton'. *Journal of Public Affairs*, 2(2): 44–56.

Keenan, Elizabeth (2007). 'Kevin 07: Labor's winning brand'. *Time*, 3 December: 24–31.

Kiss, Balazs (2009). 'The Hungarian Socialist Party winning young people'. Case Study 5.2 in Jennifer Lees-Marshment, *Political Marketing: Principles and Applications*. London and New York: Routledge, 123–5.

Kiss, Balazs and Zsuzsanna Mihályffy (2010). 'Political salesmen in Hungary'. In Jennifer Lees-Marshment, Jesper Strömbäck and Chris Rudd (eds) *Global Political Marketing*, London: Routledge, 143–56.

Knuckey, Jonathan (2010). 'Political marketing in the United States: from market- towards sales-orientation?' In Jennifer Lees-Marshment, Jesper Strömbäck and Chris Rudd (eds) *Global Political Marketing*, London: Routledge, 96–112.

Knuckey, Jonathan, and Jennifer Lees-Marshment (2005). 'American political marketing: George W. Bush and the Republican Party'. In Darren Lilleker and Jennifer Lees-Marshment (eds) *Political Marketing: A Comparative Perspective*. Manchester: Manchester University Press, 39–58.

Kotler, Philip and Sidney J. Levy (1969). 'Broadening the concept of marketing'. *Journal of Marketing*, 33(1): 10–15.

Kotzaivazoglou, Iordanis and Torgos Zotos (2010). 'The level of market-orientation of political parties in Greece'. In Jennifer Lees-Marshment, Jesper Strömbäck and Chris Rudd (eds) *Global Political Marketing*. London: Routledge, 28–42.

Lees-Marshment, Jennifer (2001). *Political Marketing and British Political Parties: The Party's Just Begun*. Manchester: Manchester University Press.

Lees-Marshment, Jennifer (2008). 'Managing a market-orientation in government: cases in the UK and New Zealand'. In Dennis W. Johnson (ed.) *The Routledge Handbook of Political Management*. New York and Abingdon: Routledge, 524–36.

Lees-Marshment, Jennifer (2009a). 'Political marketing and the 2008 New Zealand election: a comparative perspective'. *Australian Journal of Political Science*, 44(3): 457–75.

Lees-Marshment, Jennifer (2009b). 'Marketing after the election: the potential and limitations of maintaining a market-orientation in government'. Rethinking Public Relations special issue for *The Canadian Journal of Communication*, 34(2): 205–27.

Lees-Marshment, Jennifer (2010). 'New Zealand Political Marketing: marketing communication rather than the product?' In Jennifer Lees-Marshment, Jesper Strömbäck and Chris Rudd (eds) *Global Political Marketing*. London: Routledge, 65–81.

Lees-Marshment, Jennifer (2011). *The Political Marketing Game*. Houndmills and New York: Palgrave Macmillan.

Lees-Marshment, Jennifer, Jesper Strömbäck and Chris Rudd (eds) (2010) *Global Political Marketing*. London: Routledge, 278–97.

Lilleker, Darren and Jennifer Lees-Marshment (eds) (2005). *Political Marketing: A Comparative Perspective*. Manchester: Manchester University Press.

Lindholm, Mikael R. and Anette Prehn (2007). 'Strategy and politics: the example of Denmark'. In Thomas Fischer, Gregor Peter Schmitz and Michael Seberich (eds) *The Strategy of Politics: Results of a Comparative Study*. Butersloh: Verlag Bertelsmann Stiftung, 11–60.

Maier, Michaela, Jens Tenscher and Kirsten Schüller (2010). 'Political marketing in Germany'. In Jennifer Lees-Marshment, Jesper Strömbäck and Chris Rudd (eds) *Global Political Marketing*. London: Routledge, 34–51.

Marland, Alex (2003). 'Marketing political soap: a political marketing view of selling candidates like soap, of electioneering as a ritual, and of electoral military analogies'. *Journal of Public Affairs*, 3(2): 103–115.

Matuskova, Anna, Otto Eibl and Alexander Braun (2010). 'The Czech case: a Market-Oriented Party on the rise?' In Jennifer Lees-Marshment, Jesper Strömbäck and Chris Rudd (eds) *Global Political Marketing*. London: Routledge, 157–74.

Mehlman, Steve (2006). 'California's special election: political miscalculations and PR missteps'. *Public Relations Tactics*, 13(2): 12–13.

Mortimore, Roger and Mark Gill (2010). 'Implementing and interpreting market orientation in practice: lessons from Britain'. In Jennifer Lees-Marshment, Jesper Strömbäck and Chris Rudd (eds) *Global Political Marketing*. London: Routledge, 249–62.

Newman, Bruce I. (1994). *The Marketing of the President: Political Marketing as Campaign Strategy*. Thousand Oaks, CA: Sage Publications.

Newman, Bruce I. (ed.) (1999). *Handbook of Political Marketing*. Thousand Oaks, CA: Sage Publications.

O'Cass, Aron (1996). 'Political marketing and the marketing concept'. *European Journal of Marketing*, 30(10/11): 45–61.

Ormrod, Robert P. (2005a). 'A conceptual model of political market orientation'. *Journal of Non-Profit and Public Sector Marketing*, 14(1/2): 47–64.

Ormrod, Robert P. (2005b). 'A conceptual model of political market orientation'. In Walter Wymer and Jennifer Lees-Marshment (eds), *Current Issues in Political Marketing*. Binghamton, NY: Haworth Press, 47–64.

Ormord, Robert P. (2006). 'A critique of the Lees-Marshment Market-Oriented Party model'. *Politics*, 26(2) (May): 110–18.

Ormrod, Robert P. and Stephan C. Henneberg (2006). 'Different facets of market orientation: a comparative exploratory analysis of party manifestos in Britain and Germany'. 3rd International Conference on Political Marketing, 5 April 2006.

Patrón Galindo, Pedro (2009). 'The re-launch of the APRA Party in a new political era in Peru'. Case study 3.2 in Jennifer Lees-Marshment, *Political Marketing: Principles and Applications*. London and New York: Routledge, 69–70.

Patrón Galindo, Pedro (2010). 'Political marketing in a weak democracy: the Peruvian case'. In Jennifer Lees-Marshment, Jesper Strömbäck and Chris Rudd (eds) *Global Political Marketing*. London: Routledge, 202–17.

Promise (2006) *Reconnecting the Prime Minister*. Paper 21 for the Market Research Society. http://www.promisecorp.com/documents/Reconnecting_the_Prime_Minister.pdf (accessed September 2013).

Rosin, Hannah (2012). 'Rise of the single-woman voter', *Slate*, March 13. http://www.slate.com/articles/double_x/doublex/2012/03/single_women_are_the_new_swing_voters_but_which_way_do_they_lean_.html

Russell, Andrew and Edward Fieldhouse (2005). *Neither Left nor Right? The Liberal Democrats and the Electorate*. Manchester: Manchester University Press.

Savigny, Heather (2005). 'Labour, political marketing and the 2005 election: a campaign of two halves'. *Journal of Marketing Management*, 21(9/10): 925–41.

Savigny, Heather and Mick Temple (2010). 'Political marketing models: the curious incident of the dog that doesn't bark'. *Political Studies*, 58(5): 1049–64.

Smith, Gareth (2005). 'Positioning political parties: the 2005 UK general election'. *Journal of Marketing Management*, 21(9/10): 1135–49.

Strömbäck, Jesper (2009). 'From the "old" to the "new" moderates: a Swedish case study'. Case study 5.1 in Jennifer Lees-Marshment, *Political Marketing: Principles and Applications*. London and New York: Routledge: 121–3.

Strömbäck, Jesper (2010a). 'A framework for comparing political market-orientation'. In Jennifer Lees-Marshment, Jesper Strömbäck and Chris Rudd (eds) *Global Political Marketing*. London: Routledge, 16–33.

Strömbäck, Jesper (2010b). 'Political market-orientation in a multi-party system: the Swedish case'. In Jennifer Lees-Marshment, Jesper Strömbäck and Chris Rudd (eds) *Global Political Marketing*. London: Routledge, 52–64.

Temple, Mick (2010). 'Political marketing, party behaviour and political science'. In Jennifer Lees-Marshment, Jesper Strömbäck and Chris Rudd (eds) *Global Political Marketing*. London: Routledge, 263–77.

Wakefield, Bryce (2009). 'Principle versus patronage: the Lees-Marshment method and political marketing in Japan'. Case Study 3.3 in Jennifer Lees-Marshment, *Political Marketing: Principles and Applications*. London and New York: Routledge, 71–2.

Winder, Georg and Jens Tenscher (2012). 'Populism as political marketing technique'. In Jennifer Lees-Marshment (ed.) *Routledge Handbook of Political Marketing* London and New York: Routledge, 230–42.

Winther Nielsen, Sigge (2012). 'Three faces of political marketing strategy'. *Journal of Public Affairs*, 12(4): 293–302.

Winther Nielsen, Sigge (2013). 'Toward a new institutional strategy framework for political marketing'. *Journal of Public Affairs*, 13(1): 84–99.

Zeleny, Jeff (2012). 'Campaign Postscript Offers a Peek at Debates on Security and Spending', *The New York Times*, 7th December. http://thecaucus.blogs.nytimes.com/2012/12/07/campaign-postscript-offers-a-peek-at-debates-on-security-and-spending/?_r=0

3 Political market research

Practitioner perspective 3.1 on the importance of political market research

The biggest danger for political parties is where they dismiss the feelings and the thoughts of the public.

Matt Carter, PSB research and former UK Labour General Secretary, interviewed in 2007

Market research is such an integral part of any campaign. . . No campaign person can say I'm not doing any market research.

John Utting, Australian pollster for UMR, interviewed in 2008

With the exception of 'spin-doctors' no campaign phrase has ever been imbued with a greater air of nonsensical mystique than 'focus groups'. Their importance is they enable politicians to hear directly the voters' voices.

The Late Lord Philip Gould, advisor to UK PM Tony Blair, 1998

Having advised campaigns on four continents, I have seen that research-based strategies have an edge over other methods regardless of the region, culture or situation, and that every year the amount of campaign research worldwide seems to increase.

Alex Braun, US Consultant for PSB Research, interviewed in 2009

Source: Lees-Marshment (2011); Gould (1998)

As Practitioner perspective 3.1 indicates, political market research is fundamental to political marketing; it ensures that any decisions taken are well informed, and without it there would be a lot of guess work in politics. Political market research involves a wide range of qualitative and quantitative, formal and informal methods for candidates, parties and governments to understand the nature of the political marketplace. Such market research is used to understand the attitudes, behaviour, needs and wants of the public and other key stakeholders and then inform decisions about strategy, creation of the brand, policies, internal political marketing within organisations, and communication of positions with the view to inform, educate, persuade, change and reinforce existing views.

This chapter will first discuss the nature of the political market, exploring the decline of traditional forms of political participation and rise of consumerist attitudes towards political elites, before reviewing the wide range of political market research tools. Political market research (PMR) includes quantitative forms of research such as polling, surveys, segmentation (including voter profiling), big data (analytical and experimental marketing); and qualitative forms such as focus groups, co-creation and deliberative research; opposition, candidate and policy research; and informal tools including global knowledge transfer and use of public records and data. Lastly it will explore the range of ways in which political market research is used.

The political market and the political consumer

Practitioner perspective 3.2 on the challenges of the political market

What makes campaigns difficult is the shorter attention span that people have, and the flood of sensory input that they keep getting . . . you're really fighting for attention with so many aspects there.

Alex Braun, US Consultant for PSB Research, interviewed in 2009

When they do open up to communication, it is not just that sent by the party or candidate, or even particular media channels, because voters increasingly use a variety of sources of information to form their views.

Goldy Hyder, M. Hill and Knowlton, interviewed in 2009

People are tired of being put into old-fashioned political boxes. Venstre is today a broadly based party with voters in all groups . . . People do not think in terms of classes anymore but insist on being allowed to make the decisions that affect their lives by themselves. People no longer accept politicians saying 'we know what is best for you'.

Danish Prime Minister Anders Fogh Rasmussen

Membership attitudes today, particularly amongst young people, have evolved from the days when [being a member] was a form of social infrastructure. Today people want to feel they are involved in politics and that above all they have a right to be listened to – at the top.

Archie Norman, a business executive appointed as the UK
Conservative Party's Chief Executive after the 1997 General Election

As political practitioners we always need to remember that 'we' are not the target audience. We are political junkies who obsess over policy and process and we dramatically over-index on news consumption. What matters to us rarely matters to the low-engagement swing voters who decide close elections.

Patrick Muttart, Former Deputy Chief of Staff in the Canadian Prime Minister's Unit, 2013

Sources: Lees-Marshment (2011); Pettitt (2009); Lees-Marshment (2001); and top tip comment provided by practitioner by email, 2013.

The decline in traditional patterns of political behaviour

The political marketplace, which includes every aspect a candidate, party or government has to consider as well as the more obvious aspects such as how voters behave, has changed significantly since the 1960s. Practitioner perspective 3.2 indicates how there have been changes in a number of respects including how voters receive communication and the attitude of voters towards politicians. There is a substantial area of research that reports a declining respect for, and confidence and trust in, established institutions and politicians (see, for example, Norris 2005; Pharr and Putnam 2000; and Gidengil 2012, 39, 41). As

Mortimore (2003) argues, the standing of politics is low: 'politicians today are distrusted more than other professions or institutions'.

Traditional forms of political participation including becoming a member or formal supporter of a party and even voting itself is declining, and when people do vote, their choice is less predictable. The influence of traditional social groupings or cleavages, such as class, geography and family background, on voting have declined, whilst new electoral segments, such as those based on ethnicity, race, lifestyle, life cycle stage and age have emerged. In Canada, for example, deep regional and linguistic cleavages are emerging (see Gidengil 2012, 39) but in varying ways, so that as Dufresne and Marland (2012, 23) note political marketers 'can no longer split the population simply along an English and French linguistic line, especially not in cities and suburbs where immigrant populations are concentrated', and research has to be used to update understanding of allophones' attitudes, behaviour, beliefs, and values. In a number of countries, the senior market is expanding and diversifying, and Davidson and Binstock (2012, 24) argue strategists have to conduct research to keep up to date with their diverse needs. Not only are there various life cycle factors such as retirement, bereavement, giving up driving, giving up one's home, experiencing ill health and crime; older people's reaction to this varies widely and thus governmental organisations need to conduct research to better understand the different needs within this group.

At the other end of the age spectrum, Ndlovu (2013, 110) notes there is declining interest in politics amongst generation x, which creates a more pressured environment for political marketing strategists who want to communicate political messages to youth as they not only have less knowledge of politics but lack a general frame of reference and thus communication has to educate as well as inform or persuade. The way all voters receive information about politics has changed; with a move away from newspapers and television news to a diverse range of sources including online news and social media. Continual media coverage also provides an uncomfortable, unrelenting environment for political parties and politicians, especially in government. Online media outlets enable the voter to be part of the broadcast and make the news, not just watch it; and the instant nature of mediums such as Twitter encourages the public to expect an instant response from politicians. Furthermore, research by Sherman *et al.* (2008) suggests that voters do not trust any source of information on (or from) political candidates. Similarly Lloyd's (2009) research suggests that political elites cannot control how their communication is perceived. Lloyd interviewed members of the public and found that all of them regularly failed to understand, believe or agree with political communication; they form their perception of a political brand from a range of sources to obtain alternative perspectives. The attention they pay to political communication was also mitigated by other things going on in their lives. As the comment by Patrick Muttart in Practitioner perspective 3.2 suggests, political marketing practitioners need to always remember that the interest in politics amongst the general public is very different to politicians and their staff.

Political consumerism

More broadly, the public is increasingly consumerist towards political elites and institutions. As Pharr and Putnam (2000) argue, citizens have new expectations and information that have altered the criteria by which they judge their governments. The public act more like consumers, not just in how they vote, but their overall attitude to politicians – what they demand, how they want to be involved, how they question authority, how they want to be consulted and how they scrutinise lack of delivery. Consumerisation has a number of effects on politics. Voters themselves want a more tangible, rather than a rhetorical, product: hence the rise of pledge cards or contracts between the government and people. They also want more evident and instant delivery, prefer achievement to aspiration and pragmatic effectiveness to moral principle, so delivery management is increasingly important. Parties and politicians need to convey their governing capability and political promises need to be costed and realistic. As Bennett (2012, 26) notes when discussing the consumerisation aspect of personalized politics, 'individuals have become fully immersed in consumer cultures and have developed a discerning eye for their political and personal products' which 'undermines the appeal of adopting collective identifications with party, ideology, or conventional movements'. In 2013 Susan Delacourt published a book *Shopping For Votes: How Politicians Choose Us and We Choose Them* which explores how voters behave like and are treated like consumers. Although it focuses on Canada, the analysis is relevant to all modern democracies, and raises normative as well as practical questions: see Author's corner 3.1 to learn more about her book.

Political consumer behaviour

In business there is a substantial literature on consumer behaviour, but there has been surprisingly little application of such theories to politics, even though in political science there is substantial literature on voting behaviour. There is therefore much potential for research on voters as consumers and more studies are now appearing; as Williams (2012, 5) observes there were twice as many articles published in the *Journal of Political Marketing* on voters or consumers in the last five years compared with the first five years of the journal's life. What this tells us is that politicians have to convey that they are understanding of, or in touch with, ordinary people – Busby (2009, 28) notes how, given that poll questions frequently ask voters whether they perceive candidates to understand their needs or can relate to ordinary people, expectations and perceptions of ordinariness are important to voters. Research by Chiu *et al.* (2010, 35) found that in addition to party identification and demography, respondents voting behaviour choices were significantly related to personal values; specifically whether they were:

*   conscientious (sense of accomplishment, wisdom, ambitious, honest, self-controlled, logical, polite and responsible);
*   self-confident (capable, imaginative, independent and intellectual);
*   considerate (cheerful, clean, forgiving, helpful and loving);
*   affectionate (happiness, inner harmony, mature love, self-respect, true friendship);
*   artistic (a world at peace and a world of beauty).

Ben-Ur and Newman (2010) surveyed potential voters in the lead-up to the 2004 US presidential election in a southern US county and conclude that voters choose candidates on the basis of the value of the product they are offered by them. Similarly Johns and Brandenburg (2012) surveyed British voters to test their views on parties' political market-orientation and explore what voters are looking for in a party. Their research suggests that voters could not recognise the difference between a product and market-orientation, or the trade-offs between the two, when they were put in terms of parties sticking by what they traditionally believe in or changing their policies in line with public opinion. As Johns and Brandenburg conclude, voters want a bit of both orientations – a party that will stick to its core principles without being intransigent *and* a party that is responsive to public opinion but again not indiscriminately so. So parties need to respond to public opinion but without

Author's corner 3.1

Shopping for Votes: How Politicians Choose Us and We Choose Them
By Susan Delacourt
Published by Douglas & McIntyre in 2013

Shopping For Votes: How Politicians Choose Us and We Choose Them is a Canadian political book, which attempts to tell a popular history of political marketing in Canada.

The book owes some of its origins to Jennifer Lees-Marshment and her friends in Canadian political-marketing expertise, notably Alex Marland of Memorial University and Thierry Giasson.

Here is the backstory: while on a journalism fellowship at the University of Toronto, I landed in a course on material culture, which was essentially an introduction to how consumerism and shopping had changed our lives. This was the fall of 2008, and Canada was in the midst of an election. It was hard not to notice that the federal Conservatives had a much more consumer-friendly platform than any of the other parties – and that they rode to victory on it.

In the spring of 2009, the Canadian Political Science Association held a special session on political marketing at Carleton University in Ottawa, featuring fascinating presentations by Lees-Marshment, as well as Marland and Giasson. It hit me then that Canadian voters needed to read more about political marketing and consumer-citizenship. While much work had been done on these subjects in Britain and the United States, these were still very new ideas to Canadians.

So I decided to write a book – a narrative history of how marketing had infiltrated politics and how citizens had come to see themselves as consumers of government and politics. To tell the story, I had to go back to the consumer boom after the Second World War and chart how the landscape had changed in Canada at the consumer and political level.

The book is divided into three chronological parts, which (not so coincidentally) parallel the stages of a consumer transaction.

The first part, 'The Pitch', spans the period from the 1950s to the 1970s, when Canadian politicos were diving into the world of advertising and market research, giddy with the possibilities of what these new techniques would 'buy' them, in terms of increased voter support and citizen engagement. Just as Canadians were into a spending spree, inundated with Madmen-style pitches, so were the political backrooms and the voters.

The second part, 'The Bargaining', covers the 1980s and 1990s, when we saw real ambivalence about whether we wanted all this marketing and consumerism in our civic life. These were great days for pollsters and marketing experts, but Canada was also embroiled in national-unity dramas, between federalism and Quebec separatism, which kept political debates somewhat removed from consumerism and marketing.

The third part, 'Sealing the Deal', is the story of modern Canadian politics and all the ways in which Conservative Prime Minister Stephen Harper has managed to fuse marketing and governance in a way that none of his successors achieved. Not only has Harper managed to do marketing in politics, but he has also pulled it off in government too. In this third part, as well, considerable attention is paid to the ways in which data management – the tool of the consumer marketers – has been increasingly adopted by the Conservatives first as well as their rivals in Canada.

In the end, *Shopping For Votes* asks Canadians to take a closer look at political marketing and consumer-citizenship and maybe ask some pointed questions. For instance: Does the political marketplace need the same rules and guidelines as the consumer marketplace? If marketing and advertising are so crucial to political success, do we need to make sure the playing field is democratically fair? And perhaps most importantly, is there a difference between being a consumer and a citizen and, if so, how do we preserve the distinction?

losing all their core principles and policies. Case study 3.1 by Tiffany Winchester reviews the results of research into voter/consumer behaviour and recommends from this that voting decision-making is a low-involvement decision for many voters, and thus when campaigning the party in power needs to reassure those who did vote for it that their decision was wise so they consider repeating their vote at the next election; and provide clear and consistent messages which discuss their positive product aspects.

The political marketplace is therefore a very challenging one for politicians. Voters are like buyers who will switch supermarkets easily instead of building a long-term relationship of loyalty and trust with their local grocery store. In their book on *Voters as Consumers*, Lilleker and Scullion (2008, 1–2) note how society has changed. They analyse speeches made by two British prime ministers on taking office: one, Clement Attlee in 1945 and the other, Gordon Brown in 2007. They note how Attlee positioned himself as a prime minister who had tough decisions to make and warned the nation of hard times ahead. In sharp contrast Gordon Brown said he would be a prime minister that listened and responded to individuals concerns and met their aspirations. They therefore concluded that 'a prime minister can no longer just argue that they know what is best for the country and deliver that, but that they must listen to the key concerns of the public and deliver specifically measurable outcomes'. Political elites cannot take any support, including that of their own core voters, for granted; they have to work hard to get support, donations, activity and actual votes. This is why political elites use PMR so they can better understand the views and behaviour of the public – and how best to respond to it.

The market intelligence industry

- Harris interactive (US): http://www.harrisinteractive.com/
- Nielsen (US/global): http://www.nielsen-netratings.com/
- Gallup (global): http://www.gallup.com/
- PSB (Penn, Schoen and Berland associates) (US and worldwide): http://www.psbresearch.com/Abacus Data (Canada)
- Ipsos MORI (UK): http://www.ipsos-mori.com/
- Opinion leader (UK): http://www.opinionleader.co.uk/
- Opinion research (UK): http://www.opinionresearch.com/
- UMR: http://www.umr.co.nz (New Zealand) and www.umr.com.au/index.html (Australia)
- Gfk NOP (UK): http://www.gfknop.com/customresearch-uk/
- ICM (UK): www.icmresearch.co.uk/
- YouGov (UK): https://yougov.co.uk/opi/
- Digi poll: http://www.digipoll.co.nz/main.html
- Colmar Brunton: http://www.colmarbrunton.co.nz/
- IDC (global): http://www.idc.com/
- Survey USA: http://www.surveyusa.com/
- American Research Group: http://www.americanresearchgroup.com/
- Mason-Dixon (US): http://www.mason-dixon.com/public/index.cfm
- Roy Morgan Research (Australia): http://www.roymorgan.com.au/

Figure 3.1

Political market research tools

Market intelligence in politics has increased tremendously in both size and the range of methods employed. A whole range of political-public organisations conduct intelligence, both formally using outside professionals, and informally in-house. Figure 3.1 shows some of the larger well-known international companies with branches in several countries, but there are also organisations in each country who offer their own unique approaches.

PMR helps ensure politicians are well informed. Lees-Marshment (2011) notes how practitioners recalled that it is very effective at seeing through the 'hysteria' and being able to solidly say what the course of action should be. In particular it enables practitioners to see whether the daily critique common to 'planet politics' – the centre of political activity whether it be Parliament Hill in Ottawa Canada, Wellington BeeHive and parliament in New Zealand, Westminster in London in the UK or Capital Hill in Washington – is being felt by the general public.

Quantitative research: polling, surveys, segmentation, voter profiling, analytic and experimental marketing

Quantitative research uses closed questions to try to measure opinion and the strength of opinion. It provides big numbers – surface-level data. Examples include polling; consumer panels; telephone surveys; personal interviews, both door-to-door and in the street; panel studies; and mail surveys. It provides accuracy just before an election and trends over time; it is also easy to administer, deliver data and compare results. The constraints with quantitative research include the potential for bias in question design, the financial cost of the research, and that you have to know what you want to measure before you do it so it is less likely to uncover new insights.

Quantitative research has to be designed carefully to produce accurate results. It is impossible to ask everybody in the market, because the market is too big. Instead, a sample is taken. Whereas the *population* includes all elements, units or individuals that are of interest to researchers for a specific study, a *sample* is a smaller-size population: a segment of people that will reflect or represent characteristics of an entire population. There are different options for the types of question asked, including structured multiple choice; opinion scales (e.g. very happy – happy – neutral – unhappy – very unhappy); rank order (in your opinion rank the following . . .); and alternatives or paired comparisons (is x candidate lively or dull?).

Examples of political polls can be found online. The simplest polls simply ask for voting preferences, but more detailed questions give an idea of how voters perceive particular characteristics and track ongoing levels of support. For an example see Ipsos Mori's Political Monitor: see Figure 3.2 – which tracks changing opinions of British party leaders on leadership characteristics, including being good in a crisis, capable leadership and being in touch with ordinary people.

Quantitative polling is used in different ways at different times. There are a number of uses at different stages during a campaign, for example. Turcotte sets out five types of opinion polls frequently used in political campaigns (see also Rademacher and Tuchfarber 1999, 203–5; and Braun 2012, 17): see Figure 3.3.

Matuskova *et al.* (2010, 168) note how consultants working for the CSSD (Czech Social Democratic Party) in the Czech Republic in the 2006 parliamentary elections undertook a large quantitative benchmark poll of almost 3,000 likely voters in September 2005 'which created the backbone for the entire campaign strategy, and provided a blueprint for the

Ipsos Mori Political Monitor, September 2013

Q   I am going to read out some things both favourable and unfavourable that have been said about various politicians. Which of these, if any, do you think apply to . . .

	Ed Milliband %	David Cameron %	Nick Clegg %
A capable leader	28	53	24
Good in a crisis	20	47	18
Has sound judgement	32	40	27
Understands the problems facing Britain	52	50	39
Out of touch with ordinary people	49	70	56
More style than substance	41	52	51
Looks after some sections of society more than others	58	79	58
None of these	2	1	2
Don't know	5	2	6

Figure 3.2

Source: Extract/adapted from 'Labour lead of three points as Miliband's personal ratings fall to lowest ever'. http://www.ipsos-mori.com/researchpublications/researcharchive/3263/Labour-lead-of-three-points-as-Milibands-personal-ratings-fall-to-lowest-ever.aspx (accessed 18 September 2013)

campaign plan'. It asked voters' views and preferences in many areas including the political environment, party and leader attributes, government accomplishments ratings, policy proposals, spending priorities, profiles and analysis of voters and their media habits, and regional differences. The data this generated gave the campaign a detailed insight into the minds of voters and their perceptions of elites as well as what they wanted elites to do. It was used to develop the CSSD message in response, the campaign plan, and segment the voters as they sought not only to retain core supporters but to capture as many swing and undecided voters as possible.

Despite the value of polling, public opinion can be very volatile and hard to measure. Any method captures a snap judgement only, and it could be different to the actual decision or final vote. People may hold views on both sides that conflict and change. Asher (1995) notes an example of polling, conducted by the Harris organisation during the 1980 presidential primaries, that asked respondents about their preference for the candidates and then asked questions about current government issues. When the respondents were asked at the end to reaffirm their voting preferences, support for former US President Carter declined. The explanation was that, on being reminded of Carter's record, voters became more negative.

Turcotte's stages of quantitative polling research during a political campaign

1   **Benchmark poll**: Typically the most in-depth poll (in terms of sample size and number of questions) conducted prior to the official beginning of the election campaign and designed to gather information on every relevant aspect of the campaign (issues, leaders' images, voting intentions, key segments, etc.). Braun (2012, 17) notes that the results are usually presented to the campaign leadership in significant detail and help develop the overall strategic plan of the campaign, its positioning, targeting and framework for communications.

2   **Strategic poll**: Poll conducted after the benchmark poll and designed to delve into the key findings gleaned in the benchmark poll. A strategic poll is often timed in conjunction with focus group research.

3   **Tracking poll**: Small poll typically conducted on a daily basis throughout the campaign and designed to look at the dynamics of voter choice, allowing for immediate strategic changes or readjustment in tactics.

4   **Brushfire poll**: Small poll designed to focus on an emerging issue or problem during the campaign.

5   **Post-election poll**: Large poll designed to ascertain the nature of the electoral mandate and evaluate the reasons for success or failure.

Figure 3.3

Source: Adapted from Turcotte (2012, 79)

Segmenting and profiling the market

Segmentation is a crucial tool to break up the heterogeneous, mass electoral market into smaller sections which can be targeted in terms of product, message and medium. It helps cut across old left-right ideological divisions to create new groupings and can help to provide new understanding where traditional political labels no longer apply or work as effectively. Newman (1999, 263) observed how Bill Clinton's presidential re-election bid in 1996 succeeded by creating a message that appealed to the desire for an American dream across four segments of voters: rational voters, driven by their American dream expectations; emotional voters, driven by the feelings aroused by their desire to achieve the American dream; social voters, driven by the association of different groups of people and their ability to achieve the American dream; and situational voters, driven by situations that might influence their decision to switch to another candidate. Segmentation tries to identify common characteristics: see Figure 3.4. Research suggests that in some cases people choose to live in a particular area because they hold similar socio-economic, cultural and lifestyle characteristics; and geography is easy to measure and provides easy information. Psychographic segmentation is seen as more valuable because it considers the individual's actual behaviour and lifestyle rather than inferring that from other characteristics.

Segmentation selection criteria depends on the situation: in the new democracy of Ghana in Africa, for example, ethnicity and religion are important segmentation methods; Alabi and Alabi (2007) discuss how this was reflected in parties' choice of leadership and images.

Practitioner perspective 3.3 on segmenting the market

Texas is a good example, where we don't have any party registration, so we don't know whether somebody is a Republican or a Democrat ... so micro targeting is very helpful in saying OK ... somebody lives in this type of house, drives this type of car, reads these kinds of magazines, goes to this kind of church, has this many kids, and they voted in these last three elections, therefore we can make some basic assumptions about them.

Rick Beeson, RNC Political Director, interviewed in 2007

It's not enough to recognise that in any one constituency there are 15,000 people that you need to talk to in order to win the election, but it's actually that those 15,000 people may be able to be grouped into smaller groupings, each of whom has their own personal agendas and issues.

Matt Carter, PSB research and former UK Labour General
Secretary, interviewed in 2007

Segmentation *'brings target voters alive, e.g. females, 30–45, kids, in part-time work, under heavy costs of living pressures, concerned about their children's education, worried they're not spending enough time with their kids, not very interested in politics, don't read the newspaper, hate anti-smacking legislation, blind to nuances that it was a Green bill and National voted for it, etc.*

Stephen Mills, UMR Pollster to New Zealand
Labour Party, interviewed in 2009

Source: Lees-Marshment (2011, 20–1)

Basic segmentation options

Geographic	where people live, with differences between countries and regions within that country.
Behavioural:	segments based on the actions of the individual, e.g. loyalty to the party or candidate, or what benefit they seek from the product.
Demographic	age, family nature, social class, income, etc.
Psychographic	lifestyle characteristics, e.g. leisure choices, tastes, readership of newspapers/magazines; values, beliefs, attitudes, activities, interests and opinions.

Figure 3.4

Sources: adapted from Bannon (2004) and Smith and Saunders (1990)

Segmentation can also be carried out at a much more detailed level than that of the old social cleavages – as Butler and Harris (2009, 154) note, it provides 'an insight into the more precise nature of demand in the marketplace' – see Practitioner perspective 3.3. The elderly or pensioner group, for example, consists of a range of different segments with very different needs. As Davidson (2005, 1181) notes, 'someone in their 70s could be working full time and be fit and healthy, another person in their early 50s could be living with a long-term chronic condition and forced out of the labour market'. In the 2005 election, UK Labour identified different groups such as 'low-income elderly', 'childfree serenity', and 'small town seniors'. Turcotte (2012, 85) notes in the 2006 and 2008 federal elections in Canada, strategists for the Conservatives created fictional people to epitomize swing voters such as 'Dougie' – single, in his late twenties, working at Canadian Tire who agreed Conservative policies on crime and welfare abuse, but was more interested in recreation than politics and might fail to turn out; 'Rick and Brenda' – a common-law couple with working-class jobs; and 'Mike and Theresa' who were better off and could become Conservative supporters except for their Catholic background. This identified about 500,000 voters out of the 23 million eligible voters the Conservative strategy could focus on to achieve victory.

Segments should be selected strategically depending on goals and resources. As Burton (2012, 35) explains, strategic voter selection is 'the act of prioritizing members of the voting-eligible population, as individuals or as groups, in order to guide the allocation of outreach expenditures'. It helps maximise the effectiveness of resources by dividing the electorate into politically meaningful segments and estimating the benefit and costs of reaching them before identifying the most cost-effective means of accumulating enough votes to win the election. In the 2004 US presidential election, Republicans divided Michigan voters into 31 political categories, noting numbers and likelihood of voting Republican in each one, such as religious Conservative Republicans, tax-cut Conservative Republicans and flag and family Republicans, anti-terrorism Republicans, and harder to reach groups such as wageable weak Democrats (Johnson 2007). Burton and Miracle (2014) note how the 2012 Obama re-election campaign invested $25 million into data analysis to maximise the efficiency of campaign expenditures. However they also note that targeting in the US has a long electoral history, dating back to the 1930s, even if it was less scientific and lacked the more complex statistical analysis now in action. Even as far back as the late 1970s, Margaret Thatcher, the UK's first female prime minister, gained support from a new segment – the skilled working class – through a policy enabling tenants to buy their council/ state house.

Segmentation helps to create new groupings that elites might not otherwise think of. Braun (2012, 13) notes how researcher Mark Penn's company conducted a unique micro-targeting project for Republican candidate Michael Bloomberg's election campaign for mayor of New York City in 2001. At that time 70 percent of registered voters in New York were Democrats, so research was used to create a target group based on a combination of demographics, party affiliation and established attitudes and needs. This generated surprising outcomes such as that older, affluent Jewish males on Wall Street and younger, low-socio-economic status, Hispanic waitresses shared concerns on the effects of terrorism on their business and income, and thus the campaign was able to send all these groups communication on Bloomberg's security plan.

Segmentation is also used to make sure a candidate's own supporters actually turn out to vote (GOTV) which is especially important when elections are close. Knuckey (2010, 107) argues that the goal of Bush's re-election campaign in 2004 was to 'mobilize the Republican base' using the RNC's database Voter Vault to target Bush voters. He cites Matthew Dowd, chief strategist for Bush's re-election campaign, for explaining how they conducted a sophisticated analysis of what magazines people read, or what kind of cars they own or where they live, as well as what issues they were interested in. Thus:

If somebody thinks that the war on terror is paramount and it's very important, they're more likely to be a Republican these days than a Democrat. If somebody is against the war in Iraq, they're more likely to be a Democrat these days than they are a Republican.

(Frontline interview with Matthew Dowd.
http://www.pbs.org/wgbh/pages/frontline/shows/architect/
interviews/dowd.html)

Case study 3.2 by Zsuzsanna Mihályffy explores how Fidesz used segmentation to target specific voters to reinforce and mobilise their traditional supporters. Burton and Miracle (2014) also argue that the development of technology is such that individual candidates can now use segmentation, taking power back from central party organisations.

Segmentation relies on data about voters which is gathered using software such as Voter Vault, Mosaic, Demzilla and the Constituent Information Management System (CIMS), some of which are tailor-made for specific parties – the US Republicans used Voter Vault, US Democrats used Demzilla and Canadian Conservatives used CIMS. DNC staffer Parag Mehta explained how in the 2008 US presidential election, the Democrats used their national voter file 'to figure out what messages most resonated with them, so that when we sent them mail, when we made phone calls, and when we knocked on their doors, we were able to tailor the message to them' (Lees-Marshment 2011, 22). The data can also be used to ensure volunteers contact those most receptive to the party message. The voter file was built between 2004 and 2008 and the party invested about 10 million dollars in building it to ensure they had up-to-date information about voters from every single state in the country and to protect it from being lost so if a voter moved across states information would travel with them. Dufresne and Marland (2012, 26) note how in 2006 the Canadian Conservatives used cluster analysis to segment the electorate into voter types to enable precise targeting using CIMS.

Despite the growth of the industry around segmentation, voter profiling and micro-targeting, the methods are limited by assumptions made on data that may be inaccurate given the data fed into the system is often collected by canvassing by party supporters or members on the ground, and thus elites risk spending a lot of money communicating inappropriate messages to people. As US Republican consultant Terry Nelson explained:

> It's not like I have called you up on the phone and you have said 'I believe in X, Y and Z'. All we know about you is that you fall into a segment in a voter file that says there is a high likelihood that you want low taxes . . . you can't say with great specificity that they support a reduction in capital gains taxes or the earned income tax credit . . . if you take the issue of abortion you might have a segment that is 75 per cent or 85 per cent pro-life, but you don't necessarily know how pro-life . . . [so] a very hardcore message . . . [is] likely to alienate some people in that segment.
>
> (Lees-Marshment 2011, 24).

Furthermore, micro-targeting can't solve every problem. As US consultant Gene Ulm noted: 'we couldn't micro target our way out of this last election . . . you can't micro target our way out of a third of Americans strongly supporting the President. That's a brand issue' (Lees-Marshment 2011, 24).

Big data: analytical and experimental marketing

There is now a lot more data on individual behaviour available because we interact online, and new information this provides together with extensive databases built by political

Practitioner perspective 3.4 on big data in politics

A lot of the research we do, which is based on quite complex statistical theories, is sensitivity modelling ... you can almost create a kind of black box situation where you can try different options within your model ... it's only in the last decade or so that the statistical techniques have got to a stage where you can put together these models and ... [test] if you change your position on something, or if the public changes their position on an issue, how that's likely to affect voting outcomes.

John Utting, Australian pollster for UMR, interviewed in 2008

Not only are we able to choose to contact a voter because he or she is a Democrat or a Republican, or old or young, or a good voter or not, but we can also choose from a number of models. We are scoring voters on their likelihood to take an action in support of a progressive issue, or to donate. A voter is similarly scored on his or her media consumption habits and whether it is better to contact that voter by mail, phone or online.

Bob Blaemire, Founder and President, Blaemire Communications, 2013

Sources: Lees-Marshment (2011); Blaemire (2013)

parties has enabled practitioners to engage statistical modelling to predict how voters will behave in response to a range of potential actions and messages from political organisations and politicians. Data is no longer being used just for one campaign; US parties are combining data from one election to the next now to build up a long-term resource. This makes the data much more nuanced – see Practitioner perspective 3.4 – and enables analysis to explore the consequences of several courses of action the leader may take in advance of the decision.

In the 2012 Obama re-election campaign, staff analysed data to predict what communication would be most effective. Organisations like The Analyst Institute, founded in 2006 by liberal groups in the US, and the Canadian Firm Environics Analytics offer dedicated services combining data analysis and predictive modelling. They conduct randomised controlled experiments, or field experiments, to predict what will work in communication, and identify new groups of voters not discernable from other methods. It is somewhat similar to test marketing, but more sophisticated, drawing on the rapidly expanding 'big data' that online communication has made available. Friesen (2011) discusses how, in Canada, Environics Analytics creates narrow, sophisticated segments based on a host of factors, from where people live to what they buy and believe. They assign one dominant group to each area, assuming that people who live nearby tend to have similar profiles; and in Surrey North the dominant group was seen to be 'fairly well-off, blue collar, South Asian families, both Canadian-born and immigrant. They're more likely to have large households and to speak a non-official language at home. Let's call them Aspirasians.' Friesen described how, in the 2008 Canadian federal election, the Conservatives got 10 per cent of this group to shift to them, as well as just under 1,000 votes from the next two largest groups: 'Canadian Tirekickers, mostly white exurban families' and 'Rust Collars, a low-income, mobile, working-class population'. This made the difference between winning and losing. An industry of companies offering this work is rapidly growing – see Figure 3.5 – whilst market research companies diversify their services to include more experimental and predictive work.

Companies engaging in analytic and experimental marketing

The Analyst Institute https://analystinstitute.org/
US firm who worked for Obama and works for the general progressive community providing voter contact strategies and tested targeting.

Catalist https://www.catalist.us/
US company which works for the Democrats and progressive organisations, proving affordable database programmes for communication and campaigning.

TargetPoint Consulting http://www.targetpointconsulting.com/
US firm which works for the Republicans and offers services including customised data dashboards, online interactive data visualisation and info graphics.

Strategic Telemetry http://www.strategictelemetry.com/
US firm which provides micro-targeting, mapping, and data analysis services for corporations, governments, campaigns and non-profit organisations.

Environics Analytics http://www.environicsanalytics.ca/
Canadian firm which has geo-demographers, modelling statisticians and marketing experts.

Figure 3.5

Sources: Dr Michael Burton at Ohio University, and Campaigns and Elections. http://www.campaignsand elections.com/resources/political-pages/political-category/?category=Targeting%2C+Voter+Modeling+%26 amp%3B+Analysis (accessed 24 September 2013 which has a list of firms working in this area)

Experimental and analytical marketing is informing strategic campaign decisions behind the scenes. Issenberg (2012, 12) cites a range of political decisions made in response to the results of this research, such as Mitt Romney's decision to hold back on allocating resources to canvass Iowa voters because he had data to tell him how every caucus member would be likely to vote even before they had formed their decision to tell canvassers. Issenberg (2012, 5) notes how the growth of analytics has resulted in 'an ongoing, still unsettled battle between the two parties for analytical supremacy.' Work is often hidden to protect new methods to improve accuracy of the predictions but skills it involves are calculus, statistics, machine learning, and data engineering.[1]

Part of this development is built on new technology; however it is important to note that it is also about careful strategic analysis and 'little data' if done well can still be useful for candidates, as is illustrated by Case Study 3.3 by Nicholas Mignacca. Issenberg (2012, 11–12) notes how low-tech forms have emerged where, for example, a staffer on a presidential campaign figured out which buses to place ads on depending on their route and whether voters they wanted to contact would get on board. He notes (2012, 274) how in the 2008 Obama campaign an analyst had identified that, of the hundreds of variables on voters in Wisconsin which the algorithms explored, mass-transit ridership was most influential – those who rode on public transport were most likely to support Obama. They told a media planner on the campaign, and they found out that the Milwaukee transit agencies would let them target advertising according to routes, stops or depots; and working with the graphics department they combined data on the city's bus routes with that showing individuals with high support scores, and then commissioned the media/advertising agency GMMB to purchase ads on those buses. Case Study 3.3 demonstrates that 'little data' can be gained by analysing social media sites connected to local-level candidates that can then be used to inform campaign strategy and target campaign messages to suit the local electorate. Using social media to harvest free data in this way means that individual politicians can adopt a market-orientated strategy even though they don't have the big budget of national-level parties and campaigns. Thus the effectiveness of experimental marketing is not just in the data or method but the strategic thinking behind it – as is often the case with political marketing.

Qualitative research: focus groups, co-creation and deliberative marketing

Qualitative research is used to *understand* rather than measure and thus uses open-ended questions and produces narrative data. It is designed to probe more deeply than quantitative research, exploring values, beliefs, attitudes and influences behind opinions measured by quantitative methods. Qualitative research can help explore whether opinion can be changed. Examples include focus groups; semi- or un-structured, in-depth interviews; projective techniques; word associations; consumer drawings and role play.

Focus groups

Focus groups are small samples of typical consumers under the direction of a group leader who elicits their reaction to a stimulus, such as a political party. Analysis is conducted not just of what is said, but of body language. Mills (2011, 27) offers a definition:

> The political focus group is a facilitated discussion, usually amongst undecided voters ... [who have] some prospect of voting for the commissioning party. Typically in a campaign, a group would explore campaign impressions and views on critical issues, and test the messaging and campaign advertising.

Mills (2011, 36) notes how they can help test how well a policy is understood, how best to argue for it, what the weak points are that need to be defended, what the best language is and how to explain the potential impact. Focus groups can also be used to understand why a party has lost support, as well as to develop new strategy to regain votes in the future. Johnson (2007, 104) argues that they add 'a human dimension that cannot be matched by traditional survey research methods ... participants are free to express themselves, to complain, and to vent their anger.' After the UK Conservatives lost the 1997 election, a Channel 4 television programme, *Portillo's Progress*, filmed one ousted MP, Michael Portillo, travelling the country to find out why. Part of this involved a focus group run by MORI that asked former Conservative supporters to answer the question: How would you describe the Conservatives if you thought of them as a car? The answers were not particularly flattering – they included 'an old banger needing a new engine and major overhaul' and 'an old Morris Minor on bricks with no wheels'!

Co-creation and deliberative market research

Qualitative political market research has expanded very recently to include more deliberative and creative approaches. Langmaid (2012, 61) explains that co-creation uses a range of techniques 'that involve the user, or voter, in creating the solution to the problem, rather than simply voicing their demands and issues.' It holds the potential to provide higher-quality information which will be more valuable to politicians. The techniques used to generate co-creation research include two chair work, spirit walks, gossip games, role play, social dreaming and art-from-within.

Langmaid (2012, 66–7) discusses how the firm Promise used co-creative techniques when invited in February 2005 by the, then, UK Prime Minister Tony Blair's advisors, including Phillip Gould, Alan Milburn and Alastair Campbell, to understand and also find solutions to the disconnection between Blair and UK voters. The creative techniques they used not only explored the underlying feelings of voters towards Blair to help understand the problem on a much deeper level than polls would ever identify – because they took the approach of asking the public how to make things better – they also identified a potential solution to Blair's unpopularity. They asked participants to write letters to Blair: see Figure 3.6 (see Promise 2005 and Scammell 2008 for further detail).

They also used 'two-chair work', where one of the people in a chair was a voter, and the other one played Mr Blair. In the first role-play, the participants played Blair as voters currently saw him:

> I'm afraid you've only got part of the picture. From where I sit the war in Iraq was crucial to the cause of world peace. But I understand that it's difficult to see the whole thing for you. You put me in charge and I just do what I think to be the right thing. I am sure that history will prove us right in the end.

Fictional letters to Blair in expressive market intelligence by Promise

Key phrases from letter	Underlying emotion direction tone/ experience	Desires/wishes/
Theme 1: You left me!		
• E.g. you should have come home (tsunami) • You should put our people first • All the promises you made that never came to fruition	• Abandoned and unimportant	• Get back in touch • Get more involved with us/be more hands on
Theme 2: Too big for your boots/ celebrity		
• Globe-trotting holiday-makers • Celebrity hero worship (Bush) • Thought you were a people person, not a movie star	• His self importance and global lifestyle leaves me feeling inferior, undervalued	• Reorder priorities • Get back to basics
Theme 3: Reflect and change		
• You have lost sight of reality, how the person in the street lives	• Not held in mind • Uncontained • Out of control	• Think, reflect – are you still the bloke we elected?

Figure 3.6

Source: Adapted from Promise (2005)

Langmaid (2012, 66–7) explains this made it clear that the problem was that Blair was not listening any more, no longer a people person, and didn't seem to care about domestic issues; and tried to explain his position in a dismissive way.

In the second, however, participants played Blair as they'd like him to be, where 'he' acknowledged their discontent and was more humble:

> I understand your feelings and I realise that there are many who do not agree with me over Iraq . . . I still believe on balance that we did the right thing . . . [but] I solemnly promise to spend more time at home in contact with our own people and to debate these issues more seriously.

By getting volunteers to play Blair in a more ideal way as they would like to see him – that he noted public concerns and would seek to listen and explain more in future – he could be seen as a politician who would make voters feel like they were heard, not just ignored, even if the actual policy and decision did not change. Building on this research, the party enacted the reconnection or 'masochism strategy' by the Labour Party to rebrand Blair, as will be discussed in Chapter 4 on political branding, where Blair acknowledged what he had done wrong and how he wanted to be different in the future.

This more creative form of market research thus seeks to work with the public to identify solutions to problems – not negating the room for leadership decisions – but operating on a more co-operative level. Voters have responsibility to identify solutions not just complain. Langmaid (2012, 68) suggests that co-creation works best with those less informed and with less expertise – perhaps as they are more open to new ways of working in future.

König and König (2012, 48) describe another form of research, deliberative dialogue. They note how President Obama sought to make government more transparent and involve the public more through his 'Open Government' initiative in 2009; and that in Europe deliberative political marketing is getting on the governance agenda. They explore the use of citizens juries in Germany and from this argue that governments need to become more deliberative. After openly listening to voters, leaders need to explain their decision in relation to it – especially if they decide to go against what the public consultation recommended, so that stakeholders can understand why the leader has taken a different position. If they do this, they help generate more trust. König and König (2012, 50) note that deliberative forms of political marketing could prove more effective in the long term than market-oriented ones: 'even if a politician wanted to meet the wishes of the voters, it is always possible that he or she will fail. Therefore, a market-orientation cannot ensure a long-term relationship, because the voters are addressed as customers and not as citizens. Customers expect a good product, and will switch producers if the product is deficient. Empowered citizens, however, can understand why and how political decisions were made, and so failures do not destroy a long-term relationship.'

Opposition, candidate and policy research

Opposition research is conducted to identify potential weaknesses, controversies and also comparable strengths of the party/candidate and the opposition, and like other forms of market research there are companies specialising in this work. Whilst candidate research is more well known for digging up personal scandals, analysis of public documents can be as valuable to identify potential problems. Such research draws on a range of sources including elected officials' voting records, campaign contribution records, court files, personal and business records, including property records and property tax payment histories;

Practitioner perspective 3.5 on candidate research

I'm a believer in doing very solid research on yourself and your opponent, in order to know what your strengths and weaknesses are . . .[however] in one race I . . . found a complaint [that] one of the kids of the [opposing] candidate had filed one time, and there was a divorce in the family and stuff. The candidate . . . looked at that and said . . . I don't want anybody in the campaign ever talking about this.

Peter Fenn, US Democratic consultant, interviewed in 2007

[We] do opposition research on our own candidates, so now there's no surprise . . . if we know something ahead of time, we can make plans to blunt it, counteract it, do whatever we need to do to explain it . . . Americans actually care much less about their personal lives than most. What they do do though is, you know, if you're a businessman, have you run your business well? Have you ever been sued? Did you stick by your vendors?. . . there are firms that are year-round enterprises that work and do just this.

Gene Ulm, US Republican consultant, interviewed in 2007

Source: Lees-Marshment (2011, 24–6)

behavioural records such as club membership and military service; comments from previous associates, whether work colleagues, family, friends or former partners; and more recently, audiovisual footage.

Candidates can expect their entire professional career to be scrutinised, even if it wasn't in politics, and whether or not they were responsible for everything that happened. Even their education or training will be considered. Personal family issues, such as choice of school for their children (rather than the more obvious skeletons such as affairs) can be included in the campaign (Johnson 2007, 70–1), particularly if private behaviour contradicts public political positions. As the candidate is such a key part of the product, such details become important in a way that would not happen in the commercial world, where the life of the chief executive is rarely examined. Remarks made by the people politicians associate with, as opposed to just what they themselves say, can become a factor in a campaign. In May 2008, Obama resigned from the Trinity United Church of Christ in Chicago, which he had been a member of for 20 years, when controversial comments made by the pastor, the Reverend Jeremiah Wright, were widely circulated by the media and threatened to damage his brand.

As Practitioner perspective 3.5 indicates, self-reflective candidate research helps prepare candidates for attacks and helps them prepare rebuttal, so their campaign is less likely to be sent off course. In the 2004 US presidential election, John Kerry, the Democrat candidate, made his military service in Vietnam a key part of his campaign, assuming it to be a win–win characteristic. When he was attacked by a Swift Boat Veterans ad, there was no response from Kerry's team, and the media were able to continue criticism. Henneberg and O'Shaughnessy (2007, 261) note this shows 'the need for candidates to fully think out strategically their areas of vulnerability well before the beginning of the campaign'. Kerry could have anticipated the attack, as there was an 'inherent contradiction in his Vietnam-era role and his post-service militant peace activism'. Changes in policy position need to be explained: as Johnson (2007, 66) observes, while a change in position can indicate 'growth and maturity', in politics it is criticised as weakness or populism. If changes can be justified and explained, this can be defended, but the candidate risks being accused of flip-flopping, lacking certainty and conviction, or only changing their position for electoral expediency.

Any critical claim made about an opponent needs to be checked carefully before it is released, as if it lacks credibility or is proven false this can actually damage the campaign. False accusations can backfire. As Lees-Marshment (2009, 466) notes, a few weeks before the 2008 New Zealand election, Labour Party president Mike Williams traveled to Melbourne to conduct opposition research to uncover evidence linking National leader, John Key, to problematic financial management. Nothing came to light, however, and his trip became a negative media story about Labour's campaign methods rather than Key's behaviour.

Candidate research can be used positively as well as negatively: as Johnson (2007, 57–8) observes, 'it builds the case that the incumbent has established a solid record of achievement . . . and it devises strategies to protect that record'. If they are already in office, candidates' accomplishments include legislation assisted or blocked, grants obtained, votes cast, favourable ratings, supporting or criticising the government, and constituency work. Research also investigates what would attract support from different groups of people or constituents as not all behaviour is interesting to all voters (see Varoga and Rice 1999, 255).

Global knowledge transfer

> ### Practitioner perspective 3.6 on the importance of global knowledge transfer
>
> *We often say that . . . what happens in an American election will happen 18 months from now in a UK election . . . The US is a long way ahead of us in . . . how they are able to target voters and engage with voters via the internet . . . something . . . all three parties in the UK will . . . learn lessons from.*
>
> Oliver Dowden, David Cameron's deputy chief of
staff who oversees domestic policy, 2012
>
> *It's a bizarre thing to do, to fly in and go out around and villages and other places, cities around the world and then have a conversation with a political leader about their citizens.*
>
> Mark Textor, Political strategist in Australia, NZ
and the UK, 2012
>
> Sources: World Denver Talks (2012); Sunday Profile (2012)

Another source of political marketing strategies and communication ideas is global knowledge transfer: the sharing of ideas from one country to the next. Often this is associated with Americanisation or globalisation – the suggestion being that the US is the world leader in campaigning it will transplant their ideas to other countries, including less developed political markets such as new democracies. As Practitioner perspective 3.6 indicates, getting ideas from elsewhere is highly valued by political advisors, and a whole array of companies and consultants can be found travelling to Croatia or Czech Republic or China, to extol the latest techniques in electioneering. Karanfilovska (2009) notes how, after the Republic of Macedonia became independent in 1991, international organisations such as the Institute for Democracy, Solidarity and Civil Society, International Republican Institute and National Democratic Institute for International Affairs were quick to offer training. Macedonian parties received training on public relations, media, party programme building, organisational management, political analysis, political communication and pre-election campaigning.

Part of the drive behind this is the rise of campaign consultants; and as Johnson's (2007) study shows, they offer advice on a whole range of marketing activities. Political consultants work across countries which naturally encourages global transfer: UK consultant Phillip Gould and US consultant James Carville both worked on the US Bill Clinton and UK Tony Blair campaigns; Australian consultants Lynton Crosby and Mark Textor worked on the Australian John Howard, New Zealand Don Brash and UK Michael Howard campaigns. Turcotte (2012, 86) details how Canadian Conservative Prime Minister Stephen Harper's strategist Patrick Muttart, created strong ties with staff working for Howard; he visited Australia and Australian practitioners visited Ottawa as well as Harper meeting Howard himself; and Muttart has also worked on the 2010 Australian Liberal campaign. Lees-Marshment and Lilleker (2012) also identified additional practitioners who worked across countries such as Rick Ridder who advised the Clinton/Gore 1992 campaign and the Howard Dean 2000 campaign but also the UK Liberal Democrats and Australian NSW Labor Party; Mark Gill who worked in the UK for MORI and then for politicians in Trinidad at Woodnewton Associates; Alex Braun who was employed by PSB Associates in the USA but also worked on campaigns in the Czech Republic, Thailand, the Philippines and Indonesia as well as UK Labour; and Peter Fenn who worked for several Democratic presidential candidates also worked for the US National Democratic Institute in various countries including South Africa, Mozambique, Eastern Europe, Russia, Central America and South America.

Examples of shared political marketing ideas include the1999 NZ Labour Party copying the 1997 UK Labour Party's pledges cards to demonstrate delivery capability; the 2006 Canadian Conservatives copying NZ National's 2005 split blue/red billboards with 'tax' under the opposition leader and 'cut' under the conservative leader; and use of negativity, newspaper headlines, the colour red and a repetitive sound such as a buzzer or till sound in ads produced by the consultants Crosby-Textor for the Australian Liberal John Howard campaigns, NZ National Don Brash 2005 and UK Conservative Michael Howard 2005 elections. Most recently countries have copied Obama's use of social media in the 2008 US presidential election to attract donations, volunteers and votes.

The Clinton/US and Blair/UK New Labour strategy has been copied by leaders in Germany, New Zealand, Japan, Denmark and Australia. Pettitt (2009) notes how the leader of the Danish party Venstre which won power in 2001, 2005 and 2007, Anders Fogh Rasmussen, adapted political marketing lessons from UK New Labour, modernizing the party and downplaying ideology and class. Similarly Turner (2009) demonstrates how the New Labour centre-left approach to health and education, alongside conservatism on issues such as crime, welfare and tax was copied by Helen Clark in New Zealand in 1999 and more recently Kevin Rudd in Australia in 2007 when he reassured voters of his economic conservatism by stating he was not a socialist and promising tax cuts almost as large as the opposition. The 'Compassionate Conservative' product originated by the George W. Bush campaign of 2000 which sought to include a set of policies that made the party and its candidates seem more caring and inclusive such as ensuring no child was 'left behind' in education was copied by David Cameron's leadership of the UK Conservative Party when he spoke of the need to strengthen public services, ensure social justice and maintain a clean environment; and then by John Key, leader of the New Zealand National Party, who also expressed concern for a growing 'underclass' to win the 2008 election. Turcotte (2012, 86) notes that Muttart borrowed the idea of micro-targeting to identify new groups of swing voters to win power in the 2006 election from the Australian Liberal Prime Minister

John Howard, who focused on 'the battlers' – families struggling to raise their kids on a low income – to achieve victory in 1996 and four subsequent elections.

There are pragmatic questions as to whether marketing strategies developed in one country can be transplanted whole to another. Comparative political science research would argue that systemic differences would prevent the same ideas working everywhere – such as voting behaviour, party identification, political participation, political culture, the electoral system and the media, which all vary from one country to another (see Plasser *et al.* 1999, 91; Strömbäck 2007; and Lilleker and Lees-Marshment 2005). However, the most recent comparative study *Global Political Marketing* which explored the POP, SOP or MOP strategies adopted by parties in relation to systemic differences concluded that fixed systemic differences were less influential than contextual ones such as the nature of the leader, whether a party had been out of power a long time, and the internal support for an MOP strategy (see Lees-Marshment *et al.* 2010). For example, Hutcheson (2010, 221–2) argues that in Russia 'political marketing – or, to use the Russian term, 'electoral technology' (*izbiratel'naya tekhnologiya*) – is not a straightforward transfer of American or even West European expertise. There is a multi-billion dollar political consulting market with its own techniques and values.'

Furthermore, Lees-Marshment and Lilleker's (2012) research, which analysed interviews with practitioners involved in global knowledge sharing, concluded that whilst political marketing is going global and being utilised across countries, to be effective it had to be adapted to the local context, not least because of system differences: see Practitioner perspective 3.7. Political marketing ideas flow back and forth – not just from the US to other countries. Lees-Marshment (2010, 69) notes how 'Kiwi international links can work the other way: National gave John Ansell's billboards to the Australian Liberal Party who then gave them to the Canadian Liberal Party who used them in 2006. Each election is unique and thus one campaign plan cannot be transplanted to the next, even within the same country; there are also regional differences within countries that have to be taken account of. Thus Lees-Marshment and Lilleker argue that the more effective international

Practitioner perspective 3.7 on adapting ideas from global knowledge transfer

There's a rule no matter where you are that you can't make Adolf Hitler into Ghandi. You have to adapt. You can't go into a parliamentary system with a message that a candidate is independent. What you can bring is expertise in analysing a situation – what you can't bring is the cultural values from own country. So you bridge the gap by relying on local expertise so you don't impose US values; relying on local linguists – so you don't create problems in polling; and understanding the political history enough.

Rick Ridder, international political consultant, interviewed in 2007

Of course, you can take techniques and you can take polling from polling techniques in America . . . But ultimately though strategy is situational. I don't believe in absolute campaigning truths that travel . . . what worked in one country may not work in the next . . . the point of winning an election is to win the election on the basis of political projects, a set of ideas and a set of values. And they have to be distinctive to that country in so many ways.

The Late Lord Philip Gould, advisor to UK PM Tony Blair, interviewed in 2007

Source: Lees-Marshment (2011)

consultants select lessons from a range of countries to suit the particular campaign they are advising on, or look for particular tools to suit similar features within their own market. This is explored in Case Study 3.4 by Ieva Berzina, which critiques the use of global knowledge transfer in Latvia.

Informal low-cost political market research

Not all candidates and campaigns have the funds to carry out all commissioned PMR. However they can use 'free' data sources such as past election results to see how voters in geographic areas have cast votes in different election.[2] For example, in the US where there are a lot of elections for different offices, the geographic boundaries for each level of election (local, county, state, congressional and presidential/statewide) provide different pieces of information. Indirect market research on public views can be conducted by analyzing local newspapers discussion of local policy issues which would indicate what the problems are that people want addressed by government. Turcotte (2012, 77) notes that politicians and parties gather informal intelligence in various ways such as polling members via mailed party correspondence, straw polls during meetings and conventions, door-to-door canvassing and analysing letters and online feedback from constituents. Another source is analysis of past elections: a Canadian practitioner recalled how they interviewed people all across the country in the conservative party, and practitioners in the UK and the US and 'tried to get a sense of best-practices – what were the common things among failing enterprises, and what did winning campaigns have in common' (Lees-Marshment 2011, 17). Gut instinct and just observing what is happening in the local community or what people are complaining about is also a useful source of public input; as is 'little data' as discussed in Case Study 3.3.

Which method?

Best practice advice is that a range of sources and methods should be used rather than just one to reduce potential weaknesses and increase the overall value of the data collected (Lees-Marshment 2011, 20). Braun (2012, 15) argues that 'each form's usefulness depends on the current needs of a campaign and how much time is left before election day. Selecting a particular type of research should never be a mechanical process, and should always be done based on what best advances the campaign goals at that moment.' Qualitative research may be more useful to begin with or to generate new ideas or potential solutions, whereas quantitative research helps to measure opinion. Any form of research only provides a snapshot of public opinion at that time, which is why research is conducted continuously, and in different ways. The most important thing is to do it, do lots of it, and be open to new ideas that emerge from it: see Practitioner perspective 3.8.

How political market research is used

Market research is used to inform a range of activities in politics. Interviews with practitioners suggest that 'market analysis in politics is a multi-varied activity . . . the value, purposes, uses, methods and attitudes to market analysis are broad-ranging' (Lees-Marshment 2011, 41). In terms of product and brand development, PMR can identify weaknesses in a party brand as well as opportunities for development. For example, Sparrow and Turner (2001, 999–1001) discusses how they conducted both qualitative and quantitative research when working for the UK Conservative Party between 1997 and 2001.

Practitioner perspective 3.8 on what to do or not to do when doing market intelligence

Political parties that have been in power for a while will have a hard time growing their political market. As a result, segmenting and understanding the needs of those who voted for you in the past is even more important for governments in power for more than six years.

David Coletto, Abacus Data

It is better to get the wrong answer to the right question, than the right answer to the wrong question. Asking potential voters (whether in polls or focus groups) the right questions that will get them to say what actually affects their voting behaviour is critical.

David Farrar, Director, Curia Market Research

Ask people what's on their minds as you begin the inquiry. Don't launch straight into your agenda ... Almost anything, no matter how 'bad', illogical or crazy seems less so when brought into the light. Always acknowledge people's contributions whether you agree with them or think them worthy or not. Ensure that every new project contains at least one inquiry that you have not run before – whether that be a process, interaction or type of question. Surprise yourself by trying out new things. It will keep your inquiries – and your enthusiasm – alive.

Roy Langmaid, Consultant from Promise, UK, advisor
to UK Labour 2004–2005

Source: top tips supplied by email in 2013

Market research can become an integral part of the party and campaign apparatus and thus closely connected to the strategy. Turcotte (2012, 83–4) notes how market intelligence became more closely integrated into the strategic thinking by the Canadian Conservatives under the leadership of Stephen Harper after losing the 2004 election. Harper's staff thought that there needed to be a 'market intelligence structure' and thus research was integrated with strategy to keep everyone focused on meeting set goals. Patrick Muttart, a former director for a hotel chain, used research to measure public mood, test policies, and find ways to communicate the Conservative product to appeal to a sufficiently large number of voters to form government. It also uncovered new insights: when interviewed Muttart recalled how research found that right-of-centre voters respond to 'three key fanatic drivers' which were aspiration for 'something better for their families and their children' from their hard work, family, including those who get legally married and 'a sense of localism' or cohesion. They then devised their strategy to tap into those broader themes emotionally as well as cognitively (Lees-Marshment 2011, 15).

In the 2007 presidential election, the candidate Nicholas Sarkozy used a range of tools for different purposes during the campaign from January to April, such as online panels to identify why voters might leave/join a particular candidate and then test their reactions to the candidate's main TV or radio appearances during the campaign. Teinturier (2008, 150–1) explains that such intelligence was used to support the foundations of strategy using public opinion results, to select candidates, to help improve the language and create the effect of reality in political communication and to identify strong public support, which would then reduce criticisms from commentators.

Braun (2012) notes that in campaigns, research is used to inform a wide range of decisions which are both strategic, policy and communication focused. One example is making sure candidates talk about issues that voters care about most; another is which voters to target (Braun 2012, 11–12). Rottinghaus and Alberro (2005) explored how polls were used for Vicente Fox's campaign in the 2000 Mexican election to inform the selling of the candidate at key chronological points, such as to establish which candidate traits were the most desirable, identify that using a message of change that Fox could attract support and determine what was most important to voters, which was honesty, followed by reliability and good proposals. Fox connected all three in his speeches, talking of honest new faces to form a new government, declaring he was strong enough to do the job. Lees-Marshment (2011, 40) also notes how research can be used to prevent miscommunication. When interviewed, Bob Carr – a former Australian Premier – noted how they expected a negative attack campaign about land tax in that election from the opposition so they tested an advertisement that really explained how land tax used to work and how their proposals would work and testing assured them the ad was effective. However another time research prevented mistakes – when he wanted to criticise the opposition leader for having very limited experience qualitative research showed that the remotest attack on her would be interpreted by softly-committed female voters as an attack on all of them.

Polling is not confined to establishing democracies – it is also used in developing democracies (see the Abad and Ramirez's 2008 study of the Philippines, for example). Nor is it confined to campaigns – polls are also used in government. Rothmayr and Hardmeier (2002, 130–1) analysed how the Swiss Federal government used polls to inform government communication, and Birch and Petry (2012) note how government agencies commission substantial research on policy and behaviour to improve policymaking which is regulated at the federal level in the US and Canada to ensure methodological quality and objectivity. Lees-Marshment (forthcoming) interviewed over 40 practitioners involved in collecting or using political market research in the UK, US, Canada, New Zealand and Australia and noted how the UK Prime Minister's Office under Gordon Brown conducted qualitative and quantitative research on policy 'trying to test and ascertain the shifting landscape of electoral opinion and what that mean[t] in terms of [their] overall policy program'.

Limitations to the influence of political market research

Historically there have been many barriers to politicians and parties commissioning, let alone responding to, market intelligence. Wring (2005) explains how the UK Labour Party's traditional culture, mission and ethos involved education and persuasion, which made it difficult for professionals and party figures to gain acceptance for the use of marketing in presentation, let alone product design. Not every politician or party wants to just win an election – they also want to change the world. Individual politicians often think they know best and that their gut instinct is the right one – and their agenda and goals can be to advance a particular cause, not subject their behaviour to the dictates of the market, let alone the median or target voter. Kavanagh (1996, 105–10) argues that there are a number of factors that enhance or constrain the attention politicians pay to market intelligence results, such as that in power ministers are more interested in justifying existing programmes than considering where new proposals would attract market support; individual politicians and different party groups prefer one policy to another and look for results that support a particular position.

Even though the use of PMR is now more widespread, interviews with practitioners suggest that PMR is only one of many different inputs into politician's decision-making (Lees-Marshment 2011 and forthcoming). An advisor to President Bill Clinton recalled that 'he was interested in as wide a network of people informing him as he could. He wanted as many facts and opinions from informed people as he could get . . . Clinton read voraciously and would mark up articles every single day and send them around and circulate them and ask questions and stress things and want to know more about things'. Consequently Lees-Marshment suggests a model for PMR whereby the first stage is that the politician sets the goals before PMR is commissioned from several sources; consultants then offer multifaceted advice about potential actions in response; and politicians consider this along with other inputs before making their decision. The role that market research plays in politics therefore needs to be seen in context of politics and government.

Practical issues with market intelligence in politics

There are also methodological problems of accuracy with market research, and each method has pros and cons. Polls can be wrong, such as in the UK 1992 election and US 2000 presidential election. In the latter, media networks called the election result using exit polls in only a small number of precincts, saying Gore was ahead by 6.5 per cent, but they then had to backtrack as more results came in to suggest a Bush win. There is a margin of error in every poll or survey and biases against the young and 'not at homes' (see Rademacher and Tuchfarber 1999, 205–15 for further detail). In developing democracies, security risks and political culture can make it difficult to collect effective and accurate intelligence. Abad and Ramirez (2008, 273–4) note that in the Philippines, where rebels operate, interviewers have been robbed, and the lack of reliable public transport makes it hard to get to the place to conduct polling. Nevertheless, appropriate quality-control measures can help ensure polling is a reliable tool even developing democracy like the Philippines (Abad and Ramirez 2008, 280).

Despite the surge in attention on analytics the methodology it has limitations like every other new marketing tool. It is only as good as the data the party collects to feed into the system. Canvassing by party supporters or members on the ground to ascertain their opinions and political behaviour is one of the sources for political data, and this can be problematic. Furthermore, assumptions about their political opinions, judgements and response to party/candidate communication and behaviour are only that: an assumption. Candidates and parties may be spending a lot of money communicating inappropriate messages to people. Moreover, it is just a tool and its effectiveness in terms of winning elections is always going to be constrained by the attractiveness of the product being sold. Research to date has discussed how analytics may help identify who is more receptive to your policies in communication, but like polling and focus groups it could also be used to identify what such segments want from you in terms of your actual political product or brand. Or to identify a synergy between voters' wants and party/politicians' goals and vision. Otherwise, if there is a strong competitor, no amount of analytic marketing is going to sell a poor product.

Researcher bias can creep into data collection. Focus groups have been hotly debated in academic literature because of fears about moderator bias, the small sample size, and over-influence on product decisions. Sparrow and Turner (2001, 993) note how focus groups can suffer from the interviewer effect where 'the social characteristics of the moderator may have a disproportionate influence on respondents and the information they are prepared to divulge'. Savigny (2007, 130) argues that, in the case of UK Labour in the 1990s, 'Gould also used focus groups as a site to test his own ideas [r]ather than listening and collecting the opinions of the selected public . . . Gould's interventionist approach, to argue and challenge participants.' The way focus groups are run can inhibit rather than facilitate the expression of what the market wants. Additionally, they require skilled interpretation. Wring (2007, 87) argues that the problems with focus groups used by Labour between 1992 and 1997 also included that they were used to push a political agenda, leaked to the media selectively to generate support, and reported without full complexity and acknowledgement of the limitations of the focus group method.

Solutions to such problems are to commission a range of consultants to conduct market research, use several methods, and interpret it carefully. Political market research is a very important part of modern politics, but it does not dictate how politicians behave and the decisions they make.

Summary

This chapter has explored how a number of changes in the political market have altered the way that voters respond to and judge political parties and candidates, so that voters are more demanding and questioning, and their behaviour is less predictable. Additionally,

---

Best practice guide to political market research

1   Understand that voters are critical, negative, and consumerist towards political elites; and use a variety of sources of information to form their views and are questioning of them all.
2   Accept that how they vote is less predictable; if they vote is uncertain; if they volunteer it has to be on their terms, not the candidate's/party's.
3   Look for new, emerging electoral segments which political elites can respond to and gain an advantage from.
4   Understand that voters want a tangible and deliverable product and politicians need to use delivery marketing to demonstrate actual progress not just rhetoric.
5   Don't just rely on gut instinct.
6   Conduct market analysis continuously.
7   Create, respond to, and communicate with micro-targets: tiny segments that will most likely influence the election outcome, including core voters.
8   Use different methods from different sources for different purposes at different stages.
9   Use more constructive and creative research to identify solutions to problems rather than just a list of demands.
10   Analyse data to identify future needs, alternative options and test potential reactions. This can be 'big data' gathered by well-resourced organisations/candidates or 'little data' by local candidates analysing free information on their own social media sites.
11   Research all stakeholders, not just voters.
12   Adapt ideas from global knowledge transfer to suit your country and case.
13   Develop skills to interpret PMR – it's not a golden bullet just by itself.
14   Don't rely on market analysis for product ideas.
15   Use market analysis proactively to inform, not dictate, decisions and create room for proactive, visionary leadership.
16   Use PMR to inform a range of positions in response to public opinion and types of communication.
17   Understand that research does not tell you everything.

Figure 3.7

citizens appear to behave in a more consumerist manner. Such changes have encouraged parties and candidates to consider using marketing to help them achieve their goals. Market intelligence provides politicians and their staff with information that they can then use to make decisions about all other aspects of marketing, including product development and communication. Options such as segmentation, targeting and opposition research provide different ways of looking at the market. Figure 3.7 provides a best practice guide to understanding political consumers and carrying out PMR.

However PMR tools also have limitations and are not quick fixes to secure success. There remains debate about the value of market intelligence, but it is unlikely any modern candidate or party would not gather any, given the choice. Without using such methods to understand an increasingly diverse public, politicians would be relying on gut instinct and guess work, which would be more prone to bias and inaccuracy and unable to provide the detailed breakdown of the electorate now offered by computerised segmentation models. Market researchers play an important role in political marketing, and the practitioner profiles of Richard Wirthlin and Karl Rove explain their work and influence in US politics.

Market intelligence isn't a perfect conversation between government and the public, but it does go some way to bringing the two closer together. While there are democratic issues with the use of market intelligence, most of these develop because of the way elites choose to use it. Parties and politicians need to listen, interpret and respond carefully before using it to develop their product and brand.

Practitioner profile 3.1

Name: Richard B. Wirthlin
Date of birth: 15 March, 1931 (to 16 March, 2011)
Most notable job: Advisor and Pollster for US President Ronald Reagan

Description: Richard Wirthlin was a political consultant and pollster best known for his work with former US President Ronald Reagan. After being recommended to Reagan by Arizona Senator Barry Goldwater in 1968, Wirthlin helped shape Reagan's political message and strategies for the next 20 years – both in presidential campaigns and in the White House. In 1980, as chief campaign strategist, Wirthlin used polling to help Reagan build a winning coalition. One important Wirthlin strategy was the use television advertisements to highlight Reagan's qualifications before turning to attack President Carter directly. After Reagan gained office, Wirthlin went on to supervise 'The First 90 Days Project', a blueprint of policy goals and the political strategies to achieve them – the start of White House operations that would come to be known as 'the permanent campaign'. Wirthlin proved essential in taking Reagan's decisions and seeing how they might play with the public. For example, he frequently used polling and testing to analyse President Reagan's speeches – with focus group participants using dial meters to indicate what phrases and emphases they liked or disliked. Wirthlin advised Reagan for his entire eight years in office. Furthermore, Wirthlin's company, Decision Making Information (later known as The Wirthlin Group and Wirthlin Worldwide), also did polling for British Prime Minister Margaret Thatcher, among other political clients. Wirthlin's reputation among political strategists and pollsters is immense. He is seen as a pioneer in tracking research, advanced analytical techniques in polling, and the use of public values in shaping political communication. See his book *The Greatest Communicator: What Ronald Reagan Taught Me About Politics, Leadership, and Life* (written with Wynton C. Hall) published by John Wiley & Sons in 2004.

Practitioner profile 3.2

Name: Karl Christian Rove
Date of birth: 25 December, 1950
Most notable job: Senior Advisor to President George W. Bush

Description: Karl Rove is well known as a key member of George W. Bush's Presidential staff during his eight years in office. However, from a political marketing standpoint, his work in the field of 'get out the vote' (GOTV) campaigns is of more interest. After Bush won the 2000 presidential election, one of Rove's first tasks was to organise and mobilise certain key demographics who may not have voted in 2000 but may vote Republican in the 2002 midterm elections. In essence, the '72-hour project', as it came to be known, was a programme that looked to energize the conservative base and mobilise the evangelicals, Hispanics, Catholics, and other potential affinity groups to build a Republican majority. The project was used to identify and turn out the Republican base on the final three days before the 2002 midterm elections. One of the most successful components of Karl Rove's programme was its small-government ideological approach. Similar to Matthew Barzun's peer-to-peer fundraising years later, the programme worked by enthusing the grass-roots base to get involved and make a difference – helping reinforce the connection between the executive and the grass roots of the party. Each volunteer was tasked with personally getting a handful of voters from their area to the polls; voters that they were already familiar with from their church, their children's schools and their community. The programme helped the Republican Party make a net gain of two Senate seats and eight House seats, an unusual occurrence in midterm elections.

Discussion points

1   Discuss how you decide what to think about politics. What sources of information are most relied on? What does this reveal about how voters form political opinions and therefore what politics should consider when using marketing?
2   Drawing on personal experience, discuss whether and why you have been a volunteer, and whether you have been satisfied with your experience.
3   How do you decide to vote? List the different factors that influenced you, and discuss which are more important.
4   To what extent are practitioners and academics right about voters becoming more demanding and wanting to be empowered and drive the political system?
5   Create a plan for how you would conduct PMR for an election campaign, organiation or issue including when, what type, on what issues/aspects.
6   If an election were held tomorrow in your electorate/country, consider what segments might be most important and why.
7   What do you think of the new trend towards analytical and experimental marketing? Would you advise parties to follow Obama in using this to allocate resources in the next election campaign?
8   Why do politicians use focus groups and what is their main advantage over other forms of market research?
9   What are the advantages of deliberative and co-creation forms of market research? What might be the limitations?
10   To what extent is the global transfer of political marketing consultations effective?
11   List the different ways in which political market research is used in politics and discuss which you think is most valuable to a politician.

Assessment questions

Essays/exams

1 To what extent has the political market changed in recent decades, and how?
2 Explore the potential effects that the rise of the political consumer has on politics.
3 Outline and compare the nature and effectiveness of the different political market research tools.
4 How important and effective is segmentation in politics?
5 Critically evaluate the potential and limitations of analytic and experimental marketing as a new political market research tool, drawing on examples from the 2012 US presidential election.
6 What is the nature of qualitative political market research, and what are the benefits and limitations of its use in political marketing?
7 How does the role of a political consumer change when deliberative and co-creation forms of political market research are used, and what does this mean for the effectiveness of the research and politics as a whole?
8 To what extent and how effectively have political leaders engaged in global knowledge transfer, copying strategies, products and campaigning techniques from each other?
9 Outline and discuss the range of ways that political market research is used in politics.

Applied

1 Conduct and analyse market research data (whether a poll or other form) during a political campaign, using Turcotte's Stages of Quantitative Research during a Political Campaign – the benchmark poll, strategic poll, tracking poll, brushfire poll and post-election poll.
2 Conduct a strategic analytic marketing plan for a local candidate, using free online data from sources such as their emails, Facebook, Twitter and LinkedIn and make recommendations for what they should do over the next 12 months in light of this.
3 Produce a market research report for a current political leader/party/government with analysis of all publicly available market research and make recommendations for what they should do over the next 12 months in light of this. Try to take into account contextual factors such as their goals, position in the electoral cycle, constraints, likely crisis, potential positives, nature of the leader his or herself, how to manage markets (e.g. party, other MPs, media, the public, civil service).
4 Conduct a literature review of focus group methodology, then design and hold your own focus group on a particular candidate, party, government or political issue. Observe how people make judgments and reflect on the reliability of the method and your particular results.

CASE STUDIES

Case study 3.1 What politicians can learn from marketing: approaching the low-involvement voter

By Tiffany M. Winchester, Deakin University
tiffany.winchester@deakin.edu.au

When we start studying politics, or political marketing, we may begin to consider everyone thinks the same way that we do: politics is extremely important, a relevant factor in everyday life, and needs a great deal of thought and time devoted to it. However, Harris & Lock sum it up nicely: 'It is frequently forgotten by political commentators and academics that the majority of voters do not share their fascination with politics' (2010, 298). This is evidenced by declining political party membership in most countries and decreased turnouts to elections, providing evidence that interest in politics, in general, has seen a decrease. However, in Australia, voting is compulsory, meaning that regardless of interest or disinterest in voting, the voter must make a decision on whom to vote for come election time.

Consumer behaviour literature on low-interest, or low-involvement decision-making, outlines that most decisions we make are not high-involvement decisions. Therefore, marketers have come up with many strategies and tactics to appeal to the low-involvement consumer. One predictor of future behaviour is previous behaviour, possibly built upon habits which the consumer has formed as a result of using, or not using, a product or service. In consumer behaviour, using or not using a brand is referred to as 'usage', and those who use the brand are referred to as 'users'. The empirical generalisation on usage holds that consumers are strongly influenced by their past behaviour (Romaniuk *et al.* 2012); therefore, usage is a key element in decision-making.

These concepts can also apply to politics. Previous behaviours, driven by habit, influence future behaviours or the cues that trigger those behaviours. McCulloch *et al.* (2008) found that when a choice is repeatedly made it may inhibit the decision-making process and consideration of other choices, thereby influencing the candidate or party preference. Australia's compulsory voting requirement makes it more likely that voters turn out to vote regularly, creating the potential for habit formation. When canvassing, politicians and pollsters may ask 'Who did you vote for?' In this sense, they are identifying users of their political party. They then assume that if an individual voted for that party previously, that individual would be more inclined to vote for the candidate again. Therefore considering which political party was previously voted for may be important in determining who they might vote for in the future.

However, the application of usage is not as clear-cut in politics as it is in marketing. In marketing, usage is determined by asking which brands the consumer used right now, or which they had purchased over the period, for example, in the last four weeks. Politically an individual consumer does not make the 'choice', but rather it becomes a collective decision. As well, the voter may end up 'subscribing' to a political party to which they did not vote. In this case, political marketing acts more as a non-profit service provider or a subscription market whom the consumer subscribes to for a certain length of time. Therefore, all voters are users of the political party, whether they chose it or not, so a new definition of the user is required. It may be necessary to compare voluntary users (those who voted for the party in power) with involuntary users (those who did not vote for the party in power, or did not vote) (Winchester *et al.* 2013, 2012).

Key findings

Voting is a low-involvement decision – usage is a key element in voter decision-making – previous voting behaviour influences future voting behaviour

---

Voluntary users:

- Voted for the party in power
- Previous behaviour in 'using' the party in power made it more likely to repeat that behaviour
- Likely to vote for their chosen party again without much cognitive processing (for example, seeking information to increase knowledge, or considering how satisfied or confident they were with their previous choice)

Involuntary users:

- Did not vote for the party in power
- Likely to go through more in-depth stages of decision-making
- Able to evaluate the political party in power, and perhaps confirm their decision not to vote for the party in power during the next election

---

Lessons for political marketing

The study of consumer behaviour or voting behaviour within political marketing is an important one not only from a theoretical but also from a practical viewpoint. While usage does influence behaviour, usage does not mean that the party in power is more likely to be re-elected because of habitual voting. While voting decision-making is a low-involvement decision for many voters, especially young voters, they are still evaluating the political brand while the party is in power. To keep those habitual voters, or current users of the political party, when campaigning the party in power may wish to focus on confirming that the voter's previous decision was the right one, or that they had made the right choice in voting for that party. In this case, they are trying to reduce any cognitive dissonance which may have built up as a result of usage of the political party.

For the incumbent party, while there was an increase in decision-making factors for the involuntary users, it is still a low-involvement choice. Therefore, they may wish to look to using some elements of marketing tactics to approach this group of low-involvement voters. This may include campaigning on a clear and consistent message, including well-branded advertising to increase memory and recall through heuristics. They may wish to campaign on the positive aspects of their political party to build salience, without building more awareness and salience for the opposition through repeated use of negative advertising. They may also wish to focus on the switching behaviour that may occur because of cognitive dissonance, therefore campaigning on changing the vote to make it right.

Further reading

Harris, P. and Lock, A. (2010). '"Mind the gap": the rise of political marketing and a perspective on its future agenda'. *European Journal of Marketing*, 44(3/4): 297–307.

McCulloch, K. C. H. Aarts, K. Fujita and J. A. Bargh (2008). 'Inhibition in goal systems: a retrieval-induced forgetting account'. *Journal of Experimental Social Psychology*, 44(3): 857–65.

Romaniuk, J. S. Bogomolova and F. Dall'Olmo Riley (2012). 'Brand image and brand usage: is a forty-year-old empirical generalization still useful?'. *Journal of Advertising Research*, 52(2): 243–51.

Winchester, T.M. J. Hall and W. Binney (2012). 'Conceptualizing usage in voting behavior for political marketing: an application of consumer behavior'. In *Political Spaces in Eurasia: Global Contexts, Local Outcomes*, Ralph and Ruth Fisher Forum, Russian, East European, and Eurasian Center, University of Illinois at Urbana-Champaign, June 13–15.

Winchester, T.M. J. Hall and W. Binney (2013). 'The influence of usage, internal and external factor on youth voting decision-making: an SEM analysis'. In *NZ-OZ Political Marketing and Management Mini conference*, Auckland, New Zealand.

Case study 3.2 Target audience and segmentation in the 2010 Fidesz campaign

By Zsuzsanna Mihályffy, Institute for Political Science, HAS
mihalyffy.zsuzsanna@tk.mta.hu

This case study will explore the segmentation strategy of Fidesz before the 2010 general elections and the composition of its target audience. Segmentation is the principle of marketing which acknowledges differences between (groups of) consumers/voters and argues that businesses/political actors should take these into account – for example, by offering different products to different segments, or communicating with them through different channels. Consumers/voters can be segmented based on a number of qualities, the most common ones being socio-economic and geographical (age, sex, employment, ethnic background, location).

After losing the election in 2002 and spending two terms in opposition, Fidesz was likely to win the 2010 general elections. Moreover it had chances of not only forming a majority government on its own, but gaining a two-thirds majority in Parliament as well. Fidesz faced the 2010 election in an incomparably favourable situation: its popularity was on the rise, yielding an absolute majority at the European Parliament elections in 2009, and there were no strong opponents: the government was in crisis, and although new parties emerged, they seemed much too small to endanger Fidesz's victory. These, among other things, led pollsters to forecast, and leaders of the Fidesz to hope that the party could win a two-thirds majority of parliamentary seats in 2010.

From the position of Fidesz and the favourable political landscape, it followed that the party thought of citizens the old-fashioned way: firm preferences of voters, whether supportive of Fidesz or of other parties, were taken for granted. The idea was to turn towards those who had shown any kind of support towards the party at least once, while not targeting supporters of other parties, yet remaining open towards them. Hence the campaign of Fidesz was not aimed at persuasion. Neither was it aimed at trying to decipher and then follow voters' will. It was aimed at the *reinforcement* of supporters and *mobilisation*. The campaign was mild, almost boring in order to avoid protest votes from supporters of opponents. In other words, the party's segmentation strategy was built largely on *voters' previous behaviour*.

The party was working on establishing a close relationship with its core support for years. Going back in time, Fidesz started to build a supporters' database in 2004 and since then the party launched actions from time to time to expand this database, to keep it up to date and gain as much information as possible about those included in it. A few examples of such actions were the consultation series ('Consultation on the Economy', 'National Consultation' in 2005), the so-called 'Support vote' in favour of their candidate to the position of President of the Republic, various petitions, the V2006 programme to recruit financial supporters and campaign volunteers, and the collection of as many recommendation sheets as possible, in fact multiples of the necessary number.

An important step in this process was the 'Three times Yes' referendum, which was initiated by Fidesz, and in which the party's populist standpoint was supported with an overwhelming majority (questions of the referendum related to the abolition of hospital stay fees, GP visit fees and higher education tuition fees). The initiative was aimed at weakening the government, and as a result, the governing MSZP–SZDSZ coalition lost its majority in parliament, after the latter quit government. The standpoint of Fidesz was supported by more than 3.3 million votes in each of the three questions, which meant roughly 41 per cent of those eligible to vote, and over 80 per cent of those casting a valid vote.[3]

The prime target audience of the campaign was the 3.3 million voters who cast a 'Yes' vote at the 2008 referendum. A smaller part of them were strongly affiliated with Fidesz, and supported the party under all circumstances. The larger part of them were loosely affiliated, but have supported the party in one way or another at least once. In other words, Fidesz segmented the electorate based on former behaviour and only targeted those who, according to their database, have signalled some sort of support towards the party. The task of the campaign was to mobilise all of them – or as many as possible – on the side of Fidesz. The campaign relied on the core supporters to a large extent. Several campaign actions were aimed at maintaining their interest and support and making their relationship with the party even closer through fundraising opportunities, volunteer work, and special messages distributed in emails. It was obvious though that the party had to remain open to possible support from outside the target group. In addition to previous *behaviour*, the party relied on *classic sociological segmentation* as well: they targeted pensioners. The party's Senior Division launched a petition in their defence, party politicians frequently addressed them in their speech and a targeted direct mail was sent to pensioners towards the end of the campaign.

Lessons for political marketing

Segmentation and targeting are key components of campaign strategy. Segmenting the electorate based on political behaviour might seem an old trick and might not work under all circumstances, as it requires a strong party base and the potential to reinforce and mobilise those leaning towards the party. In many respects Fidesz's campaign resembled the labour-intensive campaigns of old days, but it clearly operated on marketing principles (building and maintaining a database and carrying out targeted communication based on it) which helped the party in concentrating its efforts where it paid the most.

Further reading

Szabó, Gabriella and Balázs Kiss (2012). 'Trends in political communication in Hungary: a postcommunist experience twenty years after the fall of dictatorship'. *International Journal of Press/Politics* 17(4): 480–96.

Kiss, Balázs and Zsuzsanna Mihályffy (2009). 'Political salesmen in Hungary'. In Jennifer Lees-Marshment, Jesper Strömbäck and Chris Rudd (eds) *Global Political Marketing*. London: Routledge, 143–57.

Bayer, József and Jody Jensen (eds) (2007). *From Transition to Globalization: New Challenges for Politics, Society and the Media*. Budapest: Institute for Political Science of HAS, 276.

Case study 3.3 Little data: using social media to gain market research and inform campaign strategy at local government level

By Nicholas Mignacca, University of Auckland

nmig002@aucklanduni.ac.nz

Social media is increasingly becoming central tools for communications within political campaigns, but it can also be used more strategically by local candidates as means to conduct free market research. In the New Zealand context, attention has been given to the use of social networking websites at a parliamentarian level (Blair, 2012) and in general elections (Cameron *et al.* 2013), but social media marketing in local body elections remains an overlooked area of research, just as with all countries. This case study examines Auckland candidates' use of social media in the 2013 Local Body Elections, focusing on mayoral, council and local board campaigns. The research shows that services such as Facebook and LinkedIn allow local-level candidates to collect free quantitative and qualitative analytical information that can be used to target communications to the tastes of the electorate. Social media is therefore a very practical tool for individual politicians who want to utilise market-orientated political marketing but don't have the big budget of national-level parties and campaigns.

This study collated social media data about the 464 Auckland candidates running for mayor, council and local board in the 2013 Local Body Elections, as found on the Vote.co.nz and VoteAuckland.co.nz databases. Firstly, it found that social media has become intrinsic with grass-roots New Zealand politics. Of the 464 candidates, 120 (26 per cent) integrated social media into their campaign. Indeed, 47 (10 per cent) used two or more social media; and 22 (5 per cent) displayed a sophisticated use of synchronised multi-medium social media platforms, especially targeted at maximising candidate visibility among specific voter segments. Key social media websites used to campaign in the elections were Facebook, Twitter, LinkedIn, YouTube, Google+ and Webo. In the most successful cases, an official website and Facebook advertising supplemented candidates' use of social media. Final results showed that, out of the ten candidates with the strongest social media use, six won their respective seats (Brown, R. Thomas, Krum, Cooper, Hulse and Brewer).

Secondly, it found that candidates utilised social media to help them market themselves in several ways. The greatest benefit of a social media communications campaign to local body candidates is increased visibility. New Zealand local elections traditionally enjoy lower voter turnouts than general elections and voters tend to be older. Consequently, campaigning candidates tend to focus their limited resources on targeting narrow voter-segments, politically active at a grass-roots level. In this context, social media campaigning is an attractive option as, for no cost, it provides candidates with around-the-clock personal access to voters, high visibility, and name recognition. The 2013 Auckland local body elections saw candidates creatively supplement traditional campaigning techniques such as hoardings, door-knocking and live hoardings with new uses of social media. This included Facebook, Twitter and LinkedIn links on candidate billboards; use of social media to recruit volunteers for door-knocking and live hoarding activities; and the use of Facebook and Twitter to organise fundraising events. When one considers that the Maungakiekie-Tamaki Ward was won by 7,923 to 7,049 votes, by a candidate with a combined Facebook, Twitter and LinkedIn following of 2,048 users, one can see that social networking websites' contribution to raising a candidate's profile is significant.

Furthermore, Facebook and LinkedIn help to generate free quantitative and qualitative data that can inform the candidate's marketing strategy. The rising use of Facebook public profiles and LinkedIn in local body campaigns indicates candidates are becoming increasingly aware of social media's potential for targeted, market-oriented communications. Facebook and LinkedIn both offer their users the capacity to collect diverse quantitative and qualitative data about followers, feedback to posts, and third-party connections. On both websites, one can:

1   Calculate how many people saw one's posts.
2   View how other users responded to each post in 'likes', 'shares' and 'deletes'.
3   Divide followers according to gender, age brackets and geographical provenance.

For political marketing purposes, this allows candidates to determine what posts received the most feedback, and develop consequent strategies to boost the reach of their communications, mindful of the specific makeup of the audience. In 2013 campaigning saw a rise of targeted posts with short personal messages, colourful images, and questions aimed at generating user response on candidates' pages. Additionally, as shown by Brown, Palino, Krum, and Thomas, some candidates used the data collected by their Facebook pages to conduct narrowly targeted Facebook advertising campaigns. Facebook advertising for non-profit organisations costs NZ$1 a day. For less than the daily cost of a single billboard, one can gain quotidian name recognition from 138,000 Auckland Facebook users, for three months.

Additionally, candidates can engage in strategic and synchronised multi-faceted social media campaigning. What the most clever Auckland local body campaigns demonstrated is that there is no single best all-encompassing social medium for political marketing. Rather, each medium is different, and serves a separate communications purpose. Each social networking website connects different voter segments according to demographics, occupation and personal interests, reaching people in different settings. Social media are complementary to one another, and can be connected to make up for each other's' structural limitations. In practical terms, while Facebook is by far the most popular social network website in New Zealand, its use to political marketing is different from that of Twitter or LinkedIn. Facebook is a hub for personal communications, linking people of all ages and social backgrounds. Its communications are personal, visual and informal. LinkedIn instead is rapidly emerging as New Zealand's leading corporate online social network, and complements Facebook by reaching people in a professional manner. While LinkedIn lacks the audience volumes Facebook provides, it allows targeted sectorial and one-on-one communications in a similar process to emailing (with To:, Cc:, and Bcc:). Twitter is the more fluid of the three, as it is both a formal and informal social medium depending of the context. Like Facebook, Twitter allows larger online user followings than LinkedIn. However, because of Twitter's instant newsfeed structure, the dynamics of communicating via Twitter are different to other social media. Since Facebook and LinkedIn can be synchronised through Twitter, a candidate can set up a multifaceted social media platform to access more voters in diverse settings while halving the workload.

Lessons for political marketing

In their study of social media use in the 2010 New Zealand General Elections, Cameron *et al.* (2013) found that social media had a visible effect in closely contested campaigns, often shifting the odds in favour of the candidate with the best social media strategy. This study of the way social media was used in the 2013 Auckland Local Body Elections reinforces Cameron *et al.*'s findings, showing that not only have social media communications become a central feature of New Zealand political campaigns but that they can be used to generate valuable market research data which can help candidates produce informed, synchronised and targeted marketing campaigns. With the trial of online voting commencing in the 2016 New Zealand Local Body Elections, internet-based forms of political marketing will undoubtedly grow in importance at the local level. Looking to the future, the capacity of social networking websites such as Facebook and LinkedIn to provide candidates with vital quantitative and qualitative data about their audience will become increasingly key to competing for digital votes and potentially enable individual candidates to utilise the same range of marketing tools and concepts we see in national-level campaigns.

Further reading

Blair, Sophia (2012) *Making the Net Work: What New Zealand Political Parties Can Learn From Obama*. Master of Arts thesis on online political marketing and political party participation, University of Auckland.

Cameron, M. P., P. Barrett and B. Stewardson (2013). *Can Social Media Predict Election Results? Evidence from New Zealand*. Working Paper in Economics 13/08, University of Waikato. ftp://mngt.waikato.ac.nz/repec/Wai/econwp/1308.pdf_ (accessed September 12, 2013)

Case study 3.4 Global knowledge transfer in Latvia

By Ieva Berzina, National Academy of Defence of the Republic of Latvia
ieva.berzina01@inbox.lv

Latvia is a post-Soviet country that is geographically, historically, politically, economically and culturally located between the West and Russia. After the collapse of the Soviet Union the Western support of newly established democracies took various forms including education of the political elite to conduct political campaigns, because political campaigning is the primary tool for the struggle of power in democratic society and knowledge about political campaigning can considerably influence the distribution of power in a certain country. The methods of contemporary political campaigning primarily were developed in the Western democracies; however Russian political campaigners gradually developed a distinct political consultancy school that spread outside the borders of Russia (Wilson 2005; Krastev 2006). Taking into consideration that Russia has chosen an autocratic path of development and in the last years is attempting to counterbalance the West in an international arena, it is a matter of geopolitical significance to ask which influence dominates political campaigning practice in Latvia – Western or Russian?

One way of estimating this is to clarify the sources of knowledge of practitioners of political campaigning in Latvia. Such an approach is based on the idea of global diffusion of political campaign techniques through various sources of information: the services of political consultants working abroad; training programmes of international non-governmental organisations; international networks of professional associations; international study programmes; websites; books and other sources (Plasser and Plasser 2002).

For the purpose of answering the question, 12 in-depth interviews were conducted with Latvian political campaigning practitioners. The scope of respondents included politicians that had taken part in at least one election campaign on behalf of their parties, external experts that are not members of the parties but who had been hired for at least one election campaign as consultants and public relations and advertising experts. The decision to include in the research both politicians and external experts is based on two considerations. First, in Latvian political practice representatives of the party have the main responsibility for the overall strategy of political campaigning. But they hire external experts for carrying out such important tasks as advertising material production, event management, media planning, research, etc., which means that the role of the external experts is also considerable. Second, the number of experts in political campaigning in Latvia is relatively small; therefore it was useful to interview both types of experts. In order to get a comparative perspective, one manager of a foreign non-governmental organisation who has an office in Latvia was also interviewed. All the interviews were conducted in Riga from February to April 2011, the length of the interviews ranged from 40 minutes to an hour. Theoretical background for the research was the framework of the transnational diffusion micro-level actors of the USA campaigning expertise, as defined by Fritz Plasser and Gunda Plasser (2002, 21).

The research disclosed that the main source of knowledge about political campaigning in Latvia is self-study – reading of books, publications, online sources, as well as the lessons learned in practical experience that is gained by leading or participating in political campaigns. Next in importance are the international networks of political parties and the circulation of information in those networks that also spreads information on political campaigning practices. Latvian political campaigners use the opportunities offered by the international party alliances which brings together parties with similar ideological background, such as the European People's Party, the Liberal Democrats, etc. In this respect, it is important to note that Latvian parties involve not only in the party networks of the European Union but also have co-operation with Russian political parties. For example, the party union 'Harmony Center' co-operates with the Russian party 'United Russia'; that is an indicator of geopolitical collision of the West and Russia in Latvia. Of equal importance to international party networks are the training courses provided by various foreign non-governmental organisations aimed at promoting democratic development. Several respondents pointed to the fact that they have visited training courses at the US Democratic Institute and organisations affiliated with German political parties – the Friedrich Neumann Foundation, the Konrad Adenauer Foundation and others. An interesting finding is that feature films are one of the sources that help form ideas and understanding of the way political campaigns are run and how political consultants are working.

By contrast, an unused source of political campaigning knowledge is participation in international professional organisations, such as the International Association of Political Consultants. Even the external experts of political campaigning, who might be the most interested in participation in such organisations, are not aware that such organisations exist. Of little importance also are commercial activities by foreign political consultants in Latvia. There have been some cases when Latvian politicians have used the services of the Western and Russian political consultants, but it happens very rarely due to the fact that it is expensive and external experts are not aware of the peculiarities of the Latvian political system. Academic education also is not being considered an important source of knowledge because, in the opinion of respondents, the Latvian higher education system gives an incomplete or even false picture of political reality in Latvia, since the content of study programmes is based on theories developed in the Western democracies that have significantly different political context than in post-Soviet Latvia. As several experts noted, the crucial difference between the West and Latvia is the absence of a genuine left–right dimension in the party system and in political values in the media and among the public. None of the respondents had studied abroad and did not consider the possibility of complementing their knowledge in foreign universities. As to the Western and Russian influence, the experience of Western Europe is prevailing, but there is also some US and Russian influence. Politicians and external experts of political campaigning admit that in order to build up their knowledge of political campaigning they use both sources – Western and Russian. Therefore in terms of the knowledge of political campaigning, Latvia is a mixture of the Western and Russian influences combined with its own uniqueness. The transnational sources of knowledge are used just in a limited scope, leaving an impression that the practice of political campaigning in Latvia is locally oriented and dominated by a trial and error approach.

Lessons for political marketing

- Despite the growing internationalization of political campaigning, each country has its own peculiarities. The opinion of Latvian political campaigning practitioners suggests considering the idea of 'glocalization' in the field of political campaigning.
- International party networks and organisations affiliated with them are very important micro-level actors of transnational diffusion of knowledge specifically in Europe; therefore it is worth developing the idea of Europeanization of political campaigns in contrast to Americanization. The influence of Russian political campaigning practice in the post-Soviet region can also be considered.
- International political marketing can be used in the geopolitical interests of superpowers; therefore in certain circumstances it may become an issue of national security.

Further reading

Bowler, S. and D. M. Farrell (2000). 'The internationalization of campaign consultancy'. In Thurber J.A. and C. J. Nelson (eds) *Campaign Warriors: The Role of Political Consultants in Elections*. Washington: The Brookings Institution.

Krastev, I. (2006). 'Democracy's "Doubles"'. *Journal of Democracy*, 17(2): 52–62.

Plasser, F. and G. Plasser (2002). *Global Political Campaigning: A Worldwide Analysis of Campaign Professionals and their Practices*. Praeger Publishers: Westport.

Scammel, M. (1997). *The Wisdom of the War Room: US Campaigning and Americanization*. The Joan Shorenstein Center on the Press, Politics and Public Policy, John F. Kennedy School of Government, Harvard University.

Wilson, A. (2005). *Virtual Politics: Faking Democracy in the Post-Soviet World*. New Haven and London: Yale University Press.

Notes

1 I am grateful to Dr Michael Burton at Ohio University for his advice on this and the list of analytical research firms.
2 I am grateful to an anonymous reviewer of the proposal for this second edition who suggested this point.
3 National Election Office data http://www.valasztas.hu/hu/ovi/42/42_0.html

References

Abad, Mercedes and Ophelia Ramirez (2008). 'Polling in developing democracies – the case of the Philippines'. In Marita Carbello and Ulf Hjelmar (eds) *Public Opinion Polling*. Berlin: Springer-Verlag, 267–80.

Alabi, Joshua and Goski Alabi (2007). 'Analysis of the effects of ethnicity on political marketing in Ghana'. *International Business and Economics Research Journal*, 6(4): 39–52.

Asher, Herbert (1995). *Polling and the Public: What Every Citizen Should Know*. Washington DC: Congressional Quarterly Press.

Bannon, Declan (2004). 'Marketing segmentation and political marketing'. Paper presented to the UK Political Studies Association, University of Lincoln, 4–8 April.

Bennett, W. Lance (2012). 'The personalization of politics: political identity, social media, and changing patterns of participation'. *The Annals of the American Academy of Political and Social Science*, 644: 20–39.

Ben-Ur, Joseph and Bruce I. Newman (2010). 'A marketing poll: an innovative approach to prediction, explanation and strategy'. *European Journal of Marketing*, 44(3–4): 515–38.

Birch, Lisa and Francois Petry (2012). 'The use of public opinion research by government: insights from American and Canadian research'. In Jennifer Lees-Marshment (ed.) *Routledge Handbook of Political Marketing*. New York: Routledge, 342–453.

Blaemire, Bob (2013). 'From handwritten lists to online databases – how voter files became the "big data" of modern campaigns'. *Campaigns & Elections*, 6th June. http://www.campaignsandelections. com/magazine/us-edition/371892/part_3/evolution-of-the-voter-file.thtml (accessed 21 June, 2013)

Braun, Alexander (2012). 'The role of opinion research in setting campaign strategy'. In Jennifer Lees-Marshment (ed.) *Routledge Handbook of Political Marketing*. New York: Routledge, 7–19.

Burton, Michael John (2012). 'Strategic voter selection'. In Jennifer Lees-Marshment (ed.) *Routledge Handbook of Political Marketing*. New York: Routledge, 34–47.

Burton, Michael John and Tasha Miracle (2014). 'The emergence of voter targeting: learning to send the right message to the right voters'. In Jennifer Lees-Marshment, Brian Conley and Kenneth Cosgrove (eds) *Political Marketing in the US*. New York: Routledge.

Busby, Robert (2009). *Marketing the Populist Politician: The Demotic Democrat*. Houndmills and New York: Palgrave Macmillan.

Butler, Patrick and Phil Harris (2009). 'Considerations on the evolution of political marketing theory'. *Marketing Theory*, 9(2): 149–64.

Chiu, Kevin Kuan Shun, C. Richard Huston, Hani I. Mesak and T. Hillman Willis (2010). 'The role of a psychographic approach in segmenting electorates' voting behaviour and party identification'. *Journal of Political Marketing*, 9(1–2): 34–54.

Davidson, Scott (2005). 'Grey power, school gate mums and the youth vote: age as a key factor in voter segmentation and engagement in the 2005 UK general election'. *Journal of Marketing Management*, 21(9/10): 1179–92.

Davidson, Scott and Robert H. Binstock (2012). 'Political marketing and segmentation in aging democracies'. In Jennifer Lees-Marshment (ed.) *Routledge Handbook of Political Marketing*. New York: Routledge, 20–33.

Dufresne, Yannick and Alex Marland (2012). 'The Canadian political market and the rules of the game'. In Alex Marland, Thierry Giasson and Jennifer Lees-Marshment (eds) *Political Marketing in Canada*. Vancouver: UBC, 22–38.

Friesen, Joe (2011). '"Micro-targeting" lets parties conquer ridings, one tiny group at a time'. *The Globe and Mail*, Friday, April 22. http://www.theglobeandmail.com/news/politics/micro-targeting-lets-parties-conquer-ridings-one-tiny-group-at-a-time/article1996155/ (accessed 12 June, 2013).

Gidengil, Elisabeth (2012). 'The diversity of the Canadian political marketplace'. In Alex Marland, Thierry Giasson and Jennifer Lees-Marshment (eds) *Political Marketing in Canada*. Vancouver: UBC, 39–56.

Gould, Philip (1998). *The Unfinished Revolution: How the Modernisers Saved the Labour Party*. London: Little, Brown and Company.

Henneberg, Stephan and Nicholas O'Shaughnessy (2007). 'Theory and concept development in political marketing: issues and an agenda'. *Journal of Political Marketing*, 6(2–3): 5–31.

Hutcheson, Derek S. (2010). 'Political marketing techniques in Russia'. In Jennifer Lees-Marshment, Jesper Strömbäck and Chris Rudd (eds) *Global Political Marketing*. London: Routledge, 218–33.

Issenberg, Sasha (2012). *The Victory Lab: The Secret Science of Winning Campaigns*. New York: Crown Publishing Group.

Johns, Robert and Heinz Brandenburg (2012). 'Giving voters what they want? Party orientation perceptions and preferences in the British electorate'. *Party Politics*, 22nd February: 1–16.

Johnson, Dennis W. (2007). *No Place for Amateurs*, 2nd edn. New York: Routledge.

Karanfilovska, Gordica (2009). 'How are Macedonian parties oriented?' Case study 9.6 in Jennifer Lees-Marshment, *Political Marketing: Principles and Applications*. London and New York: Routledge, 258–61.

Kavanagh, Dennis (1996). 'Speaking truth to power? Pollsters as campaign advisers?' *European Journal of Marketing*, 30(10/11): 104–13.

Knuckey, Jonathan (2010). 'Political marketing in the United States: from market- towards sales-orientation?' In Jennifer Lees-Marshment, Jesper Strömbäck and Chris Rudd (eds) *Global Political Marketing*. London: Routledge, 96–112.

König, Mathias and Wolfgang König (2012). 'Government public opinion research and consultation: experiences in deliberative marketing'. In Jennifer Lees-Marshment (ed.) *Routledge Handbook of Political Marketing*. New York: Routledge, 48–60.

Langmaid, Roy (2012). 'Co-creating the future'. In Jennifer Lees-Marshment (ed.) *Routledge Handbook of Political Marketing*. New York: Routledge: 61–76.

Lees-Marshment, Jennifer (2001). *Political Marketing and British Political Parties: The Party's Just Begun*. Manchester: Manchester University Press.

Lees-Marshment, Jennifer (2009). 'Political marketing and the 2008 New Zealand election: a comparative perspective'. *Australian Journal of Political Science*, 44(3): 457–75.

Lees-Marshment, Jennifer (2010). 'New Zealand political marketing: marketing communication rather than the product?' In Jennifer Lees-Marshment, Jesper Strömbäck and Chris Rudd (eds) *Global Political Marketing*. London: Routledge, 65–81.

Lees-Marshment, Jennifer (2011). *The Political Marketing Game*. Houndmills and New York: Palgrave Macmillan.

Lees-Marshment, Jennifer (forthcoming). 'The Democratic Contribution of Political Market Researchers'. *Journal of Public Affairs*.

Lees-Marshment, Jennifer and Darren G. Lilleker (2012). 'Knowledge sharing and lesson learning: consultants' perspectives on the international sharing of political marketing strategy'. *Contemporary Politics*, 18(3): 343–54.

Lees-Marshment, Jennifer, Jesper Strömbäck and Chris Rudd (eds) (2010) *Global Political Marketing*. London: Routledge.

Lilleker, Darren and Jennifer Lees-Marshment (eds) (2005). *Political Marketing: A Comparative Perspective*. Manchester: Manchester University Press.

Lilleker, Darren G. and Richard Scullion (eds) (2008). *Voters or Consumers: Imagining the Contemporary Electorate*. Newcastle: Cambridge Scholars Publishing.

Lloyd, Jenny (2009). 'Keeping both the baby and the bathwater: scoping a new model of political marketing communication'. *International Review on Public and Nonprofit Marketing*, 6(2): 119–35.

Matuskova, Anna, Otto Eible and Alexander Braun (2010). 'The Czech case: a Market-Oriented Party on the rise?' In Jennifer Lees-Marshment, Jesper Strömbäck and Chris Rudd (eds) *Global Political Marketing*, London: Routledge, 157–74.

Mills, Stephen (2011). 'Focus groups: myth or reality'. In Alastair Carthew and Simon Winkelmann (eds) *Political Polling in Asia-Pacific*. Singapore: Konrad Adenauer Stiftung, 27–38.

Mortimore, Roger (2003). 'Why politics needs marketing'. *International Journal of Non-Profit and Voluntary Sector Marketing*. Special issue on 'Broadening the concept of political marketing', 8(2): 107–21.

Ndlovu, Musa (2013). 'Marketing politics to generation X'. In Kōstas Gouliamos, Antonis Theocharous, Bruce Newman (eds) *Political Marketing Strategic 'Campaign Culture'*. London: Routledge, 97–113.

Newman, Bruce I. (1999). 'A predictive model of voter behavior – the repositioning of Bill Clinton'. In Bruce I. Newman (ed.) *Handbook of Political Marketing*. Thousand Oaks, CA: Sage, 259–82.

Norris, Pippa (ed.) (2005) *Critical Citizens*. Oxford: Oxford University Press.

Pettitt, Robin T. (2009). 'Learning from the master: the impact of New Labour on political parties in Denmark'. Case study 9.2 in Jennifer Lees-Marshment, *Political Marketing: Principles and Applications*. London and New York: Routledge, 249–51.

Pharr, Susan and Robert Putnam (eds) (2000). *Disaffected Democracies: What's Troubling the Trilateral Countries?* Princeton, NJ: Princeton University Press.

Plasser, Fritz, Christian Scheucher and Christian Seft (1999). 'Is there a European style of political marketing? A survey of political managers and consultants'. In Bruce Newman (ed.) *A Handbook of Political Marketing*. Thousand Oaks, CA: Sage, 89–112.

Promise (2005) *Reconnecting the Prime Minister*, Report. www.promisecorp.com/casestudies/pr_case_labour.pdf (accessed 19 March 2008).

Rademacher, Eric W. and Alfred J. Tuchfarber (1999). 'Pre-election polling and political campaigns'. In Bruce Newman (ed.) *Handbook of Political Marketing*. Thousand Oaks, CA: Sage, 197–222.

Rothmayr, Christine and Sibylle Hardmeier (2002). 'Government and polling: use and impact of polls in the policy-making process in Switzerland'. *International Journal of Public Opinion Research*, 14(2): 123–40.

Rottinghaus, Brandon and Irina Alberro (2005). 'Rivaling the PRI: the image management of Vicente Fox and the use of public opinion polling in the 2000 Mexican election'. *Latin American Politics and Society*, 47(2): 143–58.

Savigny, Heather (2007). 'Focus groups and political marketing: science and democracy as axiomatic?' *British Journal of Politics and International Relations*, 9(1): 122–37.

Scammell, Margaret (2008). 'Brand Blair: marketing politics in the consumer age'. In D. Lilleker and R. Scullion (eds) *Voters or Consumers: Imagining the Contemporary Electorate*. Newcastle: Cambridge Scholars Publishing, 97–113.

Sherman, Elaine, Leon Schiffman and Shawn T. Thelen (2008). 'Impact of trust on candidates, branches of government, and media within the context of the 2004 US presidential election'. *Journal of Political Marketing*, 7(2): 105–30.

Smith, Gareth and John Saunders (1990). 'The application of marketing to British politics'. *Journal of Marketing Management*, 5(3): 295–306.

Sparrow, Nick and John Turner (2001). 'The integrating of market research techniques in developing strategies in a more uncertain political climate'. *European Journal of Marketing*, 35(9/10): 984–1002.

Strömbäck, Jesper (2007). 'Antecedents of political market orientation in Britain and Sweden: analysis and future research propositions'. *Journal of Public Affairs*, 7(1): 79–90.

Sunday Profile (2012). Broadcast, *ABC Radio*, March.

Teinturier, Brice (2008). 'The presidential elections in France 2007 – the role of opinion polls'. In Marita Carballo and Ulf Hjelmar (eds) *Public Opinion Polling in a Globalized World*. Berlin: Springer-Verlag, 135–52.

Turcotte, André (2012). 'Under new management: market intelligence and the Conservative resurrection'. In Alex Marland, Thierry Giasson and Jennifer Lees-Marshment (eds) *Political Marketing in Canada*. Vancouver: UBC, 76–90.

Turner, Jamie. (2009). 'International political product marketing'. Case study 9.3 in Jennifer Lees-Marshment, *Political Marketing: Principles and Applications*. London and New York: Routledge, 251–3.

Varoga, Craig and Mike Rice (1999). 'Only the facts: professional research and message development'. In B. Newman (ed.) *Handbook of Political Marketing*. Thousand Oaks, CA: Sage, 243–58.

Williams, Christine B. (2012). 'Trends and changes in journal of political marketing titles 2002–2011'. *Journal of Political Marketing*, 11(1–2): 4–7.

Wring, Dominic (2005). *The Politics of Marketing the Labour Party*. Hampshire: Palgrave Macmillan.

Wring, Dominic (2007). 'Focus group follies? Qualitative research and British Labour Party strategy'. *Journal of Political Marketing*, 5(4): 71–97.

World Denver Talks (2012). Broadcast, *Rocky Mountain PBS*, 28 September.

4 Political branding

Practitioner perspective 4.1 on the importance of brands in politics

There has been quite a strong resistance to the idea that political leaders are iconic in the same way that nationally or internationally known brands are. And that people project a lot of fantasies onto them . . . Of no politicians in the UK has that been more true (truer) than of the Blairs. You only have to replay the footage of their arrival at Number 10 in 1997 to see that nothing really short of adulation was going on. So they cease to be people. And they become, you know, the best of us in a way that a brand is the best of its class. And they then, they carry all of our hopes with them.

Roy Langmaid, Consultant from Promise, UK, advisor to
UK Labour 2004–2005, interviewed in 2008

A political party leader is . . . a brand. [S]he should be aware of his brand's strengths and weaknesses, and play to the strengths and work to improve the weaknesses. [New Zealand Prime Minister] John Key is very self-aware in this department.

John Ansell, NZ Advertiser, interviewed 2007

In terms of content alone, politics is different to buying a car. However, we can learn from brand advertising, how certain instruments, concepts and images can be used to depict political content.

Matthew Machnig, Bundestag Chief of the SPD

Sources: Lees-Marshment (2011); Schneider (2004, 50)

Political branding is about how a political organisation or individual is perceived overall by the public. It is broader than the product; whereas a product has distinct functional parts such as a politician and policy, a brand is intangible and psychological. A political brand is the overarching feeling, impression, association or image the public has towards a politician, political organisation, or nation. As Cosgrove (2009) puts it, 'a brand is the overall summation that includes the logo, a narrative, a consistent set of visual images and three to five specific selling points about the products that it is supporting'. Individual perceptions of political brands are formed by the experience and communication a political consumer receives from a range of sources: 'nodes' which the public then links together to create an interconnected network of information about a political party or politician which are stimulated every time voters see or hear from a new party leader (French and Smith 2010, 462). Political branding helps the party or candidate to help change or maintain reputation and support, create a feeling of identity with the party or its candidates and create a trusting relationship between political elites and consumers. It helps political consumers understand more quickly what a party or candidate is about; and distinguish a candidate or party from the competition. However, given their complexity, political brands are hard to control or change once established. When trying to create or improve a political brand, practitioners draw on many different elements of political marketing – strategy, goals, political market research, product development and communication. Research on political branding has expanded significantly since 2008. This chapter will explore principles of effective political brands, followed by how branding is used for political leaders; individual candidates; parties; policy, government and programme branding; city and nation branding; and maintaining and rebranding political brands.

Criteria for effective political brands

As Cosgrove (2012) notes, branding can occur at different levels: the government (e.g the Obama Administration, the Harper government); the house party brand (e.g. the Democrat or Republican party); platform brands occupied by presidential candidates in each election (Obama 2008); and product brands related to policies (such as health care, bailouts and the American Reinvestment and Recovery Act). Government policies, departments and agencies; cities, states and countries are also branded to stimulate trade, investment, tourism and aid international relations. Needham (2005) details what makes a successful political brand: see Figure 4.1.

Case study 4.1 applies this criteria to the brand of the New Zealand Green Party and argues that by meeting many of the principles the party was able to create a positive, aspirational, moderate and reassuring brand and achieve far more successful results than in previous elections.

Another measure of a successful political brand is brand equity which is about how much consumers value each brand relative to the competition and explores brand awareness, loyalty, perceived quality and brand associations. A successful brand will be one that the public is very aware of, loyal to, considers highly and associates with positively. French and Smith (2010, 462) analysed the brand equity of the main UK parties: the Conservatives and the Labour Party. Both scored highly on brand awareness; reasonably on loyalty; and weak on perceived quality. Using a brand concept map to measure perceptions of the UK Conservatives and Labour amongst students in October 2007, when Labour was in power and the Conservatives in opposition, they identified both strengths and weaknesses in their brand equity. Conservative supporters provided positive comments such as 'good policies

---

Needham's criteria for successful brands

1   Brands act as simplifiers to make it easy for voters to understand what is being offered.
2   Brands are unique and clearly differentiated from the competition.
3   Brands are reassuring so voting for them is not risky.
4   Brands are aspirational and convey a positive vision for a better way of life.
5   Brands symbolise better internal values of the product or organisation.
6   Brands are perceived as credible, delivering on their promises.

Figure 4.1

Source: Adapted from Needham (2005, 347–8)

on education', 'party of fairness', 'supports green policies', 'represents middle/upper classes'; and negative ones including 'party of the 80s/dated' and 'hug a hoodie'. Labour received negative comments such as 'special relationship with USA' and 'war in Iraq'; but positive ones including 'party for the working class', 'promotes equal opportunities' and 'promotes a fair society'.

Branding political leaders

Practitioner perspective 4.2 on the need for vision in presidential brands

American people are very pragmatic. And they don't get into the intricacies of a lot of foreign policy issues. But what they do expect is to see in a presidential candidate the indications of leader, of judgement, of vision that will . . . lead to the president being able to protect American interests.

John Bolton, Foreign Policy Advisor to the Romney Campaign, 2012

To go from opposition to power you have to have people who haven't voted for you before. And often they're people who . . . don't care about politics. But you're not going to get them to come and vote for you simply by the other lot being not up to much.

Alistair Campbell, Blair advisor, 2013

When you have an unemployment rate of 8 per cent, a record number of people on food stamps or welfare, a sense that the country's moving in the wrong direction . . . it should be an easy election . . . [but] it didn't work because Mick Romney was defined before he could define himself.

Frank Luntz, US communications expert and political strategist, 2012

Sources: Whitman (2012); Campbell (2013); PolicyExchangeUK (2012)

The branding of political leaders is naturally a key focus of research on political branding. As this section will show, leader branding involves offering a simple and distinctive vision with values that connect with the target audience, that gains a strong awareness amongst the public and that stimulates positive associations. The leader needs to convey a positive brand personality with characteristics such as sincerity, openness and competence; and to be credible and actually deliver the promised brand once elected. New party leaders also need to differentiate their brand from their predecessors.

As Practitioner perspective 4.2 suggests, creating an effective political brand that offers a distinctive vision is very important for political leaders. Knuckey (2010, 106) observes of Kerry's failure to win the 2004 US Presidential election how 'he did not have a real vision for the Democratic Party'. The Democratic convention showed 'the inability of the Kerry campaign to provide a specific vision' because it lacked a clear theme other than the candidate's war record. Parker (2012) analysed the brand equity of candidates in the 2008 US presidential primaries and elections, considering brand awareness, associations, perceived quality, and loyalty to four US presidential candidates (Hillary Clinton, Barack Obama, John McCain, and Mike Huckabee) amongst registered voter segments in 2007 and 2008. Candidates with highest levels of brand equity attracted the most support from voters across both main parties. For example, whilst Clinton was perceived to be the strongest candidate brand by Democratic voters in the primaries, Obama had a higher overall brand equity from the aggregated sampled voters including those outside his party. Obama's strength was his appeal to the broader electorate and independent voters and thus leaders need to make sure their brand appeals to external as well as internal markets.

Indeed Barack Obama's 2008 brand is the most commonly known political brand. Several scholars have discussed what made the 2008 Obama brand successful. Conley (2012, 128) argues that he encapsulated many of the principles academic theorists, such as Needham, argue political brands should: the brand was simple and reassuring, centred on a rhetoric of 'hope' and possibility. The slogan 'Yes We Can' was simple but also responded to the political market's desire for change and to be optimistic that the country could go in a new direction despite the Iraq War and problematic economy. Cosgrove (2012, 109) argues that it was effective because it embodied core values that resonated with the target audience and offered tangible product aspects; thus the values were hope, change; benefits were to transform US politics and restore American democracy; and Obama himself had clear attributes such as two years' senate experience, eight years' in office in Illinois and having been a community organiser at Harvard law school. Both scholars note that Obama positioned

Authors' corner 4.1

Branding the candidate: marketing strategies to win your vote
By Lisa Spiller and Jeff Bergner
Published by Praeger in 2011

Using the 2008 Obama presidential campaign as a prime example, *Branding The Candidate: Marketing Strategies to Win Your Vote* by Lisa Spiller and Jeff Bergner will provide an overview of how political campaign marketing has evolved and how it boldly utilised a multitude of precisely targeted, high-tech, digital direct and interactive marketing strategies to effectively win the hearts, minds, donations and votes of the American consumer/voter.

This groundbreaking book addresses the most recent major development in American politics – how political campaigns have borrowed from the world of direct and interactive marketing. Political campaigns today resemble business marketing campaigns, and the consumer has replaced the voter as the target of political campaigners.

This process was taken to a new level of sophistication by the Obama presidential campaign of 2008. This book reveals the ways in which the Obama campaign utilised consumer research to create perceptions that emotionally connected with the consumer/voter. It discusses how the Obama 'brand' was created in order to respond to consumers who were eager for change and ripe for convincing. The book outlines the ways in which the Obama campaign relied on database-driven political micro-targeting and high-tech digital media to reach different market segments.

The marketing strategies of the 2008 Obama campaign are described clearly and simply, so that average readers can understand how a relatively unknown politician became an overnight national marketing success. The book addresses the process of creating a candidate/brand from the ground up and the challenges associated with managing that political brand. The book offers an account of the likely marketing tactics and techniques that will be utilised to reach American voters in future political campaigns.

Branding The Candidate: Marketing Strategies to Win Your Vote was written to empower voters to become sharper, more informed political consumers.

himself as different to the Republicans: as an outsider who can change things and as Cosgrove put it, the choice for a new generation. The creation of the Obama brand, and its relationship to segmentation, data, direct marketing and targeting is also discussed at length in the book *Branding the Candidate* by Lisa Spiller and Jeff Bergner and they provide an overview of their arguments in Authors' Corner 4.1.

Political leaders need to build up a positive political brand personality. Smith (2009) argues that events, politicians/party actions, advertising and brand users/endorsers help to form a brand's personality, as well as being impacted on by partisanship. The personification of the brand develops from that brand's observed behaviours and inferences from their actions or stated intended action. Political leaders ability to control their brand personality can be limited by their own physical attributes; younger leaders find it easier to convey change and be fresh; older leaders easier to appear reliable and capable of governing. Smith (2009, 220) argues that there are six important components of political brand personalities see Figure 4.2 – and political leaders need to try to score highly on sincerity, excitement, competence, sophistication and ruggedness.

Smith's components of the political brand personality

- *Honesty*: traits such as honest, reliable, wholesome, sincere, real, sentimental, down to earth and friendly.
- *Spirited*: being spirited, daring, imaginative, up to date and cheerful.
- *Image*: smooth, good looking, trendy, young, cool, exciting, contemporary.
- *Leadership*: the leader, confident, intelligent, successful, hardworking, technical and secure.
- *Toughness*: masculine, rugged, tough and outdoorsy.
- *Uniqueness*: unique, independent and original.

Figure 4.2

Source: Smith (2009, 220)

Guzman and Vicenta (2009) analysed the public's brand image of presidential candidates for Mexico's 2006 election, using Aaker's (1997) brand personality scale in combination with adjectives used to measure politicians' personalities by Caprara *et al.* to create a brand image framework exploring sincerity, excitement, competence, sophistication, ruggedness, energy, agreeableness, conscientiousness, emotional stability and openness (see Guzman and Vincenta 2009, 211). They surveyed a representative sample of 1,144 Mexican registered voters. Their results suggested that the most important factors were capability, openness and empathy: see Figure 4.3.

This suggests that political candidates need to develop a brand that conveys their competence, openness and empathy – thus the ability to do the job, as well as being in touch with the general public.

Cosgrove (2009) argues that successful political brands in the US have been supported by positioning and differentiation marketing to clarify their space in relation to opponents. Under President Ronald Reagan, the Republicans built a brand that stressed traditional principles such as a smaller state and lower taxes and focused on the themes of American renewal and a strong America, symbolised by a symbol of state such as a flag. The Reagan brand was so effective it became the heritage brand for the party with which subsequent leaders try to connect, such as George W. Bush who used colours and cowboy imagery similar to Reagan and took similar policy positions.

Guzman and Vicenta's principles of effective political brand personality

1   *Capability*: hardworking, intelligent, leader, successful, dynamic, energetic, enterprising, constant and responsible.
2   *Openness*: sharp, creative, innovative, modern and original.
3   *Empathy*: cheerful, sentimental, friendly, cool and young.

Figure 4.3

Source: Guzman and Vincenta (2009)

Political branding also intersects with commercial branding. Cormack (2012) notes how the home-grown Canadian coffee shop Tim Hortons 'has a formidable political role in Canadian politics. Politicians regularly flock to the restaurants; Stephen Harper in particular has publicly linked himself to the brand'. Parties target voters who get their coffee from Tim Hortons as opposed to Starbucks; there are 2,800 outlets compared with 800 Starbucks in Canada. It is part of Canadian identity, and thus politicians seek to associate themselves with it as much as Canadian Hockey. Cormack (2012, 215) argues Tim Hortons is a Habermasian public sphere: 'like a public space or village square where people congregate and talk, argue, and debate'. Canadian politicians use Tom Hortons to make political announcements – in 2010 Prime Minister Harper even chose to visit Tim Hortons headquarters in Ontario rather than attend an address to the UN by US President Obama.

However, a strong brand cannot always be delivered despite the best intended design. Busby (2012, 220) analysed Palin's campaign for the vice-presidency under the McCain ticket in the 2008 US presidential election and how she was chosen strategically to help McCain's brand and position within the market, particularly amongst women voters. At first she attracted positive public and media support as she gained credit for her high polling rating as Governor of Alaska, for being a working mother of five children, and for being down to earth. Busby (2012, 222) notes how market research identified the importance of the 'Walmart Mom' – lower-middle-class white women who shopped at the discount retailer – as a pivotal swing group with split electoral loyalties, and Palin was thought to appeal to this segment of society given she was the least wealthy of the four candidates in the race. She was marketed as an ordinary person; an 'embodiment of the social group she sought in part to represent', and initial research by the Pew Research Centre found she was seen as strong, fresh and interesting – if inexperienced. However, during the campaign several marketing issues emerged with Palin's candidacy. Palin was expected to appeal to a specific section of the market, women voters, but failed to attract significant support from them. Busby argues this was because she was, at heart, a product-oriented leader whose positions were only attractive to core Republican voters. At presidential level candidate brands need to appeal to the mainstream not just the internal market. Furthermore, campaign strategists utilised inauthentic marketing which undermined her original brand appeal, dressing her in $150,000 of clothes which contradicted her original attraction as a 'hockey' or 'Walmart mom'. This confused the brand with mixed values – elite and ordinary. When combined with the questions over her knowledge of issues such as foreign affairs, this damaged perceptions of her leadership capability which is a crucial aspect of any presidential candidate's brand. Presidential-style brands need to be authentic, coherent and believable. The Palin case raises the issue of authenticity, and whilst strategising about the brand to be created is important, it also needs to be authentic or it will not gain credibility. It is no good conducting research and asking politicians to change to suit it in a way that does not suit them and will not be convincing.

Smith and Spotswood (2013) explored the brand equity of the leader of the UK Liberal Democrats, Nick Clegg, in the 2010 election. Clegg gained positive brand awareness after he performed well in an election debate, and attracted positive symbolic meaning and values from a wide range of voters which enhanced his brand equity. He was also perceived as credible and trustworthy; and he conveyed responsiveness through listening to the questions and trying to answer them, instead of just giving a prepared answer. However, as may be expected with the leader of a smaller party, Clegg scored less well on reliability and competence, an issue which grew stronger after the party went into coalition government with the Conservatives after the election.

Maintaining the leadership brand in power is not easy. Needham (2005) also assessed US Democrat President Bill Clinton's brand performance in power: see Figure 4.4.

Needham's assessment of Clinton's brand performance

Successful brand criteria   Bill Clinton 1992–2000

1. **Simple**	• Clear communication and organisation of communication staff • But lacked clarity due to media attention on sub-issues rather than main focus on economic plan and health care
2. **Unique**	• Differentiated himself as a New Democrat; rising above both opposition and his own party • Third way, e.g. not just no tax cuts, or yes to tax cuts, but certain tax cuts
3. **Reassuring**	• Continued policy to suit new middle-class voters, e.g. middle-class bill of rights including tax cuts and help with college fees • But failed to provide reassurance as aborted social conservative campaign stance for social liberal, losing votes in 1994 midterm elections • Over time regained popularity because of public sector delivery
4. **Aspirational**	• Emphasised appeal to aspirant, hard-working families • But once in power, began to lose touch
5. **Value-based**	• Developed values agenda in later years; opportunity, responsibility and community • But damaged by Lewinsky scandal
6. **Credible by delivering on promises**	• Targeted promises • But implementation constrained by political system such as the failed health care plan • Focused on advocating action at state level, not federal • Achieved more positive perception of delivery over time

Figure 4.4

Source: Adapted from Needham (2005, 349–55)

Cosgrove (2009) also notes that Bush's use of branding became problematic because of the unfounded rationale for war in Iraq, a weak response to Hurricane Katrina and failure to pass social security reform which damaged his delivery reputation. Political leaders' brand promises must be kept or this will damage their relationship with consumers. The problems with the Bush brand in power created an opportunity for the Democrats – and then Obama specifically – to rebuild their brand however, and they began by labeling the Republican brand as corrupt and failing to deliver. In 2008 the Obama campaign adopted a specific logo using the same red, white and blue colour scheme as Reagan, around the theme of hope and change. However, as Cosgrove said, 'change' is 'a daunting promise for any branded candidate to deliver in the real world', and Obama faced the same challenge as Bush in being seen to deliver in power once he was elected.

New party leaders need to differentiate their brand from that of the former leader. Needham (2006) observes how Bush Senior and John Major failed to win a second election because they failed to offer an alternative brand offering to their predecessors. The same was true of Al Gore and is, potentially, of Gordon Brown. Gore tried to distance himself from the problems of Bill Clinton but, in doing so, could not then take credit for the achievements of the government. Political branding is not easy for successors of strong brand leaders. Another example concerns the difficulties experienced by Blair's successor, Gordon Brown, who succeeded Blair in 2007. It is harder for new leaders to rebrand in government after a particularly strong leader has gone before them without a period in opposition in which to rebuild. Lloyd (2009) notes how when Gordon Brown took over as Labour prime minister in 2007, he was encumbered by the government's record over the past ten years. As Chancellor of the Exchequer, Brown was a key part of Blair's government so could not deny responsibility for any negatives associated with the New Labour brand. After so much time in power, the brand had also become contaminated by the war in Iraq and questions over ministerial behaviour. He therefore struggled to communicate a new version of the Labour brand that was unique to him and more attractive to the public. Lloyd's research suggests that he, and any other politician in this situation, needed to draw a line under the previous administration, establishing a clear and positive point of difference from the former leader. As Case study 4.2 by Mitra Naeimi on Rouhani's campaign during the Iranian presidential election of 2013 notes, leader branding can also be carried out in a co-branding form with other candidates who offer similar features, but must sometimes distinguish between inferior and superior choices amongst all the candidates. Political leaders also need to consider how their brand relates to their party brand, which will be discussed in a later section.

Branding candidates

Practitioner perspective 4.3 on the need to tell a story with your brand

Politics is no different from business . . . The brand has to stand for something, has to be unique, and has to tell a story . . . It is not enough to have a product and a service – you have to have more. There are 10 to 20 of everything, including political candidates.

Joshua Claflin is the president and creative director of US firm Garrison Everest

Source: Swanson (2012, 73)

As Swanson (2012, 72) notes, in the US there are hundreds of thousands of races run at the local level including sheriff races, school-board races, races for city council and county commission. Hughes and Dann (2010, 86) notes how, in Australia, personal branding has helped candidates win seats at a federal and state level: at the 2007 federal election the Labor Party used celebrity candidates for nearly 10 per cent of all total candidates, demonstrating the power of a personal brand in the Australian political market. It is as important to tell a story – or a local-level version of presidential or prime ministerial vision – with candidate brands, as Practitioner perspective 4.3 suggests.

Phipps *et al.* (2010) applied brand equity concepts to local politicians in Australia, including characteristics such as brand loyalty, perceived quality (including leadership), brand associations (including value), brand personality and organisations, and awareness measures. They explored the influence that actively involved political consumers might have on a local politician's brand, through two case studies of Australian politicians, and focus group interviews with those involved in community groups in their electorate. The conclusion was that members of the public involved in communicating groups help to advocate for the brand locally, though not all politicians utilise this resource. Community brand equity is important to individual politicians at local level. Active members of the public who are well connected in the electorate help develop a politician's community brand equity through word-of-mouth advocacy; they help to convey positive messages. Thus local politicians can use volunteers and members to help build a positive brand equity over time.

Swanson (2012, 72) notes that, at local and state level government candidates' use of political marketing professional services is limited by budget constraints. Thus Dawn Steele, who operates Steelegrafix in the town of Manchester in Michigan, provides a smaller-scale designing and printing service for yard signs, campaign posters, direct mail and flyers for local candidates paying for their own campaign and, with a tiny budget of a few hundred dollars, cannot invest in strategic design. Thus not all political marketing techniques filter through the whole system. Given the smaller budgets, and focus of local businesses on being printers who produce a small number of signs without integrating political marketing concepts or strategic thinking, branding may not permeate local levels of political behaviour. Nevertheless, Swanson notes that Joshua Claflin, President of Garrison Everest which is a design firm in Denver is still trying 'to bring graphic design down from the Olympian heights of presidential politics' (74) and branding may help create differentiation with competitors. Thus the same principles of creating a vision, making sure it is unique and can convey a narrative are as important to local candidates as they are to presidential candidates.

Cogrove's (2014) analysis discusses how US candidates can use personal political branding at state level, creating a differentiated, individualised brand that responds to new emerging segments other candidates might not have responded to. Candidates need to make sure their brand has policies that appeal to new and core voters and reassures voters they can risk switching to their new brand. Personal branding allows the candidate to sell themselves to the voters instead of trying to sell a party and can therefore enable candidates to win in states where their party does not normally succeed.

Branding parties

Parties as well as leaders need to have effective brands; if they succeed in creating and maintaining an effective brand image this helps new leaders succeed in presidential, federal and national elections, even in political systems such as the US where parties are thought to be weaker than in countries like the UK. Until the decline of the George W. Bush brand, Republican branding in the US had maintained a superior position since branding under Reagan in the 1980s. Cosgrove (2012, 110) argues that Ronald Reagan created such a positive brand heritage around themes such as a strong national defence, free market

Authors' corner 4.2

Branded Conservatives
By Ken Cosgrove
Published in 2007 by Peter Lang Publishing

I never thought I'd see the impeachment of a sitting president and all through the process and after kept asking myself: 'Why did they do that?' Gradually the answer became clear: Republicans impeached Bill Clinton because it was what their customers wanted and their brand promised. Republicans had used branding in this case like any company would and had been doing so for years. Most interestingly, those in the party using these tools the most frequently and most innovatively were from the party's conservative wing. Thus was born the book *Branded Conservatives*.

The conservatives branded everything about their movement and the party they came to dominate with the result that their movement became the driving force in American politics from at least 1980 until 2008. The movement had the ideal face: Ronald Reagan. He combined the skills of an actor, baseball announcer and product pitchman. Reagan was the movement's best salesman. He remains a key part of the brand's heritage, and most contemporary Republicans endeavor to build fellowship with Reagan personally, politically and when selling policy. It is important to have such a face when developing a political brand.

Branding let the conservatives present their ideas clearly, concisely and emotively. It helped them to cut through the background noise of American life to hit their audience targets efficiently while marketing a line of variegated products to their customers, all of which shared a common brand. Branding's impact was amplified because conservatives adapted many technological innovations to politics. Plus, the many conservative groups working on specific issues allowed the movement to easily reach diverse audiences and thus was perfectly suited to the age of niche narrowcasting and segmentation.

The Republican experience shows a great political brand's ability to build a coherent package for the voter about a party and its candidates. It can build deep consumer loyalty, emotive ties and enduring relationships with the party that can insure immediate and lasting electoral success. To be a great brand, the product has to work and promises made have to be kept. The party's current woes show the impact of product failures and broken promises, absent which there might not be a Tea Party and the Democrat's leftward shift might not have worked. It takes years of hard work to build a great political brand and only a few visible missteps to destroy one.

Republicans were early adopters of new marketing technologies through early 2000s but failed be so in the web 2.0 world. Plus, their major competitor was out of power from 2000 forward and had plenty of time to study the Republican brand and how it had produced political success. The Republicans, on the other hand, were consumed by governing and became internally fractious. A Republican Party that once was an innovative force in political marketing found itself by 2012, behind in understanding new technologies and growing its market share with the result that its brand's power is not what it used to be.

economics, weak regulatory and social states, and family values which lasted for decades. Cosgrove describes his book on *Branded Conservatives* in Author's corner 4.2, which explains the impact that branding can have on a major political party's electoral fortunes.

Cinar (2011) discusses how the Turkish AKP (Justice and Development Party) won a third term in office with an increase in votes by creating a party brand that was about being trustworthy, reliable and capable of satisfying the electorate's demands through its successful delivery in government, but also co-ordinating all members in the party into an organisation built around the leader, Recep Tayyip Erdogan. Individual candidates 'were treated as personnel at the service of the party' (Cinar 2011, 108). The campaign focused on what the party brand overall would deliver rather than the qualities of individual candidates. This can cause problems for local politicians who have to fit in with the central party brand, and candidate branding will be potentially constrained by the party brand. Hughes and Dann (2010, 86) notes how, in Australia, the Liberal Party lost several popular local members in 2007 as the party leader John Howard declined in popularity. Leaders are still important to the party brand, even when they have left office (French and Smith 2010, 470).

Movements can also use branding; Miller (2014) argues that the success of the Tea Party was due partly to their use of branding as it helped citizens understand the goals and functions of the movement through memorable beliefs and tactics and played on the beliefs of individual Americans related to spending and taxing. Movements might even be able to utilise branding more easily than parties as they have a more focused, niche market, and thus branding might empower non-party organisations to compete with established political parties as they can use branding to generate support quickly.

Party branding is not always as easy to implement as it might seem in theory. Lees-Marshment (2012, 186) explored how, in New Zealand, when the Labour Party was thrown into opposition in 2008 it sought to reconnect with its internal and external market and sent a survey on branding to its members which asked them what values they wanted to see associated with the party. Options ranged from artistic, diverse, trusted and practical to edgy, sophisticated and vibrant. They were also asked to describe Labour in no more than six words, whom the brand should appeal to and how it should be visually represented. However, by the time of the election no new brand had appeared; there were a few distinctive policy positions but the party lacked an overall vision and seemed more focused on stopping what the National government was doing. Nevertheless parties do succeed in repositioning their brand. Case Study 4.3 by Lorann Downer shows through interviews with party figures, how the Australian Labor party made a cognizant attempt to rebrand the party and developed a new logo as part of a comprehensive and co-ordinated call to action to voters. It also demonstrates the importance of communication as carefully designed logos can help tell the story of a revamped brand.

Maintaining the party brand once in government is also difficult as the political brand then has to deliver. White and de Chernatony (2002, 50) argue that the UK New Labour brand 'came to be devalued when some of the important promises made were not delivered'. The brand promise in 1997 had been vague: it 'aimed to reassure, to allay fears and to convince the electorate that Labour would provide a new kind of government'. Despite effective communication, the difference between government talk and public perception of reality created negative feelings towards the whole brand.

Despite the success of the Obama candidate brand, Conley (2012, 129) argues that the Democratic party itself has struggled to adopt and link with it. In the 2010 midterm elections, the Democrat candidates running for US Senate did not connect that much with President Obama and his economic policies, for example; and there was a lack of unity in the content of their websites. This is reflective of Obama's sliding popularity and the challenge of

---

Conley's five principles of successful party branding

1 **Market research**

Parties must develop a clear understanding of the changing contours of the public's opinion of itself; including past, current and future perceptions; and then identify those segments of the public with which the party can relate and build a lasting relationship.

2 **Brand design**

The party should design and modify brand concepts in response to this research, creating a brand based on market desires as well as the party's unique history and political identity.

3 **Brand implementation**

The brand concept must reflect the input of the internal market to get support and then a broad section of a party's leadership and membership. Once established the party brand will function as a mechanism for co-ordinating the party's activities. So brand co-ordinators must develop mechanisms through which they test and gather feedback on working brand concepts from all stakeholders.

4 **Brand communication and management**

The brand must become the main prism through which the party interacts with, and is understood by, the public and be the vehicle through which the party will, when necessary, reposition itself with its target audiences.

5 **Brand delivery**

A party's brand, its promises, ideals and images must permeate the party's behaviour and be delivered in government in order to create brand loyalty.

Figure 4.5

Source: Adapted from Conley (2012, 131)

branding in government. However Conley (2012, 130) also argues that the lack of coherent Democratic brand was also a result of ineffective centralised party organisation or strategising, given that different data indicate approval from 80 per cent of registered Democrats and his economic populism remained broadly popular with the public at large up to 2010. Party branding may be harder for a party like the Democrats because of its decentralised structure and culture. Conley thus argues there are five principles of successful party branding: see Figure 4.5.

Cosgrove (2012) notes that the US republican branding under Reagan, whilst successful until George W. Bush, emerged from the top level which helped ensure consistency; but a strong party brand can make it difficult for new leaders or candidates to create their own unique identify or to rebrand the party in light of defeat. Indeed, party brands are longer-lasting than leadership or candidate brands, and are thus hard to change. Lloyd (2006) examined the uses of branding in the 2005 UK General Election and found that voters' associations with brands were predicated on previous party behaviour at past elections, not just what the parties offered in 2005 – showing the longevity of brand image. However, the leaders' behaviour had affected perceptions of the party brand – e.g. perceptions that Blair had misled the electorate over the war had coloured perceptions of the New Labour brand; and the Lib Dem leader Charles Kennedy's appearances on television comedy shows encouraged participants to dismiss the brand as not being serious enough. Although it is important to consider the brand of the party, separate from leader and individual candidates, they can all influence each other.

Policy, government and programme branding

Branding can be used to help gain support for leader's policies, their government, and government programmes. US Presidents have utilised branding to sell policies to the range of stakeholders they need to get support to get legislation passed, such as Congress, but also lobbyists, the media and the public themselves. Barberio (2006) outlines principles of presidential policy branding – see Figure 4.6.

Barberio's principles of presidential policy branding

1   Appeal to universally desired values such as strength, reliability and fairness.
2   Make claims and offer a comparison about how the policy more fully provides these values, or how the competition's offering is completely devoid of these values.
3   Encourage the consumer to see a benefit beyond the one immediately evident in the policy offered, either directly or indirectly by the use of symbols.

Figure 4.6

Source: Adapted from Barberio (2006)

Barberio (2006) argues that examples of presidential policy brands include 'The Square Deal', 'The New Deal', 'The Great Society' and 'No Child Left Behind' and are used by presidents to gain public support before engaging in traditional political combat with organisations and institutions. After all, the media and members of Congress are influenced by public opinion too. Well-thought-out phrases help to convey the values of the brand, and create symbols that resonate with voters and their values. Presidents then draw on staff in the White House Offices of Communications, Public Liaison and Media Liaison to help communicate the brand. Fritz *et al.* (2004, 19) note how the George W. Bush administration integrated 'softer, female-friendly language' within the president's speeches to suit target markets – such as 'employers' instead of 'business', 'moms and dads' in place of 'parents', and 'tax relief' rather than 'tax cuts'. However, policy branding is not fail-proof. Barberio (2006) observes that branding did not work for President George W. Bush when he tried to implement new social security reforms, despite 'the trappings of branding including high value content and phrasemaking featuring "personal" rather than "private" accounts'.

Cosgrove (2012, 114–15) argues that the Canadian Conservatives attempted to brand the government under Harper, focusing on economic policy to stimulate the economy through Canada's Economic Action Plan with its own logo featuring multicoloured arrows upward and a consistent font for its verbiage with both official languages. However government branding is not always easy and Cosgrove explores problems in the branding of the first Obama administration as he struggled to deliver promises or show quick progress in areas such as the stimulus or health care, thus failing to generate public awareness of and support for the Obama Administration brand. Both policies were complex and the President's proposals faced internal opposition within the legislature, making it hard to convey the values and benefits of such policies and thus the connection with Obama's government brand. This in turn made it harder to pass the legislation in Congress. Cosgrove

(2012, 116) contends that 'Candidate Obama represents an excellent model of what works in branded politics, but President Obama is more of a cautionary tale about branding's pitfalls'. Government branding can also attract controversy, blurring the line between government and partisan work – the Canadian media critiqued use of the 'Harper Government' brand, noting how public servants were being asked use the term 'Harper Government' to announce federal funding, policies and government projects in more than 500 news releases in the first seven months of 2013, breaching the principle of the bureaucracy being neutral (Naumetz, 2013).

Government services or programmes are also branded. Marsh and Fawcett (2011, 516–18) note how the Investors in People (IIP) standard which recognised employers that adapt good practice in people management was recently named a business super-brand. It originated from the UK government and the organisation IIP UK is responsible for promoting and developing the standard and has secured licence agreements with over 20 other countries. Procurement solutions, such as OGC buying.solutions (an agency of the UK Office of Government Commerce) – designed to improve the process for nationally sourced commodity goods and services in central government and the public sector (schools, health services, local councils) – is another example which actively sought to increase recruitment and retention of public sector customers through relaunching its brand, in April 2009, as one unified service. The government stated openly that the aim was to simplify the brand and make it more meaningful to customers, showing how there is a strong awareness of the benefits of branding in the public sector. The UK government also sought advice from a branding consultant and created a plan to market the Gateway Review Process to the UK and then overseas. A Brand Assurance Team was established in 2007 to ensure that when it was franchised the overall brand was maintained (see also Marsh and Fawcett 2012). Marsh and Fawcett suggest a number of principles for effective programme branding: see Figure 4.7.

Lastly, international organisations also use branding to advance their policy goals. Marsh and Fawcett (2011) argue that branding both labels and simplifies communication of a programme and thereby increases awareness and attractiveness of the policy package. They cite Ogden *et al.* (2003, 184) who notes how the WHO developed a programme on

---

Marsh and Fawcett principles for effective government programme branding

1   The brand should only be adopted after all relevant stakeholders are aware of its nature and have been extensively consulted.
2   Extensive documentation must be provided about the brand so that it will remain intact through franchising.
3   A Brand Assurance Team should be established to involve all relevant stakeholders.
4   The government department needs to show continued commitment to the brand.
5   There should be reviews of the policy to enable the exchange of best practice and policy learning which can help reinvigorate and strengthen the brand.
6   Franchisees need to be free to adapt the overarching brand to meet their needs as long as they accept the broad principles of the system.

Figure 4.7

Source: Adapted from Marsh and Fawcett (2012, 335).

turbuculosis that was 'explicitly intended to develop a policy package that was simple and marketable to policy makers and programme implementers'.

City and nation branding

Branding is also used to define and promote cities and nations. Place branding helps manage perceptions about regions and cities to attract tourists, new residents, and investors in the area. Eshuis *et al*. (2013, 507) note how measures to improve the management of space, organisations and finances to improve the area in relation to what people want help to create a better place which can then be promoted. Here, political branding merges with a governance strategy encompassing development, which requires working with a range of stakeholders with divergent needs and wants including hotels, the tourist board, museums, major companies and local government. City branding is not easy as designing and implementing the changes needed to rebrand can also create power struggles; Eshuis *et al*. (2013, 509) note that 'when municipal departments such as planning departments are confronted with new place marketing agencies that want to make city development more market oriented, they may be inclined to protect their turf and resist collaboration'.

Political marketing intersects international relations with nation branding, which applies the same principles to create a more positive brand and international perception of a whole country. Nation branding is a relatively new and under-researched area of academic research (Hulsse 2009; Fan 2008) but is increasingly important to help countries compete in a competitive global marketplace as a positive brand can help businesses consider investing, tourists contemplate visiting, and professionals decide to emigrate to a nation. Fan (2008, 155–56) argues that a nation's brand consists of three elements: a political brand, an economic brand and a cultural brand. A nation brand is how a country is seen in the mind of international stakeholders, and like party and leader brands, may be influenced by a range of factors including the place, culture, language, history, food, fashion, tourists' experiences, companies and famous people from that nation such as celebrities, actors and sports men and women.

Nation branding is particularly important for countries with an unfavourable image due to historical culture, wars or poor human rights records. Even if a country has changed its behaviour and systems, nation branding is needed to help update outdated images held by the rest of the world otherwise no one will notice or believe changes have really occurred. Fan (2008) argues that South Korea and Spain did this in the 1980s and 1990s, and now China is trying to do the same with the Beijing Olympics 2008 and Shanghai World Expo 2010, adding soft power to economic and military power. New Zealand has been branded as '100 per cent pure' and the national airline, Air New Zealand, has been connected with movies *The Lord of the Rings* and *The Hobbit* to increase tourism. Hulsse (2009, 294 and 302) observes how in Germany marketing has permeated foreign policy to help achieve economic goals. The slogan 'Germany – Land of Ideas' was adopted in the run-up to the 2006 football world cup, and various communications initiatives were launched around it including a 'Walk of Ideas in Berlin': a guide to over 350 locations developing innovative ideas and a welcoming film produced by the foreign ministry featuring a German model. Branding can help countries reposition themselves to remove historically negative perceptions and give them a competitive advantage in areas such as foreign investment, trade, education and tourism.

There is also an important international relations aspect to nation branding as it is an important tool in a nation's soft power which can help forge constructive relationships as an alternative way to achieve international goals. According to Fan (2008, 157) 'nation branding provides a more focused, culturally unbiased and more useful approach to creating international influence in the world' which is more effective than soft power public diplomacy discussed by scholars such as Nye (1990).

As with all other areas of branding, nation branding is not without difficulties. Nation brands, like party brands, are built up over decades and create strong brand heritages. A negative nation brand is hard to change, yet a positive nation brand can be quickly damaged. Individuals and individual companies can influence a nation's brand very positively, but if they run into difficulties this can then damage the overall brand of the whole nation, causing governments to intervene in business. In August 2013 the New Zealand brand was undermined by the Fonterra company's discovery of contamination of a component used in their manufacturing of baby formula. As Fonterra was such a big company in New Zealand, and associated with the national brand, this damaged the overall image of the country's dairy industry, not just that specific company, which led to a ban on all dairy produce from New Zealand from some countries such as Russia; and the Kiwi dollar fell for one day. The government held crisis meetings about the issue, and sent its own officials into Fonterra facilities in New Zealand and Australia, trying to control the crisis because it threatened the trade reputation of the whole nation, not just that company.

Maintaining and rebranding political brands

Practitioner perspective 4.4 on maintaining political brands

Iconic brands in politics follow similar patterns to iconic brands in the marketplace . . . what had been a good Tony, became a bad Tony. The idealisation is always followed by denigration . . . in the marketplace we do brand tracking . . . when a product or a service loses its way, if it has any sense, it instantly starts to re-engage with its customers and find out what's gone on in their psychological process that's made them leave. In Blair's case . . . it was that he hadn't, that he wasn't there for the British people, seen to be hanging about with George Bush more than he was hanging out with us.

Roy Langmaid, Consultant from Promise, UK, advisor to UK Labour 2004–2005

Source: Lees-Marshment (2011, 67–8)

To enjoy continued success, branding has to change over time. Cosgrove (2007) argues that the Republican loss of seats in the 2006 midterm elections was because of problems in delivery, but also because the Republicans 'added nothing to their brand since 2002 that was relevant to the voters' concerns. In such a circumstance, consumers will always start to look for something different and it is for this reason that old products must go away while new ones must be added.'

Rebranding in politics is very difficult yet can be crucial when a brand has attracted negative associations or a new direction is being pursued by a leader or nation that has yet to be noticed by the public. Political brands, like party ideology, are long-standing and hard to change because past behaviour creates a brand heritage (Smith 2009, 215). We can see this in the UK where Labour was perceived as incompetent in the 1980s–1990s; and the Conservatives too rough and nasty after the Thatcher-Major Government, and new party leaders such as Neil Kinnock or William Hague struggled to change the perception of their brand despite redesigning the product significantly. A party's failure in government can haunt it for a long time in opposition. After losing power in 1997, the new leader of the

UK Conservatives, William Hague, tried to change the overall brand of his party, utilising significant research and changing its organisational structure as well as communications style. Hague and the party were pictured in counter-intuitive situations to convey the message that the party had changed: Hague visited the multicultural Notting Hill Carnival, and his team were pictured in baseball caps with the 'fresh start' logo at an adventure park, trying to suggest a party that was pro ethnic minorities, women and youth and that accepted nontraditional lifestyles. However, the public was reluctant to believe this new approach, it failed to attract public support, and the rebranding strategy was abandoned midterm (Lees-Marshment 2008, 216). Smith (2009, 224) notes how in politics the nature of the market means that often just one leading political brand will control perceptions of brands including those of the competitive, and often the opposition parties find it very hard to develop their brand personality.

Negativity which is strongly attached to a party brand has to be removed before rebranding can be begun, or just a single image can reactivate the negativity in the public mind. Smith (2009, 212) notes how, because the public's concept of a political brand is created by lots of different things: 'the stimulus of seeing Tony Blair on television can activate from memory other associations such as the Labour Party, Cherie Blair, weapons of mass destruction and the case for going to war in Iraq'. French and Smith's (2010, 469–70) analysis in 2007 of political brand equity found that the key branded features for the Conservatives were David Cameron, representing middle/upper classes, and the former leader Margaret Thatcher who had not been in power since 1990. For Labour it was Gordon Brown, being a party for the working class, and Tony Blair. That, for both parties, former leaders remained an important part of the brand, shows how difficult it is to reposition a brand and change voter perception. The Thatcher association presented a big challenge for the Conservatives in particular to rebrand itself as a more modern centre-right party, given that she had been out of office for 17 years and respondents in their research were young and five leaders have been in place since her.

Thus if a leader wants to reposition and rebrand their party they need to engage in a careful, sustained and coherent effort. When UK New Labour was developed under Tony Blair's leadership, significant steps were taken to remove negative associations with the party that had lost it successive elections, such as high taxes and anti-aspiration, and replace them with key fixed policies that repositioned the brand in a new direction. Similarly Stephen Harper, leader of the Canadian Conservatives when they lost in 2004, initiated a rebranding exercise for the 2006 election, appealing to Quebec voters in particular (Pare and Berger, 2008, 51).

When David Cameron, who was the fourth Conservative leader since the party lost power in 1997, took over as leader in 2005 he sought to decontaminate the UK Conservative brand before rebuilding it; conceding past weaknesses and mistakes and that the party needed to change how it was perceived (see Lees-Marshment and Pettitt 2010, 122; Smith 2009, 210). He then focused on policy areas such as environmentalism and social welfare which the party was not normally associated with, connecting photo opportunities with action days and policy announcements so that communication and behaviour consistently conveyed the new brand position. However, the overall effectiveness of this has to be questioned given that the party did not win enough support to win a majority government in 2010 and had to enter coalition, despite the first past the post electoral system in the UK; and Christopher Pich discusses this in Case study 4.4, suggesting that that the political brand's identity revealed contradictions and tensions as well as success. Pich's research explored the brand identity of the UK Conservative brand under Cameron using in-depth interviews with party stakeholders and suggests that the Cameron brand needs to become more integrated to reach its full potential.

However, it is harder to rebrand when in office than in opposition. Governing is not easy and events tarnish and threaten the integrity of the brand. Smith (2009, 216–17) notes how problems occur 'when events are linked together in the memory of voters to form a wider pattern (schema) from which a basic personality trait is observed'. Thus with UK New Labour their original brand personality of trustworthiness and honest was threatened by a series of high-profile issues including an issue over donations by Bernie Eccleston and others for peerage titles, fast-tracking of passports for the Hinduja brothers, unfounded claims about WMD in Iraq; and you could add, more recently in 2008, rows over MPs' expense claims. Being in office presents constraints: politicians can't rebrand, redesign, restrategise from new as there is a recent history that the public, opposition and media will seize upon if they decide to change direction suddenly for no good reason. Yet freshness is important, otherwise people lose the need to vote for a politician again; Smith and French (2009, 218) note how 'there is a shelf-life with most brands'.

One example of a successful rebranding exercise was when the market relations company Promise (http://www.promisecorp.com) was asked by the UK Labour Party in 2004 to consider the problem of Labour's and Blair's declining public support (see Scammell 2008). The practitioner Roy Langmaid (2006), who worked for Promise, reports how they conducted brand analysis and qualitative research on the incumbent New Labour brand and the reputation of Prime Minister Tony Blair: see Practitioner Perspective 4.4. Promise found that people's needs in 2004/2005 were very different from when New Labour was first elected in 1997 and they were no longer so attracted to the New Labour brand, personified by Tony Blair. The results suggested that, in part, the problem was a decline in the public's relationship with Blair on a personal level, and he needed to reconnect in some way. Promise found that the public's idealisation of Blair in 1997 had turned into a negative view by 2005, with female voters characterising this broken relationship as a 'damaged love affair'. People felt that the New Labour/Blair brand had stopped listening. Langmaid notes how 'attributes such as competence, integrity and teamwork came through as three of the most important elements for any brand. These three issues had been undermined for voters by the perceived inability of the Prime Minister to listen (principally over Iraq), the divisiveness of the media and the infighting within the party'.

Promise advised the government to embark on four key strategies: show Team Labour through party figures other than Blair; be seen to deliver, especially domestically, and keep future promises manageable; make sure communications are unified within the brand; and reconnect the leadership. Promise (2006) notes how Blair did this through difficult discussions with live audiences on Channel 5 and on the BBC's *Question Time* where he sat through and listened to harsh public critique. It worked to improve Blair's reputation with the public. Politicians and their advisors need to monitor the brand before it is too late and be prepared to listen to good strategic suggestions for new ways to deal with old issues.

Summary

This chapter has explored how important branding is in politics and how it operates at the level of political leaders, parties, candidates and in government. Branding is strategic and communicative and includes creating an overall vision for what politicians can achieve, as well as forging long-term relationships with the public. Political brands are made up of a brand heritage from past behaviour, a vision, a personality with key characteristics like honesty and openness, and need to connect with target markets and deliver in power. Political brands also need to be maintained, and rebranded if needed though this is not easy given the long-term nature of brands. Figure 4.8 presents a best practice guide to doing political branding. Like most marketing techniques and concepts, as Scammell (2008, 109–10) observes, 'branding is not the elusive magic bullet to political success. There is no magic formula' but there are some key principles for success. Political branding is a growing area of political practice, and even though there are no practitioners specialising in it, staff who work in research, strategy and communications all intersect with it. The practitioner profile

Best practice guide to doing political branding

1 Understand that a political brand is an overarching feeling and impression the public has of a politician, political organisation, government or nation.
2 Public perceptions of political brands are created by experience of, and communication about, the brand from a range of sources over time which creates a brand heritage that is not easy to control or change.
3 Accept that all political figures/organisations can be seen as a brand.
4 Use political branding to change or maintain reputation, create a feeling of identity with a political organisation or figure and create a more trusting relationship.
5 Make the brand clear and coherent; differentiated; reassuring; aspirational; symbolic of superior internal values; credible and competent; sincere; trustworthy.
6 Build a positive brand equity where the public is very aware of your brand, loyal to it, consider it positively and ensure it creates positive associations.
7 Political leaders need to offer a distinctive, aspirational and visionary brand.
8 Ensure the political leader has an effective brand personality such as being sincere, exciting, competent, sophisticated, strong, open and empathetic.
9 Apply the same concepts to political candidates, but also draw on community brand equity to offset fewer resources to communicate the value of the brand on offer, and try to create differentiating brand aspects that appeal to new emerging segments that other candidates might not have responded to.
10 Create and maintain a positive party brand to help support candidates; making sure it is implemented at all organisational levels so the brand remains unified.
11 Use nation branding to help promote trade, foreign investment and tourism.
12 Brand public policy to increase the chances of implementation both nationally and internationally, ensuring success by consulting and involving stakeholders, creating a brand assurance team, providing effective documentation about the brand, showing continued commitment to the brand at government department level, and leaving room for review and adaption of the brand over time.
13 Decontaminate a negative brand before rebranding, or just a single image can reactivate the negativity in the public mind; and plan for rebranding to occur over a long period with new behaviour and policy as well as communication to make it convincing.
14 Mange the political brand's product life cycle – try to ensure it delivers, especially once in power, but expect it to decline and plan to reconnect as part of a long-term brand relationship.
15 Make sure the political brand is authentic and fits with the product and behaviour and overall strategy.

Figure 4.8

below discusses the work of New Zealand consultants Judy Callingham and Brian Edwards to help build up the brand profile of Helen Clark who became Prime Minister and remained in power for nine years.

Practitioner profile 4.1

Name: Judy Callingham CNZM
Date of birth: 1944
Name: Dr Brian Edwards CNZM
Date of birth: 4 November, 1937
Most notable job: Media Advisors to Helen Clark

Description: While Brian Edwards is probably best known in New Zealand for being a media personality, it is his work alongside his wife, Judy Callingham, in media training that is most important to those studying political marketing. Since they formed their media training company, Callingham and Edwards Limited, Callingham and Edwards have trained hundreds of high-profile individuals from all sectors of society. Most notably, Edwards and Callingham worked on the public image of then-Leader of the Opposition and Labour Party leader Helen Clark in the lead-up to the 1996 election, which had been poor over the three years Clark had been leader. While Clark was initially reluctant to change, Edwards and Callingham suggested Clark change the way she projected herself in order to promote her true personal qualities. Importantly, Edwards and Callingham highlighted Clark's tendency to treat media interviews like question time in The House of Representatives; acting defensively with an uneasy smile. Edwards and Callingham decided that the answer was to boost her confidence in front of the camera, while also highlighting her need to use less harsh punctuation and punch, and be more gentle and sweet, so that the New Zealand public could warm to her. Edwards and Callingham's work with Clark was most noticeable in the debate with Prime Minister Jim Bolger, which presented clear evidence that the public was warming to Clark's seemingly transformed personality. While Clark and the Labour Party did not win the election that year, her public image was improved greatly – helping build a leadership brand base for the party's election win three years later. 'She wouldn't have survived if she hadn't. That's the guts of it,' Edwards noted during an interview in 2001. See Brian Edwards' book *Helen: Portrait of a Prime Minister* (2001), published by Exisle; and Brain Edwards and Judy Callingham's book *How to Survive and Win with the Media: A Self Defence Course for Interviewees* (2004), published by Random House New Zealand.

Discussion points

1 What is a political brand?
2 To what extent does *x* party/politician meet Needham's Criteria for Successful Brands of being simple, unique, reassuring, aspirational, value based and credible?
3 To what extent do the brand personalities of current political leaders meet Guzman and Vicenta's Principles of Effective Political Brand Personality of being capable, open and empathetic?
4 Rate the brand personality of current leaders or parties against Smith's characteristics of honesty, spirited, image, leadership, toughness and uniqueness, and discuss what this means for the likely success of the brand.
5 Define what Obama's 2008 brand of change meant, and assess to what extent it met Needham's criteria for successful brands and whether he delivered on it in power.

6 Discuss the brand equity for current parties. What is your perception of them in terms of how consumers are aware of them, are loyal to them, consider them highly and hold positive associations of them (draw on concepts by theorists such as French and Smith 2010 and Parker 2012). How successful are they and what might they try to improve?

7 Identify the key aspects of brand heritages for political parties, and discuss the positive and negative impact this has on rebranding parties and new party leaders.

8 Think of attempts to brand or rebrand political parties, such as the UK Conservatives under Cameron, UK Labour under Blair, NZ Labour under Goff onwards, the US Republicans post 2008; and discuss to what extent they followed Conley's five principles of successful party branding of researching the market, designing the brand in response, implementing it, communicating it and delivering on it.

9 Discuss whether Obama might have had an easier ride getting health care reform through if he had branded it as Barberio suggests presidential policies can be branded. How might he and other political leaders currently in power develop a brand around key policies to gain more support and credit for them?

10 Think of examples of branding in government in terms of policies or programmes. Do you think there is a strong potential for government departments to use branding?

11 Develop a plan to improve the brand of x candidate/politician/party or government, utilising a range of branding concepts, such as the brand vision, values, personality, equity, association.

12 Identify what barriers exist to changing the current brand for a candidate/politician/party or government and how you might seek to overcome them, drawing on theories and the Blair rebranding case in 2005.

Assessment questions

Essay/exam

1 What is political branding and why do politicians and political organisations use it? Utilise theories and empirical examples in your answer.

2 Why do some political brands succeed and others fail? Utilise different concepts and tools of branding in your answer, alongside discussion of a range of empirical cases.

3 Discuss and critique the effectiveness of the brands of current politicians or parties, using the Needham criteria.

4 Discuss what brand personality is and assess how effectively political leaders develop a positive brand personality.

5 Given the challenges for local candidates to use branding, noted by Swanson (2012), how can local politicians develop an effective political brand for themselves?

6 Explore and review the brands of three political parties.

7 Compare and contrast branding by political leaders, parties and candidates, noting similarities, differences and challenges between branding in the three areas.

8 'Candidate Obama represents an excellent model of what works in branded politics, but President Obama is more of a cautionary tale about branding's pitfalls' (Cosgrove 2012, 116). Discuss this statement in light of US President Obama's (or any other president/prime minister's) brand when campaigning and in government.

9 Critically evaluate attempts by cities to create a positive brand.

10   Discuss and critique the use of nation branding in terms of its effectiveness to improve international trade and tourism, considering the potential as well as limitations of branding nations.

11   'Nation branding provides a more focused, culturally unbiased and more useful approach to creating international influence in the world' (Fan 2008, 157). To what extent is Fan correct that nation branding is more effective in promoting positive international relations than public diplomacy?

12   To what extent is it possible to rebrand a leader or a party? Discuss both the potential and limitations using a range of examples.

Applied

1   Assess the effectiveness of the brand of a candidate, politician, party, government or political organisation using Needham's Criteria for Successful Brands.

2   Assess the brand equity of a candidate, politician, party, government or political organisation using concepts by theorists such as French and Smith (2010) and Parker (2012).

3   Drawing on the theories by Smith (2009) and/or Guzman and Vicenta (2009) to evaluate the effectiveness of the political brand personality of a politician (such as honesty, spiritedness, image, leadership, toughness and uniqueness; and/or capability, openness and empathy), and make suggestions for how they might improve it in future.

4   Compare and contrast the brand of five local politicians to draw conclusions about political branding at the local level.

5   Create a branding plan for a local politician or candidate to develop or improve their political brand, taking account of the challenges for local candidates to use branding noted by Swanson (2012), but drawing on ideas from research such as Phipps *et al.* (2010) if not any *theory* of political branding.

6   Assess the political brand of *x* political parties, utilising Conley's five principles of successful party branding, determining what they are succeeding on and what they need to improve – and how they should do this.

7   Apply Barberio's (2006) Principles of Presidential Policy Branding to Obama's marketing of his health-care plan after being elected in 2008 to provide a balanced critique of the branding of health care.

8   Identify examples of branding used by government departments to brand government programmes; and drawing on Marsh and Fawcett's (2012) principles for effective government programme branding, assess their effectiveness and make recommendations for improvement in future.

9   Apply principles of branding to a city to explore the effectiveness of the city's brand and make suggestions for how it might be further developed.

10   Assess the effectiveness of nation branding by your country, making recommendations for improvement in future.

11   Explain and critique the intervention by the New Zealand Government in Fonterra's discovery of contamination of a component used in their manufacturing of baby formula in the context of nation branding.

12   Evaluate the extent to which an elected political leader such as US President Obama succeeded in maintaining his positive brand in 2008 in government once elected, drawing on both theory and empirical analysis to support your assessment.

13   Political brands often fail to deliver or decline once a leader has won power. Identify and discuss failed political brands in office, and draw lessons from them that future leaders may use to avoid such problems in office.

14   Create a plan for rebranding a politician who has been in power for more than one term, drawing on theory and empirical examples for what might work as well as what to avoid.

CASE STUDIES

Case study 4.1 Everything in moderation: the brand of the New Zealand Green Party in the 2011 election

By Jack Davies, The University of Auckland
jdav335@aucklanduni.ac.nz

Political branding has much do to with how a political party is perceived overall. Branding is relative to the comprehensive perception of the party; it goes to the psychological aspect of voters' perceptions and helps distinguish a party's values and policies from those of its competitors. Branding establishes a social connection between parties and voters, it goes not only to the rational part of ourselves but also to the irrational and emotional. As such, branding can be a powerful tool when parties aim to market themselves to potential voters.

The Green Party of Aotearoa New Zealand is an environmentalist party situated on the left of the political spectrum, and has struggled to enter parliament in most elections since its inception. However, with 11 per cent of the popular vote and 14 MPs elected, the result of the 2011 general election ushered in a new era of prosperity for the New Zealand Green Party. In 2011, it also changed its brand, utilising a more moderate overtone, but still holding its trademark environmental tinge. This case study looks at the empirical evidence from the Greens' campaign in concert with Needham's (2005) criteria for successful political branding to assist in explaining this surge in support, for what was once a party considered by many to be doomed to the left fringe of the New Zealand political spectrum.

'It's the economy, stupid!'

With an unemployment rate of around 6.5 per cent, the economy dominated the 2011 election. The Greens presented a lucid solution to the economic woes of Kiwis with a succinct 'tagline': 'jobs, rivers and kids'. While conveying to voters the Greens' environmental focus, they provided also a resonant picture of what the Greens would focus on should they be elected to government: unemployment, child poverty and fresh water quality. This aligns with Needham's principle that a clear, simple message is desirable for parties. The other strapline often used was 'For a richer New Zealand', which epitomized the Greens' new brand: a rich standard of living coupled with sustainable economic growth. Succinct, inoffensive branding such as this potentially helped to court moderate voters without jettisoning traditional conservationist supporters.

Though for many years the Greens have been regarded as ethical, if innocuous, by many New Zealanders, Co-Leader Metiria Turei stated they needed to change their brand from that of an outright environmental party to one which embraces a variety of 'modern, progressive politics', competent on economic issues. Given their past which tended to focus on ecological issues, far removed from the political mainstream, the Greens, to create an impression of competence, released three detailed policy documents clearly showing their solutions for many of New Zealand's economic problems; 2011's emphasis on 'jobs, rivers and kids', rather than 2008's 'climate change, peak oil and food safety', coupled with comprehensive policy plans, arguably created an improved aura of competency for the Greens. As Needham states, parties must be perceived as capable of delivering on campaign promises.

Despite the Greens seeking to hold a mainstream economic focus in 2011, they still managed to retain a 'green' countenance of sustainability. Their employment scheme emphasised that the 'economy *is* our environment' and so by making post-materialist issues relevant, they were able to achieve a semblance of economic proficiency coupled with ecological awareness. This is the balance however, that the Greens will need to perpetuate if they are to maintain support.

Too much stress on the environment will likely isolate moderates whereas straying too far from their roots will quarantine their base. Uniqueness and differentiation served their interests well in the election.

'For a richer New Zealand'

The Greens' campaign also sought to reassure voters that they contested the election on moral and ethical grounds. To this extent many of their policies were branded with having New Zealand's best interests in mind. Utilizing influential Kiwi actor Robyn Malcolm, they lambasted the governing National Party as a pack of short-term sellouts, with National's flagship 'Mixed Ownership' model's only purpose being to make a quick buck. The Greens further emphasised the need for sustainable infrastructure in contrast to National's preoccupation with fossil fuels, and drew attention to New Zealand's undesirable position in the OECD child poverty rankings. This assisted in convincing voters that the Greens do have New Zealanders' best interests at heart, and are perhaps the most ethically scrupulous party on the spectrum.

The Greens' 'strapline' on their billboards of 'For a richer New Zealand', successfully conveyed a sense of aspiration and hope to their target audience. This double entendre was used to not only portray a goal of economic growth and success, but one of a picturesque quality of life. This tagline was featured on each of the Greens' billboards in the election along with one of two pictures. One showed a child fishing in a river, another was of a family at a wind farm. Considering this combination, the Greens' ultimate aim of a sustainable New Zealand was successfully conveyed along with a message that was friendly to business.

Finally, the Greens' campaign reflected ecological values that have been with them since their inception, as well as more moderate, pro-business values which would resound with a wider audience. This balance was perhaps best seen in their billboards. While using emotive, natural imagery to illustrate that they are still striving for a sustainable, green New Zealand with clean industry, the tagline of a 'richer New Zealand' also reached out to voters with real concerns about the economy. While this lead to dissent from traditional supporters who feared the Greens were moving too far from their original roots, the balance struck can be seen as a moderate one. Indeed, 2011's brand successfully positioned the Greens as still holding environmental values, concerned about New Zealand's ecological status but also realistic about its economic issues; that is, the party is still green but is allowing for a degree of entrepreneurship and materialism to appeal to a wider base.

Lessons for political marketing

The evidence from the Greens' campaign strongly emphasises the impact that a positive, moderate and optimistic brand can have on voters. By countering their former radicalism with an economic focus, they achieved far more successful results than in previous elections. As voters are told to place faith and trust in parties, having a brand that is both aspirational and reassuring is very important. Moreover, a balance must be sought between balancing unique, traditional values with those with general appeal, likely to resound with a wider audience. In the case of the Greens in 2011, aspiration, hope and a policy of 'moderation in all things' was undoubtedly successful.

Further reading

Needham, Catherine (2005). 'Brand leaders: Clinton, Blair and the limitations of the permanent campaign'. *Political Studies*, 53(2): 343–61.

Turei, Metiria (2012). 'The Greens'. In Jon Johansson and Stephen Levine (eds) *Kicking The Tyres: The New Zealand General Election and Electoral Referendum of 2011*. Wellington: Victoria University Press, 135–42.

Green Party of Aotearoa New Zealand (n.d.). 'The History of the Green Party'. http://www.greens. org.nz/page/history-green-party (accessed April 7, 2013)

ONE News (2011). 'Greens clear campaign reaps success'. *TVNZ*, 24 November. http://tvnz.co.nz/election-2011/greens-clear-campaign-reaps-success-4575592 (accessed April 9, 2013)

Edwards, Bryce (2012). 'For a richer New Zealand: environmentalism and the Green Party in the 2011 New Zealand general election'. *Liberation*. http://liberation.typepad.com/liberation/2012/05/for-a-richer-new-zealand-environmentalism-and-the-green-party-in-the-2011-new-zealand-general-electi.html (accessed April 9, 2013)

Case study 4.2 How political branding affects politics: studies of Hassan Rouhani's political co-branding strategy

By Mitra Naeimi, Lund University

mitra.naeimi@gmail.com

This case study explores the branding strategies employed by Rouhani's campaign during the Iranian presidential election of 2013. It argues that, although all candidates of the 2013 election – except Saeed Jalili – attempted to say that they are new, generally they failed to introduce new brands, since the consumers perceived most of them as very similar to the 'Ahmadinejad' brand. However, by running with some new values, Rouhani established a new political personal brand. Moreover, the Construction and Reformist parties both co-branded a new brand, Rouhani, that Rouhani's campaign tied to Moderation. While the strategy was successful in wining this election, political marketing has not developed in Iran very well and campaign strategists might not be aware of the branding effects of their political strategies on long-term politics.

According to many scholars of political marketing, marketing principles of branding can be applied to politics. Many researchers and practitioners of this field of studies had particularly used branding strategies in politics and developed interdisciplinary theories such as political personal branding, political branding equity, nation branding, and so on. The presidential campaign of Hassan Rouhani attempted to build a political personal brand and also employed a co-branding strategy.

According to marketing theories, a personal brand consists of four elements: attributes, promised benefits, values and persona (Keller, 1993). Another strategy in political branding is co-branding. According to marketing theorists, co-branding is when two or more brands of different marketing organisations join in one product to increase sales (Keller, 1998). This transfers 'the positive associations of the partner (constituent brand) brands to a newly formed co-brand (composite brand)' (Ueltschy and Laroche, 2004, 91). This can have a win–win result for both constituent brands. However, another consequence of co-branding is that two constituent brands are merged in a new one and, thus, they can no longer exist as the independent brands that they were at the beginning.

Political marketing theorists have expanded marketing theories of personal branding to politics and, for instance, they have redefined four elements of a political personal brand as performance, promises, policies and personality. Also, in political branding terms, the alignment of two or more political personal brands can make a new political personal brand (political co-branding) (Hughes and Dann, 2011). However, this case study argues that the co-branding of two political personal brands from two different organisations into one can have negative consequences: the two constituent political parties no longer have their political personal brands, and in future elections, they will have to construct these anew.

Hassan Rouhani's political branding

The practices of political marketing have not emerged very strongly in Iran. Rouhani's campaign did not release the names of all the campaign strategists, just the advertising and media manager of his campaign: Mohammad Soltanifar is an expert in communication, but not in political marketing. Moreover, Rouhani's presidential campaign focused intensely on gathering voters' opinions and gradually had been releasing the survey's results. Considering these points, I can say that his campaign did not have a political marketing strategist. However, they have employed some branding strategies – it seems that they have taken these strategies as political strategies, and they were not aware that from a political marketing approach, their strategy is a political branding strategy.

Rouhani's campaign used the easiest strategy: distancing itself from the 'Ahmadinejad' brand, since the Rouhani campaign understood that the majority needed a new brand. The campaign chose as its slogan, 'A Spring behind the Winter'. Rouhani emphasised that he ran for 'hope' and 'prudence'. Rouhani's campaign attempted to center on issues in which Ahmadinejad was not successful. He claimed that he had better values and, since his ethics are better than his opponents', his cabinet will do a better job in nuclear issues than the current administration has done; he will fix the economy; and he will change the style of Iran's dealing with the world (foreign policy). In all issues, Rouhani enabled consumers to differentiate him from Ahmadinejad and other candidates. He gives the consumers the sense that they have one choice between Rouhani and the Ahamdinezhad brand, which encompassed the other similar brands/rivals – five conservatives and one independent. The only reformist candidate, Mohammad Reza Aref, withdrew and stood behind Rouhani in order to give reformists a single voice. Moreover, Rouhani emphasised that he is juristic in comparison with Mohammad Bagher Ghalibaf, his main rival, who was a police commander in the past. Thus, he emphasised that he has a calm and peaceful personality.

Furthermore, in his speeches and documentaries, Rouhani tied himself with two previous presidents of Iran, Rafsanjani and Khatami, while other rivals did not. Khatami – embodying the brand of Reformism – and Rafsanjani – the brand of Construction – also supported and co-branded Rouhani. In the new brand, Rouhani labeled himself a 'moderate.' Thus Rouhani's campaign built a brand that is new and different from Ahmadinejad but has a long history of Construction and Reformism behind it.

Lessons for political marketing

Although, in a political approach, the result of co-branding was a win-win for aligned brands – in a field dominated with conservatives, Rouhani won the election – from a political marketing approach, 'over time the two brands become linked together in a consumer's mind', and this can have negative results. Over time, Rafsanjani and Khatami will no longer epitomize the brands of Construction and Reformism, since their new aligned brand stands for Moderation. In future, if Reformists want to have a candidate in a presidential election, they will need a new brand instead of Khatami. Therefore, campaign strategists will have to train themselves in branding and co-branding and follow marketing theories more. Politicians should assess if they, as the brand of their parties, align with the brand of another party and stand for a new brand, what would happen for the brand of their own party.

Further reading

Hughes, A. and S. Dann (2011). *Influences and impacts of personal brand and political brand bi-directionality.* Academy of Marketing Conference, University of Liverpool, Liverpool, UK.

Keller, K. L. (1993). 'Conceptualizing, measuring and managing customer-based brand equity'. *Journal of Marketing*, 57(1): 1–23.

Keller, K. (1998). *Strategic Brand Management: Building, Meaning, and Managing Brand Equity.* Upper Saddle River, NJ: Prentice-Hall.

Ueltschy, L. C. and M. Laroche (2004). 'Co-branding internationally: everyone wins?' *Journal of Applied Business Research*, 20(3): 91–102.

Case study 4.3 Personal and party logos in the *Kevin07* campaign

By Lorann Downer, The University of Queensland
lorann.downer@uqconnect.edu.au

At the heart of the Australian Labor Party's successful campaign in the 2007 federal election was *Kevin07*, the personal brand built around then-leader Kevin Rudd. After the brand's launch in August, the *Kevin07* logo proliferated on t-shirts, websites, and social media. *Kevin07* was not the only new logo launched by Labor that year; a revamped party logo had been released some months earlier. Each logo played a role in a year-long strategy to revitalise the central brand of the country's oldest political party and craft a vote-winning personal brand for its newest leader.

Logos – along with devices like symbols and slogans – are brand elements (Keller 2008, 140). They help identify a brand, differentiate it from competitors, and make it 'memorable, meaningful and likeable' (Keller 2008, 140). They can also help build the equity, or value, of a brand and transfer equity between different brands owned by one organisation (Keller 2008, 433). These potential benefits drive logo use in both profit and non-profit settings, including politics (Spiller and Bergner 2011, 47). This case draws on interviews conducted in 2012.

The party logo
The Australian Labor Party certainly hoped to reap these benefits from the two new logos that it developed in 2007. Labor revamped its branding, including the logo, for its National Conference in April. The logo was updated, first and foremost, to refresh the party's image. In 2007 Tim Gartrell said the party's brand had 'copped a lot of damage' during eleven years in opposition. Among some voters, Labor was seen as fiscally-risky, union-dominated and outdated (Gartrell 2012). Nick Martin said the party 'had to demonstrate that we were new and different and reassuring' (2012). Reworking the party's visual imagery was an important way to communicate change (Gartrell 2012). A secondary consideration in changing the logo was to achieve a better fit with the global 'labour family' (Martin 2012).

The new logo retained some of the design elements from the previous two images, and evolved others. The logo used from 1980 to 1993 (Young 2004, 235), was a rectangle that featured a fluttering Australian flag in full colour. The full party name appeared above the flag in black, Times Roman font. A new logo was introduced in 1996 (Young 2004, 236). It 'still relies heavily on the Australian flag as a patriotic, nationalistic symbol' (Young 2004, 236) but omitted the British Union Jack apparently in deference to the republican views of then Labor Prime Minister Paul Keating (Young 2004, 236). The Southern Cross detail of the flag remains in its original white. The party name is replaced with the contraction 'ALP', in Times Roman font and picked out in white against the blue of the flag. While the palette remains the same, the colours are brighter and more contemporary. The overall design, too, has a more modern feel with a stylised flag. Finally, the shape is changed to an upright rectangle. A third logo, introduced in 2007, retains the colour palette and the Southern Cross. However, it now bears the name 'Australian Labor', with the second word larger than the first, and in Arial font. The overall design is more stylised and striking, with two blocks of colour in a rectangle.

Speaking of the 2007 logo, Martin said 'all the design elements – the red and blue squares, nice clean lines, very simple geometry – are great for materials' (2012). Research confirmed the logo looked 'clean and fresh and nice to voters' (Martin 2012). Labor hoped the voters' view of the logo would inform their view of the party itself, thereby building equity for the party's brand. The new logo also sent a message globally. 'The red square is a logo used by New Labour in

Britain and by a lot of European parties so it was really about . . . a reassertion of a labour identify as well' (Martin 2012). Thus, the new logo sought to restate Labor's identity as a party with roots in the labour movement and to show differentiation with its competitors. It also aimed to contribute to brand equity by presenting Labor as a contemporary party.

The personal logo

Shortly after the launch of the party logo, Labor started crafting another for the leader. 'Political parties as institutions in Australia are not the most popular things so there's only so far you can go with that, and that's why it was the *Kevin07* campaign' (Gartrell 2012). Rudd's personal brand was much stronger than the party's (Gartrell 2012). This meant that *Kevin07* could be employed on its own as a vote-puller, and alongside the Labor brand to help update the party's image (Gartrell 2012). As former Labor campaigner, Mike Kaiser, explained, Rudd 'described a modern inception of Labor'. 'His rhetoric around fairness, the way he linked it to his own biography, the way he used his foreign language capabilities as a way of talking about internationalising Australia – this was all Labor in a modern incarnation' (Kaiser 2012).

The *Kevin07* logo was an oblong with 'KEVIN07' squarely in the centre. The colour palette of the party logo was repeated, with 'KEVIN' in white and '07' in red, against a solid blue background. The use of the well-known Arial font and capital letters for Rudd's name attracted attention, like a friendly shout-out. The oblong shape and the background colour effectively acted as a frame for the leader's name. Overall, the design made for a strong image. The logo was designed to be 'something catchy, new and different' rather than 'the typical, clinical' offering from parties (Gartrell 2012). It was meant to appeal to middle Australia, and young people especially (Gartrell 2012). Using Rudd's first name identified and differentiated him from his competitor, Prime Minister John Howard. Using a contraction of the election year made it contemporary and purposeful. These factors, plus the serendipitous rhyming of name and year, made the logo memorable, meaningful and likeable. The logo featured prominently in Labor marketing to build equity in Rudd's personal brand. *Kevin07* was also co-branded with Labor to transfer some of the leader's positive equity to the party. Thus, the *Kevin07* logo aimed to simultaneously showcase the new leader and freshen up the party.

Lessons for political marketing

Carefully designed logos can help tell the story of a brand. One strong visual captured the essence of the personal brand of *Kevin07*, Labor's principal offering in 2007. Meantime, thoughtful evolution of the party logo helped update the narrative of the Labor brand. In addition, carefully deployed logos can do double duty. Judicious use of *Kevin07* in tandem with the Labor logo helped burnish the party's image. As Labor strategist Bruce Hawker (2012) noted: 'There was no need to be embarrassed about the Labor brand because Rudd polished it up'. The logos were part of a comprehensive and co-ordinated call to action to voters. It was a call the voters heeded, putting Rudd into the Prime Minister's office and Labor into government.

Sources and further reading

Gartrell, Tim. 2012. (*Pers. Comm.*) Former National Secretary, Australian Labor Party. Interviewed by telephone by author. March 15, Sydney, Australia.

Hawker, Bruce. 2012. (*Pers. Comm.*) Managing Director, Campaigns and Communications. Interviewed by author. March 12, Brisbane, Australia.

Jackman, Christine (2008). *Inside Kevin07: The People. The Plan. The Prize.* Carlton: Melbourne University Press.

Kaiser, Mike. 2012. (*Pers. Comm.*) Former National Assistant Secretary, Australian Labor Party and former State Secretary, Queensland branch of the Australian Labor Party. Interviewed by author. September 11, Sydney, Australia.

Keller, Kevin Lane (2008). *Strategic Brand Management: Building, Measuring and Managing Brand Equity.* New Jersey: Pearson Education Inc.

Martin, Nick. 2012. (*Pers. Comm.*) Assistant National Secretary, Australian Labor Party. Interviewed by author. October 11, Canberra, Australia.

Spiller, Lisa and Jeff Bergner (2011). *Branding the Candidate: Marketing Strategies to Win Your Vote.* Santa Barbara: Praeger.

Young, Sally (2004). *The Persuaders: Inside the Hidden Machine of Political Advertising.* North Melbourne: Pluto Press Australia.

Case study 4.4 Understanding the political brand identity and political brand image of the UK Conservative Party brand under the leadership of David Cameron prior the 2010 UK general election

By Christopher Pich, Nottingham Trent University

Christopher.pich@ntu.ac.uk

Since the demise of Margaret Thatcher, the UK Conservative Party failed to identify with the common ground Thatcher had held, resulting in an unprecedented four successful election campaigns. After three election defeats and three Conservative Party leaders, the UK Conservative Party had clearly failed in its attempt to modernise, to reinvent and to reconnect with the electorate. In December 2005, David Cameron was elected as leader of the UK Conservative Party, vowing to be different from previous leaders and arguing it was time to modernise and unite the party, making the UK Conservative Party electable again. He attempted to reshape the UK Conservative Party which was, at that time, perceived to be out of touch, focused on immigration and representative of the rich and privileged few. Party insider Lord Ashcroft's *Smell the Coffee: A Wake-up Call for the Conservative Party* (2005) warned the only way to electoral success was to address the 'largely negative brand image' of the Conservative Party.

To discuss the evolution of the Conservative brand under Cameron, this case will look at brand identity and image. *Brand identity* can be seen as the current and envisaged associations desired by the brands creator and communicated to the external audience. In contrast, *brand image* can be considered as the current associations perceived and formulated in the mind of the consumer often out of control of the brand's creator (Kapferer 2008; Nandan 2005). The concepts of brand identity and brand image are considered useful approaches to generate a deeper understanding of a brand from an internal and external perspective. Furthermore, they can be used to explore whether communication discrepancy gaps exist between the two concepts.

Despite the various conceptualisations of brand identity and brand image, these are often used interchangeably and occasionally misunderstood. Furthermore, a brand's envisaged identity may not be understood in the desired fashion, with separate viewpoints existing. Resulting discrepancy gaps need to be as small as possible and ultimately narrowed or eliminated in order for the brand to be considered strong, trusted and valued. Therefore, this highlighted an opportunity to apply the concepts of brand identity and brand image to explore the UK Conservative Party brand and addressed calls for more research in this area.

Political brand identity – internal

This research included 30 in-depth interviews with UK Conservative Party stakeholders such as Members of Parliament, Members of the House of Lords and Members of the European Parliament. It revealed that the political brand's identity was seen as complex, deep-seated and multilayered.

The research not only highlighted coherent and supportive elements but also contradictions, tensions and, more importantly, a limited understanding of the electorate and internal aspects of the UK Conservative Party brand identity. This was seen as largely to blame for the failure of the UK Conservative Party brand to communicate a coherent message and demonstrate a consistent approach in promoting the political brand prior and during the 2010 UK General Election.

Nevertheless, the findings also illustrated the profound nature of the UK Conservative Party's brand identity by revealing numerous 'sub-cultures' which not only revealed tensions but also strengthened the UK Conservative Party's 'broad church' position. This in turn suggested that the UK Conservative Party is an amalgamation of 'multiple individual identities' united by the core 'broad church' Conservative values yet it was often these 'multiple brand identities' that often undermined the UK Conservative Party brand.

Political brand image – external

Eight focus group discussions held with participants aged 18–24 years revealed that the *brand image* of the UK Conservative Party under the leadership of David Cameron was also complex without an authentic political message. Crucially, this was inconsistent with the existing literature on successful political brands. The application of brand image theory highlighted that the UK Conservative Party had made some progress in refocusing the image of their political brand; a key problem acknowledged by David Cameron in December 2005. Nonetheless, this research suggested that the UK Conservative Party had not managed to completely dispel perceptions of the party being of the rich and privileged, traditionally held associations especially in the minds of Conservative supporters and floating voters.

Moreover, this study revealed that the UK Conservative Party brand failed to clearly communicate a coherent political brand message. Furthermore, there was limited understanding about what to expect from a Conservative administration therefore external stakeholders often relied on their past knowledge to evaluate David Cameron's Conservative Party. Additionally, the findings highlighted that there are distinct 'multiple individual political brands', which add to the complex nature of political brands and have the potential to broaden the support base.

Looking forward, this analysis suggests that the UK Conservative Party brand needs to become an integrated, well-structured entity if it is to win the 2015 UK General Election. Furthermore, the UK Conservative Party brand identity requires close attention, particularly the lack of internal coherency. The UK Conservative Party brand image is ambiguous and remains associated with previously held perceptions and imagery. Nevertheless, this study provides deep insight into the brand identity and brand image of the UK Conservative Party and highlights some detoxification of the 'Tory brand'. Furthermore, this study uncovered a small number of consistencies between the brand identity and brand image of the UK Conservative Party. Subsequently, there is hope for the UK Conservative Party brand.

Lessons for political marketing

This study highlights the applicable nature of the concepts of brand identity and brand image to the political context. However, the concepts required appropriate adaption to suit the unique environment of application. The transfer potential of brand identity and brand image to the political arena can be used by political parties, politicians and candidates to understand the way in which the brand is presented to the electorate and how it is understood by them. The applied concepts will serve as a useful mechanism to identify consistency between the brand identity and brand image. An authentic brand integrates both components. Internal coherency is crucial for a clear and understandable brand identity. Furthermore, the need for consistency between projected identity and understood image is paramount and could be crucial to secure victory at impending elections.

Further reading

Ashcroft, M. A. (2010). *Minority Verdict: The Conservative Party, The Voters and the 2010 Election*, London: Biteback Publishing Ltd.

Kapferer, J. N. (2008). *The New Strategic Brand Management: Creating and Sustaining Brand Equity Long Term*. London: Kogan Page Ltd.

Nandan, S. (2005). 'An exploration of the brand identity-brand image linkage: a communications perspective'. *Journal of Brand Management*, 12(4): 264–78.

Schneider, H. (2004). 'Branding in politics – manifestations, relevance and identity-oriented management'. *Journal of Political Marketing*, 3(3), 41–67.

Smith, G. and French, A. (2009). 'The political brand: a consumer perspective'. *Marketing Theory*, 9(2): 209–26.

References

Aaker, Jennifer L. (1997). 'Dimensions of brand personality'. *Journal of Marketing Research*, 34(3): 347–56.

Barberio, Richard P. (2006). 'Branding: presidential politics and crafted political communications'. Prepared for delivery at the 2006 Annual Meeting of the American Political Science Association, 30 August–3 September 2006.

Busby, Robert (2012). 'Selling Sarah Palin: political marketing and the "Wal-Mart Mom"'. In Jennifer Lees-Marshment (ed.) *Routledge Handbook of Political Marketing*. New York: Routledge, 218–29.

Campbell, Alaistair (2013) Blair advisor, in conversation with Steve Richards. Propaganda, Power and Persuasion – British Library, Politics, the People and the Press, 17 May. http://www.youtube.com/watch?v=_Gu4ZEMOB78

Caprara, Gian Vittorio, Claudio Barbaranelli and Philip G. Zimbardo (2002). 'When parsimony subdues distinctiveness: simplified public perceptions of politicians personality'. *Political Psychology*, 23(1): 77–95.

Cinar, Menderes (2011). 'The electoral success of the AKP: cause for hope and despair'. *Insight Turkey*, 13(4): 107–27.

Conley, Brian Matthew (2012). 'The politics of hope: the democratic party and the institutionalization of the Obama brand in the 2010 mid-term elections'. In Jennifer Lees-Marshment (ed.) *Routledge Handbook of Political Marketing*. New York: Routledge, 124–35.

Cormack, Patricia (2012). 'Double-double: branding, Tim Hortons, and the public sphere'. In Alex Marland, Thierry Giasson and Jennifer Lees-Marshment (eds) *Political Marketing in Canada*. Vancouver: UBC, 209–23.

Cosgrove, Kenneth M. (2007). 'Midterm marketing: an examination of marketing strategies in the 2006, 2002, 1998, and 1994 elections'. Paper presented at the annual meeting of the American Political Science Association. http://www.allacademic.com/meta/p209749_index.html (accessed 19 March 2008).

Cosgrove, Kenneth M. (2009). 'Branded American politics'. Case study 5.4 in Jennifer Lees-Marshment, *Political Marketing: Principles and Applications*. London and New York: Routledge, 129–31.

Cosgrove, Kenneth M. (2012). 'Political branding in the modern age – effective strategies, tools and techniques'. In Jennifer Lees-Marshment (ed.) *Routledge Handbook of Political Marketing*. New York: Routledge, 107–23.

Cosgrove, Kenneth M. (2014). 'Personal political branding at state level'. In Jennifer Lees-Marshment, Brian Conley and Kenneth Cosgrove (eds) *Political Marketing in the US*. New York: Routledge.

Eshuis, Jasper, Erik Braun and Erik-Hans Klijn (2013). 'Place marketing as governance strategy: an assessment of obstacles in place marketing and their effects on attracting target groups'. *Public Administration Review*, 73(3): 507–16.

Fan, Ying (2008). 'Soft power: power of attraction or confusion?' *Place Branding and Public Diplomacy*, 4(2): 147–58.

French, Alan and Gareth Smith (2010). 'Measuring political brand equity: a consumer-oriented approach'. *European Journal of Marketing*, 44(3–4): 460–77.

Fritz, Ben, Bryan Keefer and Brendan Nyhan (2004). *All the President's Spin: George W. Bush, the Media, and the Truth*. New York: Touchstone.

Guzman, Francisco and Sierra Vicenta (2009). 'A political candidate's brand image scale: are political candidates brands?' *Journal of Brand Management*, 17(3): 207–17.

The Hill Times (2013). '"Harper Government" brand on 522 government news releases since December, Liberals say feds politicizing bureaucracy', 5 August. http://www.hilltimes.com/news/politics/2013/05/08/%E2%80%98harper-government%E2%80%99-on-522-news-releases-since-december-commons-report/34652 (accessed 24 September, 2013)

Hughes, Andrew and Stephen Dann (2010). 'Australian political marketing: substance backed by style'. In Jennifer Lees-Marshment, Jesper Strömbäck and Chris Rudd (eds) *Global Political Marketing*, London: Routledge, 82–95.

Hulsse, Rainer (2009). 'The catwalk power: Germany's new foreign image policy'. *Journal of International Relations and Development*, 12(3): 293–316.

Knuckey, Jonathan (2010). 'Political marketing in the United States: from market- towards sales-orientation?' In Jennifer Lees-Marshment, Jesper Strömbäck and Chris Rudd (eds) *Global Political Marketing*, London: Routledge, 96–112.

Langmaid, Roy (2006). 'Rebranding of Blair in power', Promise. http://www.promisecorp.com/people/index.htm Brand Strategy (accessed July 2008)

Lees-Marshment, Jennifer (2008). 'Managing a market-orientation in government: cases in the UK and New Zealand'. In Dennis W. Johnson (ed.) *The Routledge Handbook of Political Management*. New York: Routledge: 524–36.

Lees-Marshment, Jennifer (2011). *The Political Marketing Game*. Houndmills and New York: Palgrave Macmillan.

Lees-Marshment, Jennifer (2012). 'National and Labour's leadership, branding and delivery in the 2011 New Zealand election'. In Stephen Levine and Jon Johansson (eds) *Kicking the Tyres: The New Zealand General Election and Electoral Referendum of 2011*. Wellington: Victoria University Press, 177–89.

Lees-Marshment, Jennifer and Robin Pettitt (2010). 'UK Political marketing: a question of leadership?' In Jennifer Lees-Marshment, Jesper Strömbäck and Chris Rudd (eds) *Global Political Marketing*. London: Routledge, 218–34.

Lloyd, Jenny (2006). 'The 2005 general election and the emergence of the negative brand'. In Darren Lilleker, Nigel Jackson and Richard Scullion (eds), *The Marketing of Political Parties*. Manchester: Manchester University Press, 59–80.

Lloyd, Jenny (2009). 'After Blair . . . the challenge of communicating Brown's brand of Labour'. Case study 8.4 in Jennifer Lees-Marshment, *Political Marketing: Principles and Applications*. London and New York: Routledge, 232–34.

Marsh, David and Paul Fawcett (2011). 'Branding, politics and democracy'. *Policy Studies*, 32(5): 515–30.

Marsh, David and Paul Fawcett (2012). 'Branding public policy'. In Jennifer Lees-Marshment (ed.) *Routledge Handbook of Political Marketing*. New York: Routledge, 329–41.

Miller, William J. (2014). 'Branding the Tea Party: political marketing and an American social movement'. In Jennifer Lees-Marshment, Brian Conley and Kenneth Cosgrove (eds) *Political Marketing in the US*. New York: Routledge.

Needham, Catherine (2005). 'Brand leaders: Clinton, Blair and the limitations of the permanent campaign'. *Political Studies*, 53(2): 343–61.

Needham, Catherine (2006). 'Brands and political loyalty'. *Journal of Brand Management*, 13(3): 178–87.

Newman, Bruce I. (1994). *The Marketing of the President: Political Marketing as Campaign Strategy*. Thousand Oaks, CA: Sage Publications.

Nye, Joseph S. (1990). *Bound to Lead: The Changing Nature of American Power*. New York: Basic Books.

Ogden, Jessica, Gill Walt and Louisiana Lush (2003). 'The politics of "branding" in policy transfer: the case of DOTS for tuberculosis control'. *Social Science and Medicine*, 57(1): 179–88.

Pare, Daniel J. and Flavia Berger (2008). 'The Conservative party and the 2006 federal election'. *Canadian Journal of Communication*, 33(1): 39–63.

Parker, Brian T. (2012). 'Candidate brand equity valuation: a comparison of US presidential candidates during the 2008 primary election campaign'. *Journal of Political Marketing*, 11(3): 208–30.

Phipps, Marcus, Jan Brace-Govan and Colin Jevrons (2010). 'The duality of political brand equity'. *European Journal of Marketing*, 44(3/4): 496–514.

PolicyExchangeUK (2012) 'Political communication: new lessons from the US. Interview with Frank Luntz'. Online video, *youtube.com*, 26th November. http://www.youtube.com/watch?v= eYAuvyA216c

Promise (2006) *Reconnecting the Prime Minister*. Paper 21 for the Market Research Society. http:// www.promisecorp.com/documents/Reconnecting_the_Prime_Minister.pdf (accessed September 2013)

Scammell, Margaret (2008). 'Brand Blair: marketing politics in the consumer age'. In D. Lilleker and R. Scullion (eds) *Voters or Consumers: Imagining the Contemporary Electorate*. Newcastle: Cambridge Scholars Publishing, 97–183.

Schneider, Helmut (2004). 'Branding in politics – manifestations, relevance and identity-oriented management'. *Journal of Political Marketing*, 3(3): 41–67.

Smith, Gareth. (2009). 'Conceptualizing and testing brand personality in British politics'. *Journal of Political Marketing*, 8(3): 209–32.

Smith, Gareth and Alan French. (2009). 'The political brand: A consumer perspective'. *Marketing Theory*, 9(2): 209–26.

Smith, Gareth and Fiona Spotswood (2013). 'The brand equity of the liberal democrats in the 2010 general election: a national and local perspective'. *Journal of Political Marketing*, 12(2/3): 182–96.

Swanson, Fritz (2012). 'Small-town politics wrestles with the branding revolution ushered in by the Obama campaign'. *Print*, 66(1): 70–8.

White, Jon and Leslie de Chernatony (2002). 'New Labour: a study of the creation, development and demise of a political brand'. *Journal of Political Marketing*, 1(2–3): 45–52.

Whitman, Andrew (2012) 'Web Extra: Former US Ambassador to UN John Bolton'. *fios1.com*, 29th August. http://fios1news.com/longisland/node/17609#.Ungr0RDzqMQ

5 Internal political marketing

Internal political marketing is the hidden part of political marketing. It covers the organisation of political marketing – the structure, organisation, resourcing and staffing of offices in parties, campaigns and parliament or government; the organisation and involvement of volunteers and members on the ground; and the implementation of product change and branding. Such work goes on behind the scenes and is thus not as visible as other areas of marketing politics, but it is crucial to the resourcing, organisation and implementation of marketing strategy. Ineffective internal political marketing has the potential to derail political marketing strategies, branding and communication efforts. Successful internal activity ensures that volunteers become and remain effective activists for the party; recruits donors; ensures the right staff are in place and that new directions in the brand are accepted and complied with even if they challenge traditional party beliefs and ideals. This chapter will explore marketing volunteers including understanding volunteer demands, creating volunteer-friendly organisations, communicating with members and viewing volunteers as part-time political marketers; creating unity; relationship marketing within political parties and campaigns; fundraising; managing political marketing staff and resources; and central versus local versus volunteer control.

Marketing volunteers

As Practitioner perspective 5.1 suggests, in the 2008 and 2012 US presidential campaigns the Democrats made it as easy as possible for volunteers to get involved in campaigning for the party and then the presidential candidate Barack Obama. The principle behind this was that structures should be organised to suit the volunteer, not just the party. Volunteers, supporters or members – whatever term is used – are crucial to political success. Party members are the lifeblood of the party as Lilleker (2005, 572) argued and they carry out a number of functions including running local offices/branches, providing information about the local community and issues, campaigning on behalf of candidates and locally elected politicians, delivering campaign material, canvass voters, helping with GOTV (get out the vote), spreading the word in support of candidates through word of mouth, and donating funds to the organisation or campaign. Even in countries where there is no formal membership, mobilising grass-roots support is important, as the Obama 2008 and 2012 campaigns have shown in the US.

Understanding volunteer demands

As with voters, it is important to understand volunteer wants, needs and behaviours. As noted in the chapter on political market research, the attitude and behaviour of members

---

Practitioner perspective 5.1 on creating volunteer-friendly organisations

We created a brand new model of organising and it was called the Neighbor to Neighbor programme. What that allowed us to do is any volunteer who wanted to help Barack Obama get elected could go on their computer, and go to his website to my.barackobama.com, and on that website they could type in their home address, and Google, using Google mapping technology, could find their home, and that would find 25 targeted voters.

That's a whole different ballgame, because now I don't have to go 25 miles away to some Obama campaign office or even to another state and volunteer there. I can volunteer from my own home. I can download a list of those people, their names, their addresses, their age, and their telephone numbers; I can print a script of what to say, I can print flyers with information about Barack Obama's position on issues.

Parag Mehta, The Office of the Public Liaison Presidential
Transition Team, interviewed in 2009

As we push through the last 100 days of this election, our focus remains on helping make grass-roots organising as easy and accessible as possible for the volunteers and supporters that are the heart and soul of this campaign.

Stephanie Cutter, Obama for America Deputy Campaign Manager

Sources: Lees-Marshment (2011, 22 and 104) and Germany (2013, 88)

---

have also changed with formal membership declining and parties needing to reflect on what their members want. However, as the Obama campaigns show, it is possible to stimulate participation if the right structures are put in place. Political organisations therefore need to conduct research into volunteers needs and wants. There are different motivations for volunteering. Granik's (2005a, 2005b) research into members of a UK party, found that members scoring high on certain motivations are likely to experience higher levels of satisfaction with their role. There are three main areas of motivation:

- *social* – political party membership is seen as a means of gaining approval;
- *enhancement* – political party membership boosts the self-esteem of individuals;
- *understanding* – membership of a political party is seen as a way of learning more about politics.

If campaigns and parties create organisations that follow these principles and thus make volunteering enjoyable socially, a place to gain self-esteem and discuss politics they are more likely to attract and retain volunteers. After the UK Conservatives lost power in 1997 the new leader William Hague introduced several changes which improved the social, political and communication aspects of members. Lees-Marshment and Quayle (2001) observed how several changes were introduced after a period of internal assessment and consultation. A national membership base was created to ease communication with party members; The Conservative Network was launched to offer a social and political programme to encourage young professionals to become involved in the party; the Conservative Policy Forum was established to give members more opportunity to discuss policy and Conservative Future was created for members 30 years old and under. The Party also provided training in skills needed for candidates, such as media management, presentation and speech writing. Foster and Lemieux (2012) discussed how some Canadian interest groups also conduct market research on their members to find out which issues they want them to intervene in and what they need, as well as receiving informal feedback through members calls, emails and letters to the group. The groups also profile their members to help them meet their expectations more effectively.

Segmentation can be used on members as well as voters, as each group will have specific requirements. Bannon (2005b) argues that political relationships generally can be divided into different types: see Figure 5.1.

Internal party groups can also be segmented using segmentation according to potential levels of participation and contribution: see Figure 5.2

One way segmentation has been carried out in parties is the addition of some kind of network adjacent to formal membership in the UK. Rogers (2005, 608) argued that parties could offer supporters different alternatives to formal membership. UK Labour did just this: in Spring 2006, Labour launched a Let's Talk project and created a Labour supporters' network in an attempt to restart the Big Conversation and boost involvement in the party (Lees-Marshment 2008, 272).

Bannon's typology of volunteer relationships with their party/candidate

Relationship	Characteristics
Hyperactivist	Party activist, who is *married* into the party for better or worse
Blood brother	Blood ties, was born into the party through family association with it and treats their party as *the family*
The Idealist	Strongly held political views developed usually in an individual's early life or events, this relationship is based on *true love*
The Mutualist	Seeks mutual outcomes, but doesn't want to sign to an agreed contract, *kissing cousins*
Loosely aligned	A relationship exists but they are not fully committed to the party, the *open marriage*
Multi-relational	A voter who has more than one preference and will get involved in several parties, the *tart syndrome*
The Transient	Floating voter who moves from one party to the next, so has *one-night stands*
The Hostage	Cannot find anyone better to have a relationship with so sticks with the party anyway, the *trapped lover*
Nepotistic relationship	Seeks and gains favour from a party, so acts like a parasite in their own interests and is thus *married for money*
The Blackmailed	Coerced into supporting because the alternatives are worse and the barriers to exit maybe too high, the *forced partner*

Figure 5.1

Source: Adapted from Bannon (2005b)

Bannon's principles of political marketing segmentation by social group behaviour

Segment	Behaviour	Desired outcome	Action plan
Politicians	Political representative	Competent and re-electable	Give them a key role in strategic input and implementation
Hyperactivist	Politically active	Evangelist	Involve them in the decision-making process
Activist	Positive advocate	Loyalty	Maintain the existing relationship
Supporter	Active	Vote/member/ donor	Nurture and develop the relationship
Potential supporter/ undecided	Passive	Vote	Persuade them to become a supporter through communication
Non-voter	Inactive	Active	Communicate the importance of being an active voter
Non-supporter	Active negatively	Inactive/ non-voting	Ignore
Opposition	Negative advocate	Neutralise	Give out misinformation and use negative campaigning

Figure 5.2

Source: Adapted from Bannon (2004)

Creating volunteer-friendly organisations

Lebel (1999, 134–40) argued that volunteers need to be recruited and promoted to appropriate roles in campaigns according to their skills and performance; and also they need to be trained: see Figure 5.3.

The two Democratic primary campaigns in 2007/8 of Barack Obama and Hillary Clinton made it as easy as possible for volunteers to get involved. The Hillary Clinton campaign created an 'Online Action Centre' on the campaign website where supporters could join Team Hill, make calls using the volunteer calling tool, attend/plan an event, start a blog, join/start a group, or send a fundraising/recruiting email to a friend. Online videos were also posted on the campaign website, showing Clinton supporters in action. One humorous video showed famous movie director Rob Reiner giving volunteers tips on how to be more optimistic and convince more people to support Clinton when door knocking and making phone calls. Obama gave potential volunteers a specific goal and date such as *x* calls by Tuesday and made them actionable and realistic through easy-to-use online tools such as 'click on this button and make 20 calls from this list' (Bryant 2008). Cogburn and Espinoza-Vasquez (2011, 200–2) detailed how the 2008 website was designed in a way to make participation easy: it allowed users to scan it easily and used informal language; and it was

---

Lebel's principles of managing volunteers

1 **Planning:** plan their recruitment, roles and management, considering what motivates them.

2 **Recruitment:** consider those who fit most easily with campaign needs, including not just their attachment and commitment to a candidate but their skills; segmenting the message sent to volunteers where appropriate; taking into account what they expect to get from the investment of their time; making it easy for them to commit; contacting them within 24 hours of them offering to help to capitalize on their enthusiasm.

3 **Management:** manage volunteers like money; considering the resources available and the needs of the campaign; matching capability with the nature of the task set; including training where needed; relating volunteer activities to the overall campaign; and promoting those who display particular skills.

Figure 5.3

Source: Summarised from Lebel (1999: 134–40)

easy to find out how to get involved locally and nationally, and connect to other volunteers. The Obama 2008 website gave access to content that was user-generated, encouraging the feeling that volunteers were important too. Communication was also sent from the candidate at key moments, such as before a speech or announcement which enabled them to feel more connected with him.

Lower levels of organisation of parties need to follow suit otherwise the marketing of local politicians can be limited by the skill level and knowledge of volunteers at this level of government. Reeves (2013) explored how political marketing is viewed at the local constituency party level in the UK Conservatives and found that there was partial awareness of the scope of political marketing on aspects such as data management and targeting; and there were people involved at the lower levels with marketing skills, but they needed further training to maximize their potential contribution to the political context. Systems such as Merlin also need to be given to the local levels, otherwise party organisations are left to rely on commercial data, whereas they could be collecting their own data from the constituency to add into the central party system to make the party's targeting more effective.

Although there is a lot of attention on the use of the internet to attract voter support, it is also an effective channel for internal marketing to volunteers. Lees-Marshment and Pettitt (2014, 12) quote Matt Carter, who was involved in the 2005 UK Labour campaign, as noting how the Party utilised the internet in 2005: 'not only to convey a message, but to try and mobilise the membership, to try and give them a unique way of understanding where could they help, how could they play a part, what their role could be'. In 2012 the Obama campaign created an iPhone app for volunteers, which as Germany (2013, 88) explains, 'packaged all the functionality of a traditional campaign headquarters into a palm-sized device. It focused on very local functions, like connecting supporters to local political events, voter registration information, and polling locations.' Lilleker and Jackson (2013) analysed the websites and linked online presences of six parties (Conservative, Labour, and Liberal Democrat, Green, the UK Independence Party, and the British National Party) that stood across the UK at the 2010 general election and found that party supporters and activists were a key target market. Parties are using their websites to attract supporters and increase their activity and donations. All of the six parties encouraged visitors to the site to get involved; such as through sharing videos and pages, donating, volunteering for the campaign and promoting the party via social networks. The Conservative site had a separate website (http://www.MyConservatives.com) a network focused on volunteering and donations; as did Labour in the form of Membersnet along with an iPhone app which – like Obama's Neighbor to Neighbor programme – allowed users to discover where campaigners were working near to them and how to join in. Labour, Conservative and Lib Dem membership sites enabled supporters to have their own profile, generate their own content, comment and participate in campaign events. The Parties also used the email addresses of visitor-supporters who had given permission to send out communication to them that reinforced their support and helped to mobilise them. Case Study 5.1 by Sophia Blair explores the use of online mechanisms to increase volunteer activism in the New Zealand Labour Party, noting the limitations in practice which demonstrate that simply using online communication is not enough to stimulate participation; the principles of internal marketing need to be integrated as well.

Communicating with volunteers

As well as making it easy to get involved, it is important that volunteers feel wanted and valued. As Lebel (1999, 141) notes, 'volunteers often are at the low end of the campaign hierarchy, with the least access to the candidate and senior staff', so internal communication is extremely important to help them feel recognised and part of the overall campaign. Marketing strategies that respect and engage supporters help to mobilise supporters, who in turn increase voter support and also convey a positive image of the overall campaign.

Obama used marketing communications to mobilise his grass roots during his bid for the Democratic presidential nomination. Bryant (2008) notes how the campaign, built on the themes of hope, action and change, was good at translating such values into simple slogans such as 'Change we can believe in' and 'Yes, we can'. They spoke 'positively to the subconscious in a way that would make NLP (neuro-linguistic programming) practitioners proud.' E-communication was also effective, and run by users themselves instead of the political elites. The *Yes We Can* viral video created by Will.i.am and cYclops achieved nearly six million hits on YouTube. Mark Jurkovac, CEO of cYclops and executive producer of the video, recalls that as soon as it went viral 'we got calls from all sorts of groups saying they wanted to do their version of the *Yes We Can* and so we decided to create an online community for this kind of content' (quoted by Byrant 2008). A website (http://www.hopeactchange.com) was created and has since become a social community for Obama user-generated content, a sort of pro-Obama YouTube. Lilleker and Jackson's (2013) analysis of the UK parties at the 2010 general election found that the Conservatives, Lib Dems and British National Party created online communities of supporters, which helped to give them a space to discuss politics and create a feeling of a network – although overall websites were mostly used to get things the party wanted rather than allow open debate or control of the campaign.

The nature and style of communications techniques selected should match the requirements of each of the identified segments so as to inform, persuade and encourage continued support and involvement. Cogburn and Espinoza-Vasquez (2011, 201) noted how the 2008 Obama campaign website utilised social media tools alongside a database of details about volunteers which enabled the campaign to provide targeted messages to 'narrow constituencies and slices of their activist base'.

Viewing volunteers as part-time political marketers

Political parties have moved from seeing volunteers as foot soldiers to be directed without consideration of their needs, to realizing that creating organisational structures and opportunities to suit volunteers can make them so effective that they can help the party significantly. Van Aelst *et al.* (2012) argue that parties should consider volunteers as part-time marketers as they provide useful sources of local market intelligence and help market the party at a local level – for free. They argue that party members know and can communicate public opinion and preferences from mass to elite level; so they can provide the party with a cheap form of market research. Their research on Dutch party members found that members are more similar to voters than we might think – on several issues members had almost identical opinions and ideological positions to voters – and members thus help connect the party to society at large. Furthermore, members are open about their political affiliation and willing to spread the word and thus act as volunteer marketers for the party. Staff in the US Democrats also took this view; Lees-Marshment (2011, 18) noted that trainer Parag Mehta would tell volunteers 'come back to me and tell me what are you hearing? What are you seeing? When you knock on your neighbour's door and you have a conversation, are they frustrated? What issues are they upset about? Because we can sit here all day long and have all the polling and research . . . but nothing is more powerful than half a million neighbourhood leaders who talk to 50 of their neighbours four times over the next 14 months and who come back and tell me what they heard.'

Ubertaccio's (2012, 189) research on the US Republicans explains how the Party utilised volunteers to carry out direct face-to-face marketing which both helps to recruit and retain volunteers, providing them with solidary benefits and continual opportunities for political action. The Republicans built an effective volunteer structure to enable supporters to work in their local area, utilising existing networks to communicate with voters over time and get involved in GOTV at election time. President George W. Bush's key advisor Karl Rove worked with the Republican National Committee to create the '72-Hour Task Force' which implemented the '72-Hour Project' designed to increase the number of Republican voters by using personal campaign teams to contact GOP-leaning voters within 72 hours of the polls opening on election day. Ubertaccio (2012, 181) noted how the task force 'drew heavily on network marketing techniques to create a new organisational level of activism, the grassroots network, complete with "upline" and "downline" participants, who could more effectively reach prospective voters and increase turnout'. Similarly, as the Practitioner perspective 5.1 suggested, the success for the US Democrats under Dean – and then utilised by Obama once he became the nominated candidate – came through creating volunteer-centred structures. Instead of asking people to go along to where the party needed them, they utilised online methods to enable volunteers to help the party in the way that suited them.

Lees-Marshment and Pettitt (2014) interviewed professional party managers working in the central offices of political parties to find out how they had tried to incentivise volunteer activists in a way that helped them win elections – thus merging principles of providing avenues for participation which is good for democracy with the pragmatism of needing to win. They found that party staff created solidary incentives – incentives derived from the pleasure of being involved in politics – to mobilise volunteers, and that by involving volunteers more they could increase their activity and retention. As well as the usual internal meetings, they noted that online forums have also opened up new ways for parties to enable internal debate and quote from an interview with Cyrus Khron, who was e-marketing director for the US Republicans leading up to the 2008 election, who discussed how the party had created a website 'where anybody, regardless of party affiliation could create an account and tell us what they thought the Republican Party should represent, and we had over 13,000 comments and 180,000 people visit the site over the course of a month' (Lees-Marshment and Pettitt 2014, 10). The Party 'incorporated those entries into the platform document', even including specific comments from individuals – the first time it had ever done so – 'in such a way that somebody from South Dakota makes a comment about wind energy, and that shows up in the energy section of the platform, and instead of reading the party's decisions, actually read Americans' thoughts on it.' Whilst final policy decisions remain in the hands of the party leadership, such initiatives enhanced the link between internal party discussions and the manifesto, involving volunteers in a meaningful way.

Lees-Marshment and Pettitt (2014) also noted how Democratic National Committee (DNC) staffer Parag Mehta discussed the changing attitude of the Democrats in 2004–2008 to seeing volunteers not just as foot soldiers but as potential leaders: 'for so many years the Democratic Party has taken them for granted and used them for electioneering, but then not used them for leadership. There has been no promotion system within the Democratic Party', but to be effective – as well as democratic – party organisations need to 'empower people at the local level to make their own decisions, train correctly, to have the resources they need to get the job done'. So they gave activists access to the national voter file; not only was this good in terms of sharing information within the party it was pragmatically beneficial because the volunteers could then help to ensure the data was regularly updated. Lees-Marshment and Pettit also quote Republican Political Director Rich Beeson, who explained how the Republican National Committee (RNC) also ran training for volunteers on campaign management, campaign finance and campaign field schools so volunteers knew how to go door to door, run a survey and enter the data into voter vault.

Volunteers can also be enlisted to help create and communicate the party's message. Party staff can explain that campaign messages and positions are for voters not yet converted, and necessary to win power to achieve more principled aims. Thus, Mehta quoted by Lees-Marshment and Pettitt (2014) would acknowledge any disquiet more ideologically led volunteers might have with repositioning of branding changes, but explain how their perspective was very different as an activist and hardcore Democrat to those of voters at large. He would say 'these messages were not crafted for you. We already have you. We love you, we appreciate you, we're going to get your vote, we thank God for your vote. But these messages are not being crafted for you; these messages are being crafted for that small, narrow group of voters who are truly independent.' It doesn't mean the 'founding cornerstone principles of the party are different' but just 'how we talk about it'. That might seem superficial, but that is the reality of political communication which the party has to fit in with 'because if you want to do all the good things we talked about, you have to win the election first'. Lees-Marshment and Pettitt thus put forward a framework for increasing volunteer involvement – see Figure 5.4.

Volunteers can also be involved in government; after winning power in 2008 President Barack Obama and the Democrats sought to turn their organisation for campaign volunteers into a permanent structure, Organising for America (OFA), and ask for the public's help in campaigning for policies in government which continued into and beyond the 2012 election. OFA retained and recruited new volunteers, getting them to help lobby their representatives to get the President's policies passed and take part in action days. Figure 5.5 has an example of an email sent to encourage people to get involved after the 2012 election.

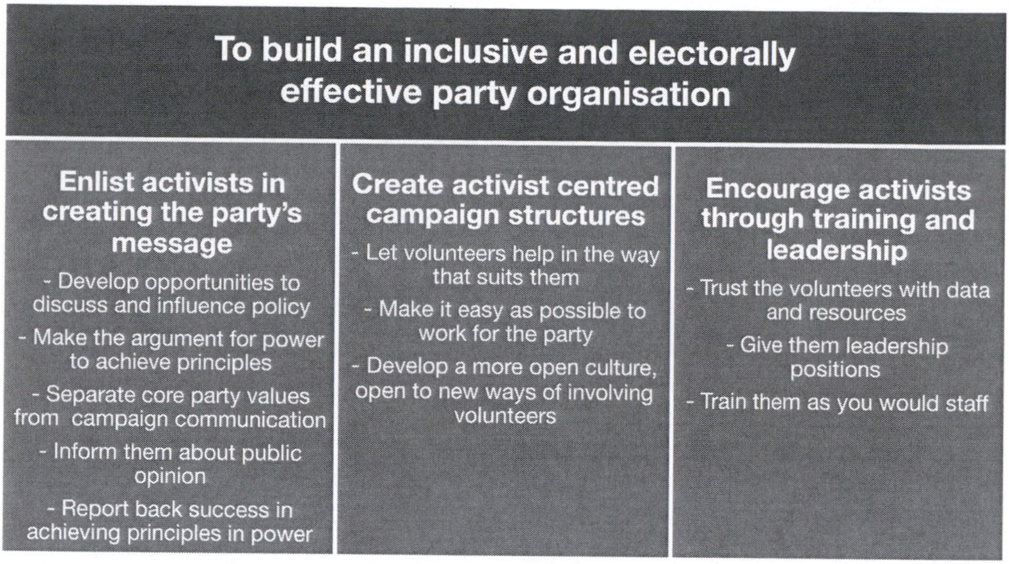

Figure 5.4 Lees-Marshment and Pettitt's framework for volunteer activism through inclusive party organisations

Source: Lees-Marshment and Pettitt (2014)

However, Spiller and Bergner (2014) argued that Obama met many challenges utilising his campaigning database once in power. Presidents therefore need to create a governance model of market-oriented database political marketing to maintain volunteer support, that is distinct from that used in campaigning. In government, parties and political leaders need to continue to carry out listening exercises with volunteers, asking volunteers for constructive feedback on how the politician/party is doing in government, to convey any problems on the ground, and to make suggestions for anything the government needs to do to reach its goals. The campaign grass-roots support networks and mobilizing voters need to be maintained, using segmentation of the supporter database to identify different needs and goals and potential contributions. Effective internal communication with volunteers through the database is needed to explain and justify any changes to election promises, convey progress on delivery in government, and create a loyalty rewards programme to motivate campaign volunteers to carry on their work in government. In this way presidents can develop a long-term relationship with volunteers in power. Volunteers can then be asked to help campaign for legislation the president wants to enact, such as communicating the constraints of government to dissatisfied voters and explaining why it is important to continue to campaign for the president.

The relationship between politicians and volunteers is changing just as it is between politicians and voters. Lees-Marshment (2013) discussed how politicians and parties have sought to work with volunteers to a greater extent, and put forward the idea of a political partnership model for political organisation. In a political partnership model, parties build permanently volunteer-oriented organisations, develop engagement to suit the user and view volunteers as a partner in the campaign: see Figure 5.6.

Organising for America's email to involve volunteers in government

From: Barack Obama [info@barackobama.com]
Sent: 31 July 2013 04:21
To: XXXX
Subject: I'm asking you

Friend –

There is only so much I can do on my own.

The special interests know it, and they're counting on you to be silent on gun violence and climate change. They hope you're not paying attention to creating jobs or fixing our broken immigration system.

And they plan to make the loudest noise when your members of Congress come home for August recess.

I'm counting on you to be just as vocal – to make sure the agenda that Americans voted for last year is front and center.

Say you'll do at least one thing as part of OFA's Action August in your community, no matter where you live.

I know it's easy to get frustrated by the pace of progress.

But it's not a reason to sit back and do nothing – our system only works if you play your part.

If you don't let your representatives know where you stand in August, we risk losing an important battle on your home turf.

So I'm asking you to speak up – commit to do at least one thing in your community during Action August:

http://my.barackobama.com/Commit-to-Action-August

Thanks,

Barack

Figure 5.5

Co-create	Co-campaign	Co-communicate	Co-consider
• Use creative and deliberative market research methods to get the public to co-create solutions with political elites	• Train and empower volunteers in parties and campaigns to take leadership and initiative	• Engage in long-term interactive and dialogic communication	• Consider public input into decision making and justify final decisions by political leaders to show public input has been reflected on

Figure 5.6 Lees-Marshment's Political Partnership Model
Source: Lees-Marshment 2013

Creating unity

In political marketing, it is not just the volunteers, but the whole party, including politicians, candidates for office and party figures, that needs to be considered if party leaders or candidates want to change the product or brand. The UK Conservatives were held back 1997–2005 because of their older, white, middle-class membership being unreflective of society. Smith (2009, 215–16) argues that party members convey the personality of a political brand; thus if there is disunity or internal criticism of a rebranding or market-oriented strategy, political marketing will be undermined and conflicting messages are sent to voters (Lees-Marshment 2001; Smith and French 2009, 213). Changing the product or brand is not as straightforward for a party leader or chairperson, who has considerably less autonomy than most chief executives leading a business. As most party leaders are elected by a range of people from the party, their position is actually dependent on those below them.

Parties have to try to increase acceptance amongst internal supporters for new products, and given that volunteers tend to have a greater ideological or emotive attachment to the party this can make it harder for them to accept new ways of operating. As Lloyd (2005) noted, part of the product is investment; people who have been members of a party for years and have gone out and trod the streets to campaign on its behalf have an obvious investment. A party leader intent on making a party or campaign market-focused risks encountering resistance from stakeholders. The UK Labour Party from 1983–1997 is a clear example of this, as internal debates raged about which direction the Party should take. As Wring (2005), who analysed the emergence and development of marketing in the party in relation to internal debate and ideological considerations, noted over the course of the twentieth century Labour held three approaches to electioneering up until Blair's victory in 1997:

1   **The educationalist approach**: campaigning was about converting people to their cause through informing them.
2   **The persuasional school of thought**: using campaigning to create an emotional response and change public opinion so it supported the party perspective.
3   **Market research socialism:** more concerned with responding to public opinion than reshaping it, introduced by the leader Neil Kinnock 1987–1992 and then taken to a new level by Tony Blair 1992–1997.

The third approach, which is more in line with a market-orientation, challenged many long-standing beliefs in the Party. Wring (2005, 116) cited a delegate who spoke out at the 1992 Annual Conference saying: 'we have allowed ourselves to be marketed by paid image-makers, but . . . we should beware of the paid image-maker. These are people, mainly middle-class graduates, who have learned their socialism from market research and opinion polls.' Tension in the party between doing what was believed to be right and winning elections continued through until Tony Blair's victory in 1997 and beyond.

Leadership, party culture and party unity are important factors in the success or failure of implementation. Gouliamos *et al.* (2013, 4) argue that campaign culture should be studied in relation to political marketing for it involves 'deep connections through shared histories and reciprocal experiences' and understandings and commitments which might impact on the effectiveness of campaigning. It can influence access to resources, knowledge and competency; as well as the propensity to learn from each campaign. Their book *Political Marketing: Strategic Campaign Culture* discusses the role of culture within campaigns in more detail: see Authors' corner 5.1.

Authors' corner 5.1

Political Marketing: Strategic Campaign Culture
Edited by Kōstas Gouliamos, A. Theocharous and Bruce Newman
Published by Routledge, Routledge Research in Political Communication, 2013

The book *Political Marketing: Strategic Campaign Culture* envisages culture as an omnipresent component of the (post)modern society, occurring on the Lifeworld (Lebenswelt) apparatus throughout various forms of communication. For us and the highly distinguished contributors from different regions of the world, the rapid expansion of globalization has led to a social and political condition that causes a resurgence of native identity and, simultaneously, the growth of cultural heterogeneity. Within this context, a guiding principle in engendering electoral campaigns is to examine the ways in which culture, politics, and society interrelate in the field of political marketing.

In the course of the book, we introduce the notion of 'campaign culture' since we consider 'culture' as a distinctive concept with transformative capacities that need further and deeper development in the engineering of the political marketing process.

By 'strategic campaign culture' we mean the dialogical protocols and spaces associated with the process of a holistic approach that identifies cultural beliefs, ideas, concepts, images, or attitudes in an attempt to modify them through the management of the political marketing platform. Such a protocol seeks to develop and integrate culturally meaningful persuasive messages that would correspond to the characteristics of a given target audience.

This may be introduced and, consequently, lead to strategic formulation of a 'campaign culture'. Indeed, understanding and adapting a broader 'campaign culture', political marketing models may be perceived as arrays of stratums of significant resources ensuing viability in human assets, forms of influence, class stratification, alternative flows of information or networking and intercultural knowledge-sharing activity.

Nevertheless, starting from a critical premise, we and the contributors proceed to locate the emergence of culture as a continuous tangible and intangible activity that attributes a corpus of consequences to the rationalization of an electoral campaign in which the cultural actors interact with new media technology as well as with the agencies of political management.

A stage of implementation or management is therefore needed in the political marketing process because political parties will not necessarily accept change, however important to win an election. Campaign teams also need to be unified. The Bush-Cheney 2004 team was, as one Republican staffer commented, made up of 'a lot of us that had been together for years. So it was one group . . . and we had one goal and that was to re-elect the President. Nothing else was more important to that' (Lees-Marshment 2011, 120). There are of course a wide range of stakeholders parties need to consider as well as volunteers, including elected politicians, office holders and candidates (see Dean and Croft 2001, 1206). Stakeholders can exert influence over different activities and decisions the party carries out; they also vary in how active or passive they are, and how much influence they have over political marketing.

After losing power in 1997, the UK Conservatives set about reforming the party and making it market-oriented again. Lees-Marshment (2009) discussed how William Hague, a former management consultant, reorganised the party, tried to recruit new members and a broader range of candidates, conducted market intelligence both formally and informally, and developed early policy priorities in response to public opinion. The party began to pursue a public services strategy in response to market intelligence, begun in major speeches made by Hague and Deputy Leader Peter Lilley in April 1999 and focusing on improving state provision of public services rather than looking to the market and simply reducing taxes. The plan was, then, to produce policy themes showing the more caring side of Conservatives. Guarantees to voters were launched in late 1999 which focused on areas of prime importance, responded to the results from market intelligence and attracted positive press coverage when first launched. However, Hague met with sustained internal resistance to the changes. Archie Norman, a successful businessman, became chief executive, opened up central office and reassigned staff, meeting internal opposition. The Party suffered from a number of defections or resignations. Speeches on the new policy direction away from Thatcherism were criticised internally as repudiating Thatcher's free-market legacy and stimulated a very negative reaction from the parliamentary party. Furthermore, membership and public support failed to increase – in fact both went down – and senior party figures joined in the critique of what Hague was trying to do. The leadership ended up scaling back on the changes, withdrawing new policies and guarantees, and abandoning the market-oriented strategy in favour of getting the core vote out. As the Conservative politician Kenneth Clarke later commented, 'from about half-way through the parliament we stopped trying to broaden our appeal, we narrowed it'.[1] Just because leaders want to adopt and implement a market-orientation, it does not mean that it will be successful – they have to get support from the majority within the party.

Achieving a market-orientation arguably takes some time, especially if it necessitates major changes in values and beliefs. It is also unlikely that the leadership will achieve 100 per cent party unity or complete acceptance of a market-orientation, but it would aim for a majority of support for the new behaviour. Marketing management literature suggests a number of guidelines for how to make the process easier: see Figure 5.7.

Another aid to easing implementation is to consider the internal market *before* completing plans for changing the product. The Lees-Marshment (2001) MOP model argues that parties should carry out internal reaction analysis, taking into account a party's ideology and history to ensure that some product aspects suit the traditional supporter market and MPs as well as new target markets; and Ormrod (2005) notes the need to consider stakeholders and members with an internal and external orientation.

Knuckey and Lees-Marshment (2005) analysed the US presidential campaign of George W. Bush, in 2000, which had reached out to new target markets, including middle-class and Hispanic voters, with policies on health care and childhood education – nontraditional Republican issues. During the primaries, he adjusted his behaviour to suit internal criticism, to ensure he would win the nomination. He tried to increase his own conservative credentials and temporarily replaced the 'Compassionate Conservative' slogan with 'A reformer with results' and stressed traditional conservative Republican themes, emphasising his belief in limited government. Once he had secured the party nomination, he moved back towards the centre and focused on issues that opinion polls showed to be of paramount concern for most Americans in the 2000 election – education, social security and health care – but alongside traditional Republican themes such as tax cuts, smaller government and a stronger military. As Medvic (2006, 23) noted, Bush's emphasis on school choice, as well as local control and accountability, fitted Republican ideology but also appealed to swing voters.

Bendle and Nastasoiu (2014) provide the first in-depth analysis of political marketing in primary elections. They note that the US primaries present obstacles to candidates by requiring them to meet the demands of their internal markets, whose views are generally

---

Guidelines for implementing a market-orientation from marketing management literature

1   Create a feeling that everybody in the party can contribute to making it market-oriented and successful.

2   Acknowledge that the party may already be doing many things that would be classed as marketing activities.

3   Encourage all members of the organisation to suggest ideas as to how the party might respond more effectively to voters.

4   Create a system that enables all forms of market intelligence to be disseminated as widely as possible through the organisation.

5   Present market intelligence reports from professionals, especially in the form of statistics, in a way that everyone in the party can understand.

6   Appoint a marketing executive (or equivalent) to handle market intelligence from within the party and from professional research firms.

7   This executive should meet various groups within the party to learn what they think about the party and voters: first, explaining his or her job position and the nature of marketing and its uses and then encouraging open discussion, inviting ideas for change within the party.

8   The importance of views other than those of the majority of the electorate and the party's history should be acknowledged.

9   Those within the party who support the idea of being market-oriented should be promoted to encourage market-oriented behaviour.

10   Emphasise that becoming market-oriented is the means to achieve the party's goal; it is not the goal in itself.

Figure 5.7

Source: Lees-Marshment (2001)

divergent to, and more ideological than, the external market – or voters in the general election. Candidate strategies to manage this internal/external market clash differ but, despite the importance of the primaries, the general election is the ultimate market. Strong candidates can resolve the internal/external market dilemma by focusing on supporters' desire to stop the other party, while weaker candidates need to convey what only they personally can offer. Otherwise candidates who are successful in getting their party's nomination will find it difficult to reposition after a primary.

Meeting the needs of both internal and external markets is not always easy however. As with all political strategies, successful implementation can depend on timing, the nature of the competition and how long a party has been out of power. Balancing demands between the two markets is difficult. Hughes and Dann (2010, 88) studied the case of Labor leader Kevin Rudd in Australia in 2007 and observed that 'the ALP remained divided between the desire to become more market-driven and desire to remain faithful to the original ideologies of the party: although a combination of both could represent a more comprehensive market-oriented strategy'. In 2007 Kevin Rudd's leadership of the ALP suggested that the party wanted to become more market-focused to achieve electorate success but without sever traditional ties with the unions. Seventy per cent of the front bench candidates had strong union or party official backgrounds (2010, 88). However the compromise created in election year soon gave way to factional debate when Rudd's opinion polls started to decline in 2010, stimulating a leadership challenge by the deputy Julia Gillard who then led labor to re-election later that year, only to be replaced by Rudd when she suffered a similar fate in the polls in 2013.

In the UK, upon becoming leader of the Conservatives, David Cameron attempted to appeal to both markets while seeking support. Lees-Marshment and Pettitt (2010) note how he appealed to external markets by creating initial new policy positions on the environment, discussing protecting and safeguarding the NHS and conveying a different persona via photo opportunities in Darfur and social action days with MPs. He met with internal criticism in various respects – environmentally friendly policies suggested a less friendly approach to business, with greater regulation: a potentially un-Conservative position. However, other policies, such as on grammar schools, were withdrawn after attracting too much discontent; and there was concern expressed that Cameron was eroding what the party stood for when backbench MP Quentin Davies resigned he argued that the Conservative Party under Cameron's leadership has 'ceased collectively to believe in anything, or to stand for anything. It has no bedrock. It exists on shifting sands. A sense of mission has been replaced by a PR agenda'. Franz Luntz, consultant, ran a focus group of floating voters on Cameron's first year as leader, and noted that: 'there is an underlying fear of 'spin' that could undermine your long-term success . . . floating voters believe you are actively engaged in a sincere effort to bring about fundamental change, and they appreciate it . . . [but] they are afraid you'll turn into the Tony Blair of 2006' (2006, in *The Daily Telegraph*). Cameron sought to appeal to internal markets by discussing social responsibility; a blend of traditional Conservatism, discussing responsibility, but also social, emphasising concern about the nature of society. He declared:

> What I say to traditional Conservatives is that we have lost three elections in a row, we have to modernise and change to reflect changes to British society . . . [but] . . . look at the centrality of what I am saying: social responsibility, parental responsibility – that the state doesn't have all the answers . . . this is a profoundly *Conservative message*.

He also continued support for some traditional policies such as government support for marriage. In the April 2007 Party election broadcast, Cameron was seen meeting and talking to a variety of people, and not just listening, but sometimes saying no to what the participants wanted, suggesting a degree of leadership alongside responsiveness. Lees-Marshment *et al.*'s (2010, 289) comparative study concluded that being market-oriented need not mean abandoning internal supporters but that party leaders need to be effective party leaders at managing the demands of the different markets to be successful in implementing a market-oriented strategy. Considering the internal market in product design is not just important to maintain party unity, it may also be essential to the long-term success of political marketing in government.

Relationship marketing within political parties and campaigns

Relationship marketing involves volunteers in creating the new product or marketing design. Party organisational research tells us that volunteers need to be incentivised, so political marketing needs to find ways to include volunteers in product design. Pettitt (2012) argues that relationship marketing concepts offer political marketers ways to nourish relationships with a party's internal market. Integrating understanding from Katz and Mair's

(1993) ideas of the three faces of political parties – the public office (party politicians in government); the party on the ground (volunteers); and the party in central office (paid party staff) – Pettitt argues that these three faces mean parties have to consider three distinct internal markets for a political party. These are distinct from external markets which obviously include voters and other stakeholders. He argues that parties can adopt a range of strategies in response to these markets: see Figure 5.8.

Pettitt (2012) acknowledges that there are pros and cons to each approach, thus practitioners need to weigh up which benefits are most valuable and which problems they can most easily cope with.

Levenshus (2010) argues that Obama's grass-roots campaign in 2008 was grounded in relationship management theory, seeking to create positive relationships. Drawing on interviews with three of Obama's campaign staff, media articles and the Obama for America website (http://www.barackobama.com), he noted how the campaign was designed with a master online strategy and localised plans which stimulated grass-roots activity. New media strategists worked closely with field organisers and were always thinking about the relationships that happened on the ground; and paid organisers worked with volunteer

---

Pettitt's strategies for involving volunteers in creating the party product

1   **Offer material incentives.**
   • Paying volunteers.
   • *Problem*: problematic as it is too expensive and fails to motivate political loyalty and attachment.

2   **A base strategy of offering purposive incentives.**
   • Giving internal stakeholders what they want, or purposive incentives, so determining the product to suit internal views not external voters.
   • *Problem*: this can lead a party to lose elections.

3   **Become an empty vessel of glittering generality.**
   • Appeal to purposive incentives in a vague sense with an empty product which appeals to a wide range of people who can project their own ideas on it.
   • Utilise virtue terms such as New Labour.
   • *Problem*: it can lead to disappointment as policy detail delivers something people did not want or expect.

4   **Dignified/empty democracy.**
   • Offer solidary incentives where volunteers get to feel involved in creating the product, whilst still considering external market opinion when making the final decisions.
   • *Problem*: activists will notice where their views are not reflected in the party's product.

5   **Effective or real consultation and democracy.**
   • Offer volunteers real democratic consultation and joint creation of the political product, so that volunteers will support and campaign for the product.
   • *Problem*: what volunteers want is not what voters want; and the realities of government require faster decisions than consultation allows.

Figure 5.8

Source: Adapted from Pettitt (2012)

Levenhus's Principles of relationship building with volunteers – from the 2008 Obama campaign

1 **Resources for relationships**: campaign managers ensured resources were in place to build relationships with the online grassroots.

2 **Openness and adaptability**: willingness to change in response to volunteers' comments, room for them to share their thoughts including disagreement in places.

3 **Volunteer empowerment**: a you-centred approach and online tools that gave volunteers the power to organise and take action themselves, so they felt like part of the team along with paid employees.

4 **Sharing volunteer best practice**: campaign staff listened to conversations and shared any useful information emerging from the most active groups with others; promoting the most effective ideas.

Figure 5.9

Source: Adapted from Levenhus (2010, 327–30)

co-ordinators on local Obama social networking groups sites to monitor and participate in conversations, rather than implement a unilateral, centralised plan. Their approach to the grass-roots was to argue that they had the power to influence the outcome of the campaign; a 'you-centred' approach', with the phrase 'Because it's about you' appearing at the top of the Action page. Levenhus (2010, 326) argued that 'Obama campaign managers highly valued the campaign's relationships with the grassroots' and thus forging a positive relationship between the campaign and volunteers was very important and seen as mutually beneficial. They sought to do so in several ways – see Figure 5.9.

Levenhus (2010, 331 and 333) thus concluded that 'campaign managers used the internet strategically to create conversation' and 'to empower, dialogue with, and build mutually beneficial relationships with publics'. This meant the campaign lost some control, so befitting Pettitt's last principle of effective or real consultation and democracy, at least in terms of input into the campaign.

Fundraising

Fundraising is an important activity that generates resources to fund political marketing activities. As with voters and volunteers, campaigns and parties need to understand donor behaviour. Political marketing research (e.g. Steen 1999, 161–4 and Bannon 2005a) suggests that several factors increase donations, including:

- affection for the candidate;
- agreement with the candidate's stance on issues or policy;
- the candidate's power to influence legislation;
- relation of donation to outcomes;
- benefits offered to the donor, such as greater access to the candidate;
- social and enjoyable fundraising events.

Various communication tools can be used in fundraising, including direct mail, telemarketing, events and the internet. There are many examples of using direct marketing to gain donations. Response rates are often extremely low, but when used in fundraising the donations gained can still outweigh the cost to make it worthwhile. Sherman (1999, 366) cites an example from the Bill Clinton presidency after his popularity dived:

> In an effort to get increased support, the firm of Malchow, Adams and Hussey was selected to handle the Democrat's direct marketing fund-raising effort. In 1995 . . . a closed-face envelope with a picture of the White House was sent to 600,000 individuals on Democratic National Committee lists. The message stressed that President Clinton said the recipient was a friend and that he or she was wanted as part of the steering committee. It was a soft call for money, with no explicit call for money until the PS at the end of the letter . . . it pulled in $3.5 million.

Direct emails were used heavily in the 2008 US presidential bid by Barack Obama to encourage donations and volunteering to help with campaigning. Anyone who signed up as a supporter or interested party on the Obama site received emails regularly that asked for both support and donations. Often the attention-seeking element of direct marketing was utilised well, with recipients asked to donate by a certain time to allow Barack to stop fundraising for one day, or before some other deadline, in emails written from Michelle Obama as well as the candidate himself. This technique was also used in 2012: see Figure 5.10.

Fundraising email appeals in Obama's 2012 presidential campaign

From: Barack Obama [democraticparty@democrats.org][1]
Sent: Thursday, November 01, 2012 11:54 AM
To: [Name]
Subject: How this ends:

[Name] –

We got outraised pretty badly in the first half of this past month by Mitt Romney and the Republicans, giving them a $45 million edge on us.

We don't know what kind of impact it will have in the final days of a tight race, but we still have time to fight back and make sure it will not be a decisive factor in this election.

[Name], I need you to make a donation of $5 or more to close the gap and finish strong. http://my.democrats.org/page/m/4052bf04/5eb3dc8/19ceacab/74b41b34/2963130561/VEsH/

I know I've asked a lot of you.

No matter how this ends, on Election Night I'll get up on stage and thank you for all the time and effort and hard-earned dollars you've put into this. But I also want to be able to tell our country that our hard work paid off, and that we will continue moving forward for four more years.

Please donate $5 or more today:

https://my.democrats.org/November<http://my.democrats.org/page/m/4052bf04/5eb3dc8/19ceacab/74b41ac8/2963130561/VEsE/

Barack

Figure 5.10

In 2008 Obama made an unusual decision to forgo public funding to get donations from individuals via social media instead. Cogburn and Espinoza-Vasquez (2011, 200 and 203–4) and Marland (2012b, 168) note how Obama succeeded in obtaining nearly $750 million for his presidential campaign by applying marketing concepts including:

- donating was made as easy as possible so the website had a simple but prominent donate button and donation checkout integrated into online advertising;
- communication via email and YouTube videos was direct, personalised and delivered before or after a key event, connecting the recipient to the candidate and campaign;
- special offers were made, such as if they donate x amount they would get something from the campaign merchandise;
- targeted search engine advertisements were placed via paid keywords;
- celebrities such as Oprah Winfrey were utilised in blogs and speeches;
- fundraising strategies responded to market research via data from online donors, those attending events and those who entered contests to win campaign merchandise.

Marland (2012b, 170) also notes how, in the 2010 congressional elections, Organizing for America encouraged supporters to create their own fundraising page and identify a fundraising goal; and a thermometer would show how much progress they had made towards achieving this. They were asked to enter friends' email addresses and the campaign then sent them an email saying:

President Obama and I are committed to changing the political process by growing an organization founded on a broad base of support from ordinary Americans. This organization is about putting the people's interests ahead of the special interests, but to do that, Barack needs help from people like you and me. I've set my own personal fundraising goal for the organization, which you can see in the thermometer to the right. Will you click the thermometer to make a donation and help me reach my goal?

Marland (2012b, 173–4) also cited an example of using online marketing to fundraise money to campaign for policy in government, whereby the Democratic Party organised a competition to vote on the best citizen-created, 30-second videos supporting health insurance policy reform; once the top 20 were selected they asked visitors to the website http://www.BarackObama.com to donate so they could be aired to the general public. The argument made by Organising for America was:

Help put the final ad on the air. In the next few days, we'll be using the winning video as the basis for a new television ad that will air across the country – and you can help, by ensuring we have the resources to make the biggest impact. With only weeks to go before the final vote on health insurance reform, we need to make sure Congress hears this grassroots message. Can you help get this message out, just when it's most critical? Please donate today, using the form on the right.

Fundraising appeals are well researched and tested; Johnson (2013, 17) notes how the 2012 Obama campaign used constant testing of email messages seeking donations, halting poor performing email requests and resending those that performed well. Candidate fundraising also draws on the efforts by political parties – the Obama 2012 re-election campaign was able to draw on efforts by the Democratic National Committee: the Obama Victory Fund was established in April 2011 which sought large donations from individual donors for both the Obama campaign and the Democratic Party. Funds were then given out to battleground states in 2012 (Corrado 2013, 65–6).

Managing political marketing staff and resources

Practitioner perspective 5.2 on the importance of long-term resourcing in winning elections

This is what I generally think about not just the RNC but also the campaign in general, the Romney campaign: I think in the year and a half that we had, I think we did a great job. Unfortunately, I think the other side did a great job for four years . . . Ultimately where this is going to lead is that we have to have a massive operation that is very granular, that is in communities across America for a very long time . . . This idea that we tear down every three years and build up for a one-year monster campaign – I just don't see that being the future. I think the future is a much broader operation for a long period of time.

Reince Priebus, RNC Chairman, 2012

Source: National Review interview quoted in Haberman (2012)

The organisation and staff involved in political marketing may be a less visible part of politics but it is an important one nonetheless as they help form and run long-term organisations necessary for political marketing, as Practitioner perspective 5.2 suggests. Marland's (2012a, 71) analysis of political marketing in the 1993 and 2006 Canadian federal elections led him to conclude that good organisation is essential for effective political marketing: 'when campaign units operate with military-like meticulousness, regularly interact, and stick to a plan with a developed product offering, they are more likely to experience marketing success than when they are disjointed, isolated, and impulsive'.

Party staff play an important part in implementing political marketing strategies and tactics. Mills (2012) argues that, although party officials do not attract as much attention as consultants or top political advisors, they play key roles in many areas of political marketing. Mills analysed work by three Australian party officials and concludes that they played significant role in a range of marketing activities including gathering market intelligence, designing the product (policy and leadership), building and using long- and short-term campaign resources, and post-campaign product delivery. Party officials can be highly effective political marketers.

As Practitioner perspective 5.3 suggests, party organisational structures need to be maintained over the long term. Lynch *et al.* (2006) argue that a resource-based view (RBV) suggests parties need to maintain strong resources, such as leadership, staff, supporters, organisation, knowledge and management. If a party develops superior performance on these aspects over the long term, it can help it outperform rivals – and so ensure it has a strong basis from which to strategise and secure re-election. Parties in government often neglect their party organisation, focusing too much on daily government business, and then turn to consider re-election only to find their party organisation is in tatters making it harder to rebuild. Wiser parties will ensure the organisation is considered a valuable resource that can help them stay in power. O'Cass (2009) also argues that parties need to develop long-term skills within their organisation including information, knowledge and skills amongst their staff and volunteers.

The Democratic Party's organisational changes under the chairmanship of Howard Dean could be considered an RBV-building activity. Lees-Marshment (2011, 106) noted how DNC staffer Parah Mehta explained that Dean's intention was to build 'a permanent infrastructure so that we didn't just keep rebuilding the party every two years'. The 50-state strategy wasn't just for the 2008 election but was done with the goal of building a more permanent organisation structure regardless of election time or whether a state was part of the top target list. Mehta worked with the state parties to build a team of constant organisers to maintain the Democratic Party so that when there was an election there was already a machine in place. Without this, the party had to rebuild a structure at each election which would just disappear and this meant that the party was not talking to the voters during the two years in between. This approach, to value the maintenance of resources over the long term, helped Obama win in 2008; as Mehta explained:

> When Barack became the nominee of our party he had all the resources and all the infrastructure to execute a massive political machine. The elements in that machine were A– the field organisers that we had hired, funded, and trained, and put to work for three years in their states, and they knew their states backwards and forwards, and they knew their districts well, they knew their constituents, they knew the ground, they knew the turf . . . And B– we built a national voter file, which the Democratic Party has never had in a presidential election . . . that had every single registered voter in all 50 states in one place, and we were able to turn that over to Barack Obama for free . . . he had a really extensive network built in before he even became the nominee.

Central versus local versus volunteer control

One pragmatic issue that arises is that, as technology offers candidates greater ability to reach supporters, it reduces control because opponents as well as supporters can use it to make their case. This can dilute the overall brand, give fuel to a rumour, or it can be helpful. Cogburn and Espinoza-Vasquez (2011, 204) noted how email campaigns by Obama's opponents sometimes went viral via YouTube, but it's influence was – fortunately for the Obama team – limited as it had to compete with spoofs of the opposition on comedy shows also spread by his supporters via social media. Volunteer-led/fluid campaign organisations might cause difficulties; Johnson (2012, 213) talked of how a more fluid model which encourages citizen input and involvement – whilst it is democratically desirable to have more people participating in a campaign – can make a campaign chaotic and also over-responsive to the whims and wishes of the moment instead of concentrating on a consistent, long-term strategy, or make it seem like the campaign has a thousand messages and no clear message at all.

Turcotte and Raynauld's (2014) analysis of the Tea Party movement suggested that political mobilization, engagement, and organising may become more bottom-up, led by volunteers on the ground rather than an organisation's central office. This could make it harder for parties and candidates to control their brand and communication. For example, whilst the obvious threat of the Tea party was to the Democrats and Obama, it is also potentially a threat to the Republican Party as it makes maintaining a clear brand very hard. The Tea Party may have made it very hard for a moderate, energetic, new market-oriented leader of the Republicans to build support from independents in future and so damaged the Republican chances of recovery also.

Nevertheless, too much centralized control can prevent individual politicians being able to respond to their local political market. In countries, such as the UK, with party-based systems, local MPs and candidates are traditionally more restricted as campaigns are national and party-based. Marland (2009) noted how Canadian constituency campaigns act like local franchises, implementing the centrally driven market-oriented strategy created by the party. Candidates are expected to promote the party leader, the label, the manifesto, the key messages, the overall brand – regardless of local electors' viewpoints. Thus Marland argued that these political franchisees 'are more concerned with getting hamburgers ready for a Saturday morning rush than they are with changing recipes' in order to win elections. However, research by Lilleker and Negrine (2002 and 2003) and Lilleker (2005 and 2006) suggests that candidates are increasingly running local marketing campaigns, having realised the negative consequences of too much central control. In some constituencies, local voters are particularly important and influential on the vote. And in the US where party organisation are looser, Steger (1999, 663, 667) notes how candidates employ their own staff and consultants and have freedom from party control to tailor their positions and issues to suit their market. Incumbents get an informal feel for their market through 'direct interactive communication with their constituents to gain first-hand information about their concerns, complaints, and preferences'. The power in the organisation of political marketing has to be carefully balanced to maximize effectiveness on all sides.

Summary

Internal marketing is an important part of political marketing. It is really crucial to create volunteer-friendly organisational structures in response to research about volunteer needs, trying to involve volunteers in the product design enough so that they accept proposed changes; to ensure that fundraising attempts reflect understanding of donor behaviour; and to make sure campaign and party organisational structures are well staffed and resourced to support political marketing activities. Without effective internal political marketing, good products can get blocked and volunteers will do less or resign, and in the long term this can undermine support for the party. Fundraising and resource management is also an important part of internal marketing that impacts on what parties, campaigns and candidates can do. Figure 5.11 offers a guide to doing internal political marketing in practice, and the practitioner profile of Matthew Barzun explores his work to raise donations for Barack Obama's presidential campaigns. Internal marketing is more subtle, behind the scenes, and does not often yield quick results; but if it can be done well the product is more likely to be supported by committed and enthusiastic members and volunteers, and the next stage of communication and campaigning, which will be discussed in the next two chapters, will be much easier.

Practitioner profile 5.1

Name: Matthew Winthrop Barzun
Date of birth: 23 October, 1970
Most notable job: Fundraiser for Barack Obama's presidential campaigns

Description: Before becoming involved in his most notable role, Matthew Barzun worked as an intern for John Kerry in 1989, then as a business executive for CNET networks. However, from a political marketing perspective, his most important role was as a key fundraiser in Barack Obama's 2008 presidential election campaign. While not the Finance Chairman at the time (a position he would hold in 2012), Barzun's efforts in 2008 helped revolutionise the way campaign fundraising is done, both in the US and worldwide. With Obama relying on raising money privately rather than through public

Best practice guide to doing internal political marketing

1   Understand that internal political marketing is important; ineffective internal marketing can derail all other political marketing efforts.

2   Research and respond to the demands, expectations, needs and behaviour of the internal market of volunteers, supporters, donors and members.

3   Create volunteer-centred structures, accepting that they can't always do what you want when you want and instead enabling them to get involved to suit themselves.

4   Help them help you even more: offer volunteers support and training, assign tasks and promote according to skills, and give volunteers leadership positions and access to data.

5   Use e-marketing and internal marketing principles to create online forums for supporters to discuss and get involved in the campaign/party, creating solidary incentives and stimulating participation.

6   Where volunteers are more representative of voters, engage them as part-time marketers, to both provide useful market intelligence and campaign on behalf of the party and to build long-term relationships that outlast the campaigns – and governments – of political candidates and leaders.

7   Use direct marketing to encourage party sympathisers to be involved in a party, designing e-marketing to enable them to campaign for the party.

8   Target online fundraising messages to suit the audience to make them more effective, and aim fundraising at active and satisfied volunteers.

9   Adapt both the concept and mechanics of donor marketing to suit the volunteer and donor cultures and regulatory frameworks within the political system.

10   Train party staff in political marketing as they have increasing influence on marketing.

11   Maintain organisation in all areas/at all levels, don't segment, to ensure a long-term infrastructure is there when needed.

12   Utilise ideology and internal views to create distinctive positions but also to win.

13   Set limits: let volunteers be involved in policy discussion, strategy and the campaign and let them influence it – but within constraints.

14   Thank them for their efforts.

15   Make the argument about the need for power to achieve moral goals.

16   Use effective internal communication to explain policy decisions and progress especially in government.

17   Get a balance between unity of the brand at central/local level and enough room for local adaptation.

18   Adopt a political partnership model, working with volunteers in government as well as campaigns.

Figure 5.11

campaign funds, Barzun was the mastermind behind building Obama's network of supporter-driven online event pages in order to co-ordinate small-dollar fundraisers. The internet donation system not only made it easy for people to donate if they so chose (both small and/or recurring payments to the campaign), it also empowered Obama supporters to do online fundraising themselves. The idea behind the system was to create incentives to encourage supporters to achieve fundraising goals. By offering various tools through the Obama campaign website, the campaign effectively used peer-to-peer fundraising. The idea was that potential donors were far more likely to donate money to the campaign if they were being prompted by their friends and peers rather than official campaign staff themselves. Barzun's revolutionary supporter-driven fundraisers helped contribute to the US$778million that the campaign was able to raise in total. Furthermore, the grass-roots-like citizen fundraisers also helped Obama establish a connection with his supporters in a way that seemed lost to contemporary politics. Barzun has since become an American ambassador, while also working as the Finance Chairman for Obama's 2012 re-election campaign.

" " Discussion points

1   Why are members or volunteers important to parties and candidates?
2   Discuss Granik's three main motivations for volunteering for parties or campaigns – social, enhancement or understanding – and discuss how effective *x* party is at meeting these needs and what they need to do to improve their organisation in this respect.
3   What advantages may come from conducting research and then redeveloping what is on offer to members or supporters?
4   Consider which party you support, either at the moment or at the last election, whether as a party member or voter. Discuss which of Bannon's (2005b) types applies: married, the family, true love, kissing cousins, open marriage, tart syndrome, one-night stands, a trapped lover, married for money or the forced partner.
5   List all the ways in which marketing can be applied to volunteers and decide which are most important and why, drawing on the examples here and any personal experience of volunteering.
6   Examine the websites of several political parties and discuss the extent to which they seem to be following Lilleker and Jackson's (2013) suggestion that the internet can be used to manage relationships with volunteers.
7   Do you think it is true that volunteers can be seen as part-time marketers? What are the arguments for and against this?
8   Discuss whether you think internal marketing can be carried out in government through initiatives like Organizing for America.
9   Why should party leaders and strategists bother to worry about creating unity in political marketing?
10 What blockages might a leader trying to implement a market-oriented strategy encounter and what can they do to overcome them?
11 Is it the leader's fault if the internal market blocks their attempt to re-market their party, or is it just bad luck and a matter of timing that they couldn't have done better to create unity?
12 How was Obama so successful in raising funds in 2008 when he sought smaller individual donations instead of large sums of money?
13 How should staff and resources best be organised to help political marketing be effective?

Assessment questions

Essay/Exam

1 Discuss ways in which parties and campaigns can create volunteer friendly organisations, utilising theory and empirical examples.

2 How effectively do parties utilise the internet to attract and retain volunteers, as suggested by Lilleker and Jackson (2013).

3 Academics such as Van Aelst, Ubertaccio and Lees-Marshment and Pettitt argue that parties should see volunteers as part-time marketers. To what extent do you think this is true?

4 How effective was Organising for America in both retaining 2008 volunteers and recruiting new volunteers in 2012?

5 How can internal marketing be used by parties and leaders in government to help them achieve policy implementation?

6 Why is creating unity important in political marketing, and what strategies have parties used to achieve this and with what effect?

7 Why is internal culture important to internal political marketing?

8 Identify cases where the internal market blocked political marketing such as the Australian Labor Party under Rudd and Gillard, UK Labour under Kinnock/Blair and UK Conservatives under William Hague. To what extent did the leaders follow the guidelines for creating unity, and what might they have done better?

9 Discuss the use of marketing in fundraising, using theory and empirical examples.

10 Discuss the nature and importance of party staff and resources in political marketing.

Applied

1 Synthesise theories on how to create a volunteer-friendly organisation (using Granik, Lebel, Lees-Marshment and Pettitt, etc.) and assess a party or campaign against them, making recommendations for improvement

2 Assess the membership or supporter network (or a sample of it) from a local party organisation, branch, association or network, in terms of how they fall into each of Bannon's (2005b) relationship typologies (married, the family, true love, kissing cousins, open marriage, tart syndrome, one-night stands, a trapped lover, married for money or the forced partner) and the implications for the party's strength of support.

3 Assess a party or campaign against Lebel's (1999) principles for managing volunteers and make recommendations for how they might improve.

4 Drawing on theoretical and empirical research, critique the effectiveness of party or campaign websites as a means to attract and retain volunteers/members, and make recommendations for how they might improve their use of online volunteer marketing.

5 Assess the extent to which a political party, group or campaign considers volunteers to be part-time marketers (Van Aelst *et al.* 2012) and how effectively they allow this resource to be utilised, making suggestions for improvement if appropriate.

6 Apply Lees-Marshment and Pettit's Framework for volunteer activism through inclusive party organisations to *x* party, assessing to what extent they are doing this, and create a plan for future development.

7 Conduct a critical assessment of the effectiveness of Organizing for America in helping President Obama in government in aspects such as policy implementation.

8 Assess a party or campaign against Lees-Marshment's (2013) Political Partnership Model, identifying strengths and weaknesses and making recommendations for how they could perform better in future.

9 Think of a party that has recently won power after using political marketing, such as becoming market-oriented or creating a research-driven brand. How effectively did they maintain unity within their party?

10 Assess the internal marketing strategies employed by party leaders such as Julia Gillard, David Cameron, Nick Clegg, Phil Goff, David Shearer, William Hague and Neil Kinnock and whether they followed suggestions in previous research for creating unity, and make recommendations for how future party leaders might be more successful.

11 Outline and explain Pettitt's strategies for involving volunteers in creating the party product, noting both the costs and benefits of each strategy. Assess which strategy x party seems to have taken in relation to its volunteers. Recommend whether they should continue to change this, based on consideration of the party goals, context, and the potential costs and benefits of each strategy in relation to them.

12 Critique a campaign website against Levenhus's (2010) principles of relationship building with volunteers.

13 Critically assess the rationale and effectiveness of the 50-state strategy implemented by Howard Dean when Chairman of the DNC, and compare it with the organisational resourcing of a current party to make recommendations for how that party might further develop its resources to help it succeed in political marketing over the long term.

CASE STUDY

Case study 5.1 Making the net work: key lessons in online political marketing

By Sophia Blair, University of Auckland
sophia.blair@gmail.com

> *Each new generation of nerds thinks it has the answer, only to run into the same brick wall of human behaviour. We must understand people and organisations before we can determine how to meld them with technology.*
>
> Frank Bannister, senior lecturer and e-democracy
> expert at Trinity College, Dublin

Over the last decade, the use of online technology has become firmly entrenched as a tool that parties deploy to increase political party participation. Yet, its efficacy is often misunderstood. Political parties regularly view the use of it as strategic, when it is merely tactical and should be should be deployed in support of a comprehensive and robust internal marketing strategy. Chris Hughes, the creator of Barack Obama's successful online social network, reflected this point when he noted 'you can have the best technology in the world, but if you don't have a community who wants to use it and who are excited about it, then it has no purpose' (quoted in McTear 2012). Online technology itself is not the key driver of party participation. Rather, party participation is increased by using internal marketing to understand and deliver what members ultimately want: a place where they can form friendships and connections with like-minded people, provide a sense of belonging and the opportunity to put their political values into action. Online technology should, then, be used as a tool to support this (Blair 2012). This case study analyses the New Zealand Labour Party's use of online technology in the lead-up to the 2011 general election to explore this idea.

Labour did not utilise online technology to engage in internal market research in any meaningful way. The few minor examples of online technology in Labour's member research were isolated, with no ongoing plan in place to understand their needs or motivations. The lack of this research was a major obstacle for increasing party political participation as internal research is critical to understand and address the needs, motivations and behaviour of party members and supporters. This information is crucial for developing a wide range of targeted participation opportunities to increase the involvement of activists.

Segmentation of members and supporters was carried out with very basic level email list segmentation at a local level. The lack of segmentation largely resulted from tensions between the local organisations and head office and the commonly held view that Labour did not need to target individual members differently. The absence of any high-level segmentation presented a problem for Labour as segmentation is a crucial part of online political marketing. It enables parties to target their members and supporters with participation opportunities and communications that address their specific motivation for belonging to the party. Labour will struggle to embed segmentation into its future use of online political marketing if it does not recognise its importance.

Labour's use of online technology to provide participation opportunities to supporters was mixed. In some cases, there was a genuine and co-ordinated push for creating a sense of community amongst members, involving them in decision making-processes, and encouraging offline participation. Open Labour NZ was a good example of this, but it still highlights the lack of infrastructure and central co-ordination within Labour, resulting in best practice examples becoming one-off events. Labour's main problem in this area was its lack of strategy, meaning that participation opportunities were ad hoc, inconsistent, and did not exploit the possibility of enhancing the opportunities that online technology can offer.

Labour's online political marketing communications were inconsistent and indicated the absence of a coherent participation narrative. Labour's online communication did not reinforce why members had joined the party, nor did they develop a long-term relationship with members. Communication needs to 'sell' party involvement as an appealing activity, using language that recipients can identify with. Labour's communications were not tailored to suit each online medium, meaning that opportunities to engage potential members and supporters in the party were missed. Labour's email communications closer to the election did well, but this success was due to the intervention of an overseas expert. It remains unclear whether the positive gains will be embedded in the long term.

Labour's attempt to incentivise and increase participation using online political marketing faced a range of challenges, chiefly an apparent lack of an internal marketing strategy. This represented perhaps the single largest barrier to participation growth. Labour did not appear to engage any members or potential members in consistent research. Furthermore, Labour's lack of research and segmentation resulted in participation opportunities being offered without the support of rigorous research. In addition, Labour's communication and branding did not align with any internal marketing strategy. Overall, Labour's ability to increase party participation was severely undermined by its lack of a coherent internal marketing strategy.

Lessons for political marketing

The use of online technology alone does not address the underlying needs and motivations of party members. Labour's use of online technology illustrates that while a variety of online tools were utilised, the lack of a comprehensive internal marketing strategy meant that they found it difficult to increase party participation using these tools. Online technology might increase involvement, but it would be ad hoc, inconsistent, and unpredictable unless parties underpin their e-marketing activities with a strong and coherent internal marketing plan.

Overall, the use of online technology alone is not the key to increasing participation in political parties. Parties using online technology for increasing participation must develop a comprehensive internal marketing strategy, placing significant emphasis on connecting supporters with the campaign and each other emotionally. In other words, parties must 'understand people and organisations' before it can 'meld them with technology.' Labour provides an excellent case study of how parties often fail to understand this simple principle, demonstrating also how resource scarcity and organisational dysfunction can undermine attempts to successfully engage in online political marketing.

Further reading

Blair, Sophia (2012). *Making the Net Work: What New Zealand Political Parties Can Learn From Obama*. MA Thesis, University of Auckland.

Cogburn, Derrick L. and Fatima K. Espinoza-Vasquez (2011). 'From networked nominee to networked nation: examining the impact of Web 2.0 and social media on political participation and civic engagement in the 2008 Obama campaign'. *Journal of Political Marketing*, 10(1): 189–213.

Dean, Dianne and Robin Croft (2001). 'Friends and relations: long-term approaches to political campaigning'. *European Journal of Communication*, 35(11/12): 1197–216.

Granik, Sue (2005). 'Membership benefits, membership action: why incentives for activism are what members want'. *Journal of Nonprofit & Public Sector Marketing*, 14(1): 65–89.

Lebel, Gregory G. (1999) 'Managing volunteers: times have changed – or have they?' In Bruce I. Newman (ed.) *Handbook of Political Marketing*, Thousand Oaks, CA: Sage, 129–42.

Levenshus, Abbey (2010). 'Online relationship management in a presidential campaign: a case study of the Obama campaign's management of its internet integrated grassroots effort'. *Public Relations Research,* 22(3): 313–35.

McTear, Euan (2012) 'Facebook, the 21st Century Ballot Box' *Glasgow Guardian*, May 5. http://glasgow guardian.co.uk/views/facebook-the-21st-century-ballot-box/

Notes

1   BBC 1, *Question Time*, 5 July 2001.
2   I would like to thank Dr Ken Cosgrove at Suffolk University for supplying me with this and other emails for this book.

References

Bannon, Declan (2004). Marketing segmentation and political marketing. Paper presented to the UK Political Studies Association, University of Lincoln, 4–8 April.

Bannon, Declan (2005a). Internal marketing and political marketing. UK PSA conference paper. Leeds, 7 April.

Bannon, Declan (2005b). 'Relationship marketing and the political process'. *Journal of Political Marketing*, 4(2/3): 73–90.

Bendle, Neil and Mihaela-Alina Nastasoiu (2014). 'Primary elections and US political marketing'. In Jennifer Lees-Marshment, Brian Conley and Kenneth Cosgrove (eds) *Political Marketing in the US*. New York: Routledge.

Bryant, Illana (2008). 'An inside look at Obama's grassroots marketing'. *Adweek*, 12 March.

Cogburn, Derrick L. and Fatima K. Espinoza-Vasquez (2011). 'From networked nominee to networked nation: examining the impact of Web 2.0 and social media on political participation and civic engagement in the 2008 Obama campaign'. *Journal of Political Marketing*, 10(1/2): 189–213.

Corrado, Anthony (2013). 'The money race: a new era of unlimited funding?' In Dennis W. Johnson (ed.) *Campaigning for President 2012: Strategy and Tactics*. New York: Routledge, 59–80.

Dean, Dianne and Robin Croft (2001). 'Friends and relations: long-term approaches to political campaigning'. *European Journal of Marketing*, 35(11/12): 1197–216.

Foster, Émilie and Patrick Lemieux (2012). 'Selling a cause: Political marketing and interest groups'. In Alex Marland, Thierry Giasson and Jennifer Lees-Marshment (eds) *Political Marketing in Canada*. Vancouver: UBC, 156–71.

Germany, Julie (2013). 'Advances in campaign technology'. In Dennis W. Johnson (ed.) *Campaigning for President 2012: Strategy and Tactics*. New York: Routledge, 81–91.

Gouliamos, Kōstas, Antonis Theocharous and Bruce Newman (2013). 'Introduction: political marketing: strategic "campaign culture"'. In Kōstas Gouliamos, Antonis Theocharous and Bruce Newman (eds) *Political Marketing Strategic 'Campaign Culture'*. London: Routledge: 1–11.

Granik, Sue (2005a). Internal consumers – what makes your party members join your election effort? Political Marketing Group Conference, London, 24–25 February.

Granik, Sue (2005b). 'Membership benefits, membership action: why incentives for activism are what members want'. In Walter W. Wymer, Jr. and Jennifer Lees-Marshment (eds) *Current Issues in Political Marketing*. Binghamton, NY: Haworth Press, 65–90.

Haberman, Maggie (2012). 'Priebus: we did the best we could in the time we had'. *Burns & Haberman* blog, 12th December. http://www.politico.com/blogs/burns-haberman/?hp=bh

Hughes, Andrew and Stephen Dann (2010). 'Australian political marketing: substance backed by style'. In Jennifer Lees-Marshment, Jesper Strömbäck and Chris Rudd (eds) *Global Political Marketing*. London: Routledge, 82–95.

Johnson, Dennis W. (2012). 'Campaigning in the twenty-first century: change and continuity in American political marketing'. In Jennifer Lees-Marshment (ed.) *The Routledge Handbook of Political Marketing*. London and New York: Routledge, 205–17.

Johnson, Dennis W. (2013). 'The election of 2012'. In Dennis W. Johnson (ed.) *Campaigning for President 2012: Strategy and Tactics*. New York: Routledge, 1–22.

Katz, Richard S. and Peter Mair (1993). 'The evolution of party organizations in Europe: the three faces of party organization'. *The American Review of Politics*, 14(4): 455–77.

Knuckey, Jonathan and Jennifer Lees-Marshment (2005). 'American political marketing: George W. Bush and the Republican Party'. In Darren Lilleker and Jennifer Lees-Marshment (eds) *Political Marketing: A Comparative Perspective*. Manchester: Manchester University Press, 39–58.

Lebel, Gregory G. (1999). 'Managing volunteers: time has changed – or have they?' In Bruce Newman (ed.) *Handbook of Political Marketing*. Thousand Oaks, CA: Sage, 129–42.

Lees-Marshment, Jennifer (2001). *Political Marketing and British Political Parties: The Party's Just Begun*. Manchester: Manchester University Press.

Lees-Marshment, Jennifer (2008). *Political Marketing and British Political Parties: The Party's Just Begun*. 2nd revised edition. Manchester: Manchester University Press.

Lees-Marshment, Jennifer (2009). 'Examples of internal blockage to market-oriented strategy: the UK Conservatives, 1997–2001'. Case study 6.2 in Jennifer Lees-Marshment, *Political Marketing: Principles and Applications*. London and New York: Routledge, 154–55.

Lees-Marshment, Jennifer (2011). *The Political Marketing Game*. Houndmills and New York: Palgrave Macmillan.

Lees-Marshment, Jennifer (2013). 'Political marketing and governance: moving towards the political partnership model of organisation'. In Emmanuelle Avril and Christine Zumello (eds) *New Technology, Organisational Change and Governance*. United Kingdom: Palgrave Macmillan, 218–34.

Lees-Marshment, Jennifer and Robin Pettitt (2010). 'UK political marketing: a question of leadership?' In Jennifer Lees-Marshment, Jesper Strömbäck and Chris Rudd (eds) *Global Political Marketing*. London: Routledge, 218–234.

Lees-Marshment, Jennifer and Robin Pettitt (2014). 'Mobilising volunteer activists in political parties: the view from central office'. *Contemporary Politics*.

Lees-Marshment, Jennifer, and Stuart Quayle (2001). 'Empowering the members or marketing the party? The Conservative reforms of 1998'. *The Political Quarterly*, 72(2): 204–12.

Lees-Marshment, Jennifer, Jesper Strömbäck and Chris Rudd (eds) (2010). *Global Political Marketing*. London: Routledge.

Levenshus, Abbey (2010). 'Online relationship management in a presidential campaign: a case study of the Obama campaign's management of its internet – integrated grassroots effort'. *Journal of Public Relations Research*, 22(3): 313–35.

Lilleker, Darren G. (2005). 'Local campaign management: winning votes or wasting resources?' *Journal of Marketing Management*, 21(9/10): 979–1003.

Lilleker, Darren G. (2006). 'Local political marketing: political marketing as public service'. In Darren Lilleker, Nigel Jackson and Richard Scullion (eds) *The Marketing of Political Parties*. Manchester: Manchester University Press, 206–30.

Lilleker, Darren G. and Nigel A. Jackson (2013). 'Reaching inward not outward: marketing via the internet at the UK 2010 general election'. *Journal of Political Marketing*. 12(2–3): 244–61.

Lilleker, Darren and Ralph Negrine (2002). Marketing techniques and political campaigns: the limitations for the marketing of British political parties. Paper presented to the UK PSA, Manchester, 7–9 April.

Lilleker, Darren and Ralph Negrine (2003). 'Not big brand names but corner shops: marketing politics to a disengaged electorate'. *The Journal of Political Marketing*, 2(1): 55–76.

Lloyd, Jenny (2005). 'Marketing politics . . . saving democracy'. In Adrian Sargeant and Walter Wymer (eds) *The Routledge Companion to Nonprofit Marketing*. New York: Routledge, 317–36.

Luntz, Frank (2006). Article in *The Daily Telegraph*, 4th December.

Lynch, Richard, Paul Baines and John Egan (2006). 'Long-term performance of political parties: towards a competitive resource-based perspective'. *Journal of Political Marketing*, 5(3): 71–92.

Marland, Alex (2009) 'Canadian constituency campaigns'. Case study 7.6 in Jennifer Lees-Marshment, *Political Marketing: Principles and Applications*. London and New York: Routledge, 190–92.

Marland, Alex (2012a). 'Amateurs versus professionals: The 1993 and 2006 Canadian federal elections'. In Alex Marland, Thierry Giasson and Jennifer Lees-Marshment (eds) *Political Marketing in Canada*. Vancouver: UBC, 59–75.

Marland, Alex (2012b). 'Yes we can (fundraise): the ethics of marketing in political fundraising'. In Jennifer Lees-Marshment (ed.) *The Routledge Handbook of Political Marketing*. London and New York: Routledge, 164–76.

Medvic, Stephen K. (2006). 'Understanding campaign strategy "deliberate priming" and the role of professional political consultants'. *Journal of Political Marketing*, 5(1/2): 11–32.

Mills, Stephen (2012). 'The party official as political marketer: the Australian experience'. In Jennifer Lees-Marshment (ed.) *The Routledge Handbook of Political Marketing*. London and New York: Routledge, 190–202.

O'Cass, Aron (2009). 'A resource-based view of the political party and value creation for the voter-citizen: an integrated framework for political marketing'. *Marketing Theory*, 9(2): 189–208.

Ormrod, Robert P. (2005). 'A conceptual model of political market orientation'. In Walter Wymer and Jennifer Lees-Marshment (eds) *Current Issues in Political Marketing*. Binghamton, NY: Haworth Press, 47–64.

Pettitt, Robin T. (2012). 'Internal Party Political Relationship Marketing: encouraging activism amongst local party members'. In Jennifer Lees-Marshment (ed.) *The Routledge Handbook of Political Marketing*. London and New York: Routledge, 137–50.

Reeves, Peter (2013). 'Local political marketing in the context of the Conservative Party'. *Journal of Nonprofit & Public Sector Marketing*, 25(2): 127–63.

Rogers, Ben (2005). 'From membership to management? The future of political parties as democratic organisations'. *Parliamentary Affairs*, 58(3): 600–10.

Sherman, Elaine (1999). 'Direct marketing: how does it work for political campaigns?' In Bruce Newman (ed.) *The Handbook of Political Marketing*. Thousand Oaks, CA: Sage, 365–88.

Smith, Gareth (2009). 'Conceptualizing and testing brand personality in British politics'. *Journal of Political Marketing*, 8(3): 209–32.

Smith, Gareth and Alan French (2009). 'The political brand: a consumer perspective'. *Marketing Theory*, 9(2): 209–26.

Spiller, Lisa and Jeff Bergner (2014). 'Database political marketing in campaigning and government'. In Jennifer Lees-Marshment, Brian Conley and Kenneth Cosgrove (eds) *Political Marketing in the US*. New York: Routledge.

Steen, Jennifer (1999). 'Money doesn't grow on trees: fund-raising in American political campaigns'. In Bruce I. Newman (ed.) *Handbook of Political Marketing*. Thousand Oaks, CA: Sage, 159–76.

Steger, Wayne (1999). 'The permanent campaign: marketing from the hill'. In Bruce Newman (ed.) *Handbook of Political Marketing*. Thousand Oaks, CA: Sage, 661–86.

Turcotte, André and Vincent Raynauld (2014). 'Boutique populism: the emergence of the Tea Party movement in the age of digital politics'. In Jennifer Lees-Marshment, Brian Conley and Kenneth Cosgrove (eds) *Political Marketing in the US*. New York: Routledge.

Ubertaccio, Peter N. (2012). 'Political parties and direct marketing: connecting voters and candidates more effectively'. In Jennifer Lees-Marshment (ed.) *The Routledge Handbook of Political Marketing*. London and New York: Routledge, 177–89.

Van Aelst, Peter, Joop van Holsteyn and Ruud Koole (2012). 'Party members as part-time marketers: using relationship marketing to demonstrate the importance of rank-and-file party members in election campaigns'. In Jennifer Lees-Marshment (ed.) *The Routledge Handbook of Political Marketing*. London and New York: Routledge, 151–63.

Wring, Dominic (2005). *The Politics of Marketing the Labour Party*. Houndmills: Palgrave Macmillan.

6   Static political marketing communication

Practitioner perspective 6.1 on the need for strategic communication in campaigns and government

What you're doing is creating a campaign which supports what the strategy is. [In a campaign] 'the big thing is to have a strategy and to stick to it. And if you're going to deviate from the strategy you have to have good reasons to be deviating from it.

Fraser Carson, New Zealand Labour Party advertiser 1993–1999,
interviewed in 2006

You have to map everything . . . the essence of a campaign is to make sure that every single possibility is talked about, thought about, so that when you're in a crisis situation you can go back to the plan and stick to the plan.

Mark Textor, Political Strategist in Australia, NZ and the UK, 2012

At the start of the year you put in place a strategy, you work out what your key messages are going to be, what your key themes are going to be and then you try to group your activity around those themes throughout the year.

Mike Munro, Former Chief Press Secretary for Prime Minister
Helen Clark, interviewed in 2006

Strategic communication is . . . never done in the moment, because most people aren't listening . . . Most people are going about their business . . . They're taking their kids to school, they're taking their mum to hospital, they're going to work . . . which is why you have to keep communicating the same things again and again and again.

Alastair Campbell, Press Secretary to UK Prime Minister Tony Blair, 2013

[Campbell brought in] a lot more of the strategic thinking about how you position the government, branding, longer term reputation, try to use all the different media, whether it's using specialist media, women's media, the internet.

James Humphrey, Former Head of corporate communications and the
strategic communications at Downing Street, interviewed in 2007

Sources: Lees-Marshment (2011); Campbell (2013); Sunday Profile (2012)

Political organisations and politicians use marketing communications all the time to achieve a wide range of goals, including improving the reputation of a government, launching a new brand, communicating a message, countering negative attacks from the opposition, educating voters, placing an issue on the agenda and increasing support for a politician or policy. Marketing helps to ensure that politicians understand who they should communicate with, when, on what topic and how; i.e. that communications are conducted strategically, as the comments in Practitioner perspective 6.1 argue is so crucial for it to be successful. Communication can be static – so simply what goes from the political organisation or figure to the public – or two-way through interactive communication between receiver and producer to form a relationship. This chapter focuses on static communication, exploring the marketing communication of candidates; campaign communication (research-led communication, market-oriented advertising, insights marketing, guerrilla marketing and celebrity marketing); communication tools (e.g. get out the vote, direct marketing, targeted communication and mobile/virtual marketing); selling policy (including government advertising and social marketing, and looking at policy concerned with involvement in war); communicating change, crisis and issues management; and integrated marketing communications.

Marketing communication of candidates

Political marketing research has explored several aspects of leader communication, including the need to make an emotional, human connection and the importance of non-verbal image. Bill Clinton appeared on MTV and *The Arsenio Hall Show* to show his human side when campaigning for the US presidency in 1992 (Ingram and Lees-Marshment 2002). Newman (2001, 210–14) argues that the relative success of the candidates in forging an emotional connection with voters in the 2000 US presidential election made the difference. Bush used his natural characteristics to connect, conveying positivity and likeability; whereas Gore showed more of a serious commitment to specific voters' concerns by talking about issues, but this lacked emotion. Schweiger and Aadami (1999, 348) argue that German leader Helmut Kohl lost support in the elections of 1998 despite delivery success in power because his image was that of an old man. Conversely it could be argued that in 2008 Barack Obama benefited from portraying a youthful, change-driven image during his bid for the Democratic nomination.

Schweiger and Aadami (1999) note how non-verbal images (NVI) marketing research can be used to understand what makes up a political image and measure responses from voters using a range of pictures representing different characteristics, both positive and negative. Figure 6.1 sets out both positive and negative image attributes that candidates can attract.

PMR can identify potential weaknesses and enable communication to be devised to reduce them. In President Bill Clinton's 1992 campaign, research suggested voters were more open to changing their view of Clinton if they heard him speak at length. Clinton therefore made frequent use of electronic town hall meetings, which allowed more direct and non-mediated access to voters, unavailable via traditional media (Ingram and Lees-Marshment 2002). Research also indicated that voters wanted Clinton to offer a New Democrat perspective that was different to Republicanism but without the old disadvantages of a 'tax and spend' liberal approach. Television commercials were created portraying Clinton and vice-presidential nominee Gore as a new generation of Democrats. Similarly, the media team GMMB responded to research about Obama in the 2008 presidential election that showed the more people learned about the candidate, the more they identified with him, and thus created videos of different length, using 60-second, two-minute and

Schweiger and Aadami's political candidate positive and negative image attributes

Dimension	Positive attribute	Negative attribute
Honesty	Honest Credible A man/woman of his/her word Transparent Reliable	Entangled in scandals Secretive
Quality	Possesses knowledge and experience Educated Capable	Lacks knowledge of how to manage a government Lacks other skills such as business knowledge or international experience
Strength	Strong Winner Carries his/her point Dynamic Successful	Weak Loser Seems to lack a backbone or the determination to get things done

Figure 6.1

Source: Adapted from Schweiger and Aadami (1999, 361)

on-demand versions, and a 30-minute special in October that drew 33.5 million viewers; they were delivered online or on the air, and via TV and radio (O'Leary 2009).

One question for candidate communication is how to market gender: whether to target branding and communication to female voters and what gendered leadership characteristics to promote. Busby's (2014) analysis of female conservative candidates notes how the 'Mama Grizzly' brand was designed to appeal to specific market segments – women generally, women suffering economically, and women who were socially conservative. However the Mama Grizzly brand was not successful in attracting women voters – most prominent Mama Grizzly candidates received more votes from male voters than female voters. Busby argues this was because whilst women voters desire masculine traits because they are important to show leadership, they also want female political candidates to show emotional and behavioural traits, so the socially conservative, aggressive Mama Grizzly brand was not as effective as had been hoped.

Campaign communication

Campaign communication taking place within the official election campaign period is more focused and includes research-led communication, market-oriented advertising, insights marketing and guerrilla marketing.

Research-led campaign communication

Here, market research continues to be used: as Rademacher and Tuchfarber (1999, 202) argue, polling is used in different ways, depending on the stage of the campaign; in the early stages it identifies what messages to send to whom, and later it measures the effectiveness of different messages to inform any necessary changes. Braun and Matuskova (2009) explored how market intelligence and strategy informed campaigning and changed the direction of the 2006 Czech elections. A year before the election, CSSD trailed ODS in public opinion polls by more than 2 per cent. Marketing consultants from the US firm Penn, Schoen and Berland Associates (PSB) changed this by being the first campaign to use market research. PSB ran focus groups with swing voters followed by an extensive quantitative benchmark poll to assess the position and support for all the parties among different voter blocks; issue importance; and reaction to potential messages and policy. The research results were used to inform the goals of the campaign and develop the strategy, message and tactical tools to achieve those goals. It identified that the CSSD has strengths such as a successful economic record in government, a more popular leader and favourable product but weaknesses including corruption and internal fighting. The campaign therefore focused on attacking ODS on policies that voters disliked and framing the campaign as being about the leadership. Messages were refined in response to continuous research throughout the campaign. As a result of this research-informed campaign, the CSSD managed to triple its support among voters, even though ODS eventually won the election, with 35 per cent compared with CSSD's 32 per cent.

Whilst there is much attention paid to election advertisements, we need to consider the marketing that goes on behind them. Ridout's (2014) analysis of US adverts demonstrates how market research is fundamental to the development of effective ads: the message and medium is designed to suit targets derived from segmentation to maximize resource effectiveness, and the ads are also tested before launch to ensure they will achieve their goals. Furthermore, he notes that ads will increasingly be subject to testing through experimental and analytic marketing research before release. Targeted ads have become very important in today's complex media environment. These findings reiterate our assertion above that political marketing techniques tend to be used in an overlapping fashion that creates a more potent end product. In this case, market research gains power when it is used in conjunction with other tools like advertising. Conversely, advertising by itself is not worth so much but when it is combined with research and segmentation of the market into target groups, and fits the overall brand and candidates product message, that is when it will be most effective.

Case Study 6.1 by Miloš Gregor and Anna Matušková on a Czech presidential candidate's campaign strategy demonstrates the value of research in setting strategy, both in terms of its success in increasing the candidates support and in the failure to identify the right questions and identify issues such as if the candidate is perceived to be a foreigner because they lived outside the country for 40 years. Comprehensive research at every stage of the campaign helps to ensure the strategy continues to be appropriate and effective.

Market-oriented advertising

Market research data, but also strategic concepts, can be used to develop advertising that will support the product. Robinson's (2006) theory of market-oriented advertising applies market-oriented principles to advertising: see Figure 6.2.

Robinson's criteria for market-orientated political adverts

Market orientation	Observable form
Voter orientation	
• Target voters identified • Sense and response to voter needs	• Images of target audience and environment featured • Images of party and/or leader interaction with target voters including images of listening and words of togetherness
• Maintenance of relationships with core voters	• Evocation of party history and myth; acknowledgement of shared characters, themes and stories • Images or words of care for core supporters • Text and wording recognizable to core supporters • Kept policy promises
• Offer in exchange for party vote	• Party vote requested and policy and leadership offered in exchange
Competitor orientation	
• Behaves according to their strategic market position (market leader, challenger, follower, niche party)	• Competition identified and targeted in messages • Policy appropriated from smaller niche parties • Concern to increase market share demonstrated • Openness to coalition arrangements demonstrated • Concern to increase market share demonstrated • Niche parties remain true to original raison d'être

Figure 6.2

Source: Adapted from Robinson (2006)

Robinson (2010) analysed the New Zealand election campaigns in 1999, 2002 and 2005 and concluded that parties which demonstrated a strong voter orientation in their political advertisements were most successful. Effective adverts demonstrated an affinity for their target voter groups by showing images of voters and the party leader interacting with them and also used words of togetherness. Less effective advertising only conveyed responsiveness to their core supporters. Case study 6.2 by Thomas Seeman explores how the New Zealand Green Party adverts in 2011 identified target audiences and conveyed responsiveness to voter needs as well as maintaining relationships with core voters, an election in which they enjoyed increased electoral success. The Robinson framework could be applied to all forms of political communication.

Insights marketing

Another use of research in communication is insights marketing, where communication is developed in response to understanding people's deepest values and fears, has been used in campaign marketing. The public relations firm Crosby-Textor first advised Australian Liberal Prime Minister John Howard to use insights or dog-whistle marketing – called dog-whistle because communication is devised only to be heard by the specific target market at which it is aimed. Such communication plays emotively on people's hopes and fears. Crosby-Textor also advised the UK Conservatives and in the UK 2005 election their election posters adopted the slogan 'Are you thinking what we're thinking?', placed under simplified messages: 'It's not racist to impose limits on immigration', and with the use of handwriting, to connect with ordinary people (see Seawright 2005, 951; Gaber 2006).

Guerilla marketing

Guerilla marketing is communication that gets attention by being unexpected and novel. Egherman (2005) discuss how Iranian politician Akbar Hashemi Rafsanjani (http:www. hashemirafsanjani.ir) utilised guerilla marketing to market his particular presidential brand by getting Iran's hip youth to act as unpaid campaign workers and engage in unconventional tactics such as wrapping themselves in Hashemi stickers, taping his poster on their backs, and going skating, thus wearing Fafsanjani campaign materials like fashion accessories. Another example is the Australian Labor campaign of 2007 where volunteers wore T-shirts with 'Kevin07' on them, gaining attention to the new leader Kevin Rudd who went on to win the election and become Prime Minister. Kevin O7 was just the name of the campaign website but became a moniker for the fresh new product being offered by Labor in 2007.

Celebrity marketing

Marland and Lalancette (2014) explore how celebrity endorsement can be an important tool of political marketing. It helps to attract attention in an environment where media and the audience is very fragmented and difficult to influence. Celebrities appeal to target markets including those whom political elites find it hard to connect with – the young, disaffected and floating voters. This can help parties and candidates get attention for their brand or with fundraising. Celebrity endorsement is widely used in US politics: they note how 600+ external celebrities supported Obama and over 200 endorsed Romney in the 2012 Presidential Election. It is also used in a targeted way by groups supportive to the candidate: YouTube videos endorsing Obama were posted by the National Jewish Democratic Council, featuring a combination of internal and external celebrities including Broadway star Barbara Streisand. Celebrities Jay-Z and Beyoncé hosted the President at a private Manhattan fundraiser and Will Smith and Jada Pinkett Smith invited the First Lady to a fundraising luncheon at their home. President Obama joined a dinner with 150 guests at George Clooney's cottage that raised $15 million in May 2012 and celebrities who had helped with his fundraising, including Clooney, Oprah Winfrey, Jay-Z, Jon Bon Jovi, Sarah Jessica Parker and Morgan Freeman, visited the White House in 2012. Celebrities can also be used to attack the opposition such as when Hollywood legend Clint Eastwood spoke to an empty chair at the 2012 Republican National Convention in a critique of Obama which got significant media coverage. There are however potential hazards which researchers and strategists should be aware of in terms of compatibility with brand; strategists have to ensure the celebrities chosen – who have their own commercial brand of course – fit with and support the political product, adding, not detracting, credibility and appeal.

Communication tools

Political marketing communication tools can make a difference where competition is even and the election is close and include get out the vote, direct marketing, targeted communication and mobile/virtual marketing.

GOTV

GOTV (get out the vote) is now a substantial part of election campaigns, using segmentation and voter profiling to get voters who support your product to actually go and vote. If the election results seem a foregone conclusion, voters might not bother to turn out; or if core supporters are dissatisfied with how a party has changed or governed, they might show their protest by not voting. GOTV is used to give supporters a reason to make the effort to actually vote. GOTV on core supporters was a crucial activity during the George W. Bush RNC era in the 2002–2004–2006–2008 elections. Republican staffer Rick Beeson explained that voter profiling enabled them to identify a very specific group of people they wanted to get to the polls. Whereas before they 'looked at it like a baleen whale and we just came along and just scooped it up like krill and just tried to turn out a lot of people' they moved to trying to turn out 'a very defined universe' – so in the 2004 US Presidential election, the focus was on hundreds of people instead of thousands (Lees-Marshment 2011, 21–3).

Using volunteers through networking marketing is an important part of GOTV. In 2002 the US Republicans created a new organisational structure for volunteers to get involved in GOTV and contact the public personally to help make the message seem more credible. Ubertaccio (2008, 517) reports how an RNC post-election report claimed that 30 million people were contacted on a person-to-person basis. In 2004 the Republicans used mixed motivators to get people out with not just the right message but also the right person: 'a volunteer knocking on their door or a volunteer calling them and saying '*Hey, I live in your neighbourhood, I just want to make sure you're going to go vote*'. They also sent a lot of mail and contacts to Hispanic females and single females with children in New Mexico because they responded to the President's 'No Child Left Behind' message. New Mexico was one of two states that voted Democrat in 2000 and voted Republican in 2004. The Democrats followed this approach from 2006 onwards.

In the 2005 New Zealand election, the Labour Party realized that the election result was going to be close and sent direct mail shots to voters who lived in South Auckland in state/council homes during the last few weeks of the campaign after analysis of electoral rolls revealed turnout was low in that region in the last election. The mail was designed as a mock eviction notice, suggesting that a victory for the opposition, the National Party would result in state homes being sold and the tenants having to find an alternative home. Turnout – and Labour votes – went up and helped to secure victory (see Lees-Marshment 2010, 71).

Another example of how GOTV was used and how it helped secure victory in a close race is San Francisco's 2004 mayoral election in the US, where candidate Gavin Newsom lost on election day but won on election night, because he received 20,000 more postal votes than the opposition (see Ross 2008). This was partly owing to an advance programme to identify potential voters and target them to submit a postal vote if they weren't likely to vote on election day. Volunteers were used to ask voters to 'endorse' Gavin Newsom for mayor in a petition, which identified 24,000 supporters who were then input into a database, and those who were not registered to vote had an application delivered by a Newsom volunteer, thereby registering 5,000 new voters most likely to support the candidate. Contacting other registered voters who had not endorsed Newsom produced another 25,000 identified as potential Newsom supporters, even though many of them lived in neighbourhoods that would not have previously been considered supportive of the candidate. Half of these voters were not certain to vote, and staff implemented a GOTV campaign through several phone or in-person contacts made until they registered for a postal vote to get them to vote by mail. By the time of the election, the Newsom campaign had already got 8,000 votes through the post. This and other GOTV activities became even more important when there was a repeat or run-off election a month later. Ross (2008) argues that the campaign taught them that voter identification should be started early as, if voters endorse early and you continue communicating with them, they will stick with you. Campaigns should also reach out to areas or communities that may not universally support you as research can identify pockets of support in even the most hostile areas.

Parties also try to move voters between different GOTV universes to become more likely supporters: Republican Rick Beeson explained that the RNC broke voters down 'into a GOTV universe, which is people we know are going to vote for us or have a high propensity of voting for us. Then we have persuasion universe. That's a group of people that we need to talk to ... We want ... them to get a significant number of persuasion contacts ... understanding that once they got a certain number of percentage contacts you could move them' (Lees-Marshment 2011, 22). Green and Gerber (2004, 137) present a practical guide to GOTV, utilising scientific evidence about what is most cost effective through an experimental research method and advise what to do and what to avoid: see Figure 6.3. They note that voting is a social act and shaped by the social environment in which voters find themselves.

However, GOTV has limitations. As Figure 6.3 shows, Green and Gerber's research suggests that partisan GOTV is ineffective, and Johnson (2013, 16) notes that both presidential candidates received fewer votes in 2012 than in 2008, and despite the billions spent on GOTV drives only 57.5 per cent of the eligible adult population voted in 2012. It is also heavily reliant on technology, and the new Republican system Project Orca, adopted in 2012, crashed throughout election day.

Green and Gerber's advice as to what to do and what to avoid with GOTV

What to do	What to avoid
• Make voters feel wanted at the polls, as if inviting them to a social occasion, using a personal invitation, if not an unscripted phone call	• Simple messages reminding people to vote when election day is near, even if the pre-recorded voices are those of famous or credible people
• Connect with voters' previous voting or expressions of interest in voting	• Information-rich messages about the election such as voter guides
• Remind them that whether they vote or not will be on record as, if others seem to be watching, people seem to be more willing to get out and vote	• Telling people why they should vote for a particular candidate or cause; partisan driven GOTV does not enhance effectiveness

Figure 6.3

Source: Summarised from Green and Gerber (2004, 137)

Direct marketing

Practitioner perspective 6.2 Ensuring online communication is direct

My 'top tip' would have to be: understand what platform(s) the people you want to reach are using, and communicate with them through those sites. People's attention is so spread between different online and offline channels (TV, radio, print, news websites, Twitter, Facebook, LinkedIn, Tumblr, YouTube, etc.) that it's important to know where those people most likely to be open to your party are, and with limited resources it's important to be able to identify and market to the channel which most influentially communicates with them.

Gavin Middleton, former staffer with the New Zealand ACT Party

Source: a top tip supplied by email in 2013

Direct marketing is a common part of marketing communications and includes direct mail, direct email, direct texts, internet ads and any other form of communication that is sent directly to the individual, personalized and written in a way to get them to act quickly. As Practitioner perspective 6.2 suggests, it responds to the behaviour of the recipient and is used to increase support, recruit new volunteers, ask for donations or get out the vote. It uses segmentation data and sample forms are heavily tested to maximize effectiveness and resources. Direct mail was the original form of direct marketing and O'Shaughnessy and Peele (1985, 115) note how it was used by previous presidential candidates, including Barry Goldwater, George McGovern, Jimmy Carter, Edward Kennedy and Ronald Reagan. The UK Conservative Party used direct mail in 1997–2001 to try to boost and widen the membership, profiling existing members and buying membership lists of names for wine clubs, garden centres and rugby or cricket clubs who had a similar outlook for a recruitment drive (Lees-Marshment 2008, 208). In the 2005 UK election, Labour produced direct mail and DVDs for particular candidates in key seats. Direct telemarketing is often used by parties and candidates utilising call centres for a range of activities, including voter persuasion, voter identification, volunteer recruitment and GOTV efforts, and the UK Conservatives set up call centres all around the country for the 2005 election. Direct marketing is also used in fundraising, as discussed in Chapter 5 on internal political marketing.

More recent forms include direct texts to mobile phones and adverts that pop up when the public is browsing a particular web page. E-forms of direct marketing offer the same potential to reach individuals directly but more cheaply. Internet advertisements that pop up when the public is browsing are designed not just to reach them but to be tailor-made to the recipient in terms of content and time. However, traditional doorknocking is still valuable: Case study 6.3 by Aleš Kudrnáč explores how a local candidate in Slovakia utilised direct face-to-face marketing by knocking on everyone's door which helped to gain informal market intelligence and communicate with voters. Importantly, it shows that it is possible to win a campaign when using mainly active face-to-face campaigning with a very limited budget.

The weakness of direct marketing is that each new innovation is copied by competitors and so loses its competitiveness, and the public becomes immune to the methodology after a while. Furthermore, the communication is only as good as the data and assumptions of the list it derives its recipients from; or the overall context of the political product. Loewen and Rubenson (2011) conducted an experiment to test the use of direct mail to communicate controversial policy positions in co-operation with the Michael Ignatieff campaign 2006 for the leadership of the Liberal Party of Canada. They randomly assigned a subset of convention delegates to receive a direct mail treatment featuring policy messages outside the mainstream of the party and surveyed the effects on delegates' ratings and preference ordering of leadership candidates. The results suggested that, contrary to theory, the impact of direct mail on voters was actually negative: receiving direct mail from the Ignatieff campaign even moved Ignatieff down in the preference rankings of some delegates. Thus the ability for leaders to use persuasive communication to gain support for unpopular arguments is limited. Lowen and Rubenson (2011, 59) explain that Ignatieff's positions on foreign policy, the constitution and fiscal federalism were well outside the mainstream of the party he was seeking to lead; communicating something supporters did not want would only harm him.

Targeted communication

Practitioner perspective 6.3 on the importance of micro-targeted communications

If the paradigm before was about being on message, the paradigm for this period is about micro-targeting. Rather than saying the same thing to everybody, actually saying something different to everybody, saying something particular and personal to the particular people who have particular concerns. It's not enough to recognise that in any one constituency there are 15,000 people that you need to talk to in order to win the election, but it's actually that those 15,000 people may be able to be grouped into smaller groupings, each of whom has their own personal agendas and issues.

Matt Carter, PSB research and former UK Labour General Secretary, interviewed in 2007

Source: Lees-Marshment (2011)

As Practitioner perspective 6.3 indicates, trying to communicate the same thing to everyone is less effective than targeting the message. Segmentation can help parties and candidates decide on which voter groups to target communication. In 1979, the UK Conservatives segmented the market – albeit more crudely than happens now – and focused communication efforts accordingly: see Figure 6.4.

The New Zealand National Party's billboards in 2008 were clearly aimed at both core and new segments – see Figure 6.5.

Case studies 6.4 by Svetlana S. Bodrunova and 6.5 by Jennifer Rayner both illustrate the importance of targeted communication. Case 6.4 explores the use of strategic communications by Moscow mayoral candidates of 2013 to reach specific markets. Case 6.5 demonstrates that the use of targeted communications by South Australian Labor in 2010 was effective because they knew where to target political messages and resources as well as who to target. Rayner thus argues that calculated and strategic geographic targeting helped the Labor government win a third in difficult circumstances.

Targeting can be used by smaller and new parties as well as older established ones. McGough (2005) illustrated how the Irish party Sinn Féin segmented the market into six different targets in 2002, understanding their different demands and adopting a different strategy for each one, where appropriate:

Targeted communication by the UK Conservatives in 1979

Target markets	Examples of communication geared to suit the target markets
Skilled working class (C2)	Saatchi and Saatchi created posters with slogans which included the infamous Labour isn't working and Britain's better off with the Conservatives.
	One newspaper advert was entitled 'Why every trade unionist should consider voting Conservative' and appealed to traditional Labour supporters.
Women	Campaign adverts were placed in women's magazines.
First-time voters	Adverts were run in the cinema to attract support from first-time voters.
Party faithful	Thatcher's speeches appealed to traditional Conservative voters.

Figure 6.4

New Zealand National's targeted billboards in 2008

Billboard wording	Target market
1 in 5 school leaders doesn't pass NCEA We'll smarten up the system	Traditional supporters and families/parents
Get them into training Not into trouble. National's youth guarantee	Traditional supporters and families/parents
Make our neighbourhoods safer Tougher bail, sentencing and parole laws	Traditional supporters South Auckland voters
Wave goodbye to higher taxes Not your loved ones	Higher earners
More doctors + more nurses = less bureaucrats	Public sector professionals

Figure 6.5

Source: Lees-Marshment (2010, 75)

1 *North – nationalist Catholics*: fanatically faithful to the party; want a socialist, 32-county Republic of Ireland. The party promoted a picture of their voters as barely free from the chains of conflict and still enduring sectarianism and intimidation from various quarters.

2 *North – Catholic community*: attracted by Sinn Féin policies on demilitarisation, policing, loyalist attacks, plastic bullets and Orange parades.

3 *Alliance and soft Ulster Unionist supporters*: the party tried to build bridges to this market.

4 *Republic of Ireland voters*: very different views from the party, so Sinn Féin focused on a socialist list of policies they wanted, rather than contemplating making any concessions to competitors. The party campaigned using an alternative language focused on change and responding to discontent among the working class and for the second single transferable vote (STV) of the middle classes.

5 *Ogra Sinn Féin – the all-Ireland youth wing*: building long-term links with the youth.

6 *Irish–American/international support*: careful packaging to the international market.

Analytic and experimental marketing can be used to test the effectiveness of communication on different target markets before it is widely released. In the 2012 presidential election, Obama discovered unlikely ways to reach appropriate targets such as cheaper advertising slots with lower audiences but consisting of viewers who were more open to voting for Obama and thus more receptive to the campaign communication (Johnson 2013, 17). Germany (2013, 81) notes how both the Obama and Romney campaign combined masses of data in real time about Americans in terms of their consumer patterns, online browsing behaviour and voting behaviour. Obama created Project Narwhal and the Dashboard canvassing programme to store and use such data. Such analysis went unseen but was, Germany argues, the most revolutionary technology tactic in 2012. Such high technology was connected to traditional grass-roots contact as well as run through new mobile communication forms.

Communication can also be targeted at specific groups such as women voters. In the 2008 Obama campaign, traditional communication was highly targeted. O'Leary (2009) notes how women were targeted by focusing on the issue of equal pay using Lilly Ledbetter, an Alabama grandmother who sued her former employer after discovering her male counterparts were paid more, via a range of media outlets including TV, radio, online, web social groups, college newspapers, video games and video on campuses. States such as Ohio had communication on issues such as gun control to reassure hunters about Obama's support of their right to bear arms and also rebut third-party groups' spending against the Obama campaign. Harmer and Wring (2013) note how US and UK politicians targeted women using labels such as 'soccer mums', 'Worcester women', 'let down woman', 'school gate mums' and 'sandwich mothers'. Communication in the 2010 UK election was placed in media outlets with high female readership such as *The Sun* newspaper or *Take a Break* magazine. They quote a Labour strategist, Douglas Alexander, for recalling how the party targeted women who were under 40, a homeowner with children living in a small city or town in the Midlands, working part- or full-time most likely in retail. The Conservatives issued a political ad which featured a woman, Julie Fallon-Smith, with her children, explaining she was married and worked part-time and was thinking of voting Conservative to try to suggest that other women voters were moving toward the Conservatives.

Leppäniemi *et al.* (2010, 21) explore a digital marketing campaign that was targeted at young voters in the 2007 Finnish general election after a senior MP decided to try to reach this new market in the 2007 Finnish general election. The campaign used 'call-to-action messages' to encourage voters to visit the campaign website, which were displayed in a range of areas including billboards, public transport, flyers, election badges and local free papers and in a local nightclub's loyalty magazine. The website itself had interactive areas such as a competition, celebrities presenting the candidate's message with specific points relevant to young people; and an online raffle and a campaign event at the nightclub. Mobile SMS was used to remind them of the events and to visit the website. The online raffle was used to draw others in: those who participated in it were asked to send an invitation to their friends, with a prize for the one who sent the most invites; and the friends received communication about the website and competition and event rather than a political message in itself.

Targeted communication is not without questions. Hersh and Schaffner (2013) explore how 'big data' is used in creating highly targeted campaign communication. They conducted experiments with the public to test their response to fictional candidates for Congress in experimental conditions; and they found that targeted appeals are not always effective and can backfire if the data is built on incorrect assumptions which end up with incorrect information about voters' group affiliations and thus create mistargeting. Their experiments also suggested that voters do not tend to support candidates who pander to their group identities. Targeted communication also has to fit the overall strategy and brand, as discussed in the book by Robert Busy in which he explores its use by populist politicians in the UK and US: see Author's corner 6.1 for further detail.

Mobile/virtual marketing

All marketing communications can be implemented via mobile communication devices. In politics, this provides a very cost-effective alternative to traditional campaigning; and the 2008 Obama campaign succeeded because it integrated technology with grass-roots activity. Cook (2010) discusses how the 2008 US campaign utilised mobile marketing in the form of SMS texts and twitter feeds and targeted the 18–29 age group. Mobile marketing helped field organisers identify volunteers they could recruit into action. It offers the potential for timely and targeted communication, and could be used to build up a positive relationship between voters and politicians. Germany (2013, 85–6) notes how in the 2012 US Presidential Election Campaign, there was a substantial growth in digital – or mobile – advertising. Communication was sent to individuals' cell phones, including when voters watched non-mobile television. Such digital advertising could be targeted using internet-user profiling. In the 2012 US election, cookies were used to track internet users after they clicked on a link in an ad or on the campaign website and then used to send ads to the individual as they browsed other sites like Facebook and CNN, making Obama's advertising more effective by being more nuanced and targeted. Mylona (2008) argues that mobile marketing could add to the public sphere if it integrated interactivity and dialogue to allow voters and politicians to exchange ideas.

Selling policy

Political marketing communication is also used to sell policy. Governments can draw on public funds to create government advertising, using research to finds ways to effectively communicate its position in a way that will increase public support. One example of this is the UK Conservative government's attempt to sell privatisation of British Telecom and British Gas, previously public utilities, to raise capital and create greater efficiency in the 1980s. Allington *et al.* (1999, 637) discuss how understanding of the desires of the market

Author's corner 6.1

Marketing the Populist Politician: The Demotic Democrat
By Robert Busby
Published by Palgrave Macmillan 2009

In the political marketplace it would be commonplace to assume that voters make rational decisions about ideological and voting choices through consideration of policy positions and how policy might influence individual lifestyle. However, in recent years there has been a marked change in how political figures, particularly political leaders, sell themselves to voters. Attention is increasingly being given to social and emotional connections that might be forged with voters by targeting niche markets related to lifestyle choices and habits. In this context the contemporary political product is a mix of policy, ideological positioning and the presentation of political candidates as individuals who attempt to socially and emotionally reflect the target constituencies that they purport to represent.

In seeking to reflect target voting groups, political leaders use an array of tools to try to create personal bonds. These include making personal lives quite transparent, allowing media coverage to show domestic and family life which reflects the social conditions and demands of contemporary lifestyles. This can include discussing and showing domestic scenarios and how menial daily tasks are still undertaken by those in positions of political power. For example, party political broadcasts in the UK were used to show Tony Blair in domestic settings. Similarly Margaret Thatcher was portrayed as an aspiring political leader who looked after her children and husband at home while at the same time engaging in a political career.

Commonly, political leaders make use of their past in political presentations. This is useful in marketing for two reasons. First, it allows a very personal recollection of events and private moments from the past which is difficult to retort. Second, events can be cherry-picked from the past to highlight the moments when there might be common bonds of associations between voters and candidates. This is particularly important for political figures who are considered to be elite or financially well off. Barack Obama, in his writings and campaigns, made reference to the challenges he faced in the past on account of his race and because of a lack of finance when starting out on his legal career.

There are, however, pitfalls in looking to be socially part of the wider populace, or seeking to make connections with target voting groups. William Hague, when leader of the Conservative party, made reference to his past drinking habits when in Yorkshire. This was greeted with disdain in the media and created the impression that he would make remarks about his past which were not entirely based on fact.

Political marketing is evidently based on factors which involve emotion as much as reason. Contemporary practices have created multidimensional political candidates who appeal to the populace as much for who they are as what policies they stand for. This has led to a multitude of appearances on chat shows to discuss non-political matters, discussion of private matters and the invention and reinterpretation of past experiences so as to reflect the varied experience of targeted niche voting blocks.

was used to sell what was once a 'radical political idea' to both business and voters. Initially, the Telecom proposal faced opposition from the Labour Party, the unions and the media. In order to gain support, communication was aimed at the general public, many members of which had never been shareholders, with appeals to individual needs and desires, showing how the public could gain from buying shares. Advertising was also emotive advertising, with positive depictions of the UK including the white cliffs of Dover. It was very successful, and all shares were sold easily. Another campaign to privatise British Gas built on the appeal to individuals with a slogan, 'Tell Sid', suggesting that the sale was good news for ordinary people, because they could share in ownership and encouraging people to spread the word themselves, depicting a range of people whispering '*tell Sid*' to each other.

Government advertising is controversial because it blurs the line between publicly funded information campaigns for the benefit of society and communication in the interest of the party in power. Young (2005) argues this line is often blurred. Studies have shown big increases in government spending on advertising in the year before an election in the UK and Australia, including advertising to support policy before it has been legislated. An information leaflet produced in June 2004 by a member of staff at the Politics and Public Administration Section, Information and Research Services in the Australian federal parliament in Canberra notes how, at one level, government advertising has an important democratic function. The public has a right to be informed about the programs which their taxes fund. However, Young (2005) notes that the Liberal government led by John Howard used at least $20 million of taxpayers' money to create ads to build support for its planned industrial relations changes before the legislation has even been seen, let alone passed by, parliament.

Raftopoulou and Hogg (2010, 1220) also express concern with the way the UK government campaign against benefit fraud did more than use concepts of social marketing to change behaviour or convey information about policy, and instead integrated political goals through the way it portrayed the general public, the Department of Work and Pensions and the viewer. They used textual analysis to critique the website and 44 advertisements between 2000 and 2005; some examples were titled 'Benefit cheats. We're just a phone call away', showing a neighbour making a call on a man walking to work. The language and images used helped to convey a particular perspective on welfare benefit and the role of the state in providing it. They conclude that such advertisements 'work to produce and sustain a particular political ideology through the exclusion of dialogue'.

Gelders and Ihlen (2010) discuss how, when politicians try out ideas in the public sphere, it can be awkward for civil servants because of the potential to be seen as partisan, which is against their professional principles. Nevertheless, government needs to build relationships with the public to survive and test ideas to see whether the public is willing to accept policy change or if it needs fine-tuning. Furthermore, sometimes advertising is the only way for government to get unpopular policies through on areas like climate change which are arguably beneficial for society in the long run. When the Labor-Rudd government in Australia proposed a mining tax, they had to face millions of dollars spent by the mining industry to lobby against it before it had become legislation.

Another form of government advertising is social marketing, which aims to utilise government advertising to change behaviours in the interests of society (see, for example, Andreasen 1995; McKenzie-Mohr and Smith 1999; Kotler and Roberto 2002), such as reducing drink-driving, smoking, child abuse and domestic violence; or increasing the use of sun cream to prevent skin cancer. Understanding the consumer first is important to the success of campaigns, but they take a long time to have any impact. Other more recent high-profile campaigns with long-term goals include the campaigns by celebrity chef Jamie Oliver to promote healthy eating at schools. Climate change is another area where social marketing can be used. Corner and Randall (2011, 1005) note how selling climate change is a difficult task as it will require significant governmental and societal behaviour changes. They note how various programmes have tried to use social marketing on climate change; such as the Australian government's *Travelsmart* which sought to reduce car usage through letters or face-to-face contact, a personalised travel plan with alternative transport via public transport, incentives, follow-up letters, offers of further assistance – all designed to suit the audience and remove barriers to them changing their behaviour. It succeeded in reducing car usage by 14 per cent.

Marketing communications is therefore an important tool of government – it can be used to change public opinion and Allington *et al.* (1999, 635–6) conclude that 'marketing, when employed in conjunction with other communication methods, has the power to change things and even to change the world order'. However, that doesn't mean it can simply persuade voters to support something they are completely against – instead research is used to identify commonalities between voter views and aspirations and elite policy positions. It could also be argued that privatisation met a need of the public: it generated significant resources to be used elsewhere, made previous public utilities more efficient and therefore enabled the public to pay less for better services, and so met demand rather than working against it, even if that demand was latent and not directly voiced.

Indeed, Corner and Randall (2011) conclude that social marketing has limitations when it comes to changing public behaviour on climate change and that environmental education and supporting citizenship might be more effective instead because they engage people at a deeper level. There are many barriers to static communication. Lloyd's (2009, 132) research on how voters receive information about political brands, for example, leads her to conclude that '"noise" emerges from sources both external and internal to the receiver and, finally, the receiver is an active participant in the generation of the "message" that ultimately contributes to consumers' conceptualisation of political brands'. Whilst there is a lot of attention paid to political marketing communications, the information source rarely communicates directly with the receiver. The public receives multiple communications from multiple senders in, to adapt Lloyd's terminology, a 'noisy cocktail'. And of course the media play a role: as Temple (2010, 268) notes: 'voters' perceptions and understanding of politics in general are also largely derived through the filters of the media'. Savigny and Temple (2010, 1053) thus argue that whilst in business communication might be more controllable, 'in politics things are different'. The media's role is to act as a critic and watchdog of government and political elites; thus 'politicians cannot simply present "messages" about their product which are directly relayed to the public' (1054).

The limited impact of government communications to the marketing of war also illustrates this constraint. Fletcher *et al.* (2009) discuss how the Canadian government launched an information campaign about the war in Afghanistan to boost support for the country's involvement in late 2006. It drew on focus groups which explored levels of understanding and beliefs about the mission and Afghanistan, and factors driving support or opposition to it. Government communication focused on using facts and information to present its case, but it was limited in its effect. The research suggests that Canadians do not just receive government information passively, but instead process it according to their individual predispositions. Another weakness in the government's communication was that it failed to connect emotionally. Similarly the use of careful communication by the, then, UK Prime Minister Tony Blair to increase support for his foreign policy was limited in its effectiveness. Holland (2012) argues that Tony Blair used highly strategic discourse to achieve support from target voters for his foreign policy. Communication was carefully crafted to resonate with target markets, with discourse connecting with the cultural make-up of Middle England with references to the moral and pragmatic leadership role for the UK in foreign policy within the context of globalisation. Intervention was presented as a logical and rational choice within a history of British global leadership. Given the lack of public support for the Iraq War and how Blair's standing declined, the effectiveness of such communication has also to be questioned.

Communicating Change

Practitioner perspective 6.4 on the slowness of communicating change

It takes a long time to get those changes across. Word of mouth is usually important. Talking to people about who you are takes longer.

Iain Duncan-Smith, former Leader of the UK Conservatives
2001–2003, interviewed 2006

Everything is very slow. People have very strong opinions of the politicians they know, very strong impressions of the parties . . . and it's pretty hard to shift those impressions.

Roger Mortimore, MORI polling company UK,
interviewed 2006

If you've got a big job – and the Conservative party has done a really big job to change perception or to win a general election – that's going to be a three- or four-year project. You can't come in shortly before the election and expect to win for them.

Damian Collins, Managing Director M&C Saatchi UK,
interviewed 2006

Source: Lees-Marshment (2011)

As Practitioner perspective 6.4 indicates, communicating change in a product or politician that has already been 'designed' or has a long history is very hard as the public already has existing images and perceptions of the brand or position. If a political product changes, it can take a long time for the public to perceive such a change. Communication needs to be linked to actual behaviour to be convincing and authentic. In the UK, when David Cameron took over leadership of the Conservative Party after the 2005 election, significant and sustained communication strategies were put in place to convey a new image of the party in response to market intelligence about what the public wanted from the party. Communication included photo opportunities of Cameron cycling to work, visiting Darfur in Africa, planting trees on a social action day, on a Friends of the Earth platform, visiting a Norwegian glacier and meeting Nelson Mandela, all of which helped to convey a new strategy of focusing on environmentalism, the poor and world affairs. The party also adopted a new party symbol, a green tree and blue sky, used the slogan 'Vote Blue, Get Green' in local elections and redeveloped the party website with fresh blue–green colours, using pictures that convey a more mainstream Britain (Lees-Marshment and Pettitt 2010).

Lees-Marshment (2011, 136–7) interviewed practitioners about the best way to communicate change and they suggested that a completely fresh style is one way to do it. Neil Lawrence, who was creative strategist for Kevin Rudd in the 2007 Australian election, recalled that the 'campaign gave a very, very fresh view of the Labor Party. We started by redesigning the entire livery for the Labor Party, which was old-fashioned . . . the style of our advertising was quite upbeat, it was positive.' Unconventional forms of communication also help attract attention to change. When asked what made John Ansell's 2005 billboards for the New Zealand National Party so successful, the leader Don Brash (2007) replied 'well, they were very unconventional . . . National Party billboards are blue, and you would never see Labour Party billboards with me on it either, but here was National putting half the billboard in red and a photograph of Helen Clark'.

Crisis management

Practitioner perspective 6.5 on the pervasiveness and importance of crisis management in government

Most of my time is spent with day-to-day crisis management . . . We're not permanently in crisis. But dealing with all the issues that arise on a day-to-day basis. I'm surprised on a day-to-day basis . . . You know there's no accounting for the conduct of individuals.

Oliver Dowden, David Cameron's Deputy Chief of Staff
who oversees domestic policy, 2012

People expect to see their political leaders involved [in a time of crisis]. A bureaucratic response is not acceptable. They want leadership. They don't want a manager.

Chris Eby, Consultant for Navigator Public Affairs, 2012

You've got to face up to what you've done . . . when we apologise, and we're sincere about it, then people will be willing to give you a second chance . . . in that whole process you've got to try and protect a reputation and a brand. It's like a chess game.

Judy Smith, Crisis Management Advisor, 2012

Sources: World Denver Talks (2012); News Hour (2012); The Daily Show (2012)

Crisis management is needed in campaigning and government. Garrett's (2014) discussion of crisis management in US campaigns highlights how crisis threatens a whole range of political marketing strategies. If, for example, there are changes to campaign finances this can create a crisis and require the strategy and resource allocation to be changed, and a cascade of failures can ensue that cause the campaign's demise. In the heat of a campaign, it is difficult to make appropriate strategic choices, and candidates may be prone to reverting to more tactical, day-to-day political marketing which can be less successful. Thus more resources need to be invested in predicting and preparing for potential crises and risks that might occur in future campaigns (see also Garrett 2009).

Crisis in an inevitable and terribly diverting part of being in government. Foley (2009, 500) notes how the former UK Prime Minister Gordon Brown 'became embroiled in a succession of crises that touched upon practically every aspect of social life. Severe political and administrative difficulties became compounded with slumps in the government's public and professional standings, which in turn fused with electoral shocks, political scandals and allegations of chronic deficiencies in the organizational integrity of central government.' This was partly due to the near collapse of the global financial system and associated economic downturn, but crisis happens in every government. As practitioner perspective 6.5 indicates, it is important that politicians get a grip of any crisis to try to limit potential damage from it. Foley argues that Brown's crisis management was ineffective because it failed to convey governing competence and stay in control of events; which of course damaged his leadership image.

Crisis management is partly about managing expectations. As Coombs (2011, 214) explains, if stakeholders believe there is a crisis because expectations have been violated, then it will become a crisis whether or not the government sees it as such. Foley (2009, 502) argues that political leaders try to influence how a crisis is perceived by the public and those within government itself. They need to try to define the crisis themselves, and offer reassurance that they understand and will act on the problem so that the public trusts their competence to manage it. Coombs (2011) argues that crises are events that have the potential to seriously damage political reputations; and that emotions play a key role in crisis, such as fear, anger, uncertainty, sadness. It is obviously harder to frame a crisis that develops quickly, not least as the public expects government to react quickly – and that is not always easy in situations such as earthquakes and tsunamis. Part of crisis management is acknowledging whether there is a problem, assigning blame and deciding whether to change behaviour in response. Coombs notes how, when a Congressman Gary Condit was found to have had an affair with an intern who was later found murdered, he might have been re-elected if he had admitted and apologised and thus apology is a key tool of political crisis management (see also Boin and t'Hart 2003 and Boin 2005).

Integrated marketing communications

Integrated marketing communications (IMC) seeks to combine and co-ordinate different communications concepts into one campaign; so it is not a separate tool or function as such, but it is a very important concept. For example, Barreto *et al.* (2011, 304–5) observe that in the 2000 US presidential election both Democrats and Republicans combined targeting to market segments and direct and indirect marketing to mobilise voters – or get them out to vote, noting that more than $10 million was spent trying to motivate Latino voters in the election. Parties created unique political adverts in Spanish, and there were 3,000 airings of such ads in states which had significant Latino populations; but they also ran GOTV campaigns using door-to-door, mail and telephone forms of direct marketing in Latino communities. Their analysis concluded that messages that are both direct and targeted are more effective: 'the strengths and weaknesses of the different elements are used to offset one another' (Barreto 2011 *et al.*, 310).

IMC thus uses a range of communications tools, mediums and strategies to achieve a common goal; overall the public or recipients of the communication then receive multiple messages which, as a whole, convey the same, unified message. Papagiannidis *et al.* (2012, 305) conclude that for the web to be used to its full potential in politics, there is the need 'for integrated political marketing communications that leverage the web for its strengths, and using it as a complementary tactic in the candidates' political marketing arsenal'. Cogburn and Espinoza-Vasquez's (2011, 203) analysis of the Obama 2008 website shows it applied concepts of segmentation, targeting and internal marketing all together and explain how a free apple iPhone app helped to generate more data for the campaign. When the application was turned on it would ask users if it could use their location. If they agreed, the iPhone would use GPS to identify the supporters' geographic location and then identify relevant local political activities in which the supporter could immediately engage. This meant that volunteers gained easy access to activities such as phone banks, staff and volunteer meetings and debates in their local area, making it as easy as possible for them to get involved. Similarly Seidman (2010, 23) argues that all communication connected effectively.

The visual logo 'communicated and reinforced his brand'; the color, imagery, typography, lighting, slogans and positive tone all fitted with the brand as being inspirational, unifying, moderate, cool and charismatic.

In the conclusion to *Political Marketing in the US*, the editors note how research demonstrated that each component of marketing was limited by each other, with different marketing tools interacting with and influencing each other's success (Lees-Marshment *et al.* 2014), suggesting there is now a move towards integrated political marketing overall. This makes political marketing more complex to research, but arguably more effective in practice.

Summary

This chapter has explored how political marketing communication can be used to communicate information about political leaders, in a campaign, to increase support in particular segments and sell policy and political change, and to manage crises. Communication involves utilising many other aspects of marketing including strategy and market analysis, to make the communication effective and suitable for the receiver. It needs to be well researched, fit with the strategy and brand and also be believable. Principles of effective static communications are laid out in Figure 6.6 in the best practice guide. Communication is a key area of political marketing practice, and the practitioner profiles below describe the work and impact of Judy Smith in the US and Alastair Campbell in the UK. The next chapter will look at more interactive and relational forms of marketing communication in politics.

Practitioner profile 6.1

Name: Judy A. Smith
Date of birth: 27 October, 1958
Most notable job: Special Assistant and Deputy Press Secretary to President George H. W. Bush

Description: Judy Smith is a crisis manager and television producer. Smith is the founder and president of Smith & Co., a leading strategic and crisis communications firm. Smith began working in the public service in 1983, notably working in several high-profile positions involving information management and media relations. However, it was her appointment as Special Assistant and Deputy Press Secretary to President George H. W. Bush in 1991 that saw her gain her most notable political marketing influence. During her tenure, Smith provided President Bush and his cabinet with communications advice on a wide range of foreign and domestic issues. Notably, Smith was instrumental in guiding the Bush administration through a number of controversial issues, including the nomination of Clarence Thomas to the Supreme Court, the 1991 Gulf War, and relations with Kuwait. Smith is known for her skill in identifing high-risk situations that often lead to marital, financial, professional or personal imprudence; her ability to anticipate potential personal disasters has allowed her to coach people prior to, as well as in the wake of, crisis. Smith was later hired to advise Monica Lewinsky during the Lewinsky scandal, as well as being involved in the congressional inquiry of Enron, and the United Nations Foundation and World Health Organization response to the SARS epidemic. Ms. Smith serves as Co-Executive Producer of the television drama *Scandal* about the world of crisis management, which revolves around the life and work of a professional fixer.

Best practice guide to doing static political marketing communication

1   Ensure there is time to think strategically about communication and campaigning.

2   Know and stick to your strategy; don't get bogged down in daily news cycle/planet politics/following the pack.

3   Identify and communicate one clear central vision which reflects the candidate's personality and makes an emotional connection with people.

4   Ensure non-verbal images convey honesty, credibility, knowledge, experience, strength and energy.

5   Don't convey 'the common touch' at the neglect of leadership and governing skills; both are important.

6   Devise communication to respond to the results of political market research.

7   Use guerrilla marketing to get attention to a new leader, policy, brand or position: use unconventional, fresh or new style, colours, label, hinge or logos to convey change, and start early.

8   Use celebrity marketing to help raise funds and draw attention to products, but do so carefully, making sure the celebrity profile matches the brand and position of the candidate.

9   Make communication market-oriented so that it features target voters, shows the party leader responding to their needs, evokes party history to connect with core voters and conveys appropriate co-operation with the competition.

10 Use market analysis to help devise communication to change public opinion or explain unpopular decisions.

11 To get the vote out, get people to talk to their neighbours over a long period outwith campaigns and individualise the communication as much as possible.

12 Make communication as direct as possible to suit the receiver's behaviour in terms of when, where, what and how.

13 Target communication in terms of medium and message, but avoid conflicting messages to different target markets.

14 Pretest communication using experimental and analytic marketing.

15 Identify initial brand strengths and ensure that campaign activities protect these.

16 Define yourself before the competition defines you and, if attacked, rebut immediately.

17 Use market research and social marketing to create effective government advertising to counter anti-legislative campaigns and promote positive public behaviour in areas such as healthy eating, exercise and drink-driving.

18 Plan communication linked with behaviour, and events, over a long period to change an established reputation.

19 In a crisis acknowledge the problem and offer immediate action to remedy it and reassure the public you are still in control.

20 Create an integrated communications plan that ties all the different forms of political communications together.

Figure 6.6

Practitioner profile 6.2

Name: Alastair John Campbell
Date of birth: 25 May, 1957
Most notable job: Director of Communications and Strategy for Prime Minister Tony Blair

Description: Alastair Campbell is a journalist and political aid best known for his work as Chief Press Secretary and subsequently Director of Communications and Strategy to former UK Prime Minister Tony Blair between 1997 and 2003. Coming from the world of (predominantly) newspaper journalism, Campbell was hired by newly appointed UK Labour Party leader Tony Blair as his spokesperson in 1994. He played an important role in the run-up to the 1997 general election, working with Peter Mandelson to co-ordinate Labour's campaign. Notably, Campbell focused on winning support from the national media, particularly from newspapers who had not supported the party in many years. After Labour won the election, Campbell set up a centralised organisation to coordinate government communication. This was done in order to maintain and project a united message delivery among all ministers. While this created problems internal to the Labour Party, Campbell followed a professional approach to media relations to ensure that a clear message was presented. This included planning stories in advance to ensure a positive media reaction. Campbell used his own experience in journalism to make sure he paid attention to detail and used sound bites effectively. For example, Campbell developed a relationship with News International, providing their newspapers with early information in return for positive media coverage. Throughout his time in Downing Street, Campbell kept a diary which reportedly totalled some two million words. Selected extracts were published in the book entitled *The Blair Years* (2007). Subsequently Campbell has released a number of books (published by Hutchinson): *Diaries Volume One: Prelude to Power 1994–1997* (2010); *Diaries Volume Two: Power and the People 1997–1999* (2011); *Diaries Volume Three: Power and Responsibility 1999–2001* (2012).

Discussion points

1 To what extent are political leaders effective at communicating an emotional connection with voters?
2 Pick several current or former political leaders and rate their non-verbal communication against Schweiger and Aadami's (1999) political candidate positive and negative image attributes of honesty, quality and strength. Who performs the best and why?
3 How does market research inform campaign communication?
4 Think of recent or well-known political adverts. To what extent do they follow Robinson's (2006) criteria for market-oriented political adverts?
5 What do you think of insights marketing in politics? Is it a problem for democracy or just another part of political communication?
6 Think of examples of guerrilla political communication and create a plan for future guerrilla communication to help a candidate or party leader gain traction for a new idea, policy, position, brand or leadership.
7 What is the main goal of GOTV, and how effective do you think it is? What resources would you recommend candidates or parties invest in it, and why?
8 What are the pros and cons of direct marketing in politics?
9 Identify examples of where politicians and parties have targeted their communication, and discuss how effective the targeting was.
10 Discuss the nature and effectiveness of targeted communication to reach women voters in recent elections.

11   Why is government advertising controversial?

12   Debate whether political marketing communications might help politicians sell good politics that is right for the country but might otherwise be rejected by the political market.

13   How does social marketing differ from government advertising, and how effective do you think it is in changing society's behaviour, such as reducing drink-driving? Is it worthwhile use of government funds?

14   How possible is it for governments to use marketing to gain support for war?

15   Think of crisis faced in recent campaigns and government. How well did politicians handle it, and what might they have done better?

Assessment questions

Essay/Exam

1   Identify and critique how marketing communications (such as research-led communication strategies, identification of strengths) have been used to forge a positive image for political leaders/candidates.

2   Discuss theories and empirical examples of campaign communication devised in relation to market research.

3   Identify examples of guerrilla political communication and discuss how effective it is.

4   What is GOTV, how is it used in politics and with what impact?

5   Review and critique the effectiveness of how direct marketing is used in politics.

6   Identify and critique targeted communication by recent political leaders and campaigns.

7   Discuss the potential and limitations of government advertising as a way for government to increase support for its policies and work.

8   Outline the difference between government advertising and social marketing, utilising theory and empirical examples.

9   Review the effectiveness of social marketing by governments in changing public behaviour, using both examples and theory.

10   Review the attempts by the Canadian, UK and US governments to use marketing communications to increase support for war in Iraq, Afghanistan and Syria, and draw conclusions about the potential and limitations to the marketing of war.

11   Discuss the importance and effectiveness of crisis management in politics.

Applied

1   Assess the non-verbal communication of a candidate or leader against Schweiger and Aadami's (1999) political candidate positive and negative image attributes of honesty, quality and strength, and conclude as to how effective their image is, and how they might improve it.

2   Assess political adverts at the last election against Robinson's (2006) criteria for market-oriented political adverts, noting strengths and weaknesses, and discuss the degree to which the degree of market-orientation found in the ads related to the election outcome.

3   Assess the use and effectiveness of GOTV amongst recent political campaigns, and from this, create a plan for a future GOTV campaign for a candidate, campaign or party.

4   Drawing on previous research into partisan GOTV, create a plan for the Electoral Commission to use GOTV to increase turnout regardless of who voters vote for.

5   Assess the use of direct marketing in all its forms – mail, email, text, internet ad – in a recent election campaign, reviewing its nature and effectiveness to achieve goals such as increase

donations, support and volunteer activity; and make recommendations for how it might be improved at the next election.

6   Assess the use of targeted communication at the last national/federal/presidential election and how effective it was, and create a plan for improved targeting at the next election.

7   Create a plan for a minor party to engage in targeted communication at the next election, drawing on examples of other parties targeted communication and an analysis of the party's goals and potential segments.

8   Identify and critique the use of communication to target women voters in the 2010 UK election and 2012 US presidential election and, from this, create a plan for how parties might target women more effectively in future.

9   Critique the effectiveness of recent government advertising to sell a proposed policy or new programme in terms of how it utilised marketing or followed the principles noted in Allington *et al.* 1999.

10   Create a plan for a government to design effective advertising for a proposed policy, utilising a range of marketing concepts and tools.

11   Assess the effectiveness of communication by the Labor government and mining companies in Australia for the proposed mining tax in terms of the way it used marketing communications principles and, from this, draw generic lessons for the appropriate and effective use of public money for government advertising, given the arguments for the need for climate change policies in Australia.

12   Create a list of principles to market war, drawing on previous successes and failures such as the attempts by UK, US and Canadian governments to gain support for the wars in Afghanistan and Syria, and taking account of the changed nature of political marketing, particularly the decline in deference towards political leaders and increased availability and diversity of political communication.

13   Review the use of crisis management by recent governments such as George W Bush's response to Hurricane Katrina, Obama's handling of the Gulf of Mexico Oil spill , and John Key's handling of the Christchurch earthquake and the Fonterra botulism scare. Critique their effectiveness and, from this, draw lessons for future governments.

14   Create an integrated marketing communications plan for a political figure or organisation for the next 12 months or for the next election, utilising a range of marketing communications concepts and drawing on theory, other empirical cases and a critique of the political figures or organisation's past behaviour, ensuring that the different types of communication are integrated together effectively.

CASE STUDIES

Case study 6.1 The presidential election in the Czech Republic: a case study of Karel Schwarzenberg's campaign strategy

By Miloš Gregor and Anna Matušková, Masaryk University[1]
Milos.Gregor@email.cz and amatuskova@gmail.com

A campaign strategy is a very complex process consisting of various interdependent processes such as market analysis, research, polling, segmentation, strategic communication, constant analysis of the political environment, and of course crucial role plays of the candidate themself.

Lastly, the strategy always changes depending on the type of election and electoral system. This case study offers insight into the 2012–2013 presidential race in the Czech Republic. Before 2013 the president was elected indirectly by parliament, so this was the first Czech direct presidential election. There was a two-round majority electoral system, a new set-up that affected campaign strategies of the candidates. Our study focuses on the campaign of Karel Schwarzenberg.

The election winner and first directly elected president was Miloš Zeman, a former prime minister and one of the favourites in the race. His opponent Schwarzenberg, however, was rather a surprising candidate: a member of the historically most unpopular government, a clear underdog with support of 6 per cent in the polls just two months before elections. Despite this he got 23.4 per cent of the vote in the first round and 45.2 per cent in the second round. Schwarzenberg was the oldest candidate in the race at 75 years old, but his campaign was considered the most professional, modern and social-media-driven yet. His campaign was also an example of grass-roots campaigning and successful implementation of various campaign strategies, which are normally associated with the USA (fundraising, GOTV, endorsement, door-to-door campaigning, etc.).

The campaign strategy

The campaign began with market analysis. Schwarzenberg's campaign was officially launched on 24 October, 2012. However, his party, TOP 09, announced his candidacy back in May 2012. The campaign team had many obstacles to face: to differentiate the candidate from his party (part of an unpopular government coalition), an electoral law with obligations such as candidate nomination, transparent accounting, an electoral committee, etc. Because of the different ways to receive a nomination, some of the candidates had to collect 50,000 signatures. Therefore some of the other teams had been active since the summer. The deadline for nomination was the second week in November, which made it very difficult to do polling, opposition research and timing, since it was unclear who would run and who would be the main opponent.

First stage – candidate introduction

The campaign had four stages (three for the first round and one for the second). The first stage was to introduce Schwarzenberg as a real candidate. The media and public (according to polling) did not consider him a proper candidate. The arguments were: his age, doubts about him taking his candidacy seriously, and his social background. Schwarzenberg comes from one of the oldest Czech-Austrian aristocratic families. Because of the communist regime he spent most of his life in Austria. After the Velvet Revolution he served as president Vaclav Havel's chancellor (i.e. the president's adviser and chief of staff). Havel passed away in November 2012, and one strategic step was to present Schwarzenberg as Havel's successor.

Various polls, surveys, and data were used in the campaign. Standard monthly omnibus surveys were used, and a benchmark survey with Millward Brown agency was crucial. The results showed a clear picture of how the political forces are divided but also what the general mood in the country is. Following the poll, a series of focus groups in Czech big cities was organised. The outcomes were once again crucial. Generally the candidate was well known, but voters could not associate him with any political results. Positively perceived was the fact that he is wealthy because, therefore, he will not steal and nobody can corrupt him. The biggest problems for focus groups were his participation in the government, his trouble speaking, and that they found him very distant and too 'noble'. So the focus was very much on explaining why he is running. The following step was to get out the story of his life. Schwarzenberg refused to talk about his successes and charity activities. This was solved through interviews with VIP supporters using YouTube (there are strict limits on using TV in campaigns).

Second stage – what will he do as your president

The second stage was launched in October and focused on introducing the presidential program, in strict accordance with the Constitution. The Constitution clearly defines the rights of presidents, and the program was based on that. At the same time opposition research was carried out analysing all the other candidates. Simultaneously, a huge data set with all possible media attacks and a list of the possible topics candidates could face were prepared. From a PR point of view, media relations were rather fine, and the candidate got rather extensive coverage in his capacity as minister.

Third stage – you don't vote for Schwarzenberg, but for change

The third phase of the campaign was launched in mid-November when it was clear who was running. There were nine candidates, two on the left; however, the center and center-right were crowded. The next step was to explain the electoral system – only two candidates get to go to the second round, and people have to decide clearly. The goal was to get the other candidates' votes. Therefore this part of campaign was less about Schwarzenberg as a candidate and more about the values he represented.

The project 'Beer with Karel' was launched, and the candidate travelled across the country to have a drink and talk with voters. A huge role was played the celebrities, musicians, and actors who supported him (in fact he got the biggest level of endorsements in Czech political elections ever). For example, there were club nights 'Clubbing with Karel', where popular music clubs were open and bands played for free.

Another big change in the country was that people were openly supporting candidates. The campaign had a rather unique logo inspired by the punk group Sex Pistols: a picture of the candidate with a pink mohawk. Created by famous artist David Cerny, it became the symbol of the candidate.

The first round ended with a concert in Prague. Twenty-four hours before the election, four out of five major newspapers openly gave Schwarzenberg their support. On Facebook he had 200,000 fans' likes, which is so far the highest number. The first round was successful, and Schwarzenberg came in second, behind by only 200,000 votes.

Fourth stage – second round: the real game has begun

The second round lasted only 14 days. The strategy was to continue the marketing push, with volunteers canvassing and staying active online. Crucial for the second round were the televised debates. The campaign became stronger and attacks tougher. Schwarzenberg in one of debates opened up topics relating to the Benes Decrees.[2] He was very critical towards this former Czechoslovak president, and reaped huge criticism from his opponent which mobilised a certain part of electorate.

Zeman's team was successful in portraying Schwarzenberg as a 'foreigner and a German', therefore somebody who does not care about Czech interests. And since Schwarzenberg decided to run a clean campaign, there was no strong response to these allegations. The media were flooded one day before the election with advertisements saying, 'Schwarzenberg is a German agent and he will support German interests in the country'.

Lessons for and from political marketing

What is the lesson to be learned? Never underestimate the 'mood' in the country, never stop analysing the data, and never stop asking – 'am I asking the right questions?' The decisive issue was the framing of the candidate as a foreigner. Clearly, the fact that he lived outside of the country for 40 years was underestimated. Another problem was that the campaign only reached voters in the big cities and was isolated from the countryside.

Case study 6.2 Rivers, kids, and jobs: market-orientated advertising from the Green Party of Aotearoa New Zealand

By Thomas James Seeman, University of Auckland

tsee009@aucklanduni.ac.nz

This case study applies Robinson's criteria for identifying a party's market-orientation through its political advertisements to the Green Party of Aotearoa New Zealand's televised opening broadcast for the New Zealand 2011 general election (Robinson 2010). Through applying this theory, we can see how the Green Party's market-orientation helped it to achieve its goal of exceeding 10 per cent of the vote (Turei 2012).

Identification of target audience

The Green Party's opening address shows its market-orientation by featuring its target audience and their environments. By using images of its target audience in advertisements, parties can use 'consumers' self-identification with advertising images to strengthen involvement with a message' (Robinson 2010). The opening address shows an ethnically diverse range of people, including groups not normally associated with the Greens, such as business people in suits and parents with children. From this we can see that the Greens were trying to expand their vote beyond their core constituency and target those who would normally vote for the centre-right National Party and centre-left Labour Party. The environments shown in the opening address were primarily urban inner-city environments and the New Zealand countryside. The featuring of inner-city environments is important as electorates that include this environment have more people that give their party vote to the Greens than other electorates. So we can see that the Green Party are targeting their traditional voter base through featuring these environments.

Conveying responsiveness to voter needs

Another way that the opening address shows their market-orientation is through showing the Green Party engaging with voters and responding to their needs. By showing the party interacting with target voters and including images and words of togetherness, a party can show that it has an affinity with those it is targeting (Robinson 2010). Before each of the Green Party's policy priorities for the 2011 election are elaborated on, there are vox pops of voters saying what they want the Green Party's policy to offer. This is followed by the respective policy that responds to the needs presented in the vox pop. By showing that they are shaping their policy in regards to voter needs, the Green Party are communicating their market-orientation.

Maintenance of relationships with core voters

By showing that the Green Party is maintaining its relationships with core voters, the opening address shows their market-orientation. Parties can satisfy relationships with their core supporters using advertising through showing they have kept their promises, evoking party history and myth, having images or words of care, and by showing consistent leadership (Robinson 2010). The opening address shows the Green Party has kept its promises through Co-Leader Russell Norman stating: 'In just the last three years . . . we've made 100,000 homes warm and dry. We've got the funding for the cycleway, the clean-up of toxic sites, for pest control and more.' Party history is invoked by Co-Leader Metiria Tuirei, saying 'New Zealand was the home of the world's first Green Party and we've been represented in parliament now for well over a decade. We're a successful, independent party and we've delivered positive change' The images of children and beautiful scenery used in this opening address are continued from the last election, maintaining consistency in message (Delahunty 2008). The Greens give a somewhat consistent leadership offer, as Norman was a co-leader at the last election, but Turei only became a co-leader after the 2008 election. However, both of them telling their personal stories at the beginning of the opening address helps to build and maintain their relationship with their core constituency.

Offer in exchange for party vote

In the opening address the co-leaders of the Green Party ask for voters to exchange their party vote for the party's political product, which also shows their market-orientation (Robinson 2010). The party vote was asked for explicitly – for example, Norman saying: 'If you want New Zealand to get a part of the clean energy action, you need to party vote Green', and implicitly through the use of the slogan 'For a richer New Zealand'.

Competitor orientation

Finally, the Green Party's opening address shows their market-orientation by acting like a party occupying their strategic market-position (see Butler and Collins 1996 and Robinson 2010). As a niche party, the Green Party shows they have stayed true to their original *raison d'être* of environmentalism in their opening address by underpinning all their policy messages with a concern for the environment. They also show a concern to increase market share and openness to coalition arrangements, both of which show their competitor orientation.

Lessons for political marketing

The Green Party has obviously learned the advantages of showing their market-orientation through their advertisements. In 2005, they did not achieve their goal when they failed to show market-orientation (Robinson 2009), but in 2011 they exceeded their own expectations. From this we can see that other niche parties should use their communications to show their market-orientation, while making sure to tie it into their original *raison d'être*, to expand their vote beyond their core constituents. While not the sole factor in determining election outcomes, using marketing to inform communications can help parties to do well.

Further reading

Butler, Patrick and Neil Collins (1996). 'Strategic analysis in political markets'. *European Journal of Marketing*, 30(10/11): 25–36.

Delahunty, Catherine (2010). 'The Greens'. In Stephen Levine and Nigel S. Roberts (eds) *Key to Victory: The New Zealand General Election of 2008*. Wellington: Victoria University Press, 83–7.

Robinson, Claire (2009). 'Market-orientated political advertising in the 2005 New Zealand election'. In Jennifer Lees-Marshment, *Political Marketing Principles and Applications*. Abingdon: Routledge.

Robinson, Claire (2010). 'Political advertising and the demonstration of market orientation'. *European Journal of Marketing*, 44(3/4): 451–9.

Turei, Metiria (2012). 'The Greens'. In Jon Johansson and Stephen Levine (eds) *Kicking the Tyres: The New Zealand General Election and Electoral Referendum of 2011*. Wellington: Victoria University Press, 135–41.

Case study 6.3 Door-to-door canvassing in local elections: case study of Ružomberok, Slovakia 2010

By Aleš Kudrná , Palacký University

a.kudrnac@gmail.com

Ivan Rončák's 2010 political campaign represents an example of a totally unknown candidate with a very limited budget who managed to win a seat. In the following text, I am describing a campaign which was heavily dependent on the door-to-door canvassing. The source of information about the political campaign is based mainly on interviews between the candidate I. Rončák and the author.

There are several important facts about the City Council elections which should be noted. First, according to law, it is allowed to campaign for 15 days only before the local elections.[3] That means that the campaign has to be very intensive and very well planned. Second, the town is divided into electoral districts according to town population with usually small a number of mandates, which provides an opportunity for a closer relationship between voters and the member of the City Council. I. Rončák's electoral district has two mandates.

I. Rončák wasn't born in Ružomberok, but he moved to this town just a few months before the elections. He has never been politically active, and according to him it became a disadvantage because nobody knew anything about him. He decided to sign up as an independent candidate who was nominated by the Conservative Democrats of Slovakia, which is minor party that has no MPs.[4] The advantage to run as a candidate of one party lies in the fact that you do not need to provide any signatures or pay any deposit prior the elections.

I. Rončák and ten other people decided to be politically active and run for a mandate in Ružomberok. They formed an informal group which was called Ružomberok Without Corruption (RWC). However not all of these candidates managed to collect enough signatures to run as an independent candidate. For this reason, they tried to find some minor political parties that would nominate them, which was also case for I. Rončák. Interestingly, their campaign did not reflect the party they were nominated by, but they managed to make their common message 'Ružomberok without corruption'.

The campaign had two separate parts for each candidate of the RWC group. The first part was collective, represented by a few posters in public buses and a total of 100 leaflets distributed in the whole town. Second, running as an individual meant that each candidate was responsible for his own success in his own electoral district. All of them did run a door-to-door campaign. It is important to mention the budget of both parts of the campaign. I. Rončák could not give an exact amount; however, he said that '*one third of the budget was spent for the leaflets and posters, about 40 per cent for door-to-door and the rest for some little advertisement in the district of a candidate. The total budget for each candidate separately was between 600 and 700 euro.*'

Usually it is recommended to do research in order to provide exact targeting, however I. Rončák did not have any specific ideas about who could or could not be voting for him. Thus, he managed to visit all of the voters of the district (800 addresses). There were always two canvassing groups operating at the same time. One group consisted of volunteers only, and the second one was a mixed group of volunteers and the candidate.

During the workdays the groups used to visit homes from 15:30 to 17:30. There were also two Saturdays and one national holiday when they canvassed from 14:00 to 17:30. Speaking of the speed of canvassing, they were able to visit seven to eight households per hour. The district consisted mostly of blocks of flats, which is actually the main reason of their speed.

Sometimes some friends who lived in the blocks of flats helped the candidate to introduce him. I. Rončák says that: '*someone from the community I have known went to knock on the doors with me to say: 'Hi, I am here to introduce my friend, who is a candidate in your neighbourhood . . . and that helped me also a lot*'. The candidate himself visited over a half of the households in the district.

I. Rončák sent two letters to each household. The first letter which was informative introduced the candidate. Also it was useful for starting a conversation after knocking on the door. After the canvassing he sent another letter which was very personalized in that I. Rončák mentioned topics they had discussed, and the letter was partly handwritten. I. Rončák divided the letter recipients into two categories. The first group of voters consisted of people who were not reached at home, thus he wrote that he had been there but he had not been able to meet them. He also added his manifesto. The second one was for people he met and from whom he had had a positive feeling; in the letter he thanked them for meeting them and encouraged them to come to the elections.

I. Rončák talked to approximately two-thirds of people who opened the door. The visit was supposed to last about five minutes. The candidate and volunteers had learned the introduction by heart. Later, he asked the voters to tell him their problems and suggestions that they would like to change. During the door-to-door campaign the visiting groups were supposed to make some notes in order to create a little database. The canvassing groups noted whether the voter opened the door, who lived there (age, gender), what was the reaction and what their opinions were. I. Rončák also had a positive experience of people knowing him before the visit, which shows another effect of door-to-door. People talked about it and the campaign had an effect even without performing it in every single household since the people spread out the word.

The elections were a great success for I. Rončák. From a totally unknown candidate with a budget of approximately 650 euro and two weeks of campaigning, he managed to win a seat. He was the second of nine candidates with 222 votes. The winner, who was a mayor at that time, got 278 votes. I. Rončák received 14.2 per cent of votes. It is obvious that his victory was absolutely dependent on his door-to-door campaign, because: '*there is no other logical way how to explain the result.*'

Lessons for political marketing

I. Rončák's case proves that even in a post-communist society it is possible to win a campaign when using mainly active face-to-face campaigning with a very limited budget. I. Rončák's candidacy shows that canvassing is very effective and can be highly recommended for unknown candidates that have no time and/or money for more expensive marketing techniques. What is more, according to this case, canvassing is suitable for blocks of flats. Subsequent to door-to-door campaigning, personalised handwritten letters seem to be a good idea as reminder of the candidate and to show that candidate care of every single voter.

Further reading

Gerber S. Alan, Green P. Donald (2000). *The Effects of Canvassing, Telephone Calls, and Direct Mail on Voter turnout: A Field Experiment. American Political Science Review,* 94(3): 653–63.

Green P. Donald and Alan S. Gerber (2004). *Get Out the Vote. How to Increase Voter Turnout.* Brookings Institution Press: Washington.

Marsh Michael (2004). 'None of that post-modern stuff around here: grassroots campaigning in the 2002 Irish general election'. *British Elections and Parties Review,* 14: 245–67.

Case study 6.4 'Humble and hard-working'? Sergey Sobyanin and Alexey Navalny as Moscow mayoral candidates of 2013

By Svetlana S. Bodrunova, St.Petersburg State University
s.bodrunova@spbu.ru

On 8 September, 2013, Moscow, the capital of Russia, elected a mayor. Or, rather, re-elected the incumbent city head Sergey Sobyanin who took the post by appointment after the infamous Yury Luzhkov's fall from grace and escape to London in 2010. The electoral procedure implied a possibility of two rounds in case of the absence of a simple majority, but Sobyanin received

51.4 per cent of the vote (of those 32.7 per cent of Moscowites who had bothered to turn out). Though being formally regional, this election grabbed unusual attention throughout both Russian intelligentsia, political and civil service classes for several reasons.

First, the overall political and communicative climate in the country may be described as a general split of the public sphere (Bodrunova and Litvinenko 2013), which was expressed in a huge wave of street protest after the State Duma and presidential elections of 2011–2012. The protest was vaguely organised but covered at least 39 cities, gathered simultaneously over 100,000 people in winter time, and was led by non-political leaders and non-systemic opposition, rather than by in-Duma parties – the so-called 'systemic opposition' to United Russia who hold the biggest parliamentary share. The protest participants were described in many publications as the 'Facebook million', 'creative class', or 'internet hamsters'; this pointed to the social network nature of the protest, which was only partly true. The truth, though, was in the fact that the protesters, unlike their counterparts in Europe or the US, did not pose economic demands; they, rather, expressed general disappointment in the regime and put up democratization demands and freedoms and human rights issues. One of the protest leaders was Alexey Navalny who would later become the only real challenger for Sobyanin. Navalny, a businessman and a lawyer, has emerged as one of the most popular Russian bloggers after he brought to light, by getting access to financial reports via minority shareholding, several cases of 'raspil' (misspending of huge amounts of state money) in major industrial and natural resources' monopolies. Before 2011, he had created the 'RosPil' investigative project based on transparent crowdfunding; after the Duma elections, he united several activist projects within this foundation against corruption.

Second, for the first time in over 20 years, the election was competitive. Six candidates were registered; Sobyanin, who till December 2012 was Secretary of the political board of the United Russia Moscow division, went to elections self-nominated. Three more candidates were nominated by parliamentary parties, and the fifth one by the Yabloko party which used to be in parliament but lost two elections in row. Alexey Navalny was nominated by RPR-Parnas, a non-parliamentary party in radical opposition to Vladimir Putin's regime. But as the four candidates besides Sobyanin and Navalny gained less than 17 per cent of votes altogether, the actual confrontation was between the candidate informally affiliated with the ruling majority and one of the leaders of the non-systemic opposition.

Third, Moscow was one of the cities that showed low support for Vladimir Putin and United Russia during the elections, and the mayoral elections were perceived as the litmus paper for how many people can actually express oppositional views – either by voting or by coming out to the streets after a Navalny loss to Sobyanin.

Fourth, Navalny's very figure raised a lot of controversies before and during the election campaign (which was short due to changes in electoral law that reintroduced direct elections for regional governors in 2013). One controversy was connected to his informal leadership in a right-wing movement called Popular Alliance (without any formal attachment, though) and his anti-migrant rhetoric that is present even in his electoral manifesto. In 2012, this factor disenchanted many of his former supporters. The second controversy was created by the state. Started in 2009 and ended fruitlessly in 2012, a criminal prosecution against Navalny was reopened; on July 18, 2013, he was sentenced to five years in prison for economic violations. But a day before Navalny registered as a mayoral candidate, the court ruled to release him temporarily to provide equal access of all candidates to the election – thus, losing the election should mean his going to jail.

Pre-election polls promised Sobyanin 60 per cent to 62 per cent of the vote, and Navalny from 11 per cent to 15.6 per cent. The latter's goal was to distract votes from the incumbent to get the second round – and to be the second preferred candidate to get into it. Sobyanin's goals seemed twofold: first, to win in the first round: and second, to ensure competitiveness of elections to get stronger legitimacy; this is why journalists discussed whether Sobyanin put pressure on the prosecutors to make them release Navalny and whether Navalny was a state agent (Glikin *et al.* 2013).

In terms of political marketing, these elections provided a rare chance in today's Russia to check whether strategies work and have any impact upon electoral result. Both main candidates employed strategic thinking that we could conceptualize as 'being H&H – humble and hard-working', but in very different ways. We address just one aspect of their strategy: audience orientation and the respective use of media.

Sergey Sobyanin had 'a silent campaign' where 'Sobyanin didn't have any personal opinion on anything' (Alexander Morozov, *Russian Journal,* chief editor) – calculated, seemingly paradoxical, for an all-Russian audience rather than for the Moscowites; the campaign left an impression that Moscow was expected to swear loyalty to the incumbent rather that to elect him. He denied participation in electoral debates on Moscow TV channels but was at least once in two days a hero of federal news bulletins where he showed up as 'krepkiy hozyaystvennik' – 'sturdy executive' who is capable of effective management and ready to bear responsibility. He barely spoke several phrases in each broadcast; Moscow spoke for him. Several big development projects were started or finished by the election. 'What is heard throughout the city is round-the-clock hooting, gritting, puffing, huffing, spitting, crackling, hammer thuds here and there, and sometimes you hear a subtle hissing of something like a sickle. Listen carefully. It's Sobyanin making his claims' (Stanislav Lvovsky, *Colta.ru* editor, on Facebook). Similarly, he had serial coverage of reconstruction activities in official *Rossiyskaya gazeta* – with headlines like 'Sobyanin commanded: Let's be off!' (reminiscent of Yury Gagarin) or 'I'm responsible for the city', portrayed full-height, with rolled-up sleeves, sometimes in a construction helmet. In national media he bore the image of the only possible mayor.

For Alexey Navalny, the campaign was much less populist than expected; not nationalism but accountability, possibility of immediate alternation of mayoral power, and informal horizontal relations with citizens were its leitmotifs. 'H&H' developed through Navalny's daily meetings with Moscowites on streets and in the subway, and campaigners' gatherings and activities at 'Navalny's cubes' – branded cubic marquees throughout Moscow. But these initiatives were hardly oriented to those who witnessed them; rather, these activities were ideal for 'sharing' and 'liking' in new media, as Navalny knew well that his main audience was there and needed a mobilizing impetus, not persuasion. Branding of the campaign was pronouncedly Western-style, as opposed to Sobyanin's post-Soviet reminiscences. As a result, he received an unexpected 27.2 per cent.

Lessons for political marketing

Two conceptual results emerged after these mayoral elections. First, in today's Russia, a non-systemic candidate put competitive strategic electoral marketing (not façade marketing!) back on stage practically by individual effort. Second, traditional 'H&H' mediatization of a campaign proved relatively less effective (60–62 per cent to the resulting 51.37 per cent) than horizontal-oriented 'new-media mediatization' (maximum 15.6 per cent to 27.24 per cent).

Further reading

Bodrunova, S. S. and A. A. Litvinenko (2013) 'New media and the political protest: the formation of a public counter-sphere in Russia of 2008–2012' In A. Makarychev and A. Mommen (eds) *Russia's Changing Economic and Political Regimes: The Putin Years and Afterwards.* London: Routledge, 29–65.

Glikin, M., L. Biryukova, M. Zheleznova (2013) 'Who's behind Navalny's release'. *Vedomosti,* July 22. http://www.vedomosti.ru/politics/news/14411861/kandidat-ot-vlasti-aleksej-navalnyj

Case study 6.5 Get the targets right and victory will follow

By Jennifer Rayner, Australian National University

Jennifer.Rayner@anu.edu.au

Geographic targeting is one way that political marketing differs distinctly from other forms of strategic marketing. In addition to identifying target demographics and market segments within the electorate at large, political parties must also segment their audience in geographic terms so that they can focus their resources on the areas that will help them achieve their electoral goals (Lilleker, 2005).

As with most other aspects of political communication and election campaigning, this process of seat or constituency targeting has become increasingly sophisticated in recent decades. Formal research and marketing techniques are now used extensively to guide both the selection of target seats and the delivery of persuasive campaigns within them. The Australian Labor Party's (ALP) campaign for the 2010 South Australian state election provides a valuable example of this constituency targeting approach at work, as the party's ability to effectively identify and protect 'at risk' seats was widely credited with saving the Rann Labor government from a predicted defeat.

In the year leading up to the 2010 South Australian state election, the second-term government was riding high in the polls and was expected to easily outdo its Liberal opponents to secure another term in office. But the party's prospects took an abrupt dive when it was alleged that Premier Mike Rann had shared an intimate relationship with a parliamentary waitress, and had then lied about the nature of their relationship both in the media and on the floor of the South Australian parliament. At the commencement of the formal campaign period, public polling showed the ALP's vote sitting level with the Liberal Party's, while Premier Rann's personal approval ratings had slumped to well below 50 per cent (Manning and Anderson, 2011).

Despite the abrupt decline in fortunes, the ALP entered the campaign with one significant advantage: a parliamentary majority of 28 seats – four more than required to govern outright. By contrast, the Liberal Party held just 15 seats, which meant that it needed to win a significant number of new seats to take office. The ALP's strategists determined that if the party could hold on to at least two of its seven most marginal seats, it would be likely to retain office as the remainder were held by comfortable margins of 10 per cent or more. The party therefore embarked upon a tightly focused campaign which was targeted almost entirely towards its own marginal seats and left sitting MPs on higher margins to absorb the brunt of expected swings against it.

In late 2009 the party carried out a substantial round of quantitative polling to test its support in different parts of the state, which confirmed that its vote was softest in the seven marginal seats of Light (held by a margin of 2.1 per cent), Mawson (2.2 per cent), Norwood (4.0 per cent), Newland (5.2 per cent), Hartley (6.2 per cent), Bright (6.6 per cent) and Morialta (6.9 per cent) (author interviews, 2013). The ALP then carried out continuous polling of these key seats right up to election day in March 2010, giving its strategists a constantly evolving picture of the mood in each seat and how specific policies or campaign events were being received by voters on the ground.

Based on this rolling sampling, the party's strategists concluded that the seats of Norwood and Morialta could not be won as the results were consistently unfavourable and showed that none of the party's campaign efforts were shifting voter intentions there. Armed with this knowledge, the party withdrew most of its centralised campaign resources from these seats and poured them into the remaining five marginals, where the research showed more promising trends (author interviews, 2013). This strategy was somewhat counter-intuitive given that Norwood and Morialta were held by higher margins than other seats within the target group; conventional campaign wisdom would suggest ceding the most vulnerable seats before those higher up the pendulum.

According to those who worked on the campaign, the ALP spent approximately 90 per cent of its total central campaign budget in the seats of Bright, Hartley, Light, Mawson and Norwood alone, bombarding voters with advertising, direct mail, leaflets, signage and other campaign materials (author interviews, 2013). The content of these materials was specifically tailored to these constituencies, as the party had also carried out qualitative focus groups with people who resided within their boundaries.

These in-depth discussions involved voters from a cross section of demographic groups, but focused particularly on identifying issues of common concern or interest across the different audience segments. Feedback from these focus groups was behind the ALP's announcement of a $445 million infrastructure project servicing these areas – the Southern Expressway – as a key election commitment, and also informed its focus on the uncertainty and risk associated with voting for an inexperienced opposition in the party's campaign advertising (author interviews, 2013).

In short, the ALP used market research to single out the seats most at risk of being lost and then focused the majority of its campaign resources there to sandbag them against the coming electoral tide. The effectiveness of this targeting strategy can be seen in the results: despite gaining only 48 per cent of the popular vote and sustaining a state-wide swing against it of 7.5 per cent, the Rann Labor government saw a net loss of just two seats and was returned to office with its majority intact. The ALP retained all five of its target seats – two with increased margins – while in non-target seats higher up the pendulum some sitting members experienced swings of between 15 and 20 per cent (van Onselen 2010).

Lessons for political marketing

The clear lesson from South Australian Labor's successful 2010 campaign is that understanding *where* to target political messaging and resources is just as valuable as knowing *who* to target them at. While it is undoubtedly important to identify key demographics or receptive market segments across the electorate as a whole, it is also critical to understand how patterns of support manifest across the different seats which make up the electorate.

Furthermore, this case emphasises the importance of formal research in identifying these patterns of support and guiding effective decision-making about target constituencies. If the ALP had relied upon external indicators such as seat margins to determine its key targets, it likely would have pulled resources from its two lowest-margin seats and continued to resource those higher up the pendulum. As is evident from the above discussion, this would have been a poor choice as the lower-margin seats actually contained a higher proportion of captured and persuadable voters. By allowing its quantitative research program to guide the selection of target seats then, the ALP ensured that its efforts were accurately focused on those seats which offered the greatest prospects for victory.

Calculated and strategic geographic targeting helped the Rann Labor government win a third term in circumstances that pointed strongly towards defeat. While not every instance of constituency targeting need be as narrowly focused or well-resourced as the ALP's efforts, this case certainly highlights the importance of understanding geographic distributions of support and incorporating this knowledge into any wider political strategy.

Further reading

Baines, P. R., P. Harris and B. R. Lewis (2002). 'The political marketing planning process: improving image and message in strategic target areas', *Marketing Intelligence and Planning*, 20(1): 6–14.

Fisher, J., D. Cutts and E. Fieldhouse (2011). 'The electoral effectiveness of constituency campaigning in the 2010 British general election: the "triumph" of Labour?' *Electoral Studies*, 30(4): 816–28.

Lilleker, D. G. (2005). 'Local campaign management: winning votes or wasting resources?' *Journal of Marketing Management*, 21(9–10): 979–1003.

Manning, H. and G. Anderson (2011). 'The 2010 South Australian state election'. *Australian Journal of Political Science*, 46(1): 157–66.

van Onselen, P. (2010). 'Secrets of the unlikely victory'. *The Australian*, 22 March.

Notes

1   Both authors were involved in the campaign. Anna Matušková worked as a strategist and Miloš Gregor was involved as an analyst. This campaign description is based on the factual experience of its authors, and the cited materials are internal campaign sources.

2   The Benes Decrees legalized the process of expelling Germans from the former Czechoslovakia after WWII.

3   The political campaign starts 17 days and ends 48 hours before the elections (law no.346/ 1990 zb.).

4   In the last whole country elections in 2009 to the European Parliament, the party received only 2.1 per cent of votes.

References

Allington, Nigel, Philip Morgan and Nicholas O'Shaughnessy (1999). 'How marketing changed the world. The political marketing of an idea: a case study of privatization'. In Bruce Newman (ed.) *The Handbook of Political Marketing*. Thousand Oaks, CA: Sage, 627–42.

Andreasen, Alan R. (1995). *Marketing Social Change: Changing Behavior to Promote Health, Social Development and the Environment*. San Francisco: Jossey-Bass.

Barreto, Matt A., Jennifer Merolla and Victoria Defrancesco Soto (2011). 'Multiple dimensions of mobilization: the effect of direct contact and political ads on Latino turnout in the 2000 presidential election'. *Journal of Political Marketing*, 10(4): 303–27.

Boin, Arjen (ed.) (2005). *The Politics of Crisis Management: Public Leadership Under Pressure*. Cambridge: Cambridge University Press.

Boin, Arjen and Paul 't Hart (2003). 'Public leadership in times of crisis: mission impossible?.' *Public Administration Review*. 63(5): 544–53.

Braun, Alexander and Anna Matuskova (2009). 'Czech Republic: Social Democrats strike back'. Case study 7.2 in Jennifer Lees-Marshment, *Political Marketing: Principles and Applications*. London and New York: Routledge, 181–3.

Busby, Robert (2014). 'Mama Grizzlies: Republican female candidates and the political marketing dilemma'. In Jennifer Lees-Marshment, Brian Conley and Kenneth Cosgrove (eds) *Political Marketing in the US*. New York: Routledge.

Campbell, Alastair (2013) 'Alastair Campbell in Conversation: Politics, the People and the Press', Public Conversation with Steve Richards. The British Library, 17th May. http://www.youtube. com/watch?v=_Gu4ZEMOB78

Cogburn, Derrick L and Fatima K. Espinoza-Vasquez (2011). 'From networked nominee to networked nation: examining the impact of Web 2.0 and social media on political participation and civic engagement in the 2008 Obama campaign'. *Journal of Political Marketing*, 10(1/2): 189–213.

Cook, Catherine (2010). 'Mobile marketing and political activities'. *International Journal of Mobile Marketing*, 5(1): 154–63.

Coombs, W. Timothy (2011). 'Political public relations and crisis communication'. In Jesper Strömbäck and Spiro Kiousis (eds) *Political Public Relations: Principles and Applications*. New York: Routledge, 213–34.

Corner, Adam and Alex Randall (2011). 'Selling climate change? The limitations of social marketing as a strategy for climate change public engagement'. *Global Environmental Change*. 21(3): 1005–14.

The Daily Show (2012). Broadcast, *Comedy Central*, 19th April. http://www.thedailyshow.com/watch/thu-april-19–2012/judy-smith

Egherman, Tori (2005). 'The Hashemi brand in Iran's elections'. *Marketing Profs*. http:www.marketingprofs.com/5/egherman1.asp?sp=1 (accessed 4 April, 2008)

Fletcher, Joseph F., Heather Bastedo and Jennifer Hoce, *et al.* (2009). 'Losing heart: declining support and the political marketing of the Afghanistan mission'. *Canadian Journal of Political Science*, 42(4): 911–37.

Foley, Michael (2009). 'Gordon Brown and the role of compounded crisis in the pathology of leadership decline'. *British Politics*, 4(4): 498–513.

Gaber, Ivor (2006). 'The autistic campaign: the parties, the media and the voters'. In Darren G. Lilleker, Nigel Jackson and Richard Scullion (eds) *The Marketing of Political Parties*. Manchester: Manchester University Press, 132–56.

Garrett, Sam (2009). *Campaign Crises: Detours on the Road to Congress*. Boulder, CO: Lynne Rienner.

Garrett, R. Sam (2014). 'Crisis-management, marketing, and money in US campaigns'. In Jennifer Lees-Marshment, Brian Conley and Kenneth Cosgrove (eds) *Political Marketing in the US*. New York: Routledge.

Gelders, Dave and Øyvind Ihlen (2010). 'Government communication about potential policies: public relations, propaganda or both?' *Public Relations Review* 36(1): 59–62.

Germany, Julie (2013). 'Advances in campaign technology'. In Dennis W. Johnson (ed.) *Campaigning for President 2012: Strategy and Tactics*. New York: Routledge, 81–91.

Green, Donald P. and Alan S. Gerber (2004). *Get Out the Vote! How to Increase Voter Turnout*, Washington: Brookings Institution Press.

Harmer, Emily and Dominic Wring (2013). 'Julie and the Cybermums: marketing and women voters in the UK 2010 general election'. *Journal of Political Marketing*, 12(2/3): 262–73.

Hersh, Eitan D. and Brian F. Schaffner (2013). 'Targeted campaign appeals and the value of ambiguity'. *Journal of Politics*, 75(2): 520–534.

Holland, Jack (2012). 'Blair's war on terror: selling intervention to Middle England'. *The British Journal of Politics and International Relations*, 14(1): 74–95.

Ingram, Peter and Jennifer Lees-Marshment (2002). 'The Anglicisation of political marketing: how Blair "out-marketed" Clinton'. *Journal of Public Affairs*, 2(2): 44–56.

Johnson, Dennis W. (2013). 'The election of 2012'. In Dennis W. Johnson (ed.) *Campaigning for President 2012: Strategy and Tactics*. New York: Routledge, 1–22.

Kotler, Philip and Eduardo L. Roberto (2002). *Social Marketing: Strategies for Changing Public Behavior*. New York: Free Press.

Lees-Marshment, Jennifer (2008). *Political Marketing and British Political Parties: The Party's Just Begun*, 2nd revised edition. Manchester: Manchester University Press.

Lees-Marshment, Jennifer. (2010). 'New Zealand political marketing: marketing communication rather than the product?'. In Jennifer Lees-Marshment, Jesper Strömbäck & Chris Rudd (eds) *Global Political Marketing*. London: Routledge, 65–81.

Lees-Marshment, Jennifer (2011). *The Political Marketing Game*. Houndmills and New York: Palgrave Macmillan.

Lees-Marshment, Jennifer, Brian Conley and Kenneth Cosgrove (eds) (2014). *Political Marketing in the US*. New York: Routledge.

Lees-Marshment, Jennifer and Robin T. Pettitt (2010). 'UK political marketing: a question of leadership?' In Jennifer Lees-Marshment, Jesper Strömbäck and Chris Rudd (eds) *Global Political Marketing*. London: Routledge, 113–27.

Leppäniemi, Matti, Heikki Karjaluoto, Heikki Lehto and Annia Goman (2010). 'Targeting young voters in a political campaign: empirical insights into an interactive digital marketing campaign in the 2007 Finnish general election'. *Journal of Nonprofit & Public Sector Marketing*, 22(1): 14–37.

Lloyd, Jenny (2009). 'Keeping both the baby and the bathwater: scoping a new model of political marketing communication.' *International Review on Public and Nonprofit Marketing*, 6(2): 119–35.

Loewen, Peter John and Daniel Rubenson (2011). 'For want of a nail: negative persuasion in a party leadership race'. *Party Politics*, 17(1): 45–65.

Marland, Alex and Mireille Lalancett (2014). 'Access Hollywood: celebrity endorsements in American politics'. In Jennifer Lees-Marshment, Brian Conley and Kenneth Cosgrove (eds) *Political Marketing in the US*. New York; Routledge.

McGough, Sean (2005). 'Political marketing in Irish politics: the case of Sinn Féin'. In Darren G. Lilleker and Jennifer Lees-Marshment (eds) *Political Marketing: A Comparative Perspective*. Manchester: Manchester University Press, 97–113.

McKenzie-Mohr, Doug and William Smith (1999). *Fostering Sustainable Behavior: An Introduction to Community-Based Social Marketing*. Gabriola Island BC, Canada: New Society Publishers.

Mylona, Ifigeneia (2008). 'SMS in everyday political marketing in Greece'. *Journal of Political Marketing*, 7(3): 278–94.

Newman, Bruce I. (2001). 'An assessment of the 2000 US presidential election: a set of political marketing guidelines'. *Journal of Public Affairs*, 1(3): 210–16.

News Hour (2012), Broadcast, *Global Toronto*, 26th June. http://www.youtube.com/watch?v =uWerl10eD2Y

O'Leary, Noreen (2009). 'GMMB'. *Mediaweek*, 19(24): AM2.

O'Shaughnessy, Nicholas and Gillian Peele (1985). 'Money, mail and markets: reflections on direct mail in American politics'. *Electoral Studies*, 4(2): 115–24.

Papagiannidis, Savvas, Constantinos K. Coursaris and Michael Bourlakis (2012). 'Do websites influence the nature of voting intentions? The case of two national elections in Greece'. *Computers in Human Behavior*, 28(2): 300–7.

Rademacher, Eric W. and Alfred J. Tuchfarber (1999). 'Pre-election polling and political campaigns'. In Bruce I. Newman (ed.) *Handbook of Political Marketing*. Thousand Oaks, CA: Sage, 197–222.

Raftopoulou, Effi and Margaret K. Hogg (2010). 'The political role of government-sponsored social marketing campaign'. *European Journal of Marketing*, 44(7/8): 1206–27.

Ridout, Travis N. (2014). 'The market research, testing and targeting behind American political advertising'. In Jennifer Lees-Marshment, Brian Conley and Kenneth Cosgrove (eds) *Political Marketing in the US*. New York: Routledge.

Robinson, Claire E. (2006). 'Advertising and the market orientation of political parties contesting the 1999 and 2002 New Zealand general election campaigns'. PhD thesis, Massey University, Palmerston North, New Zealand.

Robinson, Claire. (2010). 'Political advertising and the demonstration of market orientation'. *European Journal of Marketing*, 44(3/4): 451–9.

Ross, Jim (2008). Excerpts from: http://www.completecampaigns.com/article.asp?articleid=27 (accessed March 4, 2008)

Savigny, Heather and Mick Temple (2010). 'Political marketing models: the curious incident of the dog that doesn't bark'. *Political Studies*, 58(5): 1049–64.

Schweiger, Gunter and Michaela Aadami (1999). 'The nonverbal image of politicians and political parties'. In Bruce Newman (ed.) *The Handbook of Political Marketing*. Thousand Oaks, CA: Sage.

Seawright, David (2005). 'On a low road: the 2005 Conservative campaign'. *Journal of Marketing Management*, 21(9/10): 943–57.

Seidman, Steven A. (2010). 'Barack Obama's 2008 campaign for the US presidency and visual design'. *Journal of Visual Literacy*, 29(1): 1–27.

Sunday Profile (2012), Broadcast, *ABC Radio*, March.

Temple, Mick (2010). 'Political marketing, party behaviour and political science'. In Jennifer Lees-Marshment, Jesper Strömbäck and Chris Rudd (eds) *Global Political Marketing*. London: Routledge, 263–77.

Ubertaccio, Peter N. (2008). 'Network marketing and American political parties'. in Dennis W. Johnson (ed.) *The Routledge Handbook of Political Management*. New York: Routledge, 509–23.

World Denver Talks (2012). Broadcast, *Rocky Mountain PBS*, 28 September.

Young, Sally (2005). 'Government advertising costs us dearly'. *The Age*, 30 August. http://www.theage.com.au/news/opinion/sally-young/2005/08/29/1125302509121.html (accessed 10 April 2008)

7 Relational and interactive political marketing communication

Political marketing communication is rapidly developing to become more interactive and to build relationships, holding the prospect of lifting the citizen from passive consumer to active participant in the communication process and enhancing the public sphere. Recent technological developments in Web 2.0 and social networking change communication from a means for elites to sell a product to the public to the opportunity for the public to provide input and feedback before, during and after a politician gets into power or a political product is designed and delivered. Communication becomes more about relationship building than product selling; and about maintaining or enhancing support in government instead of just getting votes in the first place. This chapter will look at e-marketing; public relations; interactive and responsive leadership communication; voter responsibility communication and reputation management in government.

E-marketing

> **Practitioner perspective 7.1 on creating volunteer-friendly and online forms of field experience**
>
> *When you walk into a field office, you have many opportunities ... You can knock on doors, and they'll have these stats there for you ... 'here's how you compare to the rest of them'. But it's all very offline ... so what we set out to do was create that offline field experience online.*
>
> Harper Reed, CTO for Barack Obama's 2012 re-election campaign, 2013
>
> *I didn't care where ... what time ... how you organised, as long as I could track it ... [so we built] a piece of software that tracked all this and allowed you to match your friends on Facebook with our lists, and we said ... 'so-and-so is a friend of yours, we think he's unregistered [or undecided], why don't you go get him to register [or be decided]?'*
>
> Jim Messina, Obama 2012 Campaign Manager, 2013
>
> Source: Balz (2013)

E-marketing is communication via digital devices such as mobile phones and the internet that integrates understanding from market research and other marketing concepts. The success of the 2008 Obama campaign wasn't just that he used Facebook but that online mechanisms made it easy for volunteers to get involved in and help the campaign, applying principles from internal marketing and mixing online with old-fashioned field activity as Practitioner perspective 7.1 suggests.

Jackson (2005, 95, 159 and 2006) argues that effective e-marketing combines direct marketing and relationship marketing concepts over the long term, rather than just being used in short-term sales campaigning and one-off transactions. Individual politicians can use websites and email as a cheap and easy means to contact their constituents in a targeted manner to put out unmediated communication over which they have greater control because they can speak directly to constituents; as a source of market intelligence to help MPs better represent their constituents, develop their political campaigns and policy stances and build credibility and a delivery record for re-election. He suggests four criteria for effective e-marketing: see Figure 7.1

Jackson's principles for effective e-marketing in politics

1   E-political marketing is regularly used outside an election campaign.
2   Communication is tailored to the requirements of the receiver.
3   Communication is two-way and not just one-way.
4   It builds 'networks' between an MP and the constituents.

Figure 7.1

Source: Jackson (2005, 95)

E-marketing needs to be two-way – one of the reasons it appeals to the youth is that it gives them the opportunity to be involved and be active, on their own terms, in a way that suits them.

Jackson and Lilleker (2014) argue that in 2008 Obama employed effective e-marketing with interactivity that built relationships to help support the brand. Obama's 2008 marketing built on that by earlier candidates such as Howard Dean's 2004 nomination bid for which his advisor Joe Trippi created complex features to track users on his blog. Dean went on to become Chair of the DNC in Washington DC and implemented such features and principles to build up the party's organisational structure in every state so that the party was able to engage in continual communication with the public. Working with state parties, he sought to ensure there would be a team of people who were committed, trained, experienced and constantly organising at all times, creating and maintaining an ongoing relationship with voters by talking to them in between elections. Maintaining a level of organisation everywhere helped support all candidates at all levels including governors and state legislators. When Obama became the Democratic presidential nominee he had this machine already in place to build on, which he used to recruit volunteers.

In 2006, data was placed online for volunteers to access so they could run canvassing operations, organise meetings and oversee telemarketing themselves. Stirland (2008) notes that it enabled the same old-fashioned organising to be carried out but using fewer resources. Such initiatives particularly suit younger voters, who had previously been disengaged from politics. They also used this to expand their volunteer base: Cogburn and Espinoza-Vasquez (2011, 200) identified how they asked for volunteers' contact details during rallies, then sorted this information geographically, working with their regional co-ordinators to communicate directly with them after the event to get them more involved. The Obama team did grasp the idea that it can be used to mobilise, engage and interact with voters. Cogburn and Espinoza-Vasquez (2011, 203) observed that the 2008 campaign created web-facilitated, hosted meetings, peer-to-peer political campaigning and public education, and raised donations. Jackson *et al.* (2012, 293) found that the 2008 Obama campaign 'adopted key innovations where my.barackobama.com (MyBO) created literally thousands of participatory opportunities.' Obama further increased interactivity in 2012 (Jackson and Lilleker 2014).

Practitioners should therefore make sure they build this into their design and avoid less effective one-way communication mechanisms. However Jackson and Lilleker's (2014) analysis of practice in US presidential politics suggests practice has been mixed; the McCain and Romney campaigns failed to use interactivity to its full potential, using online communication to sell their product instead of involving voters in its creation and dissemination. Given that Obama won the election, it could be argued that this suggests political marketing as a whole will move towards a more relational than transactional approach. Jackson and Lilleker also found that Obama's campaign sought to move volunteers up the political loyalty ladder from being passively engaged to becoming active community members and evangelists. It also helped maintain and enhance the President's relationship with his supporters, demonstrating the importance of relationship marketing. This might have democratic positives by increasing deliberation within political communication and democratic engagement in participation, though it is not without practical problems as it reduces elite control.

Small (2012)'s study of the extent to which Canadian parties' use of Facebook met relationship marketing criteria shows similar findings. Small adapted Jackson's 2006 principles: see Figure 7.2.

Small applied this to Canadian parties in 2010, and found that the first criteria of continual updating was only met by the Liberals. Facebook was rarely used for recruitment by the Canadian parties with only the Liberals and the Greens featuring a 'take action' tab with

Small's relationship marketing criteria for Facebook

Continuous	Updated at regular intervals	Yes/No
Value	Information not easily available elsewhere	Yes/No
	Information of relevance to non-members	Yes/No
Recruitment	Membership	Yes/No
	Donations	Yes/No
	Volunteer	Yes/No
	E-newsletter sign-up	Yes/No
	Events	Yes/No
Interactivity	Feedback (Like or Comment)	Yes/No
	Wall post	Yes/No
	Discussion board	Yes/No

Figure 7.2

Source: Small (2012, 199)

links to activities including donating, becoming a member and signing up for an e-newsletter. Small (2012, 203) notes that Facebook's how-to guide for politicians states it 'is a culture of conversations, giving politicians and political campaigns/organisations a huge opportunity to get immediate feedback on various issues'. Comments were allowed on all Facebook pages of the Canadian parties but they were not interactive – the political elites did not respond to comments made by the public. Only three pages operated a discussion board. The Liberals were the most open to interactivity, offering discussion boards and allowing friends to post their own content on the party page. Thus the overall pattern was mixed in terms of following a relationship marketing strategy; some did, some did not.

Online communication by individual politicians has been less effective (see Jackson *et al.* 2012). Such principles seem not have to filtered down the different levels of the political system as yet, or perhaps the infrastructure in terms of volunteers, staff and data collection and analysis is not easy and cheap enough for all levels of politics to use it. Jackson's study of UK politicians' websites found they failed to meet these principles, as did Papagiannidis *et al.*'s (2012) analysis of political candidates' websites in Greece. In the US, Williams and Gulati's (2014) analysis of congressional-level online communication concluded that politicians failed to realize – or at least to operationalise – the potential to build long-term relationships. E-marketing was not being used permanently to build relationships, or interactively, or to build social networks. Whilst some candidates and staff recognised the need to use social media more strategically, most needed to integrate marketing principles within their online communication, such as conducting market intelligence with feedback to the campaign and segmenting the market to target campaign messages to specific groups. This research suggests that non-presidential campaigns face challenges in using the full potential of e-marketing.

Turcotte and Raynauld's (2014) work on the use of Twitter by the populist Tea Party shows how online communication may be used to enable political movements to engage in marketed messages amongst the grass roots. Movements can use Twitter to generate highly targeted, emotive communication amongst individuals at the grass-roots level and to build up grass-roots support. Social media enables and encourages followers to communicate between themselves to build up a movement, instead of relying on one charismatic leader: a hyper decentralised network of individuals and organisations. Other movements may use e-marketing in this way to bring attention to, and increase support for, neglected issues amongst the general public and elites – such as interest groups advocating gay marriage or wanting to raise awareness of child trafficking; or increasing public support for policy measures such as emissions trading schemes and carbon taxes to halt climate change.

Like all new tools, e-marketing cannot guarantee success unless it is placed within the context of an effective strategy and product or brand. Middleton (2009) argues that 'while technology makes it possible to run large campaigns effectively to niche audiences at low cost, it is not a sufficient condition for electoral success'. He worked for the ACT Party in New Zealand and oversaw the use of technological tools to reach voters including weekly email newsletters, online petitions, website forums and subscribable subject-based news lists which allowed voters to register their interest in particular issues and receive updates; and a customer relationship management (CRM) database approximating Voter Vault with information on every registered voter derived from public and party data sources, including residential and postal addresses, an occupation group and socio-economic code, age range, presumptive gender and residential mesh block. Communication was then sent to target groups and any feedback added to the CRM database to create voter profiles to which were sent low-cost, targeted, policy-related communication. However, such efforts were to no avail when the party's strategic position was challenged by National, the main party, moving to the right of centre and adopting positions which attracted ACT voters. Faced with this threat, ACT reverted to traditional campaigning – doorknocking, candidate speeches – to win an electoral seat and return two Members of Parliament. Middleton therefore warns that although technology helps to maintain a group of warm supporters and data on them informs communication, contextual and strategic considerations can prove more important in an actual election.

Jackson *et al.* (2012, 296) contend that comprehensive e-marketing may be more suitable and more effective when political elites use it to forge positive relationships with their supporters. Their research identified that some parties, such as the Conservatives and Lib Dems in the UK, offered community-oriented forms of online communication to their members. Thus more traditional communication which is aimed at persuasion and providing information is more appropriate for voters who know little about the party or candidate, whereas relational forms of communication are suited to the internal market who already have high levels of knowledge and interest. Turcotte and Raynauld's (2014) work also suggested that different elements of political marketing – segmentation, targeting, internal marketing, e-marketing – can be combined to create powerful volunteer support building mechanisms on key political issues, which might be used by parties, interest groups or movements. Thus e-marketing helps to reinforce existing relationships, and it is effective within the long-term context.

Public relations

Public relations (PR) is about initiating a series of communication events designed to build and maintain a positive relationship between a political organisation/figure and its/their stakeholders. It is carried out over the long term, involves multiple events, and is not confined to an election campaign or a single piece of communication such as advertising. As Strömbäck and Kiousis (2011, 1–2) note, although the academic study of political PR is relatively new, the practice is old, going back as far as 64 BCE, through the American Revolution and to the work of Edward Bernays in the mid-twentieth century. However, most literature on PR is about the corporate sector so their book, featured in Authors' corner 7.1, sought to outline the nature of the field and the practice of political PR.

Strömbäck and Kiousis (2011, 4) review definitions of PR and note that there are several key characteristics running through such definitions, and thus PR is about:

- the management of communication between an organisation and its publics (or stakeholders);
- the relationships between an organisation and its publics which should be mutually beneficial;
- the management of the reputation of an organisation.

Political PR goes beyond media management and encompasses interactive, ongoing communication to develop long-term relationships. Political PR is therefore defined as 'the management process by which an organisation or individual actor for political purposes, through purposeful communication and action, seeks to influence and to establish, build, and maintain beneficial relationships and reputations with its key publics to help support its mission and achieve its goals' (Strömbäck and Kiousis 2011, 8). Because PR should be mutually beneficial, it is about organisations and their publics understanding each other's interests and reducing the conflict between them and is thus more about creating trust, satisfaction, openness and involvement.

Authors' corner 7.1

Political Public Relations: Principles and Applications
Edited by Spiro Kiousis and Jesper Strömbäck
Published in 2011 by Routledge

While political marketing, political communication, and public relations have always been closely intertwined, public relations strategies and tactics are more ubiquitous today than ever before. Still, there is neither much theorizing nor empirical research on *political public relations*, which can be broadly defined as the management process by which an organisation or individual actor for political purposes, through purposeful communication and action, seeks to influence and to establish, build, and maintain beneficial relationships and reputations with its key publics to help support its mission and achieve its goals.

Much public relations research is focused on the use of public relations by commercial businesses, whereas much political communication research neglects or only briefly mentions the use of public relations. Furthermore, political communication scholars seldom display any deep understanding of public relations theories, whereas public relations scholars seldom display any deep understanding of what makes political communication and policymaking different from other areas of inquiry. Thus, although there are exceptions, the general rule is that there is not much theorizing and research that manages to bridge the gap between political communication and public relations theory and research.

To remedy this and advance the field of *political public relations*, this book sought first to map and define the field; and second, to bring together scholars from various disciplines who study different aspects of political public relations. Major topics covered in the edited book include the history of political public relations, news management and media relations, agenda building, presidential public relations, corporate issues management and political public relations, political marketing, strategic framing in political public relations, political crisis communication, relationship cultivation and political public relations, government communication, public diplomacy, global political public relations, digital political public relations, and political public relations and the future.

In general, the review of political public relations in the book suggests that it is a noteworthy topic meriting scholarly attention for theoretical development and empirical testing. Unlike many other areas of inquiry, it draws on a rich interdisciplinary foundation from fields such as public relations, political science, political marketing, and political communication. The most important shortcoming within political public relations research is that most public relations theories and concepts have seldom or never been applied in the context of political public relations. To do so, and extend political public relations to domains seldom investigated, should be one of the most important priorities in future research on political public relations. Not only would it increase our understanding of political public relations per se; it would also test the validity of public relations theories beyond traditional contexts. In conclusion, it is hoped that the book can serve as a springboard for future research on the emerging area of political public relations research.

There are a range of different publics: situational publics, non-publics, latent publics, aware publics and active publics. Lieber and Golan (2011, 56) explain the difference:

- non-publics are those that don't face any similar problem, or if they do they don't recognise it or organise to do anything about it;
- latent publics are those face the same problem but do not recognise it or do anything about it;
- aware publics have the problem, are aware of it but fail to act on it;
- active publics are those who have the problem, recognise it and seek to do something about it.

Marketers therefore need to identify and monitor the behaviour of these different publics in order to decide how to use PR to build beneficial relationships with them. Jackson (2012, 271) notes that it is not about promoting a specific political product, but building and maintaining positive relationships with key audiences through dialogue, consideration of the receiver of communication and reputation management. There are several aspects to PR which Jackson explores through identifying the different schools of thought in the literature: see Figure 7.3.

The pragmatic and democratic implications of these vary; some are closer to more conventional views of PR as short-term persuasion, whereas others are more about fostering true dialogue, debate and free information and, through this, positive long-term relationships. Parties, candidates and governments may choose different approaches at different times – reputation management may be more useful for governments than opposition parties, for example. Jackson (2012) applied these concepts to candidates standing for 12 seats in Devon, a region in south-west England, but found that there was very little evidence of

---

Jackson's political PR approaches

1 **Relations with publics** – focuses on using research to identify the best message to send to the right audience.

2 **Grunigian** – strategic two-way communication based on feedback to build positive relationships.

3 **Hype** – seeks to make a noise through publicity for short-term benefit.

4 **Persuasion** – seeks to change opinions and behaviours through promotion campaigns.

5 **Relational** – develops influential relationships through issue and crisis management to ensure a positive long-term reputation.

6 **Reputation management** – similar to relational except includes other activities such as lobbying and aims to shape public opinion and organisational image.

7 **Relations in publics** – use of issues management and internal communications to develop a public sphere to debate free-flowing information.

8 **Community building** – creating a sense of a community through two-way communication, issues management and community affairs.

Figure 7.3

Source: Adapted from Jackson (2012, 273–4)

the more relational or community building types of PR, with greater focus on persuasion but also reputation management, whilst less indication of hype forms of PR.

Political PR includes a range of tools such as information subsidies, agenda building and message framing. Information subsidies make it easy or low cost for people to get access to information. Lieber and Golan (2011, 60) discuss how the Obama presidency

---

Authors' corner 7.2

Public Relations and Nation Building: Influencing Israel
By Margarlit Toledano and David McKie
Published by Routledge in 2013

Public Relations and Nation Building: Influencing Israel tells the previously untold story of the role of PR, and its interplay with nation building, in the birth and evolution of Israel. Achieving nationhood in 1948, Israel is still a relatively new state established by Jewish immigrants from around the world who have been settling there since the end of the nineteenth century, when it was part of the Ottoman Empire. We argue that the Zionist movement succeeded in establishing the state thanks to a phenomenally persuasive, and international, communication campaign. It included motivating diaspora Jews to immigrate, enlisting the support of international public opinion through professional lobbying, and uniting new immigrants from 70 different cultures into one society. It also involved inventing new Israeli traditions, language and identity rooted in the Jewish culture and faith. Pre-state and post-state Zionist institutions used PR and Hasbarah (literally 'explanation' in Hebrew, meaning a form of soft propaganda), to enlist the Israeli population in the huge nation building challenge. Professional communicators employed by Zionist institutions staged events and provided narratives, resonant symbols and emotional messages to inspire the sacrifice of individual goals, and sometimes lives, for the sake of the Jewish state. As well as analysing the effort of the Israeli government and national organisations to enlist the support of internal publics, the book describes how they used branding, strategic communication and public diplomacy to influence international public opinion and to try to improve the image of Israel in the eyes of the world. Nevertheless, we call into question the ability of even the best professional communication to satisfactorily explain such difficult realities as 45 years of occupation and the denial of basic human rights to the Palestinians.

As a result, we caution that, in any strongly nationalistic climate, PR can be too easily pressed into the service of government propaganda and urge PR practitioners, activists and media workers to contribute jointly to more democratic societies: we actually describe how the values that characterized the Jewish public sphere in the diaspora, before the establishment of the state, were intensified by the nation building effort led by the Zionist institutions; and how then, later on, these were taken up by the government of Israel and carried over to the present. More positively, we identify how specific circumstances in Jewish disaspora and Israeli life enabled strong fundraising and lobbying functions in advance of PR in other parts of the world. Nevertheless, that early and heavy emphasis on solidarity, exclusiveness and unity as well as the blurring of the lines between Israel's journalists and politicians, encouraged uncritical support of the national institutions and government. It actually inhibited the development of open liberal democracy, tolerant of dissident voices and respectful of individual human rights. This interdisciplinary study embeds PR in Israel's cultural, economic, political and social environment and draws heavily on biographies, histories, journalism, media, memoirs, politics and social studies.

used social media to make information about the health-care bill easy to access; given it was available 24/7 it helped ensure anyone could access information whenever they liked and thus help create a consensus towards supporting the legislation.

Message framing tries to influence how an issue, event or situation is perceived amongst elites as well as the public. Hallahan (2011) notes how linguist George Lakoff trained the US Democrats to use certain works, narratives and metaphors to convey the desired story over the long term; and after worldwide international talks world leaders will speak in public to convey their interpretation of events. Governments can also frame attributes, such as a rising number of homeowners being a good sign for the economy; or they can frame the size of a risk. Framing can also influence perceptions of responsibility such as whether the public should blame a political leader for a bad situation. Hallahan (2011) points out how, when there was a big oil spill in the Gulf of Mexico in 2010, framing was used so that BP was to blame not President Obama although there was critique the US government should have regulated the industry more heavily and enacted greater attacks on BP with regard to fixing the leak.

However Strömbäck and Kiousis (2011, 18–19) argue that the political environment is more contentious and may present challenges to this more positive form of PR. Furthermore, it does not always succeed. Tedesco (2011, 84) discusses US presidents' ability to influence the media agenda and notes that, despite the central position of the president in political discourse, their scope to control the agenda is constrained; even after the 9/11 terrorist attack in 2001 the president did not demonstrate agenda building capacity. Such capacity depends on the president's approval ratings and personality, and the issue, amongst other factors. Similarly Eshbaugh-Soha (2011) notes how the US President utilises a communications office, press office and office of public liaison in order to engage in political PR. Such extensive staff enables strategic and planned communication to reach out to different publics and respond to public expectations. This helps the president manage public expectations, convey the work the president does and build support for policies. However the evidence suggests the ability of such staff to influence the agenda has been limited and recommends that presidential PR needs to become more targeted to narrow groups.

Additionally, the practice of political PR is often very limited and narrow in scope. Xifra (2010) notes that political PR is also not just about media management or a set of techniques despite practitioners they interviewed in Spain claiming so, thus indicating that one barrier to effective political PR is the limited understanding of party staff involved in communications. Baines (2011, 116) observes that the UK Blair government 1997–2010 was criticised for engaging in more persuasive forms of PR to influence its image through symbols rather than substantive behaviour. The book on PR and nation branding by Margalit Toledano and David McKie discusses how PR has been used in public diplomacy to try to build a more positive perception of countries such as Israel but with questionable intentions and impact: see Authors' corner 7.2 for a summary of their arguments which raise a number of normative issues.

Interactive and responsive leadership communication

A recent section of political marketing research suggests that leadership communication needs to become interactive and convey responsiveness more effectively. Lloyd's (2012) analysis of communication in the 2010 UK general election concludes that voters thought there were more opportunities for two-way communication with their politicians such as by Twitter, telephone and email, talk radio and radio phone-in. Political leaders need to engage in meaningful dialogue with voters and so communication should be designed in to enable this and show that politicians have listened, reflected and acted on it. Robinson (2012) argues that it is important that political communication shows voters interacting with leaders as this can impact on how voters perceive politicians. She analysed non-verbal messages conveyed by images of leaders, such as through face-to-face address, exploring the clothes on the leader, the setting of the communication and the distance between the leader and the camera lenses which impacts on how close the viewer feels to the leader. She cites the example of UK Conservative Leader David Cameron being pictured, in the 2010 election, with a shirt but no tie, in a middle-class family backyard, talking directly to camera. Such communication is designed to suggest a politician is honest and friendly and voters can trust them. Other forms of communication – such as when a leader is one-on-one with a journalist, being interviewed in a studio, or in a small or large group – can also be analysed. When politicians are in small groups they can try to convey leadership using hand gestures like handshaking and waving, making physical contact (e.g. hugging) and facial expressions (smiling). Robinson advises that, for example, images of leaders in small groups suggest they can relate more widely to and care for others.

Elder (2014) puts forward a framework for how to convey a market-orientation once a leader is in power. Political leaders need to adopt more reflective forms of communication, especially where they are showing leadership, to maintain public support. Rhetorical indicators of qualities include listening, leading, honesty, common goals and governmental context: leaders need to convey that they are listening through responsiveness and reflectiveness; they need to show leadership; yet be honest and authentic; convey the common goals and benefits of their decisions and the context of social and governmental variables. In Case Study 7.1 he analyses the use of such communication by President Obama in his first term. In government, communication of the context as well as leadership is important as politicians can't simply research the market and offer voters what they want. Modern political leadership, within a marketised environment, thus calls for a more modern form of communication. Leaders cannot just get into power then do what they like – not even when they had a clear mandate for their proposals. Consider the case of George W. Bush who ran in both 2000 and 2004 on Social Security reform as a policy offering yet never managed to ever implement it. More hierarchical and authoritative forms of leadership communication such as: '*I am the leader, I need to follow my conviction*' no longer prove effective. This is an important lesson for political leaders in the US and indeed all around the world. Thus leaders need to find new forms of communication to convey the realities and challenges that leadership in government necessitates. Obama's mini-documentary called *The Road We've Travelled* did this: it was a groundbreaking piece of communication which discussed the difficulties of being president to help remind voters so their judgement on performance could be conducted within the right context. This is also important for delivery marketing, which will be discussed in the next chapter.

Voter responsibility communication

As outlined in the first chapter, there has been a move from transaction-based campaigning to transformational whereby voters are called to action to get involved in campaigning and government. Obama used the word 'we' – *Yes WE can* – in his 2008 campaign but also in his 2012 re-election campaign where he said: 'If there's even one thing we can do – even one life we can save – we have an obligation to try'. When calling for volunteers to get involved again in 2012 a series of ads were launched saying 'Are you in?', and supporters talked about how Obama could not do it all himself, he was President; it was up to his supporters to take the lead to win re-election. Similarly he issued an advert in the election called *Young Americans are Greater Together* that discussed the achievements of Obama's first administration which they themselves should be proud of. Johnson (2012, 211) notes that campaigns are becoming open-sourced in that volunteers are getting involved in campaign design and implementation, and this holds the potential for voters to feel they are participating in the campaign. They can share their ideas online with candidates, talk with others, share their experiences and feel a sense of ownership.

Reputation management

Reputation is the overall assessment the public might make of all the information they receive about a political organisation – a wide range of sources including imagery, party origins, its policies, speeches, advertising, media commentary, personal discussions (see Davies and Mian 2010, 345). Government itself needs to use marketing communication to manage its reputation over the long term. Whereas crisis communication discussed in the previous chapter is very focused and short term, reputation management is, like PR, about efforts to support the brand's image over the long term. Once a politician is in power, they are held more responsible for what happens and what goes wrong. Managing problems is, therefore, even more important as they can damage the overall image of credibility of a government, which relates to delivery and trust.

In government, consultants work to maintain a leader's image, even where scandals and failures of policy occur. The same management of a politician's personal characteristics in a campaign for office can occur in power. Newman (1999, 88) observes how Bill Clinton's advisors dealt with a number of scandals during his presidency 'by carefully crafting an image of himself as leader in charge and almost above the rumour mongering of the media about his sex life'. He focused on what was important and, amazingly, he did not lose public support, despite continual criticism from the opposition. Davies and Mian (2010, 345) discuss the reputation of UK parties in 2001 and 2005, and note how the Liberal Democrat Party's reputation was of being moderate and informal; the Conservative's chic, more ruthless, quite macho and less agreeable relative to their other scores. Labour was seen as more competent and enterprising in 2001. In party systems such as the UK, the reputation of the party is affected by that of the leader, and vice versa; they are separate but linked.

As discussed in previous chapters, communication was used to try to restore Tony Blair's relationship with voters in 2004–2005 because it had been damaged as he became increasingly dismissive of public input and argued he was the leader and knew best what was right for the country. Communication enacted for the reconnection strategy sought to change the way Blair spoke and appeared to listen to voters; so he was pictured receiving strong public criticism, and when he spoke he acknowledged public concern with his decisions and showed respect for those who opposed him, and he used phrases such as 'working in partnership with the public'. This reconnection strategy helped to rehabilitate Blair's overall image. Scammell's (2008) research identified that Labour improved its opinion poll rating over the campaign, increasing its lead over the Conservatives as the best party to deal with the issues of the economy, health and education; and Blair improved his advantage over the opposition leader Michael Howard. It increased the female vote by 8 per cent. After winning the 2005 election, Mr Blair said outside Number 10: 'I have listened and I have learned. And I have a very clear idea of what the British people now expect from this government for a third term'.

Summary

This chapter has explored more relational forms of political marketing communication including public relations, e-marketing and reputation management by political leaders, political parties and governments. This type of communication is long term, and seeks to build and maintain positive relationships between politicians and the public. It is also more interactive as it enables the public to communicate with the politician and can be used to stimulate face-to-face communication and volunteer participation. A best practice guide to relational forms of political marketing communication is given in Figure 7.4 and is followed by a practitioner profile of Joe Trippi who revolutionised how to use the internet to recruit volunteers. Communicating delivery is also an important factor of using political marketing in government, and the next chapter focuses on this.

Best practice guide to relational and interactive political marketing communication

1 Use voter-driven communication with visuals that respond to and connect with voters.
2 Use two-way communication to develop a relationship with the public and make them a participant partner, not passive.
3 Utilise e-marketing to build positive relationships, allowing interaction and stimulating volunteer involvement.
4 Understand that using new technology is not in itself as important as using it in the right way and connecting it to an effective and strategic brand.
5 Utilise e-marketing to reinforce existing relationships with supporters.
6 Create a PR strategy to suit the nature of the organisation or political figures' publics (non, latent, aware and active).
7 In government, choose the PR strategy to suit the goals – whilst listening and responding to feedback helps to build positive relationships, if the goal is to implement chosen policies, persuasive and hype approaches are more suitable to help maintain support and avoid crisis.
8 Politicians need to be shown interacting with the public.
9 Leaders in power need to use responsive communication conveying listening, leading, honesty, common goals and the governmental context.
10 Utilise long-term communication to manage a politician's reputations.
11 Make sure communication is authentic and believable.

Figure 7.4

Practitioner profile 7.1

Name: Joe Trippi
Date of birth: 10 June, 1956
Most notable job: Campaign worker/Consultant

Description: Joe Trippi is an American Democratic campaign worker and consultant who has worked on a number of presidential campaigns over the last 35 years. Having worked on several local election campaigns in California, Trippi joined the national campaign staff of Senator Edward Kennedy's presidential bid in the late 1970s. Since then Trippi has worked on the presidential campaigns of

Walter Mondale, Gary Hart, Dick Gephardt, Jerry Brown and John Edwards. However, from a political marketing standpoint, his most notable work was as the campaign manager for former Vermont governor Howard Dean's bid to become the Democratic nominee for the president of the United States in 2004. It was as the manager for this campaign that Trippi gained recognition for his use of innovative internet strategies. Notably, Trippi was largely responsible for the creation of an official campaign blog and the use of Meetup and other social networking technologies to raise more money, mainly through small-dollar donations, than any other Democratic nominee. He has also used such internet channels to organise thousands of volunteers to do door-to-door campaigning, write letters to possible voters, distribute flyers and organise local meetings. While Dean replaced Trippi as campaign manager on January 2004, Trippi's internet strategy laid the groundwork for many campaigns in the years to come, including that of Barack Obama in 2008. Trippi subsequently started his own consultancy, Trippi & Associates. See his book *The Revolution Will Not Be Televised: Democracy, the Internet, and the Overthrow of Everything* (2004), published by HarperCollins.

Discussion points

1   Identify the marketing elements in the use of the internet by Obama's 2008 campaign.
2   What is political PR and how can it help create positive relationships between the government and the people?
3   Identify the non-publics, latent publics, aware publics and active publics for a party or politician.
4   Discuss the potential and limitations for political PR to help create and maintain a positive reputation for politicians and governments.
5   What is interactive political communication? Think of some examples from recent elections.
6   Discuss whether voter responsibility communication will expand in the coming years.

Assessment questions

Essays/exam

1   What are the principles of effective e-marketing and to what extent do parties and candidates follow these in their online communication?
2   Define the nature of political PR and explore how politicians and governments have sought to use it to achieve more positive relationships with their publics.
3   Explain why political PR is not about promoting a product but building positive relationships, using theory and empirical examples to support your answer.
4   Explain and illustrate Jackson's different political PR approaches.
5   Discuss the potential and limitations for political leaders to use interactive communication.
6   Discuss and critique the ways in which reputation management has been used to promote or restore a leader's image in office.

Applied

1   Apply Jackson's relationship marketing email criteria to the use of email by elected representatives, and discuss how effectively they are using email, making recommendations for improvement and further development.

2   Assess a party's or a politician's Facebook page against the relationship marketing criteria by Small (2012), and make recommendations for future development.

3   Identify the publics that a political leader or government needs to build a positive relationship with using Lieber and Golan's (2011) explanation, and critique how they have used political PR to reach each one, making suggestions for improvement.

4   Assess which of Jackson's political PR approaches a government uses, with what impact and, therefore, which seems to be the most effective.

5   Critique the range of political PR activities used by a recent or current government and make suggestions for how they might improve their strategy in future.

6   Devise a PR plan for a local politician, using guidelines and ideas from the cases presented in this textbook.

CASE STUDY

Case study 7.1 Communicating contemporary market-oriented leadership in government: Barack Obama

Edward Elder, University of Auckland
eeld001@aucklanduni.ac.nz

Background

Assuming office introduces political leaders to a whole new set of social, political and logistical constraints not present in opposition (see Ormrod 2006, 112–15), such constraints can hurt a governing leader's ability to maintain the image of being in touch with their public (Lees-Marshment 2009). However, more recent research suggests that governing leaders don't have to blindly follow public opinion to be perceived as being in touch as long as their communication suggests they are talking *with* the public rather than *at* them. Such practices also allow governing leaders to show strong, decisive and honest leadership (Robinson 2006; Scammell 2007, 185–6). This case study highlights some important findings from analysis of US President Barack Obama's verbal communication around the issue of reforming US health care through the Patient Protection and Affordable Care Act (also known as 'Obama care') during his first term in office. It does so through the framework for market-oriented governing leaders' communication, which is briefly outlined in the following table.

Framework for market-oriented governing leaders' communication

Quality shown through rhetoric	Communicate through rhetoric by ...
Listening/in touch	• Respectfully acknowledging concerns and criticisms. • Talking about positive working relationships with political elites from other major parties. • Communicating an understanding of target audience.
Leading	• Communicating delivery. • Communicating ideological positioning. • Using words and phrases associated with strength.

Quality shown through rhetoric	Communicate through rhetoric by . . .
Honesty/authenticity/ trustworthiness	• Talking about non-political personality. • Showing an openness to questioning. • Using inclusive pronouns.
Common goals and benefits of decisions	• Focusing communication on how the decision will benefit the target audience rather than focusing on the problem(s) being resolved. • Highlighting an overall goal trying to be achieved that resonates with the target audience.
Social and governmental variables	• Talking about other potential options not chosen, and why this was. • Communicating reasoning behind the decisions made. • Outlining the decision-making process, including the variables involved.

Obama communicating Obama care

Listening/in touch

Obama effectively used verbal communication around Obama care to suggest he was in touch with the American public. This could best be seen in his communication suggesting a respectful acknowledgement of public opinion; especially in his response to criticism questioning whether Obama care was a government takeover of American health care. Typically, in response to such criticism, Obama would acknowledge the concern as 'legitimate' before asking the critical question again; communicating his willingness to put himself in the position of a person who would ask the question. Furthermore, Obama would take the time to explain why he disagreed with the argument. Such communication may be decoded as Obama showing some level of respect for the opposing argument, without agreeing with it.

Leadership

Obama successfully used verbal communication to imply his strong leadership characteristics. Notably, Obama's communication suggesting 'delivery' was substantial. A major theme in Obama's communication was the message that 'we must and will get this done'. This is not surprising considering much of Obama's communication on the issue came prior to the passing of Obama care. Such communication was often used in Obama's final remarks during speeches and press conferences prior to the bill being passed. In such communication Obama would specifically note his desire to 'deliver on health care'. Obama would verbally communicate this message with a stern tone, further implying the determination he felt. Such communication may have helped Obama show leadership characteristics in two specific ways: by implying personal conviction and strength through his determination, and by presenting Obama as a leader who will attempt to deliver on the promises he made prior to being elected.

Honesty/authenticity/trustworthy

Obama's ability to communicate honesty, trustworthiness and authenticity can best be described as mixed. However, Obama was very effective in using the Obama care issue to communicate his non-political personality. This was often achieved by linking the issue to the struggles his mother faced with the US health-care system when she was battling cancer. By communicating a story that affects him directly, the viewer may have felt as though they were gaining a better understanding of Obama as a real person, rather than simply a political figure. Such a connection is often linked to feelings about whether that person is trustworthy (Lilleker 2006, 79). Thus, by communicating a real-life example of how the issue under discussion affects him personally, Obama may have been lending validity to the idea that he can be trusted. In doing so, the American public may be more willing to accept a polarising idea such as Obama care.

Common goals and benefits of decisions

Obama successfully communicated the benefits of decisions as well as goals that would resonate with the American public on the Obama care issue. However, Obama may have communicated the benefits of these decisions too much. In the analysis, rhetoric was coded under the heading of 'communicating benefits of decisions' more than any other single heading by a large margin. This overwhelming dedication to such communication seemed to taint many media texts that otherwise strongly suggested Obama possessed market-oriented qualities. In other words, the lasting impression left on the audience by the media text may have been that it was 'Obama selling his decisions' rather than 'Obama talking about the issues with the American public'. In essence, such communication implied that Obama was trying to simulate market-oriented behaviour rather than actually being market-oriented.

Social and governmental variables

Obama was somewhat successful at using verbal communication to outline the social and governmental variables around Obama care. In particular, the President's communication on the decision-making process was often very detailed. Obama's communication often outlined the remaining process needed to achieve health-care reform. In doing so, Obama highlighted the complexity of the process, why health care reform was difficult to achieve and why it would take time. In essence, by communicating these variables in front of the bill being passed, Obama attempted to manage public expectations.

Lessons for political marketing

In sum, US President Barack Obama's verbal communication around the issue of Obama care partially followed the framework for market-oriented governing leaders' communication. However, as suggested above, Obama was normally successful in following the advice of the framework on the most important and effective ways to communicate the qualities associated with market-oriented behaviour. This suggests that Obama learnt some lessons from the failings of the governing leaders that came before him; in particular, the failings of their communication strategies. However, further investigation around other case studies is needed to understand if these findings are isolated to Obama and the issue of Obama care, or a global trend for market-oriented governing leaders.

Further reading

Lees-Marshment, J. (2009). 'Marketing after the election: the potential and limitations of maintaining a market orientation in government'. *Canadian Journal of Communication*, 34(2): 205–27.

Lilleker, D. G. (2006). *Key Concepts in Political Communication*. London: Sage Publications.

Ormrod, R. P. (2006). 'A critique of the Lees-Marshment Market-Oriented Party model'. *Politics*, 26(2): 110–88.

Robinson, C. (2006). *Advertising and the Market Orientation of Political Parties Contesting the 1999 and 2002 New Zealand General Election Campaigns*. PhD, Massey University, New Zealand.

Scammell, M. (2007). 'Political brands and consumer citizens: the rebranding of Tony Blair.' *The ANNALS of the American Academy of Political and Social Science*, 611(176): 176–92.

References

Baines, Paul (2011). 'Political public relations and election campaigning'. In Jesper Strömbäck and Spiro Kiousis (eds) *Political Public Relations: Principles and Applications*. New York: Routledge, 115–37.

Balz, Dan (2013). 'How the Obama campaign won the race for voter data'. *washingtonpost.com*, 29 July. http://articles.washingtonpost.com/2013–07–28/politics/40858951_1_president-obama-david-plouffe-barack-obama

Cogburn, Derrick L. and Fatima K. Espinoza-Vasquez (2011). 'From networked nominee to networked nation: examining the impact of Web 2.0 and social media on political participation and civic engagement in the 2008 Obama campaign'. *Journal of Political Marketing*, 10(1/2): 189–213.

Davies, Gary and Takir Mian (2010). 'The reputation of the party leader and of the party being led'. *European Journal of Marketing*, 44(3–4): 331–50.

Elder, Edward (2014). 'Communicating contemporary leadership in government: Barack Obama'. In Jennifer Lees-Marshment, Brian Conley and Kenneth Cosgrove (eds) *Political Marketing in the US*. New York: Routledge.

Eshbaugh-Soha, Matthew (2011). 'Presidential public relations'. In Jesper Strömbäck and Spiro Kiousis (eds) *Political Public Relations: Principles and Applications*. New York: Routledge, 95–114.

Hallahan, Kirk (2011). 'Political public relations and strategic framing'. In Jesper Strömbäck and Spiro Kiousis (eds) *Political Public Relations: Principles and Applications*. New York: Routledge, 177–212.

Jackson, Nigel (2005). 'Vote winner or a nuisance: email and elected politicians' relationship with their constituents'. In Walter W. Wymer, Jr. and Jennifer Lees-Marshment (eds) *Current Issues in Political Marketing*. Binghamton, NY: Haworth Press, 91–108.

Jackson, Nigel (2006). 'Banking online: the use of the internet by political parties to build relationships with voters'. In Darren G. Lilleker, Nigel Jackson and Richard Scullion (eds) *The Marketing of Political Parties*. Manchester: Manchester University Press, 157–184.

Jackson, Nigel A. (2012). 'Underused campaigning tools: political public relations'. In Jennifer Lees-Marshment (ed.) *The Routledge Handbook of Political Marketing*. London and New York: Routledge, 271–85.

Jackson, Nigel and Darren G. Lilleker (2014). 'Brand management and relationship marketing in online environments'. In Jennifer Lees-Marshment, Brian Conley and Kenneth Cosgrove (eds) *Political Marketing in the US*. New York: Routledge.

Jackson, Nigel A., Darren G. Lilleker and Eva Schweitzer (2012). 'Political marketing in an online election environment: short-term sales or long-term relationships?' In Jennifer Lees-Marshment (ed.) *The Routledge Handbook of Political Marketing*. London and New York: Routledge, 286–300.

Johnson, Dennis W. (2012). 'Campaigning in the twenty-first century: change and continuity in American political marketing'. In Jennifer Lees-Marshment (ed.) *The Routledge Handbook of Political Marketing*. London and New York: Routledge, 205–17.

Lieber, Paul S. and Guy J. Golan (2011). 'Political public relations, news management, and agenda indexing'. In Jesper Strömbäck and Spiro Kiousis (eds) *Political Public Relations: Principles and Applications*. New York: Routledge, 54–74.

Lloyd, Jenny (2012). 'Something old, something new? Modelling political communication in the 2010 UK general election'. In Jennifer Lees-Marshment (ed.) *The Routledge Handbook of Political Marketing*. London and New York: Routledge, 243–56.

Middleton, Gavin (2009). 'ACT New Zealand Party and the limits of technological marketing'. Case study 7.4 in Jennifer Lees-Marshment, *Political Marketing: Principles and Applications*. London and New York: Routledge, 186–8.

Newman, Bruce I. (1999). *The Mass Marketing of Politics*. Thousand Oaks, CA: Sage.

Papagiannidis, Savvas, Constantinos K. Coursaris and Michael Bourlakis (2012). 'Do websites influence the nature of voting intentions? The case of two national elections in Greece'. *Computers in Human Behavior*, 28(2): 300–7.

Robinson, Claire (2012). 'Interacting leaders'. In Jennifer Lees-Marshment (ed.) *The Routledge Handbook of Political Marketing*. London and New York: Routledge, 257–70.

Scammell, Margaret (2008). 'Brand Blair: marketing politics in the consumer age'. In D. Lilleker and R. Scullion (eds) *Voters or Consumers: Imagining the Contemporary Electorate*. Newcastle: Cambridge Scholars Publishing, 97–113.

Small, Tamara (2012). 'Are we friends yet? Online relationship marketing by political parties'. In Alex Marland, Thierry Giasson and Jennifer Lees-Marshment (eds) *Political Marketing in Canada*. Vancouver: UBC, 193–208.

Stirland, Sarah Lai (2008). 'Inside Obama's surging net-roots campaign'. In *Wired*, 3 March. Excerpts available at http://www.wired.com/politics/law/news/2008/03/obama_tools (accessed 1 April, 2008)

Strömbäck, Jesper and Spiro Kiousis (2011). 'Political public relations: defining and mapping an emergent field'. In Jesper Strömbäck and Spiro Kiousis (eds) *Political Public Relations: Principles and Applications*. New York: Routledge, 1–32.

Tedesco, John C. (2011). 'Political public relations and agenda building'. In Jesper Strömbäck and Spiro Kiousis (eds) *Political Public Relations: Principles and Applications*. New York: Routledge, 75–94.

Toledano, Margalit and David McKie (2013). *Public Relations and Nation Building*. London: Routledge.

Turcotte, André and Vincent Raynauld (2014). 'Boutique populism: the emergence of the Tea Party movement in the age of digital politics'. In Jennifer Lees-Marshment, Brian Conley and Kenneth Cosgrove (eds) *Political Marketing in the US*. New York: Routledge.

Williams, Christine B. and Girish J. 'Jeff' Gulati (2014). 'Relationship marketing in social media practice: perspectives, limitations and potential'. In Jennifer Lees-Marshment, Brian Conley and Kenneth Cosgrove (eds) *Political Marketing in the US*. New York: Routledge.

Xifra, Jordi (2010). 'Linkages between public relations models and communication managers' roles in Spanish political parties'. *Journal of Political Marketing*, 9(3): 167–85.

8 Political delivery marketing

Practitioner perspective 8.1 on the importance of delivery

When I talk to opposition politicians one of the measures I now have in my head about whether they are really serious about running this country is whether they are already thinking about how to do delivery.

Michael Barber, first Head of UK Delivery Unit

You can be a bit more free and easy with following the polling in opposition, especially if you are a minor party, but a major party still faces the constraints of having to govern in future.

Stephen Mills, interviewed in 2009

It's important to keep the language of delivery in the mindset of the politicians and their staff.

Keneally, interviewed in 2008

We were a little bit slow to get into the different mindset that you need in government . . . [what was] more important was . . . this is what you're going to do in a year, this is what you're doing in three years, this is what you want to do over a parliament.

Alastair Campbell, Press Secretary to UK PM Tony Blair, 2013

Source: Lees-Marshment (2011); Campbell (2013)

Political marketing is most commonly associated with efforts to win an election, but if a politician wins power, they need to deliver if they want to implement promised changes and maintain public support. As Practitioner perspective 8.1 suggests, delivery is incredibly crucial now. Citizens now want to see tangible political outcomes; there has been, as Butler and Harris (2009, 158) comment, a 'shift from the abstract to the tangible; from the consideration of principles to the emphasis on the immediate outcome'. Delivery marketing is not easy in government – either to achieve in its own right or to get credit from voters for that achievement. As Rehr (2013, 37) notes President Obama found it difficult to explain the benefits of the Affordable Care Act, not least as the wordy and complex legislation made it 'virtually impossible to explain'. This chapter discusses delivery challenges (the constraints of government and public perceptions of delivery); managing expectations pre-election; making delivery happen in power (through legislation, system changes and working with the bureaucracy); managing problems in delivery and communicating progress and success.

Delivery challenges

Practitioner perspective 8.2 on the challenges of government

Before you know it, you find that everyday problems have crept up on you and made their presence felt. Ministers are dragged into dealing with issues and media explosions. They have to attend events abroad, meet with pressure groups and participate in protracted meetings in parliament.

Mogens Lykketoft, Minister of Foreign Affairs and Finance in the Danish Nyrup

Source: Lindholm and Prehn (2007, 19)

The constraints of government

Government throws up unpredictable issues such as war and economic turbulence that constrain the ability of politicians to carry out previous promises. Bill Clinton, elected in 1992 in the US as a New Democrat, tax-cutting, middle-class president, found once in office that the actual deficit was far worse than they had previously been informed and what they had promised to do was impossible. After 9/11, George W. Bush's *Compassionate Conservatism* agenda from the 2000 election was pushed to the background in favour of the 'war on terror'. Additionally once parties and politicians are elected into power they are more likely to be blamed for any problems that occur, even those beyond their control. As Johnson (2013, 3–4) notes, on winning power in 2008:

> President Obama inherited a financial and economic mess from his predecessor, an auto industry about to collapse, and layoffs and job cutbacks reminiscent of the 1930s ... January 20, 2009, Barack Obama was sworn in as the forty-fifth president of the United States; that month 839,000 Americans had lost their jobs.

On one hand there are more resources, with the bureaucracy now employed to help the politician or party work in office. However, government involves a whole range of organisations, departments and units, and the legislative process itself can thwart election promises being converted into action. The fight to pass – and retain – Obama's health-care legislation, leading to a government shut down in 2013, was an obvious recent example of this, and Rehr (2013, 25) notes how Obama's challenges in his first term included changing the Washington culture, handling an aggressive ideological media, justifying economic policies that seemed to have little impact on the economy and managing the increase in Republican politicians after the poor performance of Democrats in the 2010 midterms. Politicians also have to work with the civil service to develop and implement policies and legislation and are subject to input from a range of stakeholders including lobbyists who try to influence its detail. The pressures and demands are intense, as Practitioner perspective 8.2 indicates.

Political consumer perception of delivery

Another challenge is that it is hard to get credit from voters for delivery. Political consumers may not always evaluate politicians' delivery objectively, fairly or clearly. By the end of

Practitioner perspective 8.3 on the difficulties getting credit from voters for delivery

The media deliberately obstruct the link between government and hospitals/NHS [and when government has delivered] they don't credit the government for it.

Alastair Campbell, Press Secretary to UK Prime Minister
Tony Blair, interviewed in 2005

We used to do a lot of campaign training, and one of the skits we used to show is that snippet from The Life of Brian, you know 'What did the Romans ever do for us? Apart from roads, sanitation, and education, and law and order . . . what have they done for us lately?' We used to show that skit from The Life of Brian to our campaign directors and leaders, and MPs, because it's a bit like that. What have you done for me lately? And I think in some ways, that's the challenge of government, and in some ways the heartening part of government. It's always, what have you done for us lately?

Eric Roozendaal, Australian Campaign Manager and politician,
interviewed in 2008

Source: Lees-Marshment (2011)

Obama's first term the President was, as Johnson (2013, 1 and 3) puts it, 'the beleaguered president': despite his success in passing the $831 billion stimulus bill and national health care (Obama care), neither attracted public approval, and on election day voters approved Obama's performance by just 2.8 percent over those who disapproved. Michael Barber (2007, 369–71) who headed the first UK Delivery Unit explains that 'citizens have to see and feel the difference and expectations need to be managed'. Even if they have positive experiences, they do not give voters credit for it. A poll in October 2006 revealed that voters thought the health service had got worse, not better, during UK Labour's decade in power, and that much of the government's huge extra investment in health care has been wasted. Yet, the public's personal experience of using NHS services is nonetheless overwhelmingly positive: 71 per cent of people say that their family and friends have had a good experience (Glover 2006).

A blockage in this process is the media: they don't want to take positive success stories; they see their role as being to find the problems, not the solutions. Temple (2010, 268) notes how, although the final stage in the political marketing process is delivery, the media play a key role in interpreting government success. The media see their role as being to note problems rather than carry success stories. Practitioners note how significant this barrier is – see the Practitioner Perspective 8.3 by Blair's former press secretary Alastair Campbell. Temple (2010, 269) notes how whilst the media are generally neutral towards commercial products, politics is different:

> No one shouts at the television their hatred of Heinz baked beans and their commitment to Crosse & Blackwell's alternative product . . . Politicians and political parties have a much tougher and fundamentally different ride in the media . . . the representatives and messages of political parties are subject to intense scrutiny and criticism.

Furthermore, demand is insatiable. Even when voters do give credit for successful delivery, they then want more. In his last party conference speech as UK Prime Minister in 2006, Tony Blair noted:

> I spoke to a woman the other day, a part-time worker, complaining about the amount of her tax credit. I said: Hold on a minute: before 1997, there were no tax credits, not for working families, not for any families; child benefit was frozen; maternity pay half what it is; maternity leave likewise and paternity leave didn't exist at all. And no minimum wage, no full-time rights for part-time workers, in fact nothing. 'So what?', she said 'that's why we elected you. Now go and sort out my tax credit.'

As Practitioner perspective 8.3 indicates, Australian campaign manager Eric Roozendaal would use the clip *What have the Romans ever done for us?* from *The Life of Brian* when training staff in his party about delivery to get over the point that voters always want more. This is the problem with delivery – you succeed, but then people want more. It's how progress happens, but it presents continued challenges for government; and thus delivery marketing is needed to try to manage expectations and communicate success.

Managing expectations pre-election

Practitioner perspective 8.4 on setting out clear promises that can be linked with outcomes

In order for delivery to be a political asset, the electorate needs to understand what your promises are and they need to have expectations of what those outcomes are . . . they have to be clear enough so that the voter links the outcome with the expectation or the promise. We were able to say 'We came to power, we promised five big things, and we have delivered five big things.'

Patrick Muttart, Former Deputy Chief of Staff to
Prime Minister Stephen Harper, interviewed in 2009

You have to tell them the impact . . . people don't really want to know the details, they just want to know you've got a plan of action . . . how it's going to change their day-to-day lives.

Frank Luntz, US communications expert and political strategist, 2012

Source: Lees-Marshment (2011); PolicyExchangeUK (2012)

The first aspect to marketing in government is the consideration of delivery before the election. Political marketing is not just about promising what voters want but ensuring the product is achievable, even if parties are trying to be market-oriented (Lees-Marshment 2001). As Esselment (2012b, 134) notes 'achievability is part of stage three in the political marketing process for a MOP, but its importance must be underscored'. Product development must also be realistic. Lederer *et al.* (2005) showed how part-marketing by the populist Freedom Party (FPÖ) in Austria, between 1986 and 2002 under the leadership of Jorg Haider, to get it into power in a coalition unravelled once in government. Although the FPÖ became the second strongest party in 1999 and entered government with the People's Party, Haider had promised unachievable products before election, such as the proposition of a flat tax in 1999, which they were unable to secure agreement for in the coalition.

At the next election in 2002 they lost almost 65 per cent of their former voters and were reduced to 18 seats. Case study 8.1 by Iordanis Kotzaivazoglou provides a timely exemplar of why politicians need to avoid over promising and failure to deliver, by exploring the situation in Greece. The case demonstrates how important it is that the product is designed according to what is possible, not voters' unrealistic desires.

In recent years, politicians and parties have developed a range of ways to convince the public they are capable of delivering and to manage expectations. One tool is pledges, contracts or guarantees. One of the earliest examples of this was the 1994 midterm Contract with America put forward by the House Republicans in the US, gaining considerable votes but also a degree of a mandate to then dominate Congress for the rest of Bill Clinton's time as president. Canadian examples include the Liberal Party of Canada's Red Book in 1993, the Ontario Progressive Conservative Party's Common Sense Revolution in 1995, and the Conservative Party of Canada's 'five priorities' in 2006 (Esselment 2012b, 123). Tony Blair's Labour Party in the UK issued a contract and credit-card sized pledges, both to get into government and then when in power: see Figure 8.1.

In this case the pledges changed over the three terms. They changed from outputs (what government would achieve) to inputs (what government would put into the system). Inputs are easier to control than outputs. They also changed from the second to third term to general rhetorical pledges which were very vague on the front side, and on the back the measurements were flexible, e.g. 'mortgages as low as possible', so they failed to be as effective in managing expectations. Nevertheless pledges and contracts have been copied around the world: Helen Clark adopted them for her Labour Party in New Zealand in 1999. Unlike Blair, she retained their more specific nature over time in government, and, in 2005, the pledges promised: no interest on student loans, a final date for treaty claims, an increase in the rates rebate, KiwiSaver, 250 extra community police, more cataract and major joint operations, and 5,000 more modern apprenticeships.

The use of contracts raises broader issues such as trust – an aspect governments care about deeply, because trust is essential to maintaining a positive relationship with voters in the long term. Steen (2009) explored the use of contracts in Danish politics by the Liberal Prime Minister Anders Fogh Rasmussen who, like Clark, copied delivery concepts from Tony Blair, noting how important it was to deliver promises otherwise politicians risk losing voter trust. He created a Partnership with the People: 6 specific pledges under slogans such as 'You know, we will make it happen': 1.5 mia. dkr extra to hospitals; 500 mio. dkr extra for homecare; one-year flexible maternity leave; a firm and fair immigration policy; a consequential judicial policy; and a tax freeze. The party won power in the 2001 election, but also scored higher on perceptions of trust. Steen reports how surveys demonstrated that confidence in Danish politicians had improved 13 per cent from 1999 to 2005; and the need for politicians to demonstrate delivery through contractual politics had increased.

As Practitioner perspective 8.4 suggests, if delivery promises are clear and then achieved once in power, it helps to manage expectations and get credit for those achievements. Lees-Marshment (2011, 170–1) cites Canadian consultant Leslie Noble who noted that for Premier Mike Harris' campaign he said '*look, we'll give you a money-back-guarantee. If I don't do this, I'm going to resign.*' All the candidates actually signed a pledge and they stuck to it, so when it came to re-election the number-one characteristic was that Harris did what he said he'd do, which gained public support even if they didn't like other attributes – 'that was a great brand characteristic to have'.

Delivery measures are not always successful, however. They can create problematic pressures in government. Lees-Marshment (2011, 150) quotes Australian consultant Robert Griggs who noted that the promises made in Australian NSW Premier candidate Bob Carr's

Blair's New Labour Party credit card pledges 1997–2005

1997 Pledges	2001 Pledges	2005 Pledges
1 We will cut class sizes to 30 or under for five-, six- and seven-year-olds by using money saved from the assisted places scheme.	1 Mortgages as low as possible, low inflation and sound public finances.	1 Your family better off.
	2 Ten thousand extra teachers and higher standards in secondary schools.	2 Your child achieving more.
2 We will introduce a fast-track punishment scheme for persistent young offenders by halving the time from arrest to sentencing.		3 Your children with the best start.
	3 Twenty thousand extra nurses and 10,000 extra doctors in a reformed NHS.	4 Your family treated better and faster.
3 We will cut NHS waiting lists by treating an extra 100,000 patients as a first step by releasing £100 million saved from NHS red tape.	4 Six thousand extra recruits to raise police numbers to their highest-ever level.	5 Your community safer.
		6 Your country's borders protected.
4 We will get 250,000 under-25-year-olds off benefit and into work by using money from a windfall levy on the privatised utilities.	5 Pensioners' winter fuel payment retained, minimum wage rising to £4.20.	
5 We will set tough rules for government spending and borrowing and ensure low inflation and strengthen the economy so that interest rates are as low as possible to make all families better off.		

Figure 8.1

campaign in 1995 made government difficult. They said they would 'halve the waiting list within eighteen months or Bob would make Andrew resign. We essentially did it, but it blew the budget out, lasted about three months before the waiting lists went skewed again.' And any form of pre-election delivery needs to be consistent and followed through. When in opposition in 1999, the UK Conservative Party launched a number of guarantees as part of its Common Sense Revolution, responding to market intelligence. However, if such commitments are to mean anything and have impact on the public, parties need to stick with them. Unfortunately the Tories did not and, as Lees-Marshment (2008, 326 and 331) notes, by the time of the election the guarantees had all but disappeared following a period of statements from senior party figures that watered them down or abandoned them entirely.

When pledges, contracts or guarantees are implemented effectively though, they help to focus voters' and politicians' minds on what is most important. Politicians are saying: '*at the very least we will get these few things done*'.

Making delivery happen in power

Delivery relationships

Actually delivering requires politicians to engage in careful negotiation and relationships with a range of stakeholders connected to government. One of the most well known cases of failed delivery was health care by Bill Clinton, whose package was blocked when it went through Congress despite it being a visible part of the product he offered to voters and won election for. Newman (1999, 99–101) suggests one factor was that, whereas opposers of the plan articulated their argument very cleverly, utilising symbolic people called Harry and Louise which gave a face to their campaign, the Clinton government never did.

Esselment (2012b, 133) argues that the Canadian Conservatives were successful in 2004–2006 because they gave the bureaucracy clear instructions on what policies to prioritize and the Privy Council Office (PCO) helped the government fulfil its commitments. Kevin Lynch, an experienced public servant, headed the PCO and drove implementation from there. Similarly, Lees-Marshment (2011, 176) notes that New Zealand Government staffer Grant Robertson recalled how talking to civil servants about the product promises works:

> One thing we did do after the 2005 election is that I actually sat down with the Prime Minister's departmental officials, the bureaucrats and we actually went through the manifesto and said what are we going to be able to do to implement these things. And of course a lot of them said oh we're already doing it or whatever but it wasn't an exercise that happened after 2002 or 1999, as far as I can tell you.

Delivery units

In 2001, after winning his second term, Tony Blair declared that it was 'very clearly an instruction to deliver' and established the Prime Minister's Delivery Unit (PMDU) at the centre of government. Esselment (2012a, 304–5) notes how it was staffed with 40 individuals and reported directly to the Prime Minister. The PMDU monitored the implementation of policies that the Prime Minster himself had identified as personal priorities, such as health, education, crime and transport and tried to help ensure that the government met its targets. It helped drive implementation, improving relationships between government departments. An analysis of the success of the Blair government in delivering on the 1997 pledges by the television channel Channel 4 (2007) gave it a 4/4/5/4/2 score out of 5; an analysis of the 2001 promises scored 3/3/4/4.5. Difficulties discussed included unintended consequences and negative implications from targeting waiting lists instead of waiting times. The analysis also noted that the 2005 pledges were so vague – such as 'your country's borders protected' – they could not be fact checked. However, overall the analysis concluded that 'the government's record on its pledges is not bad – most have been achieved, in name at least'.

Australia copied the idea of a delivery unit, creating a Cabinet Implementation Unit (CIU) at the centre of government in October 2003. As Peter Hamburger (2006), Department of the Prime Minister and Cabinet, wrote:

> It is no longer enough for those advocating major policy to have a good idea . . . the Government demands that we think through our ideas and how they are going to be implemented.

The Australian NSW state government also created a delivery unit under the premier, Morris Iemma. Lees-Marshment (2011, 169) interviewed Ben Keneally who headed it, and Keneally argued that Iemma did this to copy Tony Blair to improve service delivery with the goal of achieving 'delivering measurable change and performance'. It was effective because it had the leaders' support, linking administrative progress with electoral goals. The Queensland government also created an Implementation Unit in March 2004. Esselment (2012a, 306) observed how the delivery unit model has been adapted to state level in Australia and in the US including the state of Maryland and the city of Los Angeles, and she argues that 'delivery units can thus keep a majority government focused, even in its second or third mandate, and can assist coalition partners by doggedly pursuing the implementation of its agreed-upon agenda, thereby minimizing conflict between the parties and contributing to a productive government partnership'.

Delivery by minority governments

Delivering in a minority government is harder because the product design is compromised to form a coalition before governing even begins and then the major party lacks majority control of the legislature. In 2010 Julia Gillard secured re-election as Australian Prime Minister but only through breaking her promise not to implement a tax on carbon in order to secure support from the Greens and Independents to form a government. This clear breaking of a promise scarred her entire term as leader. Nevertheless Esselment (2012a) analysed delivery by the Liberal minority under Paul Martin (2004–2006) and the Conservative minority under Stephen Harper's first term (2006–2008) and found that both succeeded in delivering a number of promises. Martin's government succeeded in eliminating the democratic deficit, creating a national childcare system, fixing health care and a new deal for cities. The national system of childcare required the co-operation and consent of the sub-national governments but was still successful, whistleblower protection legislation helped the democratic deficit, a health accord was reached with the provincial premiers and C$600 million was diverted from federal gas tax to cities. Esselment (2012a, 307–8) argues that this was aided by Martin's experience in government, positive relationships with state politicians, good financial resources in government, and that the Liberals learnt quickly that they needed to work with the opposition. However after a scandal, Stephen Harper became Conservative Prime Minister in 2006 with five clear priorities:

1   Reduction in the goods and services tax (from 7 percent to 5 percent).
2   Childcare allowance for families with children aged five and under.
3   Stronger government accountability measures.
4   Criminal justice reform.
5   Patient wait times guarantee.

Harper was relatively untested and unknown, and sought about focusing on quick delivery of some of these promises to establish legitimacy. The GST reduction and childcare allowance was passed in the first budget and took effect in July 2006. The government passed the Federal Accountability Act to deal with the liberal scandal and address a general concern with government accountability in December 2006. As Esselment (2012a, 309) notes, this then meant that the Conservatives delivered three major policy items within the first year of government. The last two promises were more difficult. The justice reforms got delayed through the parliamentary committee system so the government responded by creating the Tackling Violent Crime Act, framing it as 'for or against' crime in Canada, and it was passed in early 2008. However, the patient wait times guarantee was never fully delivered, and the government adapted it to make it more flexible and then declared success. Nevertheless, overall the image was of a government that delivered and it won re-election (though still as a minority government) in 2008.

Esselment concludes that whilst the obvious argument is that delivering is more difficult in a minority government, these cases suggest minority governments can be successful. She argues that this may in part be psychological in so much as it forces the government to focus on delivery: 'delivery takes on heightened importance since the government is at the mercy of parliament; a vote of no confidence is a continuing threat and, should the governing party be thrust into an early election, a record of some achievements is critical to a new campaign' (2012a, 309). She argues though for generic principles to achieve delivery: see Figure 8.2.

Esselment's model for successful political marketing delivery

1   Create a separate 'delivery unit' to drive implementation.
2   Focus on delivering a few campaign promises almost immediately for 'quick wins' to create an early record of achievement.
3   Work with opposition parties to get legislation through parliament.
4   Build relationships with those who will affect delivery – staff in government departments, opposition parties and lower levels of government such as provinces, states or devolved parliaments.
5   Communicate delivery of policy promises with memorable events and photo opportunities.
6   Repackage and reframe promises if needed to make it unpopular to oppose them.
7   Continue market research while in government to monitor public perception of delivery progress.

Figure 8.2

Source: Adapted from Esselment (2012a, 311)

Implementing policy

Delivery management doesn't just stop with the passing of legislation. Even after Obama succeeded in passing his health-care plan, his staff engaged in another stage of delivery marketing to ensure the policy is implemented in the sense that the public actually take out the new health insurance on offer (see Klein and Kliff 2013).

Managing problems in delivery

> ### Practitioner perspective 8.5 on managing failures in delivery
>
> *It's the willingness to say we didn't get that right. That's very hard in politics. Because politicians never, ever want to say we got anything wrong. And the reality of that is voters know that, they know you're going to screw some things up, so why are you pretending you got everything right? You'd be far better off saying yes; we missed that one so we're going to fix it.*
>
> Ben Levin, former staff in the Canadian provincial governments
> of Ontario and Manitoba, interviewed 2008
>
> *Use a three-step approach to communicate that you have:*
> 1 *Recognised and spotted the problems straight away*
> 2 *That you're doing something about it*
> 3 *That you're doing something about it to make sure it doesn't happen again*
>
> Eammon Fitzpatrick, Former media advisor and consultant,
> interviewed in 2008
>
> *Number one is that people need someone to blame. Someone to hold accountable. And you don't spend that much time on it, but you've got to talk about why it happened. Number two is they expect the solutions and they don't expect political rhetoric . . . tell them what you're going to do.*
>
> Frank Luntz, US communications expert and political strategist, 2012
>
> Source: Lees-Marshment (2011); PolicyExchangeUK (2012)

Failure in delivery undoubtedly causes concern for politicians and strategists as it threatens the chances of re-election. However, it is impossible to ensure that 100 per cent success will be achieved. In business, this is known as the service delivery gap; as Newman (1999, 37–8) explored, there are gaps 'between quality specifications and service delivery', different constraints such as situational influences (e.g. the House of Representatives shifting from the president's party to the opposition midterm), and the bureaucracy of government stops candidates from delivering even if they want to. Even where they understand market demand and accept the need for a problem to be solved, they may be incapable of doing anything about it: 'politicians are much more vulnerable to this gap than are other service industries as a result of the unexpected situations to which politicians always must respond' (Newman 1999, 38).

Others – such as those in Practitioner perspective 8.5 – argue it is best to be honest about failures. Patrón-Galindo (2004, 116) studied the first term of Peruvian President Alejandro Toledo after he won power in 2001. Although most election promises were achieved within a year or so of getting into power, people's expectations were not satisfied, and his popularity declined, owing also to problems such as a personal scandal and perception that rhetorical, vague statements led to complicated situations. One cause of the fall in public support was that he took too long to acknowledge the problem he faced. Patrón-Galindo (2004, 122) observes that 'it was a mistake on his part to take so much time' to decide to be honest; he could have chosen instead to declare at 'a time chosen by him and not fixed by circumstances' and which was more favourable to him. This speaks to the need for a degree of honesty and admission of weakness or failings by leaders to maintain public support.

Esselment (2012b, 129) discusses how the Harper Canadian Conservatives handled failure to keep their promise not to tax income trusts – a specific pledge in their campaign. In 2006 Finance Minister Jim Flaherty reversed this decision, arguing that businesses had increasingly used income trusts as a way to avoid paying corporate taxes. Instead of pretending or ignoring it, they addressed it directly and visibly, facing up to the fact that they were breaking a promise and trying to explain why and leaving the public to decide whether to trust them again. The Department of Finance also released information about how the financial circumstances had changed since the election. In a similar way New Zealand Prime Minister John Key did the same with New Zealand National's decision to increase GST (Goods and Services Tax) which they had also promised not to. However, Key went one step further: he introduced the idea into the public sphere, discussing the pros and cons in various media to test public response to the idea before deciding to go ahead with it. They also linked the proposal to their frustrations with limited progress on improving living standards within the context of the global recession and how they had done as much as they could. Arguably this approach worked: Key's public standing increased between October 2008 when elected and October 2010 with a media poll showing an increase from 38 per cent thinking he was more honest than other politicians to 67 per cent; and from 55 to 70 per cent thinking he had sound judgement (Lees-Marshment 2012, 185).

Communicating delivery progress and success

Delivery needs to be communicated as well as actioned. In his delivery manual Barber (2007) outlined the need for delivery reports, setting targets, consideration of delivery chains, an assessment framework and sample presentations to the media. Governments seek an increasing range of tools to communicate progress in delivery. These include annual or progress reports, newsletters within each electorate, constituency branch or ward, talking about delivery in interviews and speeches and online communication.

Showing progress if not completion

Communication of early achievements helps to gain trust. Hughes and Dann (2010, 88) observed how once in government the Australian Labor Party under Kevin Rudd placed emphasis on early delivery milestones to demonstrate performance and gain the public's trust, producing a document on its first 100 days in office. A few years into his first term, President Obama was pictured amidst building infrastructure projects, showing that progress was being made on the recovery. To be effective, communication about product delivery must use clear visuals and Esselment (2012b, 135) argues that when a key part of a product is delivered this should be announced as part of a strategic communications plan. She notes how the Canadian Conservatives achieved this by placing a bright blue '5%' GST sticker onto a cash register in a retail store – a strong visual that can stay in people's minds.

Governments try to show what progress has been made whilst conceding there is more to do – thus encouraging voters to give them credit for what had been successful but reason to vote them in again to do more. Lees-Marshment (2012, 184) notes how, when seeking re-election in 2011, the New Zealand National Government adopted the slogan 'building a brighter future' which tied in with their aspiration, brighter future theme when first elected in 2008 but argued delivery was in process – it was being built, on the way. Billboards talked of 'Rebuilding Christchurch'; 'Staying strong on crime' and 'Building better public services'. This helped their argument to voters to give them a second term to complete the process. In 2001 the UK Labour Government listed accomplishments such as 'child benefit has been increased', 'NHS waiting lists reduced by 100,000'; but they finished with the phrase 'The work goes on. Vote Labour'.

Conley's (2014) analysis of Obama's delivery marketing in his first term demonstrates the importance of delivery marketing in government, both to ensure that promised policy gets legislated and help build support for re-election. Conley noted that delivery is a story that has to be told – and sometimes defended – in relation to what is promised on the campaign trail. Communication of success was not carried out throughout the term very effectively, and Obama's health-care delivery strategy failed to reap the rewards for successful delivery. What Obama did succeed in doing was more effective communication in the run-up to the election. In campaign year Obama issued a series of adverts called *Keeping his word* on issues such as hate crime legislation; credit card reform; extending unemployment insurance; early childhood education; making college affordable; lowering the cost of Medicare prescriptions; equality for LGBT Americans; health coverage for young Americans and creating manufacturing jobs. This helped to remind voters what he had succeeded in achieving, but future presidents need to engage in such delivery communication sooner: as Conley concludes, importance of a properly managed delivery process within market-oriented politics cannot be overstated.

Giving voters credit for delivery

In the UK, the Labour government gave credit to voters for helping achieve change when seeking re-election in 2001, with adverts picturing ordinary voters with slogans such as 'I did it. I created new jobs for a million people.' In the 2012 election, Obama issued an ad called *Young Americans are Greater Together* which listed achievements including ending combat operations in Iraq, getting rid of the military policy on homosexuality 'don't ask don't tell', comprehensive health becoming a reality and wall street being reformed; and the President said 'all that is thanks to you'.

Delivery in coalition

Communicating delivery in coalition is difficult for both major and minor partners. Major parties have to take care to compromise enough to keep their minor partner satisfied with the arrangement, but it can constrain their ability to deliver on everything they promised. Rudd (2005) notes how the New Zealand Labour Party tried to ensure it gave credit for delivery of certain policies to its junior coalition partner, the Alliance, during 1999–2002, such as the establishment of the 'People's Bank' as a subsidiary of New Zealand Post and the introduction of paid parental leave. It does not always work out to be an advantage to take part in a coalition for the junior partner. More protest-type minor parties can end up losing their original voter support. Lederer *et al.* (2005) note how the Austrian FPÖ which entered coalition government in 2000, then found itself with a problem as its scope to design its own product was considerably limited. Furthermore, it had attracted support by opposing the government; once part of the government, it lost this support. They found it impossible to gain delivery of their promises, as they were inexperienced in bargaining to get their policies accepted by their coalition partner. Credit for any popular policies was given to the Conservative People's Party (ÖVP) instead.

The UK Liberal Democrats issued a party political broadcast in September 2012 noting their achievements in coalition government with the Conservatives after being elected in May 2010, such as the scrapping of identity cards and the shutting down of the national identity database, the removal of income tax for low earners, cutting of emissions and extra funding for poor children at school. However key elements of their brand – such as changing the electoral system to PR – were not successfully delivered after they lost a referendum to implement a system different to that the party themselves most desired, and their overall competency for delivery has been threatened by having to compromise to fit in with Conservative policies such as those on student fees and loans.

Individualising delivery

Lees-Marshment (2011, 181–3) identified that practitioners increasingly try to individualise delivery success and impact. The argument made is that people don't live in the state on average; they live in locations and they experience services in locations. Governments need to convey what has been achieved more individually. UK Labour's 2005 online manifesto had a personalised section where you could type in your address, your age, your family status and your working status. You would get the benefits that you personally would've seen and benefits in your local community: more police on the beat, more teachers in your local schools, more doctors and nurses, etc. You also got what their future commitments would be to you personally.

Lees-Marshment (2011, 183) also quotes Simon Pleasants who worked in the New Zealand Prime Minister's office as noting how they collected and supplied local data on national developments to go to local MPS to use. For example, if they had administrative articles about school funding or early childhood education grants being given out, this would normally be announced by the minister but not get any interest in local media: 'the *Gisborne Herald*'s not going to be interested in that. The *Manukau Courier* isn't going to have interest in that at all ... so, what I [do] would be to follow the local stats, numbers ... and make up a whole lot of local media releases and fit those out to the local MPs'.

Politician's delivery

Individual politicians can also communicate their own delivery. As with governments, they can also make examples individual. One US consultant Lees-Marshment (2011) interviewed, noted how an incumbent in a governor's race in Michigan in 2006 wasn't getting credit for the work done to get new jobs. The auto industry which the state was dependent on was declining and so voters complained that they didn't see any progress on jobs. The consultant found that they had to give specific examples of what the governor had done. They had to point out that the governor had gone to Japan abd got ten companies to come and invest money to build a plant in the state; and how Google opened their East Coast place in Michigan which would employ 1,000 people. When they told those individual stories and they were able to get a lot of traction – they were where we were able to get people to agree he had achieved something.

One Australian Labor MP, Tanya Plibersek, issued leaflets in the 2010 election with specific statistics related to local areas, such as $150 million to build a new Chris O'Brien Cancer Centre at Royal Price Alfred Hospital in Camperdown; $3 million to support the rebuilding of the Wayside Chapel; and $2 million to help redevelop South Sydney Youth Services in Waterloo. Such specific examples help to show action in an area that is more visible to local residents. In the US, Steger (1999, 668–9) observed that, given the decentralised structure which means they act individually, elected officials in Congress are able to claim credit for a number of activities in their state, such as:

- fixing funding formulas to the benefit of their market;
- pressurising bureaucrats who decide who qualifies for funding;
- securing tax breaks for their constituents;
- opposing potentially damaging regulatory legislation;
- helping the public with problems with government and agencies and fighting for benefits and grants.

The resources of being in office also help congressmen and -women provide effective services for constituents, which both delivers and gains credit for delivery. UK MPs issue annual delivery reports (see Lilleker 2006). Lilleker (2006, 212–14) argues that, at a local level, an incumbent candidate's success in delivery in terms of the service they have provided for their constituents can affect the outcome of the election. MPs carry out casework for their constituents, or campaign to attract industry or other funding, such as from the European Union, or create networks between associations; all of which can create a positive reputation for a politician when they face re-election.

Lilleker (2009) explored how one UK Labour MP, Jim Knight, MP for Dorset South, used communication to weather the unpopularity of the incumbent Blair government in the 2005 general election. Knight conducted local market research through extensive media monitoring to discover the issues of the area. Anything he could deliver a solution to was communicated to voters. He was featured regularly in the local newspaper, supported local campaigns such as a campaign to reduce deaths on the roads and reported how he had dealt with 5,953 individual pieces of casework solving the problems of local voters. He personalized his campaign, focusing on local delivery, arguing that to get people to vote for him again he had to be seen to deliver and then re-contact those who supported him at the last election. Lilleker's research into voter perception showed the MP was overwhelmingly seen as the '*best representative for me and my community*' and the '*candidate who best addressed my concerns*'. Knight built an image as a representative who solved the problems of those whom he represented.

Butler and Collins (1999) also argue that MPs in Ireland try to improve their service delivery to provide a degree of immunity from electoral swings that may move against them. Local politicians focus on the implementation of politics on the ground, in a way that affects people's daily lives and may therefore gain their attention, even when they may appear to ignore national or federal politics. While MPs cannot enact substantial change in the public sector individually, they can help represent and support constituents in bringing complaints to government departments and fighting for benefit entitlements (see also Butler and Collins 2001).

Case Study 8.2 by Renisa Maki looks at the innovative forms of delivery marketing by mayors, which not only included localising achievements but also unconventional communication including the use of a cake to celebrate a record 10 million users of the train in one year and statistics about delivering new buses on banners placed on the buses themselves as they are driven around the city. In this way they created 'signature moments' advocated by the first director of the UK Delivery Unit, Michael Barber. National-level delivery tactics can be also used at lower levels of government.

Summary

Delivery is an increasingly important part of political marketing as we move towards greater focus on the change that politicians achieve. It starts with ensuring that pre-election promises are costed and achievable and clear to help convey that politicians are ready to govern and manage expectations. Once in power, politicians need to overcome constraints of government such as the pressures and need to build good relationships with the bureaucracy and get legislation passed in order to make delivery happen. Any failures need to be carefully managed, and success has to be communicated at individual levels to get traction with the public. Figure 8.3 puts forward a guide to effective delivery marketing in practice. Delivery management and marketing is an area of practice that will grow in future decades; and the practitioner profile below details the impact of Michael Barber who oversaw the creation of the first delivery unit in the UK under Tony Blair. The next chapter explores the democratic implications of all aspects of political marketing in depth.

Best practice guide to doing political marketing delivery

1   Think about delivery before you fight the election.
2   Create key pledges or priorities to build credibility that can be delivered easily once in power, which will help build initial support to help mitigate more difficult delivery.
3   Convey management and governing abilities.
4   Once in power, sit down with bureaucrats after election and go through promises and priorities.
5   Facilitate networks, relationships, and conversations to prevent fallouts, stepping on people's toes and so forth, and get legislation delivered.
6   Create delivery units to help success.
7   Create the will to succeed among those doing the delivery: give examples of progress and successes, don't blame them publicly, ensure tasks and goals are clear, work with not against them.
8   Utilise different forms of communication over long periods to overcome media barriers to communicating product change and delivery.
9   Communicate a sense of progress over time.
10   Be honest about problems or failures in delivery; but then propose a solution.
11   Use government public opinion research to improve policy development and monitor implementation to ensure that it meets original aims.
12   Communicate real-world, individualised cases of delivery to voters; localize central government stories and statistics.
13   In coalition/partnership, make sure all parties can show some delivery.
14   Understand and accept that demand is always going to be insatiable – this helps society progress.

Figure 8.3

Practitioner profile 8.1

Name: Sir Michael Barber

Date of birth: 24 November, 1955

Most notable job: Prime Minister's Chief Advisor on Delivery to UK Prime Minister Tony Blair

Description: Michael Barber is an educationist and political advisor. Barber came from a teaching background before eventually holding a number of higher executive positions within the British education system. During the first term of the Blair-led Labour government, Barber served as the Chief Adviser to the Secretary of State for Education on School Standards. However, from a political marketing standpoint, Barber's most notable role was as the Prime Minister's Chief Advisor on Delivery to Tony Blair from 2001 to 2005. Reporting directly to the Prime Minister, Barber headed the Prime Minister's Delivery Unit (PMDU). In this role, Barber's main responsibility was to work with government agencies to ensure successful implementation of the Prime Minister's priority programmes. This included translating reform into results, and ensuring that citizens could see and feel the difference the delivery was making. As head of the PMDU, Barber, along with a handful of colleagues, developed a set of processes that, over time, turned out to be a major innovation in government delivery management. Simply, the department asked five questions, repeatedly and persistently, until they received satisfactory answers. The five question were:

1   What are you trying to do?
2   How are you trying to do it?
3   How, at any given moment, will you know you are on track?
4   If you are not on track, what are you going to do about it?
5   Can we help?

Barber worked on building trusting relationships with the departments, taking the view that they shared responsibility for the outcomes. They developed techniques that could help solve problems, such as rapid reviews and delivery-chain analysis. Barber wrote a book about his experience in the PMDU, titled *Instruction to Deliver: Fighting to Reform Britain's Public Services* (2008), published by Methuen.

Discussion points

1   Why is marketing in government difficult?
2   Do you think voters give politicians credit for delivery?
3   How have politicians sought to manage expectations for delivery before getting elected? How effective do you think these are?
4   How effective do you think pledges, contracts and guarantees are to make the product seem more deliverable and manage expectations?
5   What factors do political leaders have to bear in mind when trying to make delivery happen once elected?
6   To what extent do you think the current government has followed Esselment's model for successful political marketing delivery?
7   How effectively to you think politicians manage failures in delivery?

Assessment questions

Essay/exam

1 How effective do you think current governments are at communicating their delivery progress? What do they need to improve on, and how might they do this?
2 How successfully did Obama communicate his delivery during his first term (2008–2012) and at the 2012 election?
3 Have you seen examples where your local politician has tried to communicate delivery? How have they done it – did they individualise results, show progress – and how effective did it seem to you?
4 Discuss the difficulties and potential solutions to marketing delivery in government.
5 Discuss the different relationships and stakeholders involved in making delivery happen in power, using both theory and empirical examples such as US President Obama's fight to pass Obama care.
6 'Delivery units can thus keep a majority government focused and can assist coalition partners by doggedly pursuing the implementation of its agreed-upon agenda, thereby minimizing conflict between the parties and contributing to a productive government partnership.' To what extent do you think Esselment is correct that delivery units help governments deliver?
7 Critique the way that governments have communicated delivery progress and success using literature and empirical examples.
8 In what ways have governments and politicians sought to individualise delivery success and progress to make achievements relevant to people in their day-to-day lives, and how effective is this.

Applied

1 Assess the pre-election delivery marketing of a major party and how effective it was at managing expectations and helping get credit once promises were delivered, and from this draw guidelines for the future.
2 Critique Obama's management of stakeholder relationships in the delivery of Obama care once elected in light of recommendations from existing research on that and other cases of successful and failed delivery, and draw up generic lessons from this for future government's delivery management.
3 Assess the delivery marketing of a current government against Esselment's model for successful political marketing delivery, and suggest how they might improve in future.
4 Critique governments' management of failures to deliver or when they renege on promises and, from this as well as existing literature, identify principles of effective delivery problem management.
5 Compare and contrast the effectiveness of delivery communication of progress and success by at least three governments such as the Obama presidency, Harper's Conservatives, Cameron's Conservatives and John Key's Nationals and Rudd/Gillard's Labour. Drawing on this and academic research, devise lessons for future governments about how to communicate progress and success.
6 Analyse five different incumbent politicians' communication of their delivery during an election campaign, discussing whether it follows guidelines in the literature or shows any new trends, and provide guidelines from this for future communication of delivery success.

CASE STUDIES

Case study 8.1 The importance of delivering: lessons from Greek reality

By Iordanis Kotzaivazoglou, Technological Educational Institute (TEI), Greece
ikotza@jour.auth.gr

This case study aims to demonstrate the long-term results of a party making campaign promises that are what the voters desire but that cannot be delivered once it comes to power. The underlying theory is that of the Market-Oriented Party (Lees-Marshment 2009) and the data are drawn from Greek experience and the choices made by PASOK (Panhellenic Socialist Movement) in 2009–2011.

Outline of events

In mid 2009 PASOK, as the official opposition party, had a steady lead in the polls. The New Democracy government headed by Prime Minister Kostas Karamanlis was shaky. Elected with a mandate to 'rebuild the state', that is, to create a smaller, more effective and less corrupt public administration, it had not only failed to achieve this aim but had made the situation it inherited even worse (Kotzaivazoglou and Zotos 2009).

The global economic crisis that broke out in 2008 found the Greek economy perilously weak. The slenderness of its parliamentary majority prevented the government from taking the decisions needed to protect the country, despite the warnings from international institutions and the European Union. It chose instead to conceal the problem for a while longer and keep itself in power. The pressing state of affairs, however, eventually forced Karamanlis to call an election, which was held on 4 October 2009.

During the campaign period, Karamanlis publicly admitted that the economy was in a peculiarly difficult position, although without describing the true state of affairs and the real magnitude of the problem. Contrary to customary practice for governing parties in Greece he promised no handouts, at least at the start. He spoke of austerity and tried to tell the voters, albeit in veiled terms, that steps would have to be taken to face the looming financial crisis.

PASOK, according to all the polls the unchallenged favourite, adopted a different strategy, following a market-oriented approach. The product it offered was based on market intelligence and accepted by its members. At that stage the majority of voters wanted to spin out their false prosperity by whatever means, disregarding the long-term prospects for the country. PASOK's leader, Papandreou, told the people what they wanted to hear: that austerity measures would drive the country into prolonged recession. Assuring the voters that 'the money is there', without specifying where, he promised that with a 100-day programme and targeted actions he could help the Greek economy recover (Kotzaivazoglou, 2011).

PASOK won nearly 44 per cent of the vote in the 2009 elections, well ahead of second-place New Democracy, a result that enabled it to form a single-party government. The new government began by giving handouts to specific social groups but soon realised that this was leading nowhere. After a brief period of embarrassment and inertia more and more members of the government began to admit that the country was in dire financial straits, among them Papandreou himself who announced that austerity measures would have to be imposed. But he needed a good excuse for reneging on his campaign promises. He chose to lay the blame for the situation on the previous government, accusing it of deliberately concealing the true state of the economy and presenting misleading data. He claimed that he had been a victim of misinformation and that he had not been aware of the truth about the Greek economy before the elections. A few months later, however, this was publicly refuted by senior officials of the European Union and international institutions, who stated categorically that they had briefed him on the subject well in advance of the elections.

The decision to publicize the true state of the economy and to paint it in such dramatic colours effectively froze almost all significant economic activity in the country and borrowing became impossible, forcing Greece to turn for assistance to the International Monetary Fund and the other members of the European Union (Kotzaivazoglou, 2011).

After some months of negotiation it was decided that the country should be placed under the superintendence of the 'troika', a tripartite support mechanism formed by the International Monetary Fund, the European Commission and the European Central Bank. From the beginning, however, the policy adopted seemed unlikely to succeed: the national debt would rise to dubiously manageable heights, while the economy would plunge into recession.

The Papandreou government, however, chose to present things differently. As it would do time and again in similar circumstances, it presented this development as a huge government success. It did not inform the public of the measures that would be taken, clearly fearing the political and social cost. Instead, it constantly denied almost every hint of new measures until they were actually adopted, when it laid the blame squarely on the troika. All it actually did was impose severe cuts in salaries and pensions and stiff increases in taxation, making no real attempt to address the basic problem of structural reform.

The Papandreou administration remained in office for roughly a year and a half after the signing of the memorandum, and nearly two years after assuming the reins of government. Papandreou stepped down as premier under strong pressure from within the party, other European Union countries and the public. The life of his administration was marked by a surge of social reaction and widespread disturbances. The country fell into deep recession and lost much of its prestige. Reports in the foreign media routinely spoke disparagingly of Greece.

Throughout the period of the Papandreou administration, polls recorded increasing public discontent with the government's performance. The majority of the people felt deceived, and in June 2012 when, after a short spell of coalition government, fresh elections were eventually held, PASOK – its new leadership notwithstanding – found itself in third place, having lost more than 30 percentage points and fallen into a decline.

Lesson for political marketing

The lesson to be drawn from this case study is clear: a party of power that deliberately promises policies that it cannot deliver may benefit in the short term, but in the long run it will probably lose. Party policies should, therefore, be rooted in what is possible and not based solely on what the electorate wants. This case study also raises certain questions that both theorists and practitioners of political marketing should consider:

1 What positions should a potential governing party adopt, during an election campaign, towards a looming crisis when the interests of the country demand sacrifices from the voters?
2 To what extent can a government adopt unpopular policies that kindle reaction and unrest and possibly a threat to democracy?
3 What chance does a party or a government have if it speaks frankly to the country when the people are unaware of the magnitude of the problem and judges on the basis of personal interest?

These are questions that cannot be answered on the basis of this case alone. The experience yielded by the practices of other parties in other countries could be helpful in reaching the best answers to them. They do, however, draw attention to the complexity of the decisions faced by those engaged in political marketing and the importance of pursuing an ever-deeper analysis of its principles and applications.

Further reading

Kotzaivazoglou, Iordanis (2011). 'Political marketing in the Greek context: does market orientation exist?' *International Review on Public and Nonprofit Marketing*, 8(1): 41–56.

Kotzaivazoglou, Iordanis and Yorgos Zotos (2009). 'Political marketing in Greece'. In Jennifer Lees-Marshment, Jesper Strömbäck and Chris Rudd (eds) *Global Political Marketing*. London: Routledge, 128–42.

Lees-Marshment, Jennifer (2009). *Political Marketing: Principles and Applications*. London: Routledge.

Case study 8.2 Marketing mayors in government: Graham Quirk and Len Brown's delivery communication

By Renisa Maki, University of Auckland

rmak012@aucklanduni.ac.nz

This case study examines Brisbane Mayor Graham Quirk's and Auckland Mayor Len Brown's innovative strategies for delivery communication. As incumbents, both embarked on creative initiatives to convey their delivery progress across diverse mediums. Ranging from a musical jingle, report documents, magazine publications, YouTube channels, bus advertisements, guerrilla marketing, signature moments and social media, both Quirk and Brown successfully demonstrated the impact of delivery for local constituents.

Mayor Graham Quirk

Mayor Quirk's campaign slogan itself conveys delivery: 'Getting things done, delivering for you'. This slogan was communicated using a myriad of mediums to maximise impact. For instance, an upbeat musical jingle was composed for 30-second viral video advertisements on Team Quirk's YouTube channel. The jingle uses the campaign slogan in its lyrics: *'Getting things done in our city, our city; Being the best we can be, our city; Our vision is strong as our dream for this city, our city; Delivering for you; The team that works is Team Quirk, Team Quirk!'* The jingle is played alongside video of Quirk delivering election pledges. Captions conveying delivery such as 'modern and reliable public transport, bikeway and park upgrades' are accompanied with emotive film sequences of families playing in parks and a woman waving to neighbours when recycling her rubbish. The first camera shot of Quirk depicted him on a hilltop perusing the Brisbane skyline during sunset, determinedly putting on his suit jacket with the caption 'Graham Quirk: Getting things done'. The slogan was also reiterated on the online spaces of social media sites. Team Quirk's official Facebook page cover photo includes all his campaign staff wearing matching blue T-shirts with the slogan printed on the front under each person's name. These personalised T-shirts are an effective initiative since they are eye-catching and simultaneously convey both delivery and loyalty to Quirk. The slogan is also used on Twitter, with the information: 'Lord Mayor Graham Quirk and his team – Getting things done and delivering for you in Brisbane'. Repeatedly using this slogan is an effective marketing strategy as it directly addresses delivering in power, hence satisfying political consumers.

Similarly, an effective strategy is printing advertisements on the object of delivery itself. Quirk's election pledge included tackling traffic congestion and improving suburban roads. Thus, when the 500th new bus was completed, Quirk advertised this delivery using large banners printed onto the buses stating: 'We've delivered 500 new buses! More buses, more comfortable, more often'. Emblazoned on the vehicle itself, as these buses drive around Brisbane, they are a constant reminder of Mayor Quirk's marketing in government and communication of delivery.

Quirk's official website also communicates delivery. The central element of the website is a photograph of Quirk with his signature alongside the statement: 'I'll be working hard to make our city the best it can be'. This has connotations of a legal binding contract, and the personal pronoun 'I'll' reflects his personal effort rather than that of his team. The website includes reports and press releases on delivery progress.

Mayor Len Brown

Mayor Brown's 'vision' for Auckland is to make it the world's most liveable city. This statement influences his delivery communication and inspired the Auckland Plan legislation, consisting of strategies to improve conditions in the city. Brown launched these plan drafts and made them available for public feedback and consultation. Animation experts were hired to produce high resolution before-and-after images of the city, depicting Brown's vision for progress. All this data was collated into an attractive progress report. This was available for the public to download, including enticing visual graphics and photography. Furthermore, a council web page was dedicated to a timeline of every meeting the council had on the Auckland Plan. The transparency of progress was shown by providing detailed minutes of every meeting. Butler and Collins (2001) note that politicians seek to show they are better at managing service delivery. The time between formal election campaign periods is when service delivery is the principal focus. By using feedback reports and providing details of his meetings to the public, Brown demonstrates service delivery on his promised vision for Auckland.

Another tactic for service delivery is to create signature moments. In July 2011, train passengers travelling to Auckland's Britomart station were greeted with cake from Brown to celebrate a record 10 million train passenger journeys in one year. The number has been called a 'significant milestone' by Auckland Transport Chief Executive David Warburton. The signature moment was created by a large cake in the shape of a train, along with an edible marzipan Mayor Brown figurine leading the way in front of a sign saying 'To be continued', implying his delivery in government would continue on. Better public transport and increased numbers were part of the Auckland Plan, and this signature moment was an effective way of displaying service delivery. The simple act of sharing slices of cake with citizens at the train station innovatively celebrated and communicated Brown's delivery progress.

Brown also partook in guerrilla marketing techniques. Collaborating with Broadway musical *Wicked* Australia-New Zealand cast, Brown used the stage production as a platform for conveying delivery. He published a letter to the public as part of the official programme for the show. The letter says: 'Major events play a key role in helping Auckland become the world's most liveable city .... To my fellow Aucklanders, enjoy these great events that help make our wonderful Auckland lifestyle so special'. Brown also transformed Auckland into New Zealand's own 'Emerald City', as he pushed the plunger to bathe Auckland Town Hall, Aotea Square and the Civic theatre in green light. The event was an innovative public relations stunt. Such collaboration with a musical as part of a delivery communication strategy is an effective guerrilla marketing initiative; being original and creative in inception.

Furthermore, Brown contributed to a monthly magazine entitled *Our Auckland* to communicate delivery progress in an aesthetically designed, glossy publication. Housing developments, newly built community centers and restored heritage sites are publicised. The magazine also advertises upcoming events for citizens to participate in around the city, emphasizing how Auckland is a flourishing and enjoyable place to live.

Lessons for political marketing

- For mayors, emphasising love of their city and visually depicting civic identity is effective within delivery communication. Work the fabric of the city into delivery communication, using imagery from key city monuments or participating personally in city cultural events. Such emotive visual cues help entrench positive public opinion locally.

- Communicate progress using creative platforms. Invest in hiring staff from creative industries such as Fine Arts, Advertising and Design to function as a think tank for developing innovative strategies.
- Be specific about how delivery has affected each neighbourhood. Emphasise the 'local' aspects of delivery as these will differ from region to region.
- Communicate delivery enthusiastically across diverse mediums, conveying it as a personal passion and commitment to your city.

Further reading

Butler, Patrick and Neil Collins (2001). 'Payment on delivery: recognising constituency service as political marketing'. *European Journal of Marketing*, 35(9): 1025–37.

Lilleker, Darren (2006). 'Local political marketing: political marketing as public service'. In D. Lilleker, N. Jackson and R. Scullion (eds) *The Marketing of Political Parties*. Manchester: Manchester University Press, 206–230.

http://www.grahamquirk.com.au/

http://www.lenbrownformayor.co.nz/

References

Barber, Michael (2007). *Instruction to Deliver*. London: Politicos.

Butler, Patrick and Neil Collins (1999). 'A conceptual framework for political marketing'. In Bruce I. Newman (ed.) *Handbook of Political Marketing*. Thousand Oaks, CA: Sage Publications, 55–72.

Butler, Patrick and Neil Collins (2001). 'Payment on delivery: recognising constituency service as political marketing'. *European Journal of Marketing*, 35(9/10): 1025–37.

Butler, Patrick and Phil Harris (2009). 'Considerations on the evolution of political marketing theory'. *Marketing Theory*, 9(2): 149–64.

Campbell, Alastair (2013). 'Alastair Campbell in Conversation: Politics, the People and the Press', Public Conversation with Steve Richards. *British Library*, 17th May. http://www.youtube.com/watch?v=_Gu4ZEMOB78

Channel 4 News (2007). 'FactCheck: Labour's Election Pledge Cards', http://www.channel4.com/news/articles/politics/domestic_politics/factcheck+labours+election+pledge_cards/507807 (accssed 18 July, 2013)

Conley, Brian M. (2014). 'Does Obama care?: assessing the delivery of health reform in the United States'. In Jennifer Lees-Marshment, Brian Conley and Kenneth Cosgrove (eds) *Political Marketing in the US*. New York: Routledge.

Esselment, Anna (2012a). 'Delivering in government and getting results in minorities and coalitions'. In Jennifer Lees-Marshment (ed.) *The Routledge Handbook of Political Marketing*. London and New York: Routledge, 303–15.

Esselment, Anna (2012b). 'Market orientation in a minority government: the challenges of product delivery'. In Alex Marland, Thierry Giasson and Jennifer Lees-Marshment (eds) *Political Marketing in Canada*. Vancouver: UBC, 123–38.

Glover, Julian (2006). 'Labour support at lowest level since Thatcher's last election victory', *The Guardian*, 25 October. http://www.theguardian.com/politics/2006/oct/25/uk.polls

Hamburger, Peter (2006). 'The Australian Government Cabinet Implementation Unit'. In *Improving implementation: organisational change and project management*. ANZSOG/ANU. http://epress.anu.edu.au/anzsog/imp/mobile_devices/ch18.html (accessed 11 April 2008)

Hughes, Andrew and Stephen Dann (2010). 'Australian political marketing: substance backed by style'. In Jennifer Lees-Marshment, Jesper Strömbäck and Chris Rudd (eds) *Global Political Marketing*, London: Routledge, 82–95.

Johnson, Dennis W. (2013). 'The election of 2012'. In Dennis W. Johnson (ed.) *Campaigning for President 2012: Strategy and Tactics*. New York: Routledge, 1–22.

Klein, Ezra and Sarah Kliff (2013). 'Obama's last campaign: inside the White House plan to sell Obamacare'. *The Washington Post: Wonkblog*, July 17. http://www.washingtonpost.com/blogs/ wonkblog/wp/2013/07/17/obamas-last-campaign-inside-the-white-house-plan-to-sell-obamacare/ (accessed 18 July, 2013)

Lederer, Andreas, Fritz Plasser and Christian Scheucher (2005). 'The rise and fall of populism in Austria – a political marketing perspective'. In Darren G. Lilleker and Jennifer Lees-Marshment (eds) *Political Marketing: A Comparative Perspective*. Manchester: Manchester University Press, 132–147.

Lees-Marshment, Jennifer (2001). *Political Marketing and British Political Parties: The Party's Just Begun*. Manchester: Manchester University Press.

Lees-Marshment, Jennifer (2008). *Political Marketing and British Political Parties*, 2nd edn. Manchester: Manchester University Press.

Lees-Marshment, Jennifer (2011) *The Political Marketing Game*. Houndmills and New York: Palgrave Macmillan.

Lees-Marshment, Jennifer (2012). 'National and Labour's leadership, branding and delivery in the 2011 New Zealand election'. In Stephen Levine and Jon Johansson (eds) *Kicking the Tyres: The New Zealand General Election and Electoral Referendum of 2011*. Wellington: Victoria University Press, 177–89.

Lilleker, Darren (2006). 'Local political marketing: political marketing as public service'. In D. Lilleker, N. Jackson and R. Scullion (eds) *The Marketing of Political Parties*. Manchester: Manchester University Press, 206–30.

Lilleker, Darren G. (2009). 'Local political marketing: connecting UK politicians and voters'. Case study 7.5 in Jennifer Lees-Marshment, *Political Marketing: Principles and Applications*. London and New York: Routledge, 188–9.

Lindholm, Mikael R. and Anette Prehn (2007). 'Strategy and politics: the example of Denmark'. In Thomas Fischer, Gregor Peter Schmitz and Michael Seberich (eds) *The Strategy of Politics: Results of a Comparative Study*. Butersloh: Verlag, Bertelsmann Stiftung,11–60.

Newman, Bruce I. (1999). *The Mass Marketing of Politics*. Thousand Oaks, CA: Sage.

Patrón-Galindo, Pedro (2004). ' Symbolism and the construction of the political products: analysis of the political marketing strategies of Peruvian President Alejandro Toledo'. *Journal of Public Affairs*, 4(2): 115–24.

PolicyExchangeUK (2012). 'Political communication: new lessons from the US. Interview with Frank Luntz'. Online video, *youtube.com*, 26th November. http://www.youtube.com/watch?v= eYAuvyA216c

Rehr, David R. (2013). 'The challenges facing Obama'. In Dennis W. Johnson (ed.) *Campaigning for President 2012: Strategy and Tactics*. New York: Routledge, 25–42.

Rudd, Chris (2005). 'Marketing the message or the messenger?'. In Darren Lilleker and J. Lees-Marshment (eds) *Political Marketing in Comparative Perspective*. Manchester: Manchester University Press, 79–96.

Steen, Jens Jonatan (2009). 'When politics becomes contractual: a case from Denmark'. Case Study 8.3 in Jennifer Lees-Marshment, *Political Marketing: Principles and Applications*. London and New York: Routledge, 230–2.

Steger, Wayne (1999). 'The permanent campaign: marketing from the hill'. In Bruce Newman (ed.) *The Handbook of Political Marketing*. Thousand Oaks, CA: Sage, 661–86.

Temple, Mick (2010) 'Political marketing, party behaviour and political science'. In Jennifer Lees-Marshment, Jesper Strömbäck and Chris Rudd (eds) *Global Political Marketing*. London: Routledge, 263–77.

9 Political marketing and democracy

Political marketing is a pervasive force in our lives; it influences the policies politicians pursue, the opportunities they give to people to be involved in campaigns and party organisations, the staff they employ, the way they communicate and the way they govern and lead. Given this, many scholars and media commentators have raised concerns that it influences democracy negatively; and political marketing does indeed raise many issues, but along with problems there is also the potential for it to strengthen the functioning of political systems and society. What makes the difference is how political marketing is practised. It is important that we are all aware of both the negative and positive implications political marketing can have so that those who practice political marketing make informed choices as to how they decide to use it. This chapter will explore the positive and negative impact of political marketing on a range of areas: political leadership; citizenship; political participation; power and representation; policy; and principle and ethics.

Political leadership

Practitioner perspective 9.1 on the value of the public's views

Voters tend to be pretty rational, rational in a way that serves their interests. I think they tend to be pretty consistent . . . people are pretty true to their value system.

Matt Carter, PSB research and former UK Labour
General Secretary, interviewed in 2007

I spend a lot of my time talking with members of the public. . . they're just as smart as you or me. Sometimes even smarter, you know? . . . These people aren't dumb, or they're not stupid, they're not even fickle.

John Utting, Australian pollster for UMR, interviewed in 2008

They're wise, they're understanding . . . the idea of irrational self-interested actors is nonsense . . . people vote from a pamphlet of reasons – emotion, values, sort of intuition is crucially important, a sense of right and wrong as well as self-interest.

The Late Lord Philip Gould, advisor to UK PM Tony Blair,
interviewed in 2007

There is something in it for them if there is something in it for the future generations, if there is something in it for less advantaged Canadians.

Alexandra Evershed, Ipsos-Reid, interviewed in 2009

Source: Lees-Marshment (2011)

In a democracy, politicians are expected to provide leadership – to have a vision of how society can be a better place, create proposals to achieve that vision and enlist the public in supporting the changes necessary to make it happen. There are two main areas of concern about the potential impact of political marketing on leadership: first that it encourages political leaders to listen to the public whose opinion has many weaknesses; second that it prevents politicians showing leadership on unpopular issues.

A market-oriented strategy is criticized for putting too much trust in public opinion, which has its own weaknesses; an issue made more visible by complex, inter-governmental, international issues, such as war. Behind this argument are concerns about how the public forms its opinions and also how it articulates them. Lane (1996, 47–9) argues that, compared with political elites, the mass public is generally less interested in politics and less likely to discuss politics; less supportive of open discussion of conflicting opinions and more willing to forbid discussion of policy issues considered to be sensitive; less tolerant and more punitive towards disliked groups and less able to weigh the costs of policies supported.

However, as Practitioner perspective 9.1 suggests, practitioners argue that voters are not fools and can make good choices and thus research into their views helps democracy work more effectively. Academics have also argued in support of public input. Headley *et al.* (2011) note that old arguments – that citizens were not capable of providing input into foreign policy due to its distinct nature from domestic policy, their ignorance and volatility, and that foreign policy needed to be reserved for elite experts who would best decide what was in the national interest – have been eroded by several changes. First, the division between domestic and foreign policy has been eroded as global issues arise that transcend both, such as security, climate change and the financial crisis; and second, citizens are more aware about events overseas thanks to the internet and other communication developments. New research on public opinion on foreign policy has challenged the view it is fickle and imprudent. Furthermore, as Chapter 3 on PMR discusses, more constructive and dialogic forms of market research may integrate elements of deliberative democracy and thus enable more mature input from the public, which overcomes these issues.

In terms of restricting leadership, the concern is that political marketing strategy encourages leaders to consider existing voter demand instead of creating their own ideas for future possibilities, and market research tells them what policies to favour or avoid depending on their popularity instead of what might be right for society. In their acceptance speeches for the nominations to run for the 2000 US presidential election, both Bush and Gore tried to argue they should not use polls in decision-making, with Gore arguing that 'the Presidency is more than a popularity contest. It's a day to day fight for people. Sometimes you have to choose what's difficult or unpopular'; and Bush, 'I believe great decisions are made with care, made with conviction, not made with polls, I do not need to take your pulse before I know my own mind'. When Ed Miliband took over as Labour leader in the UK in 2010 he promised 'we will not be imprisoned by the focus groups. Politics has to be about leadership, or it is nothing' (quoted in Mills 2011, 31).

Such proclamations – despite the extensive use of market research by politicians before deciding their positions and communication – is reflective of negativity towards the use of focus groups, amongst other market research tools, and indeed the whole concept of listening to the general public, which is apparent in the public sphere and academic literature. Mills (2011, 31) notes the Australian media in the run up to the 2010 Australian federal election talked of a 'narcotic reliance on focus groups' causing a 'decline in political courage' by converting political leaders into followers and creating politicians who 'won't get out of bed in the morning unless they have had a focus group report to tell them which side of the bed to get out'. There were also concerns that the Clinton presidency in the 1990s left the US Democrats with a vacuum of policies, lacking a clear vision or ideology. Newman (1999, 41) notes how Bill Clinton wanted to push for a bill to protect gay service members in the military at the start of his presidency, but many interest groups were against it so he had to pull back even though he had promised to do it during his campaign.

However Mills (2011, 31–2) argues that anyone who really knows how politics works would know that PMR is 'only a small part of the complex mix of factors that drive political decision-making'. Strategy and market research can be – and often is – utilised by politicians to help them show leadership; to identify and better understand potential opposition to a desired changed and thus find a way to explain and justify a vision to navigate around that opposition and implement it amongst the constraints that democratic elections and governing presents. Lees-Marshment (2014) interviewed political market researchers and found that their role was much more constrained, with their views being just one of many inputs that politicians consider before making decisions.

Political marketing strategy is not just about following public opinion or trying to lead it, for both normative and pragmatic reasons. A market-orientation is about responding to voter demands in such a way as to achieve organisational goals – including change and policies adjusted to suit the internal market. Mortimore and Gill (2010, 255) argue that 'leadership judgement is also indispensable to an MOP' not least because of the way the public judges politicians:

- the public can be wrong about the practical consequences of the policy choices they espouse – yet they hold responsible the politicians that implemented them;
- they can be unfair in their judgment of government performance – so that the criteria for achieving popularity is not delivery but the public perception of delivery.

The conclusion to the *Routledge Handbook of Political Marketing* argues that a lot of the criticism about opinion research is misinformed about the reality of practice (Lees-Marshment 2012a, 378–9). Research-informed communication is used by politicians wishing to find to a way to adjust and communicate their policies to achieve certain policies. Goot (1999) detailed how the Australian Liberal-National coalition was able to use polling to inform its desire to implement an unpopular policy – selling off the publicly owned phone company Telstra. Pre-decision-making polling suggested the party would lose votes with the privatisation policy. However, market intelligence also suggested two ways to make the proposal more attractive: it showed strong public concern with public debt and the environment. Coalition leader Howard, therefore, announced that funds from such a sale would go towards reducing the public debt and environmental projects, and the proposal therefore appealed to voters concerned about the environment. Therefore Goot (1999, 215) concludes that market intelligence 'may be just as effective as a means of working out how to galvanise support, neutralise opposition or convert those who might otherwise be reluctant to see things the party's way'.

Modern political leadership is therefore about listening but not just following: it requires reflection on the views of a range of stakeholders before making strategic decisions (Giasson *et al.* 2012, 252). Lindholm and Prehn (2007, 56) quote a Danish minister who said 'the art is to lead the flock, but not to move so far ahead that you disappear from sight, nor disappear in it'. Lees-Marshment (2012b, 168) argues that in a political marketing context, therefore, politicians need to be reflective leaders:

A reflective political leader will use market research proactively to achieve change as well as power. They will listen to public opinion, utilizing a range of market research methods, and for different purposes, reflect on demands whilst considering other factors and interests, and then react reflectively to market research by taking a range of positions in response.

Reflective leaders will use market research proactively to help them identify the scope for a change in public opinion and understand potential opposition before reflecting on the research results. Decision-making involves responding reflectively to such market research and includes a range of positions between overriding opinion and completely following it; and communicating their reflectiveness: see Figure 9.1.

Reflective leaders will sometimes need to give up, but only after having fully researched the market, considering a range of potential responses and trying to achieve key visionary change in some areas. Phillip Gould, had a more nuanced perspective with the benefit of

Model of a reflective political leader

Phase 1 Conduct market research proactively for a range of purposes
Commission and utilise high-quality research to understand public opinion on a range of aspects and for a range of purposes including to:

- identify existing public opinion and understand it more deeply;
- identify the scope for public opinion to change;
- predict public reaction to a change or new policy;
- identify and understand opposition to a position to inform communication.

Phase 2 Reflect and consider how to respond to public opinion
Use market analysis to inform, not dictate, decisions and take into account other factors including:

- realities and constraints of government;
- other stakeholders such as party members, expert advisors, interest groups, the media;
- the leader's vision for change.

Phase 3 Respond reflectively to market research
Respond to market research in a range of ways such as:

- consciously overriding public opinion;
- giving the public time to adjust to the change;
- using strategic communication to try to change opinion;
- adjusting position slightly or significantly;
- following public opinion 100 per cent.

Phase 4 Communicate reflectiveness
Explain leadership decisions and show awareness of and respect for any opposition.

Phase 5 Monitor and adjust
Monitor reaction to leadership decisions and actions and explain further or modify position if opposition continues.

Figure 9.1

Source: Adapted from Lees-Marshment (2012b, 169)

more experience and hindsight when interviewed in 2007, ten years after UK New Labour's first election victory:

> It's absolutely crucial to listen in modern politics, but equally important to lead . . . you have to balance flexibility and resolution . . . The art of . . . modern politics is . . . being able to perfectly blend these two together and to make them work.
>
> (Lees-Marshment 2011, 92)

Another democratic aspect of political marketing and leadership is gender: female candidates for leadership roles. Literature on gender in politics suggests that women face challenges in conveying leadership traits needed to win high office. Market research might encourage certain strategies in relation to gender. The HBO documentary *Game Change* suggested that gender was a core part in the strategic selection of John McCain's running mate for the 2000 US presidential election, and Sarah Palin's characteristics including being well dressed, attractive and having a large family were played out in the campaign. Busby (2009, 163) notes how she associated herself as a 'Walmart mom' to appeal to white working women with children and a 'hockey mom' to appeal to working-class or blue-collar workers; a gendered form of segmentation focused on key groups thought to be potential switchers in the campaign. However, although Palin's selection as vice-presidential candidate boosted the Republicans in the polls, initially she performed badly on standard leadership traits such as understanding the demands of office and policy detail (Busby 2009, 164). However, Burrell (2008, 752) explored how Hillary Clinton fared in public polling on leadership characteristics or traits in her bid for the Democratic nomination and found that she did better on masculine then feminine traits. So this suggested that 'competency, strength, and experience, which once were viewed as the biggest hurdles for women candidates to surmount in the minds of the public, proved not to be the disadvantage they once were'. However, interestingly, Clinton did find it hard to convey feminalist traits at the same time; so it could be that the new problem for women will not be that they struggle to be seen as doing 'male' parts of the political leader's job but that in doing so they fail to convey their female aspects, such as empathy, which male candidates now demonstrate just as well as their male traits.

Cardo and Lees-Marshment (2013) explored political marketing strategies used by female politicians either bidding for leadership positions or already in them with regard to their gender, including the strategies of Sarah Palin, Hillary Clinton, and Prime Ministers Helen Clark, Julia Gillard and Margaret Thatcher. They concluded that gender has to be a part of political marketing as it's part of the candidate and part of the product/brand, but gendering political marketing is a double-edged sword. If female or male aspects of women leaders are played up it can backfire. Gender needs to be marketed in a balanced and authentic way. They note how John McTiernan, who had been Blair's advisor, became advisor to Australian Prime Minister Julia Gillard and helped arrange for her to be pictured in the *Australian Women's Weekly* in June 2013; but the reaction to this was mixed, not least as she was pictured knitting a present for the royal baby. The problem was that knitting did not ring true with her reputation for being a feminist; and she was a republican and so anti monarchy. Equally, as Busby (2012) reports, whilst Palin's initial attraction was as an ordinary woman who connected with women who shopped at the discount chain Walmart, the Republican McCain campaign dressed her in expensive clothes; such false communication did not ring true what either candidate was about and used gender in a problematic way. Female politicians should be marketed as they are, and convey a balance of female/male leadership characteristics.

As Braun (2012, 18) argues, despite the importance of political marketing research 'it is always up to the individual politicians how they use it'. It helps ensure leaders listen but politicians need to find that balance between principled leadership and responding to voters desires. Political marketing does not remove the need for any leadership – what it can do is ensure that whatever decision is taken is carried out after leaders have listened and reflected.

Citizenship

Citizenship is about collective obligation and community; the need for debate, discussion and exchange of ideas to obtain the best solution to problems; and the allocation of resources according to principle and the desire to change and improve conditions. Political marketing is also criticised for treating voters like consumers – creating a product to suit public demand – and thus seen as a threat to citizenship and thus harmful to democracy. Lilleker and Scullion (2008, 4) explain how consumerism seems antithetical to traditional notions of voting and its role in democracy: 'voting is implicitly an act with ethical values and morals attached as any individual choice will also take into account the broader impact on others of that choice'. In contrast consumerism encourages people to be selfish and focus on their individual concerns. Treating voters as consumers does not guarantee equality. Consumer and customer concepts ignore the big issues of politics, such as fairness and social justice. Aberbach and Christensen (2005, 234) note that 'neo-liberal reforms have a market logic that downplays or even disregards the legal and moral aspects of citizenship that were emphasised in the republican (and what we have also called the collective) concept of the citizen role'. The consumerisation of politics has also made it harder for politicians to get credit for delivery. Stephen Mills, a pollster in New Zealand, recalled how 'sometimes in groups I've run through a list of achievements of governments and you can see slightly rueful voters who had been rubbishing the government start to change their minds a bit as the list of what they had forgotten is conveyed' (Lees-Marshment 2011, 187).

Political marketing scholars have engaged in such a debate, and Figure 9.2 summaries the opposing views presented by Savigny (2008) and Scullion (2008).

One potential solution to this is to see voters as political consumers – a mixture of citizen and consumer (see Lees-Marshment 2008). Scullion (2008) argues that the differences between the consumer and citizen can be minimised, and political consumers can come to expect a share of responsibility and blame when things go wrong if they appreciate a link between their own choice and the outcome. He also argues in Scullion (2010, 289) that 'the actual life experience of individuals reveals a messier interface where we, often unintentionally, take on citizenly roles in market spaces and that our consumer experiences contain civic qualities'. This can enhance rather than detract from citizenship.

It is possible when consulting the public that values can still be integrated. Broader frameworks of discussion consultation (such as deliberative democracy frameworks) may produce more realistic demands, in the interests of the community not just the individual. Co-creation also asks that the public work in a more citizenly way to create solutions – Langmaid (2012, 74) argues that co-creation both moves away from the idea that elites know best and beyond the idea that politicians find out what people want and then develop a product to give it to them. Instead both the public and politician work together to create the solution. Langmaid (2012, 75) thus argues if co-creation were adopted more widely in politics, it could potentially transform citizen–state relationships and increase trust in

Scholars' debate on the pros and cons of treating the voter as a consumer in politics

Scullion: pro treating the voter as consumer	Savigny: against treating the voter as consumer
1 Citizenship can exist within a consumer culture.	1 The relationship between government and consumer is not straightforward.
2 Consumer sovereignty gives the public power, perhaps more power than as a citizen, which meets rather than erodes democratic ideals.	2 Referring to the public as consumers of politics can marginalise them from the process of politics.
3 Consumerism gives people a stronger voice, empowers them and increases their efficacy.	3 Individuals are not always able to pursue and maximise their own self-interest.
4 The market is self-regulated, whereas traditional politics is rule based.	4 It reinforces the new right emphasis upon markets as the best way to create solutions to societal problems.
5 Market populism is anti elitist.	5 Politicians only consider consumer wants to suit their goals; political marketing satisfies the goals of politicians rather than the wants of the public.
6 It can encourage greater participation in politics, as people are asked to call government or other organisations to account; the market enables all to participate; it is non-discriminatory.	6 Politicians focus on those who will affect elections/support rather than everyone, alienating some consumers from the political process, and reducing participation.
7 Consumerism in politics can create avenues for the public to take on civic qualities; considering broader public issues and accepting responsibility for shaping their own lives.	7 Removing the notion of the citizen removes obligations as well as rights.

Figure 9.2

Sources: Adapted from Scullion (2008) and Savigny (2008)

politicians, as political leaders would no longer be expected to find the answer to everything. Even if parties consult the public, they can still play the role of aggregating demands to ensure that decisions are taken for the collective good, not just the individual. Political marketing can be used as a balance between consumer demands and producer judgment.

Political participation

There is a democratic argument that political elites should consider the internal market. In some countries and organisations, party members traditionally play a significant role in internal party democracy, participation, policymaking and campaigning. They therefore develop loyalty and attachment to a party and what it stands for. They participate because of a 'belief in a common societal goal' (Lilleker 2005b, 571). As Dean and Croft (2001, 1207) observe:

The enigma for a political party is how to allow the diversity of party members, activists and elected members a say in the nature of the 'product offering', while still maintaining a degree of apparent unanimity for the consumption of less-controllable groups.

Lilleker (2005a, 2005b) explored the consequences of market-oriented political marketing at the party leadership level on internal party democracy and concludes that it reduces the amount of policy decisions which are open for debate because the dictates of the market are more influential on leadership decisions. Lilleker argues that, when it became market-oriented, UK New Labour lost volunteers because its promises were devised to suit middle-class voters who did not want working-class based politics; and he found that members felt there had been a lack of consultation and they had been disenfranchised. Pettitt (2009), however, argues that it is just not always possible to consult effectively with the internal market if a party is going to use marketing to win an election. Even when leaders engage in careful internal marketing there will always be dissent as, if the product was adjusted to suit internal views, it would never be market-oriented enough to win support from the external market, namely voters. There is always a price to pay for electoral success through political marketing.

An alternative argument is that political marketing need not prevent debate. Later on in power, UK Labour responded in some way to discontent among its members: during 1997–2001 changes were made within the party with the aim of making members more involved. Members-only sessions were introduced at the annual party conference to ensure members had a chance to air their views without damaging the party externally. Online forms of interaction, which Obama demonstrated in 2008 and UK parties started using in 2010, may offer a more effective avenue for participation. As Chapter 5 on internal political marketing suggests, parties are finding ways to apply internal marketing and market-oriented concepts that create a volunteer-focused organisation that helps people participate in the way that suits them.

This might not be quite the same as policymaking through the membership, but e- and internal marketing has increased political participation. Johnson (2012, 209) notes over 2 million people participated via MyBO (My.BarackObama.com) in 2008, and they contributed 400,000 blog postings; 35,000 volunteers were recruited, and they held 200,000 offline events. This gave voters a much greater opportunity to participate; not only can marketing help mobilise them it can enable them to mobilise themselves. Marland (2012, 172) also argues that Obama's 2008 and 2010 use of marketing in fundraising made it easier for people to get involved, thus increasing civic engagement; and Ubertaccio (2012, 187) argues that internal direct marketing could, if used to its full potential, stimulate participation. Lees-Marshment (2012a, 379–80) argues that relationship and direct marketing can be used to mobilise volunteers, activists and members, which can increase participation in the political system and challenges the usual 'party and participation decline' thesis in non-political marketing literature.

Whilst marketing communications is traditionally about selling a message and product, the evolution to more interactive forms of communication and campaigning has also increased participation opportunities. Lloyd (2012, 255) concludes that in the 2010 UK general election there were new channels of communication that enabled two-way dialogue. This gave voters a voice where previously they had felt that none existed, and politicians were able to hear voters' unmediated response to their actions and decisions. Similarly, direct marketing can be used to identify and mobilise supporters if aimed not just at floating voters but party sympathisers, thus stimulating participation. Johnson's (2012) discussion of the twenty-first-century campaigning model suggests that organisationally they will become more flexible, with greater volunteer involvement but also influence and self-mobilisation. Van Aelst *et al.* (2012, 159–60) argue that seeing volunteers as part-time marketers involves ordinary people in politics 'not only as spectators but as co-producers' and thus enhances the idea of participatory democracy. Where members are more in line with voters anyway, they can be employed as part-time marketers and be involved not so much as foot soldiers but as co-producers of the campaign. Lees-Marshment (2012a, 380–1) observes that voters are therefore becoming part of the conversation instead of just being a passive recipient and this can help to improve political engagement and participation. Similarly, Lilleker and Jackson (2011, 171) argue that political PR of the CPR (corporate PR) type encourages political practitioners to take a strategic long-term approach to PR, which would be more positive for democracy as it would engage citizens in the political process (see also Ledingham 2011, 243–50).

Representation

Political marketing may skew representation. One of the problems with using market segmentation, for example, is that it enables, and arguably encourages, politicians to target certain groups whose support they need – rather than represent the public as a whole. This renders the vote of some groups worth more than others, which goes against core democratic principles of equal rights to participate in the electoral process (Savigny 2008). Savigny (2007) argues that this happened in the UK when New Labour conducted and responded to focus groups from certain segments of the population so that the party was only listening to certain groups in society – 'Tory switchers' – who were not representative of the electorate at large. Lees-Marshment and Marland (2012, 341) also contend that micro-targeting in Canada could mean the needs and wants of the public 'can become subservient to the emphasis placed on appealing to a narrow band of the electorate that shares ideological values with a political party'. As Lilleker (2005a, 23) puts it:

> Segmentation of the market and targeting of communication are to some extent responsible for causing a division in society: those to whom politics belongs and those whom politics has abandoned.

In the 2011 Canadian federal election, parties such as the Conservatives, Liberals and NDP (New Democratic Party) targeted specific ethnic groups such as South Asian, Punjabi, Mandarin and Chinese voters.[1] Voters themselves responded with the community group producing a mock video of Michael Jackson's song *Beat It* called *Go Ethnics Go*, complaining about politicians being featured with ethnic voters – they just wanted to be seen as Canadian. Lyrics in their song included 'They never ask you what you do around here; don't wanna know your name . . . see the truth behind the lies . . . you have a choice, you better speak when you can; don't wanna be an ethnic, be Canadian . . . we are not an ethnic vote!' (Avvy Go and The Colour of Poverty 2011). CBC Radio ran a programme exploring this, discussing the politics of courting the so-called ethnic vote as our political leaders learn to walk the very fine line between listening and pandering.[2] Another of the complaints raised by participants in the CBC Radio programme was that targeting was only carried out superficially in terms of photo ops rather than policies – so instead of politicians seriously attending to the demands of minority groups, they simply want to be seen to be targeting them. If targeting is to be effective, it needs to run through the product, brand and communication, otherwise it risks rejection from the market for being too superficial.

Burton (2012, 45) acknowledges the problems with selective outreach but also notes that segmentation and targeting can also stimulate participation by under-motivated and less informed citizens. Similarly Mills (2011, 35) argues that focus groups with soft and undecided voters 'are a highly effective means of bringing forward the views of voters who are mostly outside any political insider communication channel'. Binstock and Davidson's (2012) research in segmentation strategies in the retiree or pensioner segment in the US and UK demonstrated that it can be used by elites to better understand a seemingly homogenous group and thus represent voters more effectively as well as make appropriate decisions for a changing society:

> Segmentation can ... serve as a tool to open up a dialogue about the meaning of retirement and later life, negotiating a response to the transformation of older voters from excluded minority to a position where politics and government delivers a socially equitable response to the new policy challenges.
>
> (Binstock and Davidson 2012, 30)

Another positive example of the use of segmentation is that by McGough (2009) who notes that the use of marketing techniques by the IRA-linked party Sinn Féin in Northern Ireland enabled the party to build its support quickly, and thus succeed in political – as opposed to terrorist – activities. They used segmentation to create a coordinated system of research-led, targeted communication on the party message, but also collected market intelligence through talking to voters which fed back into campaign strategy. Furthermore, they trained campaigners in political marketing often in military-style settings – what McGough (2009, 289) calls 'an organised and disciplined system of education in democratic political activism' – with those who completed the training able to deliver a consistent and co-ordinated party position on a wide range of policy areas. In delivery terms, voter complaints were addressed such as through solving transport difficulties for the elderly, which built up local delivery credibility. McGough argues that political marketing was used by Sinn Féin as a weapon of persuasion targeted not only at the voters but at the British public and government, demonstrating the legitimacy, inevitability and support for the political demands of the armed struggle. McGough speculates therefore that if Sinn Féin can use political marketing in this way, so can groups such as Al Qaeda to gain a democratic position; as he puts it 'the extremists may gain far more advantages through democracy than they ever did through the bomb and the bullet' (2009, 290). The combination of terrorist groups and political marketing can seem uncomfortable, but it might also have positive democratic effect. The link between research and war or peace is also discussed in the book on peace polls by Colin Irwin (2012).

Burton and Miracle (2004) also suggest that the growing ability of individual candidates to use segmentation and voter targeting tools, instead of it being in the hands of traditional party organisations, means that marketing tools that originate as highly skilled and expensive and therefore only available for elites will over time become available to all regardless of resources or power. This makes political marketing a more democratic activity. As political marketing techniques – and with them, political power in terms of votes, public support, issue dominance and policy change – become more available to the masses, they could help minorities or the under-represented challenge incumbent traditional elites.

The use of marketing communications to persuade the public to support an elite position may undermine representation. Branding and research-led communication may give elites more control over the public and narrow choice and limit debate because it requires uniformity and tries to change public opinion. It can also be argued that utilising market intelligence to make communication as effective as possible helps politicians sell the best, but unwanted messages. Young (2005) argues that government advertising raised many democratic issues. It is expensive and is only one-way from government to the citizen. Furthermore, it offers a benefit to incumbents and borders on modern propaganda. Young contends we need to question this expenditure of public funds:

> Now that the Federal Government is frequently listed as the top advertiser in Australia – outranking commercial giants such as Coles, Myer, Holden and McDonald's – it is time to question how our Government chooses to communicate with us and how much that costs us (not only financially but also democratically).

Marketing communications can also be seen as manipulative, with insights and direct marketing being designed to play on emotions and research enabling political elites to get inside the heads of voters. Dermody and Hamner-Lloyd (2006, 128) argue that 'the way in which promotional marketing tools and concepts are being used in election campaigns, with the emphasis on creating distrust and suspicion of the competing parties, does not bode well for the future of democracy in Britain'.

However, whilst government communication can be misused in politics, it can also be used ethically. Gelders and Ihlen (2010, 61) argue that government communication about potential policies can be part of a democratic process whereby the government learns about citizens' views and needs, and public relations is needed throughout the policy process. Similarly, branding of government policy is about branding of elites within government and thus securing support for the implementation of policies that politicians have offered and received a mandate for in elections, which could be good for democracy. The branding of public policy, such as that on HIV/AIDS, can make the policy easier to implement and achieve a positive public mood. Simply getting elites to think of politics as a brand can encourage them to connect more effectively and create a more authentic offering built on core values of relevance to the public.

Overall, a market-orientation that places voter satisfaction at its heart elevates the citizens' position in the political process. It makes elites more responsive to market. Those in power are aware of public reaction when making decisions. For example, Fell and Cheng (2010, 187) argue that the trend towards more market-orientation for the leading parties in Taiwan is good for democracy because it has made the parties become more responsive to public views. Mills (2011, 36) argues that focus groups can help governments ensure their policies and services meet the needs of citizens more effectively. Lilleker (2005b, 570) observes how the design of party policy around voter groups' needs and wants may help strengthen democracy itself in new and emerging democracies. Continued marketing can also help government stay in touch or reconnect and thus avoid public opinion being dismissed by leaders in power for a long term. As Sparrow and Turner (2001, 995) argue, focus group research is now 'up-turning many assumptions made by elite politicians about the political world as experienced by ordinary people'. Lees-Marshment and Marland's (2012, 341) research through interviews with Canadian practitioners notes that whilst there are number of problems with political marketing there are also positives: 'that consultants utilise market research means they play a role in bringing public views to elite attention', and careful elite response 'can help voters feel listened to and promote a more trusting citizen-state relationship'.

Building on this basic argument, some scholars have argued that the more relational forms of political marketing may have more democratic potential. Henneberg and O'Shaughnessy (2009, 13) argue that a political relationship marketing approach would lead to positive implications for democracy where voters are consulted more often, party members turned into stakeholders and those who are better informed are actively solicited for ideas on policy. Headley *et al.*'s (2011, 16) discussion of public input into foreign policy and democracy makes a similar argument, noting that if citizens put forward their views in a reasoned and deliberative process they will provide more valuable inputs in policymaking than they can via short-term market research. They cite some examples of governments trying initiatives to allow more public input into foreign policy development, such as a Europe-wide deliberative poll 'Tomorrow's Europe' in October 2007 and the Canadian Department of Foreign Affairs and International Trade holding e-discussions to give the public input into policy in 2010. Henneberg *et al.* (2009) argue that political marketing could be allied to the political theory of deliberative democracy.

Policy

Political marketing can encourage more focus on short-term solutions – what the market wants for the next electoral period – rather than what is right for the country in the long term. The market-oriented concept of political marketing may conflict with the need for long-term solutions because there is a conflict between immediate consumer wants and the long-term welfare of citizens. Certainly, market research and market-oriented strategies can encourage politicians to avoid dealing with difficult policy issues. Paré and Berger (2008) analysed the Canadian Conservative's adoption of a market-oriented strategy in the lead-up to winning the 2006 election. They raised the concern that the Conservatives avoided discussing all the issues society needed them to address, avoiding dealing with contentious policy considerations. It has to be questioned whether the Canadian electorate really got what it needed and wanted or the market-oriented approach was used to help the Conservative Party to get what it needed and wanted. Excessive following of public opinion generally can also undermine creativity in policy development. As Paleologos (1997, 1184) argues: 'herein lies the depressing and harsh reality of a poll-driven society. This is what it means for each and every one of us. Such a society ignores creativity. It overlooks new ideas. It prohibits change and true reform.' He argues that polling is unlikely to uncover new ideas. The use of global knowledge transfer as a source of policies may also limit policy development.

There are also a number of democratic issues to consider with branding and designing the product to suit the market (Needham 2005; Barberio 2006; Scammell 2008; French and Smith 2010, 461). On the negative side it may oversimplify communication so the public gives support to the brand without looking into the detail, such as policy, or questioning elite behavior; and so it can narrow the political agenda. Brands tend to play on emotion rather than rational debate. Marsh and Fawcett (2012) note that branding of one policy may attract more political support and money for that policy area at the expense of another equally/more important area. Marsh and Fawcett (2011, 524, 527) also argue that it might be used to legitimate elite decisions in a way which undermines representative and parliamentary democracy and might encourage more managed than responsive government. Nation branding also has issues; Nimijean (2006, 69) argues that branding of Canada 'had an explicitly political dimension. Reframing debates about public policy in terms of "Canadian values" had effectively reduced the scope of ideological diversity in Canada.' Hulsse (2009) contends that the increase in foreign image policy means that PR and marketing instruments are prioritised as the means to successful government.

One particular example that raises democratic issues is when, in 2002, a team of strategists from the American political consultant firm Greenberg Carville Shrum, including James

Carville and Jeremy Rosner, advised a campaign for presidential candidate Gonzalo Sanchez de Lozada (or Goni for short) in Bolivia, an economically depressed country in South America with a long history of political chaos. This was depicted by a fly-on-the-wall documentary by Rachel Boynton called *Our Brand is Crisis*. It showed how the team of consultants was almost 'imported' into South America to help revitalise the image of President Sanches de Lozada, who had become very unpopular between 1993 and 1997, to help him be re-elected for a second time. The country faced economic crisis, and it was not easy to rebrand Goni. The opposition on the left, Evo Morales, was previously a leader of the coca leaf-growers' union and he presented strong competition. Goni was seen as arrogant in contrast, as seen from results of focus groups and polls. The campaign tried to reduce the election to a simple brand. Goni barely won the election, with just 22.5 per cent of the vote and, once in office, remained stubbornly out of touch with the general needs of the market. His term ended with large-scale demonstrations and riots (see http://www. ourbrandiscrisis.net/). The case provides a fascinating insight into how advisors work, the use of focus groups and polls to create a strategy, as well as potential ways to reform a poor image, but particularly in a global context. It raises many issues of the transplantation of US techniques and approaches into emerging democracies in particular and highlights concerns about political marketing transfer without adaptation. Strategists import more than just campaigning advice, because Goni was a western-educated, wealthy businessman who privatised Bolivia's economy and created social security and they support his aim to reinstitute capitalism. The results of the election and subsequent events in the country raise many issues.

However Birch and Petry (2012, 350) argue that government public opinion research can help ensure that policy is effective in achieving its goals; and also monitor policy as it is implemented, helping to improve the effectiveness of government policies. It can help clarify the wants and needs of citizens, segments or policy target groups, and how best to meet those needs. Marsh and Fawcett (2012) similarly concede that branding public policy might bring increased attention to public health issues like HIV/AIDS, or mean that the policy is easier/cheaper to implement because public acceptance is increased and therefore so is compliance with good health behaviour. Other scholars argue that branding helps provide differentiation between political products, thus creating choice for voters; and it can generate unity and help legislation get passed. O'Cass and Voola (2010) argue that branding helps create distinctiveness; it offers functional utility and adds value.

Delivery marketing can distort policy implementation. In governance terms, the rise of delivery units and a focus on delivery management can cause problems as these focus efforts on certain targets at the expense of others. Communication can also dominate government as opposed to actual delivery. However, if politicians are more focused on delivery then it can be seen as good for democracy, with a move from rhetoric and promises to action and change.

Principle and ethics

Politicians have always had to consider principle versus pragmatism. By the definition of democracy they cannot simply do what they believe to be right for we do not accept only one person has the right to make decisions about how our world is run. To win power, the nature of the political marketplace dictates that they have to consider the views of the public and other stakeholders, thus they have to balance principle and pragmatism. If they remain purely principled, they risk never gaining the power to achieve any of the change they believe in. Even in power, leaders are constrained: Newman (1999, 41) notes how

Bill Clinton's desire to introduce legislation to protect homosexuals in the military was prevented by strong opposition. Politicians thus have to balance principle and pragmatism all the time. They are helped in their decisions by political advisors, who are often seen as a hidden, undemocratic source of power. The rise of political marketing has encouraged greater use of professional consultants who can advise on how to use the ever-growing range of marketing techniques in politics. Advisors are there to win or because they are paid, and most are not formally part of the democratic process. Johnson (2007, 226) notes that, for some political consultants, ethics questions have 'no bearing on what they do'. However, all advisors can do is advise; the final decisions always rest with the politician. Thus Johnson (2007, 227) concludes that any real abuse in campaigns 'falls on the shoulders of the candidate'. Analysis of practitioner experiences through interviews with key advisors suggests that any influence is considerably constrained. Lees-Marshment's (2014) interviews with over 40 political professionals in the UK, the USA, Canada, Australia and New Zealand suggest that PMR can play a positive democratic role because in practice it is a diverse, complex and nuanced activity which provides valuable research-informed advice to politicians on the consequences of potential actions, but without dictating their final decision. Whilst there is, no doubt, bad practice out there, PMR can facilitate two-way communication, link elites to the public, enable elites to have a more informed view of public opinion before they make decisions, explore different ways forward and help political leaders find a way to make a good policy more publicly acceptable and achieve important societal change – such as Obama's health-care plan.

Fundraising is another area of dilemma – such as whether to accept large donations that provide the necessary resources to fund marketing activities but then might lead to an actual, or a perception of, influence over the candidate or party. Marland (2012) explored whether fundraising can be conducted in an ethical way, arguing marketing can be used to fundraise in an ethical manner if it is non-intrusive and transparent: see Figure 9.3.

Marland (2012) discusses to what extent the 2008 Obama campaign team sought to utilise ethical marketing to obtain donations. On the negative side, the Obama campaign prioritised its goals to gain donations over the interests of donors themselves. It also asked supporters to help raise funds themselves which could be seen as exploiting supporters'

Marland's framework for good practices when using marketing in political fundraising

- Clear, achievable policy promises made.
- Donors choose/informed how money spent.
- Donors voluntarily connect with each other.
- Easy to opt out of pledges.
- Factual websites with objective information.
- Information shared with inquiring journalists.
- Monitoring of fundraising progress.
- User-requested mobile marketing.

Figure 9.3

Source: Excerpt from Marland (2012, 173) – see original for questionable and bad categories of practice

positive feelings towards candidates to get them to fundraise on behalf of the campaign. In 2010 Organising for America used similar strategies and could be seen to encourage exerting social pressure on peers to donate or using emails of friends without their consent.

On the other hand the campaign and organisation offered various psychological, social and material benefits, creating fun and an emotional connection, and empowering volunteers to be involved in fundraising. In 2008 volunteers who got involved enjoyed an 'insider status' and received campaign updates and 'yes we can' ringtones. In 2010 Organising for America put the control and credit in the hands of the volunteers, stating:

> Your own personal fundraising page will put the financial future of this organization in your hands. You set your own goal, you do the outreach, and you get credit for the results.

In 2008 material incentives were also offered such as virtual gifts (e-wallpaper), campaign paraphernalia, backstage passes at campaign events and even a flight to celebration of the election results and a ticket to the presidential inauguration. Thus Marland concludes that, overall, the Obama 2008 and 2010 fundraising campaign behaved in an ethical manner in that there was no sign of any harm emerging, but it could have done better in terms of avoiding exertion of peer pressure, ensuring informed consent was present in every aspect of information sharing and avoiding capitalising on supporter's emotional attachment to the campaign and candidate.

Another area where the principle/pragmatism dilemma arises is political ideology. Political marketing has been criticised for leading to the end of ideology. Ideology is like an applied philosophy: it puts forward an idea of how things should be. It provides a framework of principles from which policies can be developed. In political parties, ideology is intended to provide an enduring foundation for policy development. Savigny (2008, 83) notes how ideology 'plays a significant role in the political process', because values and beliefs 'about the proper distribution of resources, and what a society should look like, underpins the notion of politics'. Lees-Marshment (2001, 1) argues that because of political marketing parties 'no longer pursue grand ideologies, fervently arguing for what they believe in and trying to persuade the masses to follow them. They increasingly follow the people.' The Market-Oriented Party concept could be interpreted as encouraging parties to abandon all ideology in favour of developing a product to suit the market. UK New Labour was critiqued in 1997 for lacking political ideology as the leadership had sought to remove many of Labour's long-standing policies on issues such as public spending and taxation which had been developed in response to the party's ideological traditions. Tony Blair even conceded in a party election broadcast on 27 May, 2001 that he was criticised for lacking principles; commentators argued he had overridden his party's traditional values in order to lead it to electoral success in 1997.

There is also a general sense that political marketing encourages politicians to lose their authenticity. Busby (2009, 10) notes how candidates' background is important to voters, and is thus 'purposefully modified' with flaws and low social standing promoted instead of 'excellence and exceptionalism' to respond to voters' desire that politicians seem to be in touch. When the UK Prime Minister David Cameron was being communicated before the 2010 election, the Labour opposition produced the *Dave the Chameleon* advert, trying to show how he had changed position to suit every whim or fad. Knuckey (2010, 106) notes how Kerry's changing position on voting for money for the Iraq War enabled him to be labelled a 'flip-flopper' by the Republican opposition. Smith and French (2009, 219)

Authors' corner 9.1

The Political Marketing Game
By Jennifer Lees-Marshment
Published by Palgrave Macmillan in 2011

The Political Marketing Game identifies what works in political marketing, using academic literature and 100 interviews with practitioners in the UK, US, Canada, NZ and Australia including former advisors to world leaders – US Presidents George W. Bush and Bill Clinton, Canadian Prime Ministers Stephen Harper and Paul Martin, UK Prime Ministers John Major, Tony Blair and Gordon Brown, and NZ Prime Ministers Helen Clark and John Key and Australian Prime Minister Kevin Rudd. Drawing on this collective wisdom, and featuring direct quotes from the practitioners themselves, it identifies how to play the political marketing game effectively. The book covers all aspects of political marketing, but three particularly important areas are market research, how it is used, and overall strategy.

To win the political marketing game, elites first need to use a wide range of market research sources, consultants and methods for all stakeholders, not just voters. Analysis should encourage solution-oriented feedback not just voter demands and seek to identify unity of opinion, possibilities for change and solutions to problems. Segmentation can be used to create new groups in the market using a range of factors (geography, demography, family, lifestyle, political views, internet usage and voter profiling) and help politicians better understand emerging and diversifying new groups in society.

Second, market analysis needs to be used to inform product development and communication with great care. Politicians can use it to confirm the existing position; check a new direction is gaining support; suggest adjustment, make specific changes or wholesale change; as well as to identify where it is not possible to change opinion. Research is also used in communication to understand the general picture; identify the most popular product aspects and the issues people care most about to focus on in communication; communicate issues politicians care about; sell policy; check assumptions; or test negative communication. Segmentation can help identify new groupings politicians should represent; a part of the market that has been ignored; or how to tailor internal offerings to volunteers. Leaders should use market analysis proactively to achieve their vision and broader goals.

Third, political strategy needs to be laid out clearly but still be flexible so it can evolve as circumstances change. Branding and competition management should be used to create distinctive, visionary products, creating choice for voters. The product, brand, position and communication need to be authentic, or voters are unlikely to support it. Political marketing remains crucial in government where elites need to mark out time to review the strategy and use research to help prevent them becoming out of touch. They also need to communicate delivery progress with clear demonstrable claims in a way that is relevant to the individual.

The main lesson from this book is that winning the political marketing game is about using marketing in a way that blends principle and pragmatism to enable political leaders to take voters with them as they try to achieve important change in the interests of society, balancing listening with leading, and forging a more positive relationship of partnership between government and the governed.

note how, for consumers to see a political leader's brand as authentic, it needs to be seen as disinterested; driven by core brand values of importance to consumers' lives instead of power-seeking motives.

However, Lees-Marshment and Lilleker (2001) examined the extent to which New Labour was a party with values or a skilfully manufactured entity designed to win elections, by considering the history of the party as well as its behaviour in 1997. They suggest that, despite the changes made under Blair to policy and the apparent newness of the policies, not all ethos – i.e. Labour's sense of historical identity developed through tradition and experience – was removed. Blair did integrate elements of Labour ideology such as neo-liberalism, communitarianism and socialism, while policy was developed to suit the reality of changing circumstances, such as capitalism, but with a Labour approach such as social justice. Another defence is that political branding could help restore ideological elements that some commentators fear have been lost. Lilleker adapted Kapferer's (1997) pyramid model of brand identity to politics and argued that a party's history, traditions and ethics, including its roots and history, form the inner kernel of any brand. Lilleker (2005a) argues that UK New Labour did not change the kernel or core concepts. For instance, changes to Clause IV had symbolic significance, but little practical impact on policy; indeed, changes to the kernel were not necessary, because Labour's ideological kernel was aligned with current market demands for supporting the public sector. The changes that did occur were largely within the area denoted by Kapferer as 'promises', not a redefinition of ethos. The book *The Political Marketing Game* concludes that it is possible to use political marketing in a way which balances pragmatism with principle: see Author's corner 9.1.

Within all campaigns and parties there is tension between doing what is right and winning an election; and marketing, by informing product development in response to market demands, exacerbates this and alongside it a feeling that something may be lost in the attempt to respond to the market, or segments of it, to win control of government. Savigny (2008) argues that the rise of political marketing has led political parties to adopt the ideology of marketing itself. She contends that as political marketing is based on the analogy that 'parties behave as businesses, voters as consumers, all operating in a political marketplace', and this in turn is based on the managerialist, rational-choice, neo-classical economic perspective, this introduces such concepts into the political sphere (2006, 83). Certainly the use of business-originated language, tools and concepts in politics suggests a change in the way politics is conducted. This returns us to the issue of political leadership. Political marketing, and public input generally, does not negate the need for elected politicians to make decisions. What is hard to get right is that balance – and that is the challenge for all of those who practice political marketing: see Practitioner perspective 9.2.

Practitioner perspective 9.2 on the importance of authenticity

In all forms of political communications, be true to yourself or your cause. Over time, over the top messages or 'spin' can degrade your brand. Be true.

Simon Rosenberg, President of NDN (New Democratic Network).
He is a veteran strategist and communications expert in Washington.

Source: supplied as top tip in email in 2013

Summary

Political marketing plays a substantial and significant role in democracies all around the world, impacting on policy, the behaviour and decisions of political leaders, opportunities for participation, citizenship, and representation in a broader sense. These implications can be both positive and negative for democracy – many scholars note that it all depends on how practitioners choose to use political marketing (Giasson *et al.* 2012, 250; Dufresne and Marland 2012, 37; and Small 2012, 207–8). The main argument running through this chapter is there are good and bad options, or less good/less bad options – see the best practice guide in Figure 9.5. It can be used to achieve important change that helps societal progress. Or it can be used to stifle debate if politicians lean towards being too pragmatic. Making the right choice is not easy to determine or do; but practitioners should at least be aware of them all and make informed and considered choices. The latest research suggests that it is possible to use political marketing democratically – see Figures 9.4 and 9.5 – but practitioners have to know and choose this.

Figure 9.4 Playing the political marketing game democratically

Source: Lees-Marshment (2011, 222)

One final point is that the democratic impact of political marketing also depends on those political elites are marketing to. As Mortimore and Gill (2010, 259) argue 'the weakness here is not in the marketing model but in democracy itself: an MOP is no more than the most efficient expression of the democratic will. If there is a danger here, it does not rest in the possibility that parties might become market-oriented but that the will of the voters might cause market orientation to lead to wrong choices. In other words, democracy is dangerous because the public is not always right; and we knew that already.' To a significant extent, the potential and limitations of political marketing lie in the hands of the political market itself, and thus we all have a responsibility to reflect on our own attitudes, values and behaviours as we play our role in the political marketing game.

Best practice guide to doing political marketing democratically

1. Listen to the public despite the potential weaknesses in public opinion.
2. Use methods that will increase the value of the opinion collected.
3. Consult those who can offer more informed opinion such as professionals, service users, people living with the problem.
4. Provide the public with information and a sense of the constraints of government.
5. Avoid letting segmentation lead to responding to some voters more than others; use it to find under-represented interests instead.
6. Use research to help address some difficult issues even when they are unpopular.
7. Use market analysis to increase participation and engagement.
8. Use market research to understand public opinion to inform a balanced leadership strategy.
9. Use voter-driven communication to reach and inform the public.
10. Understand the citizen is developing from a passive consumer to active participant.

Figure 9.5

Discussion points

1. Does political marketing really threaten leadership?
2. Should voters be treated as consumers?
3. 'The easy thing to do, frankly, is to hit the button on exactly what the public wants to hear ... The responsibility, though, in the end, particularly in the case of war, is to do what I believe to be the right thing for the country. I can't do it simply on the basis of the number of people who demonstrate, or on the basis of this opinion poll or that opinion poll. You've got to do, on an issue like this, what you genuinely believe to be right for the country, and then pay the price at the election if people disagree with you' (Tony Blair, *Tony and June*, Channel 4, 30 January, 2005). To what extent do you agree with Tony Blair? Do the public not consume war enough to be adequately informed about the complexities of international relations, war strategy, the realities of the battleground and the interplay of global forces to make the right decision?
4. Do you agree that segmentation and micro-targeting damages democracy by making some votes worth more than others?
5. Does marketing destroy internal democracy, or can it help it?

6   Discuss whether you think political marketing damages or enhances the policymaking process.

7   How does branding both damage and enhance policy in democracy?

8   To what extent can politicians decide for themselves when to follow their own convictions and focus on a new issue? Could an advisor guide them so they are never too soon, but also never too late, to raise a change-the-world position?

9   Do you think that Obama's use of marketing in fundraising was ethical?

10   Does political marketing really destroy ideology or could political branding revive it?

11   How would you try to balance principle and pragmatism if you became a political marketing practitioner?

Debates

Hold your own debate for and against a proposition such as:

1   Market-Oriented Parties are bad for democracy.

2   Being responsive to voter opinion when in opposition is fine, but, once in power, politicians have to decide what is right according to the information they get in government.

3   Voters should not be treated as consumers.

4   Market intelligence, far from being an instrument that gives the public a voice in a democracy, is a method by which politicians and economic elites manipulate people to buy their products and/or give them their votes.

5   Political marketing leads to the end of ideology.

6   Political marketing is inherently damaging for democracy.

7   The democratic problems with political marketing are the fault of the market – i.e. YOU!

This can be carried out by dividing the class into two sides (with small groups within each side if the class is large), one for and against. Each group should be asked to devise a list of points to support their side. Consider both practical (what is) and ethical (what should be) considerations. They should then present their argument to the class and then open discussion for debate, holding an open vote at the end.

Assessment questions

Essay/exam

1   Discuss the impact of political marketing on democracy, using theory and empirical examples.

2   To what extent does market research and market-oriented strategies threaten the notion of political leadership?

3   Examine the use of gender-related marketing for recent women politicians who have sought and/or gained power, and discuss the democratic and pragmatic implications.

4   To what extent does the notion of the consumer threaten the notion of the citizen, and why does this matter?

5   Outline and discuss arguments, examples and theories to support both Scullion's and Savigny's arguments for and against treating voters like consumers, and come to a conclusion as to which argument is stronger.

6 To what extent does political marketing reduce or increase participation in politics?

7 Is segmentation a tool that damages democracy by giving some voters more power in elections than others, or that helps elites better understand new groups in society?

8 To what extent does political marketing restrict or enhance policymaking?

9 Why does government branding attract controversy, and do you agree that it blurs the line between government and partisan work in a way that is problematic for both governance and democracy?

10 Is Marland (2012) realistic in suggesting that fundraising be carried out in an ethical manner?

11 Savigny suggests that political marketing has imposed an ideology all of its own on politics: review the impact of political marketing on ideology in politics.

12 To what extent could political marketing, a recent theory of empirical party behaviour, be allied to deliberative democracy, a modern addition to political theories of democracy, as Henneberg *et al.* (2009) suggest?

Applied

1 Assess the democratic nature of a political figure or organisation's use of political marketing using Lees-Marshment's rules on how to play the political marketing game democratically, making suggestions for future improvement.

2 Critique the use of gender-related marketing strategies for the Australian Prime Minister Julia Gillard and, from this, devise pragmatic lessons for how to market women leaders more effectively.

3 Apply Lees-Marshment's (2012) model of a reflective political leader to a current or recent politician in government, and assess the extent to which they followed this and what this means for the effectiveness of their political marketing leadership.

4 Critique the use of segmentation by parties in a recent election in terms of whether it gave some voters a more powerful vote than others; making suggestions for how segmentation can be used more democratically in future.

5 Assess the internal marketing by a political party in terms of its provision of participation opportunities in democracy, and make suggestions for how it might improve its participation within the pragmatic constraints of political marketing.

6 Assess the fundraising of a party or campaign against Marland's (2012) framework for good practices when using marketing in political fundraising (or his core principles of using marketing to fundraise ethically 2012, 169) and suggest how it might make its fundraising more democratic.

7 Create a training manual for practitioners to guide them in how political marketing can be used democratically as well as pragmatically.

Notes

1 See http://www.cbc.ca/thecurrent/2011/04/19/some-political-ads-targeting-the-ethnic-vote/index.html for examples.
2 http://www.cbc.ca/thecurrent/episode/2011/04/19/the-ethnic-vote/

References

Aberbach, Joel D. and Tom Christensen (2005). 'Citizens and consumers'. *Public Management Review*, 7(2): 226–45.

Avvy Go and The Colour of Poverty (2011). 'Go Ethnics Go', *youtube.com*, 12th April. http://www.youtube.com/watch?v=T5UE0SgN5ic (accessed October, 2013)

Barberio, Richard P. (2006). *Branding: presidential politics and crafted political communications..* Prepared for delivery at the 2006 Annual Meeting of the American Political Science Association, 30 August–3 September.

Binstock, Robert H. and Scott Davidson (2012). 'Political marketing and segmentation in aging democracies'. In Jennifer Lees-Marshment (ed.) *Routledge Handbook of Political Marketing*. London and New York: Routledge, 20–33.

Birch, Lisa and Francois Petry (2012). 'The use of public opinion research by government: insights from American and Canadian research'. In Jennifer Lees-Marshment (ed.) *Routledge Handbook of Political Marketing*. New York: Routledge, 342–453.

Braun, Alexander (2012). 'The role of opinion research in setting campaign strategy'. In Jennifer Lees-Marshment (ed.) *Routledge Handbook of Political Marketing*. New York: Routledge, 7–19.

Burrell, Barbara (2008). 'Likeable? Effective Commander in Chief? Polling on candidate traits in the "Year of the Presidential Woman"'. *PS: Political Science & Politics*, 41(4): 747–52.

Burton, Michael John (2012). 'Strategic voter selection'. In Jennifer Lees-Marshment (ed.) *Routledge Handbook of Political Marketing*. New York: Routledge, 34–47.

Burton, Michael John and Tasha Miracle (2014). 'The Emergence of voter targeting: learning to send the right message to the right voters'. In Jennifer Lees-Marshment, Brian Conley and Kenneth Cosgrove (eds) *Political Marketing in the US*. New York: Routledge.

Busby, Robert (2009). *Marketing the Populist Politician: The Demotic Democrat*. Houndmills and New York: Palgrave Macmillan.

Busby, Robert (2012). 'Selling Sarah Palin: political marketing and the "Wal-Mart Mom"'. In Jennifer Lees-Marshment (ed.) *Routledge Handbook of Political Marketing*. London: Routledge, 218–29.

Cardo, Valentina and Jennifer Lees-Marshment (2013). *Marketing Gender: Strategies for Marketing Female Political Leaders*. Presentation at the NZ-OZ Political Marketing and Management Mini conference, University of Auckland, 31 August.

Dean, Dianne and Robin Croft (2001). 'Friends and relations: long-term approaches to political campaigning'. *European Journal of Marketing*, 35(11/12): 1197–216.

Dermody, Janine and Stuart Hamner-Lloyd (2006). 'A marketing analysis of the 2005 general election advertising campaigns'. In Daren G. Lilleker, Nigel Jackson and Richard Scullion (eds) *The Marketing of Political Parties*. Manchester: Manchester University Press, 101–31.

Dufresne, Yannick and Alex Marland (2012). 'The Canadian Political Market and the Rules of the Game'. In Alex Marland, Thierry Giasson and Jennifer Lees-Marshment (ed.) *Political Marketing in Canada*. Vancouver: UBC, 22–38.

Fell, Dafydd and Isabelle Cheng (2010). *Testing the Market-Oriented Model of Political Parties in a Non-Western Context: The Case of Taiwan*. Chapter 12 in Global Political Marketing edited by J Lees-Marshment, Jesper Stromback and Chris Rudd, Routledge, 175–188.

French, Alan and Gareth Smith (2010). 'Measuring political brand equity: a consumer oriented approach'. *European Journal of Marketing*, 44(3/4): 460–77.

Gelders, Dave, and Øyvind Ihlen, (2010). 'Government communication about potential policies: public relations, propaganda or both?' *Public Relations Review*, 36(1): 59–62.

Giasson, Thierry, Jennifer Lees-Marshment and Alex Marland (2012). 'Challenges for democracy'. In Alex Marland, Thierry Giasson and Jennifer Lees-Marshment (eds) *Political Marketing in Canada*. Vancouver: UBC, 241–56.

Goot, Murray (1999). 'Public opinion, privatization and the electoral politics of Telstra'. *Australian Journal of Politics and History*, 45(2): 214–38.

Headley, James, Andreas Reitzig and Joe Burton (eds) (2011). *Public Participation in Foreign Policy*. Houndmills: Palgrave Macmillan.

Henneberg, S. C. and N. J. O'Shaughnessy (2009). 'Political relationship marketing: some macro/micro thoughts'. *Journal Of Marketing Management*, 25(1/2): 5–29.

Henneberg, Stephan C., Margaret Scammell and Nicholas J. O'Shaughnessy (2009) 'Political marketing management and theories of democracy'. *Journal of Marketing Theory*, 9(2): 165–88.

Hulsse, Rainer (2009). 'The catwalk power: Germany's new foreign image policy'. *Journal of International Relations and Development*, 12(3): 293–316.

Irwin, Colin (2012). *The People's Peace: Pax Populi, Pax Dei – How Peace Polls are Democratising the Peace Making Process*. http://www.peacepolls.org/cgi-bin/greeting?instanceID=1 (accessed October 2013)

Johnson, Dennis W. (2007). *No Place for Amateurs*, 2nd edn. New York: Routledge.

Johnson, Dennis W. (2012). 'Campaigning in the twenty-first century: change and continuity in American political marketing'. In Jennifer Lees-Marshment (ed.) *Routledge Handbook of Political Marketing*. London and New York: Routledge, 205–17.

Kapferer, Jean-Noel (1997). *Strategic Brand Management*. London: Kogan Page.

Knuckey, Jonathan (2010). 'Political marketing in the United States: from market- towards sales-orientation?' In Jennifer Lees-Marshment, Jesper Strömbäck & Chris Rudd (eds) *Global Political Marketing*. London: Routledge, 96–112.

Lane, Robert E. (1996). 'Losing touch in a democracy: demands versus needs'. In Jack Hayward (ed.) *Elitism, Populism and European Politics*. Oxford: Clarendon Press, 33–66.

Langmaid, Roy (2012). 'Co-creating the future'. In Jennifer Lees-Marshment (ed.) *Routledge Handbook of Political Marketing*. New York: Routledge, 61–76.

Ledingham, John A. (2011). 'Political public relations and relationship management'. In Jesper Strömbäck and Spiro Kiousis (eds) *Political Public Relations: Principles and Applications*. Abingdon: Routledge, 235–53.

Lees-Marshment, Jennifer (2001). *Political Marketing and British Political Parties: The Party's Just Begun*. Manchester: Manchester University Press.

Lees-Marshment, Jennifer (2008). 'Managing a market-orientation in government: cases in the UK and New Zealand'. In Dennis W. Johnson (ed.) *The Routledge Handbook of Political Management*. New York: Routledge, 524–536.

Lees-Marshment, Jennifer (2011). *The Political Marketing Game*. Houndmills and New York: Palgrave Macmillan.

Lees-Marshment, Jennifer (2012a). 'New directions in political marketing practice, political marketing and democracy and future trends'. In Jennifer Lees-Marshment (ed.) *Routledge Handbook of Political Marketing*. New York: Routledge, 366–86.

Lees-Marshment, Jennifer (2012b). 'Political Marketing and Opinion Leadership: Comparative Perspectives and Findings'. In Ludger Helms (ed.) *Comparative Political Leadership*. Houndmills and New York: Palgrave Macmillan, 165–85.

Lees-Marshment, Jennifer (2014). 'The democratic contribution of political market researchers'. *Journal of Public Affairs* (forthcoming).

Lees-Marshment, Jennifer and Darren Lilleker (2001). 'Political marketing and traditional values: "Old Labour" for "new times"?'. *Contemporary Politics*, 7(3): 205–16.

Lees-Marshment, Jennifer and Alex Marland (2012). 'Canadian political consultants' perspectives about political marketing'. *Canadian Journal of Communication*, 37(2): 333–43.

Lilleker, Darren G. (2005a). 'Political marketing: the cause of an emerging democratic deficit in Britain?' In Walter W. Wymer, Jr. and Jennifer Lees-Marshment (eds) *Current Issues in Political Marketing*. Binghamton, NY: Haworth Press, 5–26.

Lilleker, Darren G. (2005b). 'The impact of political marketing on internal party democracy'. *Parliamentary Affairs*, 58(3): 570–84.

Lilleker, Darren G. and Nigel Jackson (2011). 'Political public relations and political marketing'. In Jesper Strömbäck and Spiro Kiousis (eds) *Political Public Relations: Principles and Applications*. Abingdon: Routledge, 157–76.

Lilleker, Darren and R. Scullion (eds) (2008), *Voters or Consumers: Imagining the Contemporary Electorate*. Newcastle: Cambridge Scholars Publishing.

Lindholm, Mikael R. and Anette Prehn (2007). 'Strategy and politics: the example of Denmark'. In Thomes Fischer, Gregor Peter Scmitz and Michael Seberich (eds) *The Strategy of Politics: Results of a Comparative Study*. Butersloh: Verlag Bertelsmann Stiftung.

Lloyd, Jenny. (2012). 'Something old, something new? Modelling political communication in the 2010 UK general election'. In Jennifer Lees-Marshment (ed.) *Routledge Handbook of Political Marketing*. New York: Routledge, 243–56.

Marland, Alex (2012). 'Yes we can (fundraise): The ethics of marketing in political fundraising'. In Jennifer Lees-Marshment (ed.) *Routledge Handbook of Political Marketing*. New York: Routledge, 164–76.

Marsh, David and Paul Fawcett (2011). 'Branding, politics and democracy'. *Policy Studies*, 32(5): 515–30.

Marsh, David and Paul Fawcett (2012). 'Branding public policy'. In Jennifer Lees-Marshment (ed.) *Routledge Handbook of Political Marketing*. New York: Routledge, 329–41.

McGough, Sean (2009). 'Political marketing, democracy and terrorism: Ireland highlights the dangers'. Case study 10.3 in Jennifer Lees-Marshment, *Political Marketing: Principles and Applications*. London and New York: Routledge, 288–90.

Mills, Stephen (2011). 'Focus groups: myth or reality'. In Alastair Carthew and Simon Winkelmann (eds) *Political Polling in Asia-Pacific*. Singapore: Konrad Adenauer Stiftung, 27–38.

Mortimore, Roger and Mark Gill (2010). 'Implementing and interpreting market orientation in practice: lessons from Britain'. In Jennifer Lees-Marshment, Jesper Strömbäck and Chris Rudd (eds) *Global Political Marketing*. London: Routledge, 249–62.

Needham, Catherine (2005). 'Brand leaders: Clinton, Blair and the limitations of the permanent campaign'. *Political Studies*, 53(2): 343–61.

Newman, Bruce I. (1999). *The Mass Marketing of Politics*. Thousand Oaks, CA: Sage.

Nimijean, Richard (2006). 'The politics of branding Canada: the international-domestic nexus and the rethinking of Canada's place in the world'. *Revista Mexicana de Estudios Canadienses*, 11: 67–85.

O'Cass, Aron and Ranjit Voola (2010). 'Explications of political market orientation and political brand orientation using the resource-based view of the political party'. *Journal of Marketing Management*, 27(5/6): 627–45.

Paleologos, David A. (1997). A pollster on polling. *American Behavioral Scientist*, 40(8): 1183–9.

Paré, Daniel J. and Flavia Berger (2008). 'Political marketing Canadian style? The Conservative Party and the 2006 federal election'. *Canadian Journal of Communication*, 33(1): 39–63.

Pettitt, Robin T. (2009). 'Resisting marketing: the case of the British Labour Party under Blair'. Case Study 6.4 in Jennifer Lees-Marshment, *Political Marketing: Principles and Applications*. London and New York: Routledge, 158–60.

Savigny, Heather (2007). 'Focus groups and political marketing: science and democracy as axiomatic?' *British Journal of Politics and International Relations*, 9(1): 122–37.

Savigny, Heather (2008). 'The construction of the political consumer (or politics: what not to consume)'. In Darren G. Lilleker and Richard Scullion (eds), *Voters or Consumers: Imagining the Contemporary Electorate*. Newcastle: Cambridge Scholars Publishing, 35–50.

Scammell, Margaret (2008). 'Brand Blair: marketing politics in the consumer age'. In D. Lilleker and R. Scullion (eds), *Voters or Consumers: Imagining the Contemporary Electorate*. Newcastle: Cambridge Scholars Publishing, 97–113.

Scullion, Richard (2008). 'The impact of the market on the character of citizenship, and the consequences of this for political engagement'. In D. Lilleker and R. Scullion (eds), *Voters or Consumers: Imagining the Contemporary Electorate*. Newcastle: Cambridge Scholars Publishing, 51–72.

Scullion, R. (2010). 'The emergence of the "accidental citizen": implications for political marketing'. *Journal of Political Marketing*, 9(4): 276–93.

Small, Tamara (2012). 'Are we friends yet? Online relationship marketing by political parties'. In Alex Marland, Thierry Giasson and Jennifer Lees-Marshment (eds) *Political Marketing in Canada*. Vancouver: UBC, 193–208.

Smith, Gareth and Alan French (2009). 'The political brand: a consumer perspective'. *Marketing Theory*, 9(2): 209–26.

Sparrow, Nick and John Turner (2001). 'The integrating of market research techniques in developing strategies in a more uncertain political climate'. *European Journal of Marketing*, 35(9/10): 984–1002.

Ubertaccio, Peter N. (2012). 'Political parties and direct marketing: connecting voters and candidates more effectively'. In Jennifer Lees-Marshment (ed.) *The Routledge Handbook of Political Marketing*. London and New York: Routledge, 177–89.

Van Aelst, Peter, Joop van Holsteyn and Ruud Koole (2012). 'Party members as part-time marketers: using relationship marketing to demonstrate the importance of rank-and-file party members in election campaigns'. In Jennifer Lees-Marshment (ed.) *The Routledge Handbook of Political Marketing*. London and New York: Routledge, 151–63.

Young, Sally (2005). 'Government advertising costs us dearly'. *The Age*, 30 August. http://www.theage. com.au/news/opinion/sally-young/2005/08/29/1125302509121.html (accessed 10 April, 2008)

Index